JAPAN'S MODERN MYTH

ROY ANDREW MILLER

Japan's Modern Myth

THE LANGUAGE AND

BEYOND

WEATHERHILL
New York & Tokyo

First edition, 1982

Published by John Weatherhill, Inc., of New York and Tokyo, with editorial offices at 7-6-13 Roppongi, Minato-ku, Tokyo 106, Japan. Protected by copyright under terms of the International Copyright Union; all rights reserved. Printed in the Republic of Korea and first published in Japan.

Library of Congress Cataloging in Publication Data: Miller, Roy Andrew. / Japan's Modern Myth. / Bibliography: p. / Includes index. / 1. Japanese language. 2. National characteristics, Japanese. / I. Title. / PL523.M494 495.6 81-16213 / ISBN 0-8348-0168-X / AACR2

Contents

Preface

I generally put off reading the preface to a book until after I have read the book; since I always write my own prefaces last, I apparently have fallen into the habit of also reading other people's last, which is not good. I hope the reader of this book will not have this particular bad habit of mine, because I believe that a clue as to why this book seemed necessary and important to write, as well as a hint as to what the book attempts to do and why, will be useful to the reader.

It came as something of a jolt to me this morning when, preparing my notes for this preface, I suddenly realized that I have been occupied with the Japanese language on a daily basis, in one way or another, ever since I was nineteen—which, not to put too fine a point on it, was hardly yesterday. Not a day has passed during this entire period (apart from a brief, abortive flirtation with Chinese and Tibetan in the mid-1950s) when I have not used the Japanese language either in order to earn my living or else simply in order to live or, most often, in order to do both. Nor has a day passed when I have not, in one way or another, been struck by something startling, something unexpected, about the language and about the ways in which it is used.

First, of course, it was mainly the language itself that gave me trouble. That gradually got easier; but as I began to understand more and more of the content of what people said and wrote, I also began to feel that I was understanding less and less about its context—about why they said and wrote what they did.

Finally, about ten years ago, I began to realize that the longer all this went on, the less I was actually understanding about many of the things that I read or heard talked about in Japanese—not the words or the grammar or even the literal sense, of course, but rather what it all really *meant*, in the larger sense of how it all eventually fit into Japanese life and society. I came more and more to believe that it is quite as necessary for a student of

Japan to study how and why the language articulates itself into the other facets of Japanese culture as it is to study the language itself. I soon found that it would be necessary for me to do most of this study on my own—the kind of study that is now often called sociolinguistics—and that there was little in print that could help me, though of course I did begin to read everything I could locate, especially everything published in Japanese, on the subject.

The more I read about and studied these sociolinguistic questions, the more I came to feel that simply being able to speak, read, and understand Japanese was probably the smallest part of the problem. Indeed, these practical linguistic skills on their own, so long as they remain uninformed and undirected by some fairly precise sociolinguistic cautions, seem likely to lead nowhere—except possibly to more and more mutual misunderstanding and mutual mistrust between Japanese and foreigners, and we already have more than enough of that, without going to the trouble of learning a foreign language in order to add to it. I also began to believe that translation alone, unless elaborately safeguarded by commentary and explanation—particularly but not exclusively the translation of literary works—generally does more harm than good for our understanding of Japan. But that is another problem that must eventually be treated in another book. At any rate, I was encouraged to continue with these studies largely because it seemed to me that the more they were advanced, the more the possibility of the rest of the world's misunderstanding Japan would be reduced.

The potential of what I have here called Japan's modern myth for causing serious, often quite destructive, misunderstanding of contemporary Japanese life and culture still seems to be enormous. The purpose of this book is to further the understanding of Japan on the part of non-Japanese by trying to explain, describe, analyze, and put into accurate historical perspective some of the more striking manifestations of that myth before the myth can generate even more serious international misunderstanding than it has already caused.

I am hardly naive enough to think that any real possibility exists of slaying this durable mythic dragon by sitting here in Seattle and writing books about it in a foreign language. But that really does not bother me very much, because actually I am not all that much concerned about whether or not the myth continues to thrive and flourish. Partly this is because I suspect that the myth is already quite invulnerable to any campaign that might be mounted against it, and I am not interested in contests with impossible odds. Partly also this is because whether or not the myth is allowed to continue to proliferate and propagate itself is in a sense almost entirely the business of the Japanese themselves, and so they must in the final analysis do with it as they will.

All that I am really concerned about in this are the interests and under-standing of the rest of us: the "foreigners" who must live in the same world with Japan, and who sometimes also find ourselves, from time to time, living *in* Japan.

There is plenty in Japanese society, culture, and life for us to study and struggle to understand; there is plenty there to admire and emulate; there is also plenty there to dislike and eschew. None of these tasks is made any easier when the modern myth of the Japanese language gets in the way of our understanding of Japan. But when the myth of the language is cleared away at least in part, then sometimes the going can be made a little easier. That alone is the entirely modest goal of this book, which is intended to be a contribution to mutual understanding between Japan and the West, particularly to understanding between Japan and the United States. I hope the reader will be able to keep that goal in mind as he or she goes through the book, because it is sincerely meant.

This is not my first published exploration of some of these problems, even though it is my first attempt to relate them to the framework of a modern sustaining myth of society. My first substantial publication in this area was a "policy study" commissioned by the American Enterprise Insti-tute in 1975 and published in 1977 by AEI and the Hoover Institution on War, Revolution and Peace under the title *The Japanese Language in Contem-porary Japan: Some Sociolinguistic Observations.** In this book I explored the utility of a classic system for defining the mystical experience—which I took over intact from William James's *The Varieties of Religious Experi-ence*—for classifying and categorizing many of the characteristic and striking things that the Japanese say about the Japanese language. These are always interesting in and of themselves, of course, but they are mainly of value for the light that they can throw upon the sociolinguistic attitudes with which Japanese society approaches its own language.

The same year in which the AEI-Hoover Institution monograph appeared,

---

*Stanford, California, 106 pp. The somewhat pompous title under which this monograph appeared was the AEI's idea, not mine. I originally titled the book *The Japanese on Japanese,* since in it I mainly studied the kinds of things that the Japanese say and write about their own language. But Ben Wattenberg, Laurence Silberman, Milton Friedman, and the other fellows at the AEI are a pretty serious bunch, and they were concerned that a book entitled *The Japanese on Japanese* might be mistaken for a specimen of exotic Far Eastern pornography, so the title had to be changed, because the AEI takes a dim view of pornography. As, I am certain, would also have the thirty-first president of the United States, who founded the Hoover Institution "to investigate evils of the doctrines of Karl Marx." What Karl would have said of all this, it is difficult even to guess.

I also published a somewhat technical article on the question of *kotodama,* the so-called "spirit of the Japanese language," which is further explored in chapter 7 of the present book.* This article included additional materials of sociolinguistic interest that had turned up in the course of my research for the AEI monograph but that were either too involved or too technical to be included in that publication. In it, I treated the *kotodama* idea historically but also in the context of the large amount of contemporary writing and thinking about the nature of the language that distinguishes so much of contemporary Japanese academic and intellectual life. It was also in this article that I first explored the question of the relationship between much of the modern writing and thinking about Japanese and the ideology of the infamous *Kokutai no Hongi* tract, a fascinating and illuminating direction of study that the present book is able to explore in somewhat more detail.

With the perspective gained by writing these two preliminary studies of the Japanese language in contemporary Japan, I began to realize that while my analysis of the contemporary Japanese sociolinguistic response to the Japanese language as a variety of the classic mystical experience still had much to be said in its favor, it did not really tell the whole story. At first my self-doubts in this connection were no larger than the proverbial cloud on the horizon, the size of a fist. What set them swiftly expanding until they darkened my entire sky was the opportunity that the Japan Foundation extended to me to participate in the international conference on teaching Japanese as a foreign language, held under their auspices in Tokyo and Osaka in March 1978.

I honestly cannot recall any similarly short period of time during which I was able to learn so much that was new and surprising. I became convinced that in the modern Japanese response to the Japanese language there was something over and beyond the mysticism that I had earlier analyzed. Soon I was reminded of what Ernest Jones, the pupil and biographer of Sigmund Freud, had written about constitutional monarchy—that it had arisen to satisfy emotional starvation, that people decided to preserve kings in order "to satisfy the beneficent elements of the mythology in man's ineradicable unconscious that will enable us to deal better with the more troublesome elements." Now I knew that it was to the mythic, rather than to the mystic, that I would have to turn if I were to make further progress in rendering Japanese sociolinguistic behavior comprehensible to the rest of the world. I do not now wish to suggest that the mythic analysis totally replaces the mystic, or even that it is necessarily superior to it; but

---

*"The 'Spirit' of the Japanese Language," *Journal of Japanese Studies* 3:2 (Summer, 1977): 251–98.

I do believe that a clear understanding of the myth and how it came to exist is equally as necessary as is the understanding of the mysticism that earlier occupied me; hence, the present book.

There is more, much more, to this myth of the Japanese language—more that is important for our understanding of Japan, and more than I have been able to sketch in this book. For example, a colleague recently suggested to me that it would be useful to explore the connection between the myth of Nihongo and totalitarianism. He is disturbed by what appears to him to be a paradox between Japan's obviously open, democratic forms of government and politics and the well-documented penchant of totalitarian systems for making their subject peoples believe things that are normally, and obviously, beyond belief—things like the myth of the Japanese language. How, he asks, can this happen in a nontotalitarian society; and I am not sure that I have the best answer, though several possibilities do suggest themselves.

First of all, while I completely agree that there is much in this connection that appears to border upon paradox, at the same time I wonder if the real connection between the compulsion to believe in a sustaining myth and totalitarianism is quite as mechanical as it may sometimes appear to be from a cursory reading of recent history. As I have already suggested above, it seems to me that the compulsion toward mythic belief goes rather deeper than that, putting down its roots in places so dark and murky that they can easily escape the oversight of any form of government, whether totalitarian, democratic, or what-have-you. I also suspect that much of this apparent paradox is only superficial and that most of it arises when we mistake the open, democratic forms of government and politics in Japan for the substance of Japanese life and culture, both of which continue to impress me as being ultimately and eminently totalitarian to their core.

If I am correct in this analysis, then perhaps that in turn helps to explain why the myth has found such rich soil in which to propagate itself in postwar Japanese life. Perhaps the paradox of a compelling mythic fixation managing to flourish in the midst of an ostensibly democratic society is, after all, only apparent, not real, because the society is actually not essentially democratic. Certainly there is a lot here still to study, and a lot also that no one yet understands very well. I hope that some of those who read this book will be encouraged to take up the further studies of these and related questions. In order to understand Japan, the world needs all the help it can get.

Any book that, like this one, has occupied the author by fits and starts over a period of several years would under normal circumstances carry a fairly lengthy list of acknowledgments. A lot of people have obviously helped me in one way or another to write this book, and surely it would only be proper to thank them by name for their assistance. The difficulty with this book is that so many of the people to whom I am most indebted for materials and ideas are Japanese friends, many of whom have responsible positions in the Japanese academic establishment. I am really very much afraid that to mention any of them by name here might very well—in consideration of the book's thesis and content—single them out for vindictive retribution by their peers. Most Japanese academics are fortunate enough to enjoy pretty secure positions, but no one in any society is probably ever *that* secure.

So rather than run the risk of exposing many of my best friends in Japanese academia to possible retaliation by their colleagues—which would certainly be a poor way in which to thank them—I have decided to refrain entirely from acknowledging individually any of my many Japanese friends and colleagues to whom nevertheless I am, as always, deeply in debt. They know who they are, and they know how greatly I appreciate their help. Their secret is safe with me.

I presume—or is "hope" the better word?—one need not be quite so cautious where "foreigners" are concerned. At the University of Washington, my colleagues Donald Hellmann and Susan Hanley have been consistently encouraging, even though they must have grown increasingly tired of hearing about the myth of Nihongo. No one in Seattle could have been more helpful than Kenneth Pyle, director of the university's School of International Studies. But I must put on record that I count the substantial financial support that he was able to direct toward the writing of this book as second in importance to his continued and supportive friendship, particularly during more than a few periods of dark days.

In Japan, I particularly have to thank Donald Richie and Holloway Brown —Donald for encouragement and ideas, Holloway for more of the same, as well as for the hundreds of newspaper clippings that he has sent me over what is beginning to seem like an equal number of years. But most of all I have to thank Meredith Weatherby. It was in the course of a talk with him in March 1978, when my head was still spinning from everything that was going on at the Japan Foundation's "International Conference on Teaching Japanese as a Foreign Language," that we decided that this book had to be written; and it was also Meredith who managed to keep me at it when it seemed, more than once, easier to let the whole thing go by the boards. It certainly is not Meredith's fault that it eventually *was* written, but without his help and encouragement, it never would have been.

Seattle, Washington
November 1981

JAPAN'S MODERN MYTH

Where there is no disagreement, there is no activity.
—Fr. Rolfe, Baron Corvo (1860–1913).

CHAPTER ONE

The Making of the Myth

The Japanese language has a unique position among the languages of civilized countries. That is, there is absolutely no other language of a similar nature.
—Haruhiko Kindaichi, *Nihongo,* 1957; translated by Umeyo Hirano, *The Japanese Language,* 1978

FOR MOST people in the world today, the language that they speak, and write, and otherwise employ in their daily lives is a matter of no special concern. Language for most of us is simply something that our society and our culture both take completely for granted. We all spend much of our school days learning to read and write; but once our formal education is completed, unless we are professionally concerned with an occupation like advertising or publishing that makes special use of language, most of us hardly give language a second thought for the rest of our adult lives.

This is as it should be. Each different variety of language is itself essentially nothing more than a social convention. This is simply another way of saying that each language, indeed every language, is really nothing more than a tremendously involved but nevertheless quite arbitrary set of signs or symbols; but the signs or symbols that constitute language do not have significance or meaning in and of themselves. They mean something—and language itself means something—only because, in each individual instance, a given society has agreed upon what they should mean—at the same time and in the same way that the society in question has in the first place agreed to employ the given language to serve as its principal social convention.

The linkages between language and the world in which it is employed—or, more simply put, the meanings that language expresses—are arbitrary.

3

Most modern societies and most modern cultures recognize this arbitrary nature of language at least implicitly, and the benign neglect that most modern societies and cultures afford to language is nothing more than one expression of the way in which most societies recognize that language is indeed an arbitrary social convention. The world today is a busy place. Most of us simply do not have either the time or the energy for fussing about purely arbitrary social phenomena; and so most of us, and most of our societies, leave our language alone.

Few significant exceptions are to be found, at least in the West, to the general rule that most modern societies usually take the language that they employ for granted. In the Occident, probably the only important deviations from this rule are provided by the French. The French admittedly do profess to treat their language with particular care and respect and enjoy demonstrating the delicacy of their feelings in this connection on every possible occasion, typically by pretending not to understand a word that a foreigner says so long as he or she makes the most infinitesimal error in pronunciation.

But the French also profess to be deeply concerned most of the time about the condition of their livers, an internal organ that most other Europeans, and all North Americans, would have the greatest difficulty in even locating on an anatomical sketch of the human body. So perhaps their exaggerated concern for the French language is also only a national idiosyncrasy and hardly represents a significant deviation from the usual pattern of Western civilization and culture on this score. For almost all of us, our language is simply something we use, something we understand, and something that exists. Otherwise, we generally pay it no particular attention at all.

But when we look away from the West and turn our attention instead to contemporary Japanese society, we find something quite different—something that, at first glance at least, is quite surprising. Modern Japanese life actively concerns itself with the Japanese language to a degree that will unquestionably astonish any Western observer who encounters this state of affairs for the first time.

For most modern Japanese, and indeed for modern Japanese society and culture in general, the Japanese language is not simply a language. It is not merely a social convention, something that the society and the culture can use and then forget about. Above all, the Japanese language in modern Japan is never regarded simply as a set of social conventions arbitrarily agreed upon. For modern Japan, the Japanese language is a way of life, and the enormous amount of speculation, writing, and talking about it that goes on at every level of Japanese life constitutes an entirely distinctive and marvelously self-contained way of looking at life.

In modern Japan, the Japanese language is never allowed to be taken for granted, not by anyone, not for a single moment. It is constantly being made the subject of scrutiny, the target of self-examination and of soul-searching. The language not only serves the society as a vehicle for daily communication, but it also manages, as we shall see, to be a cult and myth as well. Since the Japanese language does have this remarkable role within contemporary Japanese society, any attempt on our part to understand modern Japan will necessarily run into more than one stone wall of serious misunderstanding unless we also pay serious attention to the ways in which the Japanese themselves pay such unflagging attention to their own language. Anything that the Japanese uniformly agree to be as important as the language is for them must also obviously be important for us, if we are to advance our own understanding of Japan in any significant manner. This book is mainly concerned with furthering the understanding of Japan and of the Japanese by a survey of some of the more striking and unusual aspects of the modern Japanese social concern for the Japanese language.

Japanese authors, social critics, and intellectual leaders are especially fond of focusing their attention upon the ways in which certain aspects of Japanese life and civilization differ from similar or parallel aspects of life and civilization in the West. When it comes to the way that contemporary Japanese civilization treats and regards the Japanese language, they have their work cut out for them. The Japanese today approach their own language in a way that is impressively, and importantly, different from the way in which any Western nation approaches its language, even making all due allowance for the sensibilities of the language- and liver-conscious French.

To the Japanese today, the Japanese language is not simply the way they talk and write. For them, it has assumed the dimensions of a national myth of vast proportions. Like anyone else, the Japanese are perfectly entitled to their own mythology. They are free to work out any system for sustaining their own intellectual and national aspirations, so long as that system does not impinge upon or endanger the mythologies and aspirations of others. What we aim at here is not to point out this or that aspect of the new national myth of the Japanese language, as it may be seen to be flourishing in modern Japan, with the idea of identifying areas in the development of this myth that may appear, to the foreign observer at least, to be fraught with danger for the future of Japanese life. Such frightening aspects of the myth certainly do exist, but they must ultimately be the concern of the Japanese themselves.

What we aim to do here is rather to explore some of the origins of this new myth of modern Japan, in the hope that, by learning something of where this myth came from, we as outsiders may in the process also begin to learn something of its implications for this world that we all—including the Japanese—must continue to live in together.

We will also try to describe some of the ways in which this modern myth of *Nihongo* (the word simply means the Japanese language) is being nurtured in Japan today, partly for the light that these may throw upon the make-up of contemporary Japanese culture and civilization, and partly for what they can do to help the rest of us understand the often startling and bizarre forms in which the myth of Nihongo confronts us in our dealings with Japan and with the Japanese.

Since much of the modern myth of Nihongo is still in the process of being generated in Japan today, we will find in the course of our consideration of this problem that we enjoy what is, in a certain sense at least, a remarkably interesting and privileged position. Myths of all kinds, even a nationally embraced, nation-sustaining myth like that of the Japanese language, generally are available to the interested onlooker only in retrospect. Most often we can only view them when they are over and done with, and when no one but a scholar of the past really cares about what elements may once have made them up, or about what people once felt about them. Although history is always interesting, it can rarely hold a candle to real life.

But with the modern myth of Nihongo, we are not dealing exclusively with history; here we are dealing with real life, as it is being lived in Japan today. The myth of course has deep historical origins, and we will have to devote some attention to these sources that go back into the Japanese past. But what we will find to be particularly fascinating about the myth is that it is an ongoing concern in the here and now: it is a myth still in the process not only of being believed and honored but also of being formulated and created. When we study Nihongo, the modern myth of Japan, we are studying something that is currently very much alive, something quite close to the heart of much of contemporary Japanese life, culture, and national sentiment.

All this means that we enjoy a particularly privileged status, since we are being allowed, as it were, to be present at the growth and elaboration of a major modern myth. To be so privileged is not unlike finding oneself present at the sudden explosion of a new volcano or the mighty upheaval of other similarly impressive geological forces, such as the emergence of a totally new island from the depths of the ocean. Many people have seen volcanoes, many have stood on islands, but how many can claim that they were there when either was in the terrifying process of formation? In the case of the modern myth of Nihongo, many of the mysterious underground forces and pressures that are currently in the process of bringing it into existence may still be plainly observed in operation.

From the beginning of our investigation of this curious situation, it is important that we keep in mind a few ground rules relating to myths in general, and to the role they play in all our lives. In the first place, the Japanese today are by no means unusual, or unique, simply because they have evolved

—and are now most busily engaged in further refining and perfecting— their own modern myth; nor are they unique in their national decision to relate so much of their contemporary life and culture to a myth. All of us— every modern individual, every modern society and every living social unit— live in terms of one myth or another. Strip away all our myths and few of us today, anywhere in the world, could go on living as individuals, much less as societies.

These myths by which we all live sometimes seem to be the only fixed elements in a spiritual and intellectual landscape otherwise filled with shift- ing, transitory, and thoroughly undependable elements. Take away our myths and our life too soon becomes impossible. How many Americans were helped to survive, for example, through the years of the Great Depres- sion by the myth of American frugality, homespun virtue, and the inevitable triumph of hard work and self-reliance? These were the myths that made at least moderately palatable many a supper of bologna bits and flour gravy in America of the Depression years. Whether or not a myth is true hardly mat- ters. What matters is that it is believed; and, much like what the Christian church calls a sacrament, if one believes in it, then it does work.

Such sustaining myths are often entire systems of what might be termed "enabling beliefs," whole bodies of thought and opinion more or less uni- formly held at sometimes widely varied levels of society. They supply the mental cohesiveness and ideological unity that any human group requires for its survival. Once out of the Great Depression, and with another world war safely behind them, Americans for a significant period of time sustained themselves with the new myth of their own monopoly over atomic weap- ons and nuclear power. Meanwhile, the Soviets (simultaneously engaged in proving the fallacy of that particular myth, by the way) were themselves sustained by the myth of Marxism-Leninism, and by the related myth that they were in the business of "building socialism."

Shortly thereafter, in China, an enormous myth concerning the om- niscience of Chairman Mao, and teaching the utter infallability of his pro- nouncements on every possible variety of subject, would be brought into being in order to help provide some of the sustaining force necessary for the birth of yet another would-be world power.

So the first thing that we must understand about all these sustaining myths is that the modern Japanese are by no means unusual, much less unique, simply because they too have one. Many people, indeed most people, do. What does set Japan and the Japanese apart, as we shall see in more detail below, is the way in which their modern sustaining myth focuses almost exclusively upon the Japanese language, often to the extent of apparently neglecting most of the extralinguistic features of the very society and culture that it has come into being in order to sustain. Language is an important aspect of all human culture, but at the same time it is not equivalent to culture, nor does its importance rule out the role of other, extralinguistic elements in a given culture. The inordinate emphasis that the modern Japanese sustaining myth places upon the Japanese language is not only out of proportion to the role of language in society and culture; it focuses upon language so sharply that, finally, it is the language itself that becomes the cardinal element in the structure of the myth.

To find parallel examples, either past or present, of sustaining myths of societies that, like the modern Japanese, find the major raw materials for their intellectual fetishes in such an ostensibly simple and matter-of-fact entity as the language that the society employs daily is difficult indeed. It is not the fact of having such a myth that sets Japan apart from the other members of the modern family of nations; rather, it is the principal subject matter of the myth itself that identifies it as something both singular and remarkable and that at the same time sets the Japanese apart.

The second important matter that must be kept in mind in examining this modern Japanese myth of Nihongo is another aspect of the classical characteristics of all mythology. We ought not to expect that any myth, this modern one of contemporary Japan included, will be simple or one-dimensional. In particular, we must not expect that it will be rational. A myth that was any of these things simply would not work in its role of providing a solid, unshakable mythic foundation to which the society concerned can secure itself.

If a myth is to support a society, or even to sustain an individual, it must be able to respond to a variety of needs. Sometimes these needs press in from one direction, sometimes from another. A perfectly consistent, rational description or view of any human or natural phenomenon—for example, the straightforward statement that water boils at 100° C—cannot serve as a sustaining myth. It may be true, but it is too simple to be of use to society in the way that a sustaining myth must be of use.

Myths are not scientific descriptions, nor are they rational accounts of what happens in the world around us. In order to respond to the needs of individuals, and to answer the requirements of societies for systems and forces that will sustain them, all myths must be infinitely flexible. Usually this means that they must be prepared to bend to the point of incorporating substantial numbers of directly opposed, and even at times quite mutually contradictory, positions. Science is rational but myth is not. Science can only deal with light or with dark, but it cannot accommodate both at the same time. For example, computer technology can deal with the most complex situations or the most involved mathematical problems, but only in simplistic terms of "off" and "on," or "yes" and "no," and arrives at its solutions by building up enormous accumulations of such simple units. (In the machinery of the computer, these become the presence or absence of an electrical impulse, the "on" or "off" situation of an electronic circuit.)

A myth is different. It can be both "on" and "off" at the same time. It can make room for light and dark simultaneously. It is not hampered by considerations of elementary rationality or superficial consistency. So long as the sustaining myth "works"—and it "works" so long as it is believed, again because of its essentially sacramental character—no one will question why or how it manages to incorporate quite contradictory elements and points of view at one and the same time.

Myths can accommodate both good gods and bad ones; myths can and do make room for the simultaneous operation of evil and good. The American sustaining myth of Depression days found room for the evil of wicked bankers foreclosing farm mortgages, explaining it as the natural, expected consequence of "big business" and "moneybags," at the same time that it had room for the unquestioned virtues and righteousness of the dispossessed.

In fact, myths seem to work even better when they do incorporate a substantial number of self-contradictory positions, since human life, which they are designed to sustain, is itself often bewildering and self-contradictory. The modern Japanese sustaining myth of Nihongo, as we shall see, incorporates a substantial number of self-contradictory elements. For example, it sometimes stresses that the language around which it has been erected is perfect, unique, and superior to all other languages; but simultaneously, and for other ends, it may equally stridently announce that the Japanese language is imperfect, vulnerable, and visibly coming apart at the seams, hardly likely to last the night.

So long as we do not place such mutually contradictory claims in their proper context, and so long as we do not relate them to their role as necessary parts of the modern myth of which they are all parts, we run the risk of jumping to false conclusions about the people who say such self-contradictory things. Often one positive claim is hardly out of their mouths before the next negative one has followed it. Naturally we are tempted to conclude that the people concerned either all have phenomenally short memories or else are simply stupid. But it happens that neither is actually the case.

The vendors of the modern myth of Nihongo in contemporary Japan are none of them in the least stupid. They know precisely what they are doing, and they are very good at it. Nor do they have short memories. To the contrary: we shall be able to demonstrate that their pronouncements on these and related subjects actually encompass a bewilderingly vast range of fact and fancy, stretching over more than a thousand years of human history.

We will continue to sell these modern mythmakers short—and, even more important, we will continue to underestimate their importance for any understanding of modern Japanese society and how it works—until we place them and their work in true relationship to the sustaining myth of modern Japan. Our understanding of the overall issue will also be delayed until we realize that that myth itself has all the necessary properties of any full-fledged myth—including, most importantly, this property of fruitful self-contradiction.

The following chapters of the present book will give the reader some idea of the wide variety of expression, both explicit and implicit, in which this modern myth of Nihongo appears. So many illustrations of the different forms in which the myth appears are available at all hands that the principal problem, in each of the subsequent chapters, has generally been how to keep the examples quoted to demonstrate the inner workings of the myth within a reasonable limit of space. For every variety of example that is cited below, a hundred more of the same could have been quoted; what the reader will find in this volume is only the tip of the iceberg.

But before we turn to specific examples and illustrations of this modern sociolinguistic sustaining myth of Japanese society in action, it will be useful to describe briefly a few of the major categories of media and distribution methods by means of which the myth does its work in Japan today. Like the different forms assumed by the myth itself, these too are so numerous as almost to defy categorization. Nevertheless, some attempt at bringing order out of the tremendous abundance of these materials must first of all be made, if the reader is ever to be able to put the examples that are quoted later into their proper perspective.

Whatever form the myth takes, and however it is circulated—whether through the printed page or through newer mass media such as TV and radio—the mythic message that remains the heart of the matter is always the same. The myth itself essentially consists of the constant repetition of a relatively small number of claims relating to the Japanese language. All these claims share one concept in common—something that we may call the "allegation of uniqueness."

All these claims have in common the allegation that the Japanese language is somehow or other unique among all the languages of the world. This is the basic myth, and all the other guises that the myth assumes, depending upon time, place, and context of particular circumstance, are simply reworkings of this same, unchanging theme. From this essential claim of absolute uniqueness, for example, it is only a short step to simultaneous claims to the effect that the Japanese language is exceptionally difficult in comparison with all other languages; or that the Japanese language possesses a kind of spirit or soul that sets it apart from all other languages, which do not possess such a spiritual entity; or that the Japanese language is somehow purer, and has been less involved in the course of its history with that normal process of language change and language mixture that has been the common fate of all other known human languages; or that the Japanese language is endowed with a distinctive character or special inner nature that makes it possible for Japanese society to use it for a variety of supralinguistic or nonverbal communication not enjoyed by any other society—a variety of communication not possible in societies that can only employ other, ordinary languages.

It is neither possible nor useful to attempt to draw hard-and-fast boundary lines that would separate each of these claims of the myth from the others. Each of them tends to encroach immediately upon the mythic domain of all the others; and, indeed, each of these allegations is really only a different way of expressing any one, as well as the sum total, of the others. Nevertheless, the attempt just made to isolate out a number of individual allegations upon which the myth centers does probably have its uses; at the very least, there are hardly any important manifestations of the myth that cannot be classified under one or another of these general areas of allegation just listed.

But when, as it often does, this or that representation of the myth does not appear to fit very well into any of the above subordinate allegations, we must always keep in mind that, after all, all these claims are really only reworkings of the one original, essential allegation of the myth—the allegation of uniqueness. This is the basic assumption upon which the entire myth is founded; it is scientifically baseless, as are all the subordinate allegations that depend upon it; but that, of course, does not in the least interfere with its successful operation as a major sustaining myth for modern Japanese society.

These major subordinate allegations of the myth—these unlimited variations upon the basic, essential theme of the uniqueness of the Japanese language—are circulated throughout modern Japanese society by an almost equally wide variety of media. The Japanese probably publish, and sell, and actually read, more books, magazines, and newspapers than any other nation in the world today. Almost every adult Japanese is literate. This means that virtually everyone in the society of sufficient mental competence to be able to learn to read has been taught to do so; and what is even more surprising, almost everyone who has been taught to read actually does read.

Japanese daily newspapers enjoy tremendous circulations, as do also a wide variety of popular weekly magazines. Even quite difficult scholarly books in Japan often achieve substantial sales among the general reading public, while it is not at all unusual for a popular nonfiction book concerned with the Japanese language to chalk up sales well above the ten thousand mark within a few weeks of publication and to continue to sell at an equally brisk clip for many months.

With the increasingly dense urbanization of more and more of Japan's limited land area, more and more Japanese spend part of each working day crowded into commuter trains, buses, and subways, going to and from their jobs. A daily commute of two hours or more in each direction is a commonplace for workers at all levels of society employed in such urban centers as Tokyo or Osaka. Some may reach their offices and factories in a shorter period of time, but others will spend even longer getting to and from the job.

Once they leave school, most Japanese do the bulk of their reading under these conditions. If the hundreds of riders and readers in a commuter train or subway car ever lift their eyes from the books, magazines, or newspapers in which they are engrossed, they find that the carriage is festooned with advertisements for more of the same. The average paperback book or weekly magazine often is just long enough to last for a day's commute, or at the most for two or three. Japanese publishing is an enormously important, profitable business, with a potentially huge captive audience available for its product.

Those elements of the myth of Nihongo that are circulated through the medium of the printed page are to be found busy doing their work at every level of this enormous publishing industry. The myth receives serious academic treatment by serious academics in the form of deadly serious academic publications—papers and monographs that are designed essentially for academic audiences but are nevertheless often printed, published, and even eventually sold in quantities that would be the envy of any American trade-book publisher. Many of the authors of this type of material are university professors, while others, including a number of the most successful and most important makers of the myth of Nihongo, are employees of government-supported research institutes and similar organizations particularly concerned with the professional study and cultivation of the Japanese language.

In modern Japanese society, it is not necessary to be a successful author of books and articles in order to be a university professor or to be a staff member of one of the many government-supported institutes or other organizations that have as their sole purpose the academic pursuit of the Japanese language. Just as in North America, many of the professors at Japanese universities on every level, and most of the civil-service employees of specialized research institutes, do little more writing than the minimum involved in signing the receipt for their monthly salaries. And in Japan, where automatic bank transfers are now the rule rather than the exception, even this necessary minimum has gradually been rendered obsolete.

But if all university faculty and research-institute staff do not actually write and publish, the reverse is emphatically not true. No one can be a successful author in this important and lucrative Japanese market unless he or she has the credentials of either university or research-institute affiliation. The Japanese are eager to buy and read books on almost every level of difficulty about the myth of Nihongo; but they are only interested in them so long as they are by "experts," and their definition of expert is a person who is either a university faculty member or is employed by the civil service as a member of a government-supported research institute.

These exemplifications of the myth of Nihongo found on the printed page—whether in the form of serious, scholarly tomes or easy-to-read paperbacks for the commuter trade or signed articles in weekly magazines and daily newspapers—all sell exceptionally well. The academic author who manages to break into this business, and whose work survives in the market-place, soon becomes financially very well off. After all, he or she already has one full-time, permanent, quite well-paid position to start with, either on a university faculty or at the civil-service research institute to which he or she is attached. But publishing an even moderately successful book or weekly-magazine series about the myth of Nihongo will immediately bring in cash royalties that may quite easily amount to many multiples of the individual's annual salary. Nor does the work involved in such writing and publishing in any way interfere with holding down the individual's other, full-time position. Far from it. In both instances, such writing and publishing is regarded as an important part of the job—indeed, the most important part of the position that the author nominally holds elsewhere.

Readers who are not well acquainted with Japanese academic circles or with Japanese society in general, and particularly readers who do not have firsthand experience of the avidness with which the ordinary Japanese reader will frequently buy quite expensive books—and then equally often actually read them!—will probably find much of what goes on in Japan in this con-nection either difficult to understand or difficult to believe. The enormous sales often enjoyed by murky academic publications will come as one surprise; so will the enormous prestige of any author who can add "Univer-sity of X" or "Research Institute of Y" to his or her name. To understand the great popularity, wide circulation, and enormous potential profits involved with the transmission of the myth of Nihongo by the print media in modern Japan, it is necessary to forget everything that one may have learned or experienced about American academic life and particularly about American academic publishing. In Japan, all this is quite a different game.

Much the same must also be said about the newer, less traditional media that are equally involved in the contemporary circulation of the myth of Nihongo in modern Japan. Radio is still an important element in much Japanese life, particularly in mountainous areas—and Japan is mostly a land of mountains—where even the superb technology of Japanese television transmission is still unable to get a clear signal into many homes. But of course, in many urbanized areas, TV is *the* important nonprint medium.

Japan has the highest per capita permeation of TV sets of any country in the world, and, to the visitor at least, most of them seem to be turned on at full volume at any given time. Both TV and radio reach hundreds of thousands of Japanese for an average of several hours per day. And hardly an hour goes by on either medium in which the myth of Nihongo does not raise its head one way or another.

Most obvious of all, of course, are the many hours of overtly cultural and educational programs scheduled daily on both TV and radio in Japan, not only on the several TV channels and radio frequencies that are operated by the Japanese government solely for educational purposes, but also on the even more numerous privately operated, purely commercial facilities. Having spent so much of their lives in one variety of schoolroom or another, the Japanese early acquire a wide spectrum of favorable conditioned reflexes to the outward forms and discipline of education that often lasts them the rest of their lives. For most of childhood, they are told that they must not play but study. Their home is a classroom, and the classroom is where they feel most at home. The result is that even after their formal schooling finally comes to an end with university graduation, many adult Japanese feel secretly guilty for the rest of their lives whenever they spend any substantial amount of time doing anything that is not ostensibly connected with studying or with some sort of formal schooling.

Japanese TV and radio both respond in two different ways to this lingering Pavlovian reflex of horror at enjoying oneself. Both media actually schedule a surprisingly large number of hours of formal educational and cultural programs, which the viewer or listener can enjoy with a clear conscience, since they are plainly labeled educational. But both media also customarily deck out pure entertainment programs in educational garb, to lull their audiences into a false but comforting sense of relaxation: it is all right, they say in effect, to enjoy the following program because it is not really entertainment, it is actually education. Relax, and study hard!

As so often, we may note here with interest that a strikingly sharp contrast exists between Japanese and American tastes and practices. On American TV and radio, educational and cultural programs can be successful only if they are made to resemble pure entertainment formats as much as possible. Any suggestion of formal education, any hint of the university classroom or lecture hall, on national public radio or educational TV in the United States is the kiss of death. Educational and cultural programs are often quite popular with American viewers and listeners, but only if they are presented in such a way that their educational intent is elaborately disguised. Instead, they must be passed off as far as possible in conventional show-business terms.

In Japan just the opposite is true. Show business stands the best chance with Japanese TV and radio audiences when it masquerades as education.

This frees Japanese audiences from the inhibitions resulting from their countless childhood years of rigidly enforced study and permits them to enjoy themselves with a clear conscience. And even while, because of the interesting complex of sociological factors just sketched, much of the educational and cultural format of Japanese TV and radio is little more than just that—a thin window dressing of educational content designed to put the audience at its ease—nevertheless a considerable amount of it is actually serious and is seriously followed by a substantial number of Japanese. Within the large amount of time allotted for such education and culture on Japanese TV and radio, programs dealing with one aspect or another of the myth of Nihongo play an important role, if only because their content or subject matter is broad enough to interest almost every element in the audience available for such enlightening entertainment.

Many of the most successful authors of print-media versions of the myth of Nihongo are also frequent, and much appreciated, performers on TV and radio. They appear on talk shows, publicizing their most recent books on the uniqueness of the Japanese language, in much the same way that American movie celebrities and political figures employ American TV for similar purposes of self-publicity. The only major difference is that in the case of these Japanese examples, the person who appears on the TV screen actually has written the book in question, and he or she will actually be interviewed, often at surprising length, about the content of the book being publicized. The Japanese audience would feel seriously cheated if it did not get a long, often rather technical and involved lecture about the subject at hand, and the audience is rarely disappointed.

At other times the format and the media presentation will be much more direct. Japanese educational TV is especially fond of long, lecturelike talks that are simply presented "cold," with not even a minimum of window dressing. Indeed, the intent of many producers seems to be to make these programs appear as much like a university classroom as possible, a goal in which they mostly succeed marvelously well.

Professor X or Lecturer Y appears on the screen seated before a small table that is generally decorated with a bit of imported Turkish carpet and the obligatory flower arrangement. The speaker is always shown in the company of a docile young lady who will introduce him to the audience and then sit just at the edge of the camera's range, in the same attitude of respectful, almost worshipful attention that the producers of these programs assume will also be that of their audiences. Professor X or Lecturer Y proceeds to talk very carefully on the subject announced for a very long time, sometimes reading from a manuscript, sometimes squinting at what must be rather poorly written cue cards. Little if any of the presentation will be relieved by graphics or other visual diversions of any sort. After all, this is educational TV; it is supposed to be educational, and education is not supposed to be interesting.

The modern myth of Nihongo is always a popular subject for these long solo talk sessions that occupy much of the Japanese TV scene. It more than meets all possible requirements for the genre, since it is a field in which there are many well-known experts; it is a field that everyone recognizes as being important and educational; and it is a field in which no one expects that anything will be said that is in the least either fun or interesting.

But such deadly earnest exercises are not the only way in which the myth finds its way into the electronic media. Almost every other variety of radio and TV program format is equally fair game for the myth, and it manages to surface in many other, ostensibly quite frivolous exercises such as quiz shows, contests, and soap operas, with equal persistence and equal impact. The more one watches Japanese TV and the longer one listens to Japanese radio, the more one is struck by how often the subject of almost any program turns to the Japanese language—and when the subject turns to the language, the myth of Nihongo is never far behind.

The mention of a foreign country, the mention of a foreign language, the mention of any aspect of verbal communication that in any manner, shape, or form might possibly involve anyone who uses the Japanese language is enough to trigger the myth. It is always present and potentially active somewhere, if only just below the surface, and always ready to make itself instantly felt, like the red-hot lava that lurks beneath the newly congealed surface of a volcanic eruption. One has only to break through its thin surface crust to be badly burned.

It is, of course, impossible to cite specific statistical data that would tell us, for example, just how many of the thousands of books or how many of the thousands of magazine and newspaper feature articles published every month in Japan are devoted to one aspect or another of the myth of Nihongo. Looking through the stock of the average Japanese bookstore—and Japan has, without any question, the largest, best-stocked, most avidly patronized bookstores of any country on earth—one soon gains the impression that the percentage of total publishers' output devoted to this particular subject is very large. The same is true of radio and TV. Watching Japanese TV for any length of time, or listening to radio in Japan, one soon gets the strong impression that a surprisingly large segment of the available air time is given over to lectures on the special qualities of the Japanese language or to other programs in which the myth of Nihongo manages to express itself in one way or another. But this too must necessarily remain on the level of overall impressions; precise data are not to be had.

Nevertheless, some indication of how very widespread the media presentations of the modern myth of Nihongo actually are may be gained from what might be termed the "slop-over" phenomenon. Since the myth of Nihongo is, by the terms of its internal self-definition, something that is ostensibly only of interest and value to Japanese living totally within the confines of contemporary Japanese society, we might expect that its media representations would also limit themselves to the context of Japanese society. But in actual fact, nothing could be further from the truth.

One need not live in Japan, or even be able to read Japanese newspapers, magazines, and books, to have many of the most striking manifestations of this modern sustaining myth forcibly brought to one's attention. One does not even have to have seen a single Japanese TV program, or ever to have listened to Japanese radio programs, to have encountered the myth in most of its representative aspects. Indeed—and this is the most curious paradox of all—one need not know a single word of the Japanese language, or to have ever been closer to the Japanese islands than Lake Woebegone, Minnesota, to have been confronted with a rich sufficiency of the myth in its manifold adumbrations.

It is here that we have the best, as well as the most reliable, measure of how all-pervading the myth is within Japanese society itself. When we see how it "slops over" in this fashion and how frequently it goes out of its way to confront totally unrelated, often remote, and generally disinterested places and peoples with its eccentric assumptions and allegations, then we have the best possible measure for its total permeation throughout domestic Japanese life and culture.

The myth has become such an all-pervading part of Japanese life today that it is now all but impossible to export anything that relates to Japan in the intellectual sphere without also picking up and transmitting a sizable dose of the myth along the way. The infection is far too widespread to be easily contained; the merest contact is sufficient to pass it on.

It is unfortunate that we lack hard statistical information about the numbers of books in circulation that elaborate upon the myth of Nihongo. One would like to know how many hundreds of magazine and newspaper articles are written and printed each week dealing with the same subject. The totals for TV and radio time occupied by the myth each week would without question be impressive figures indeed. But in the absence of such data, we must make do with what we have. And what we do have is this "slop over" of the myth, taking it into what are, by any rigorous set of definitions, irrelevant foreign areas. But this same "slop over" obviously provides us with an excellent means for estimating the statistical aspect of the impact of this myth on modern Japanese life. Quite equally obviously, that impact is immense.

Of all the examples of this media "slop-over" phenomenon that might be cited, probably the most striking are those provided by the English-language public-relations journal published under the title of *Japan Echo* and widely distributed by Japanese embassies and consulates throughout the world. We shall see later on in this book some of the questions that are raised by the official sponsorship and special interests behind this particular journal. What especially concerns us here is the surprisingly large amount of space that it has devoted, in almost every issue since the *Japan Echo* began publication in August 1974, to English-language versions of articles originally published in Japanese books and magazines elaborating upon one or another facet of the modern myth of Nihongo.

Officially sponsored public-relations organs like the *Japan Echo* claim that they are trying to "inform the rest of the world of the truth about Japan." The editors make a selection of what appear to them to be the most important, the most informative, and the most "correct" articles and books originally published in Japan in Japanese for the Japanese reader. These articles the editors then have translated into English and offer them in turn for the information and edification of the foreign reader.

But what is most surprising about all such publications is the way their editors seem incapable of sticking to their own official subject for more than a few pages at a time. Their avowed goal is to "tell the rest of the world the truth about Japan." This task they of course interpret to mean repeating the well-worn arguments for the limitless expansion of Japanese products into the world's markets. But almost at once they seem to lose sight of this, their official purpose for publishing, and end up instead offering the reader a selection of generally cryptic translations of murky articles from the Japanese print media about this or that facet of the myth of Nihongo. They may begin by urging that everyone else in the world accept unlimited amounts of Japanese exports and try to justify continuation of the strict limitations that the Japanese themselves place on all varieties of imports. But before one realizes it, their argument mysteriously shifts one way or another to—the myth of Nihongo!

The foreign reader of such pages can only conclude—if indeed he or she makes any sense out of this at all—that somehow it is necessary to understand the allegedly unique nature of the Japanese language in order to become a good customer for Japanese TV sets and economy-size automobiles. Or is the message that if one understands how difficult the Japanese language allegedly is, this will make one happier when Japanese exports invade one's own markets and destroy domestic production? Will unemployed assembly-line workers in Detroit really be much solaced after they have read about how the Japanese language has a special spirit that no other language possesses—and will they believe it, even if they read it?

When we observe how much of what survives the extensive process of editorial selection to appear at last in the pages of such organs as the *Japan*

Echo still ends up being related in one way or another to the Japanese language and to the modern myth of Nihongo, we get some idea, albeit necessarily a somewhat indirect one, of just how important the myth is in the purely domestic Japanese mass media. If it were not, there would be no way in which to explain this striking "slop-over" phenomenon.

Nor do these "slop overs" of the myth into quite irrelevant foreign contexts limit themselves to the pages of such official public-relations organs as the *Japan Echo*. Anything that is as universal within a culture as is this modern myth of Nihongo simply cannot be kept at home. Sooner or later substantial samples are bound to find their way into the export market in one form or another, often to the bafflement of those abroad who find themselves at the receiving end.

Potential American customers for educational films recently received a direct-advertising brochure from a Tokyo film company that touted its wares along the following lines: "Our international sales managing director who graduated from Columbia College recommended us a year ago to produce a series of films relating to the mastery of the Japanese language and the understanding of our complex culture. . . . He suggested that it is very difficult for American students to learn Japanese conversation as well as the contents of Japanese morality. . . ."

How many non-Japanese readers of this brochure must have said to themselves: What a puzzling way in which to try and sell a product! Perhaps the readers of this advertising matter were initially lulled into a sense of security, or at least into a feeling of the familiar, by that deft introduction of the "international sales managing director who graduated from Columbia College." But then something strange begins to happen to the message, if not to the medium. If this Columbia College graduate is really all that keen on helping foreigners master the Japanese language and "understand our complex culture," why in the world does he then make his pitch from the position that it will actually be very difficult for American students ever to learn the very things that his company is now proposing to teach them? The reader will only begin to wonder what this "international sales managing director" really studied at Columbia College. Surely it cannot have been advertising psychology. This last question only becomes more profound, and more unanswerable, when the reader encounters the strange coupling of conversation with morality that follows immediately thereafter.

If the reader is unfamiliar with the teaching and assumptions of the modern myth of Nihongo, he will find all of this simply incomprehensible. (And if he also happens to be a graduate of Columbia College, he may well fire off an angry letter to the dean, asking what in the world they teach foreign students there these days.) But if he understands something of the mythic assumptions that underlie this and similar profusions of the contemporary Japanese approach to all sociolinguistic questions, he will be forced to admit that the whole strangely ordered presentation of this brochure actually does mean something: it fits in exactly with the overall outlines of the myth.

As we shall see later in the present book, it is the myth of Nihongo that inextricably links language and Japanese morality, just as it mistakenly but inextricably links language with race and culture at every turn. It is the myth that argues that there is a need for foreigners to learn the Japanese language but also simultaneously claims that the Japanese language is so uniquely difficult that it is all but impossible for anyone to learn it, whether Japanese or foreigner. Every perplexing theme hinted at in the advertising brochure cited above is intimately bound up with the modern myth of Nihongo. If we separate the text of this advertising message from the myth, it means nothing. But once we view it in the mythic context, it testifies vividly to the permeation of the myth throughout modern Japanese society —that same permeation that explains all the examples of the "slop-over" phenomenon already described. Which is not, of course, to imply that all this is not a very curious way to go about selling anything.

At its heart, then, the modern myth of Nihongo is linguistically inaccurate and scientifically misleading. It is inaccurate and misleading because it is based upon the erroneous equation of what are actually quite separate entities. The myth does its work by equating the Japanese language with Japanese race and also by equating Japanese race with Japanese culture. Each of these equations is entirely contradicted by everything that modern linguistic science and common sense as well have to teach us today. We know that language is not the same as race. We also know that language is not identical with culture: it is a part of culture.

All this means in turn that the linguistic scientist, or for that matter even the interested, informed layman with no special linguistic training, is liable to write off the entire sociolinguistic phenomenon of the myth of Nihongo as simply silly, or at least as unimportant for understanding Japan. Unfortunately it is neither. Nothing that Japan takes as seriously as it takes this myth can be disregarded if we are to begin to understand contemporary Japanese society and culture. Demonstrating a few of the major ways in which this myth is important for understanding Japan is the immediate goal of each of the chapters that follow.

CHAPTER TWO

The Kernel of Truth

Lastly, concerning the Japan Tongue, the same sounds no less lofty than brave, and expresses sufficiently the high ambition of the Speaker, being full of Vowels and Consonants. —Arnoldus Montanus, *Atlas Japannensis,* London, 1670

IN ORDER to understand the nature and role of the modern myth of Nihongo in contemporary Japanese life, we must constantly remind ourselves that since this entire body of folk belief and social convention is actually a sustaining myth of modern Japanese society (in the sense of this expression as briefly sketched in the previous chapter), the myth itself may be expected to have a hard, irreducible kernel of truth at its heart. All successful myths do. None of them are made up out of whole cloth. No effective sustaining myth, and particularly no myth that is designed to operate for very long periods of time, can do its work, or for that matter even survive, if it lacks this kernel of truth, a core of actual fact.

The most important thing, however, at the very outset of this entire consideration of the truth that does underlie the modern myth of Nihongo, is to understand that the existence of this kernel of truth does not mean that the myth itself is true. It only means that the myth can, and does, operate successfully in its role of sustaining society. If the myth itself were true, it would not have to operate as a myth. There would, in that case, be no need for the mythic elaboration of fanciful, irrelevant layers painstakingly built up to surround and protect the kernel of truth that is at its heart, not unlike the way in which an oyster builds up a protective layer of secretions in order to protect itself from the irritation of a grain of sand.

The elements of truth at the heart of the myth are real enough, but that

21

does not make the myth any less mythic. And perhaps it is no accident that the Japanese were the first people in the world to perfect a technique for artificially reproducing the until-then-natural, uncontrolled process of introducing a solid, irritating substance into an oyster in such a way that it would eventually become the center of a lustrous pearl. We shall see below that the techniques by which Mikimoto first produced his cultured pearls are, by and large, not all that much different from the way in which the modern practitioners of the myth of Nihongo go about ensuring that durable layers of mythic materials will be encouraged to solidify about a few hard kernels of linguistic fact.

Examples that demonstrate the way in which all successful myths must necessarily be built up around kernels of actual fact are not difficult to identify. Nor is it difficult to prove that without such a kernel of truth at their center, even the most superficially pleasing and apparently well-worked-out myths disappear almost as soon as they are generated. Totally factless myths, far from sustaining ideologies and societies, are usually unable even to sustain their own weight for very long.

A fairly routine feature of American life is the spontaneous generation of a millennial myth, according to which the world is predicted to be coming to an end in the fairly near future, generally within a few weeks from the time of the prediction. Adherents of the myth sell or give away their possessions (often to the considerable profit of the mythmakers) and gather in some scenic spot—the tops of hills or conveniently accessible mountains being favored for the purpose—there to await the end of the world. But the end does not come. The predictions are false. The millennial myth has always shown itself to lack the unyielding kernel of truth that a myth must have at its center if it is to survive as a vehicle for other ideas.

We can only contrast the failure of such insubstantial myths as those predicting the end of the world at a specific time and place with the enduring success of the true myths of our time, or for that matter with those of any time. The true myths do survive, and they sustain the people who believe in them, because they incorporate elements of truth. Again, it must be stressed that this does not mean that the myths themselves are true: a toad with a diamond in its head is still only a toad, not a diamond with warts. But it does always mean that the true myth, the one that survives and sustains, necessarily incorporates elements of fact, and also even of truth, somewhere in its depths.

When we confront the evidence that modern Japanese life provides both for the survival and for the sustaining élan of the myth of Nihongo in every sphere—political, economic, intellectual, educational, the list is all but endless—one of our first tasks will be to recognize that deep within this myth there are elements of truth and then to try and find out what those elements are. Such identification is no mere intellectual game or pastime. It is only by identifying such elements and by bringing them out into the open that the myth may be shown for what it is and eventually defused of its mystical power and magical adumbrations. Once we can dislodge the diamond from within the toad, we need no longer fear that the creature will be able to harm us.

In other words, if we are to make any genuine progress in understanding the myth of Nihongo and its importance in modern Japanese society, one of our first tasks must be to try and see just what some of these kernels of truth that lie at the heart of the myth of Nihongo actually are. We need have no fears about whether or not such kernels actually exist. There really is something to all the talk one encounters about Japanese being "unique" or "special" or "unusual and distinctive among all the other languages of mankind." If there were not, then the myth of Nihongo would be able neither to survive nor to work. And one need not know much about modern Japan to realize that it clearly does both. The myth survives, just as surely as the myth works. So there must be something to it, but what?

Before considering the linguistic reality that underlies these kernels of truth about which the myth focuses itself, a few concrete examples of the sort of thing that is at issue here will probably help a great deal to clarify the entire question. The examples that follow all belong to a single and quite simple category: they all represent the sort of Japanese linguistic evidence that is commonly cited by Japanese authors and scholars today in support of their position, which is one of the keystones of the modern myth of Nihongo, to the effect that Japanese is a distinctively "rich" language. It is so rich, in fact, that its very richness is sufficient to set it apart from, and also to render it superior to, all the other languages of mankind.

Such alleged demonstrations of richness often begin, for example, with such a simple English word as "life." The modern myth of Nihongo will point out that, corresponding to this single English word, the Japanese language has a far richer array of vocabulary items, each of which, to be sure, means life, but each of which also refers to life in a somewhat more precise and more elaborate fashion.

Thus Japanese has the word *seimei*, which means life but with specific semantic reference to the continuation or survival of the life process in the human individual as a living entity. Hence *seimei* is the word for life in such expressions as *seimei hoken*, or life insurance, since *seimei* is the particular variety of life that insurance insures. Hence also, *seimei* is life as in expressions meaning to lose one's life, etc. But Japanese also has the word *jinsei*, which equally means life, but this time with sole reference to human beings. Either an animal or a man can lose *seimei*, but only human beings can lose, or even risk, their *jinsei*. Furthermore, there is also the Japanese word *inochi*, which also means life, but which represents a still further disembodied, abstracted concept of the same. For example, *inochi* is the word to be used for the life of flowers, or blossoms, particularly Japan's characteristic flowering cherries: *hana no inochi mijikashi,* "the life of a blossom is fleeting."

I recall a discussion with a number of Japanese scholars of the Japanese language, trying to decide which of the many Japanese words for life might best be used to translate the title of the American illustrated weekly *Life,* if a Japanese edition of the magazine should ever be contemplated. Actually, the tentative conclusion reached in that discussion was that none of the many Japanese words easily available, and all meaning life in one way or another, would really fill the bill. A Japanese edition of *Life* would most likely have had to be called *Raifu,* taking over the English word intact and simply making it conform to Japanese pronunciation rules (*r* for *l,* final -*u* since no Japanese word can end in *f,* and so on). In other words, not only was the Japanese language of great richness in respect to the availability of terms meaning life, but it was potentially even richer than it appeared to be, since it was apparently quite willing to add still another term to its already large repertory in the form of this loanword *Raifu.*

It is surely not difficult to imagine the interpretation that the myth of Nihongo has placed upon this and other cases where the language has a rich profusion of vocabulary items, all equivalent to what is often in a given Western language, especially in English, expressed by a single undifferentiated term. For "rice," Japanese has *ine* (rice in the seed bed, field, or sheaf), *kome* (hulled and polished rice, but still uncooked), *gohan* (steamed, cooked rice), *meshi* (a somewhat macho term for the same), and *raisu* (from English). This last word is now used when it is eaten with a fork or spoon from a flat, Western-style plate as part of a somewhat Western-style meal, as in *karē raisu,* "curry (and) rice," or, most unambiguously, in *pan mata wa raisu,* "(the meal comes with) bread or rice," a conventional phrase found on most menus in Japanese restaurants serving non-Japanese-style food. When the contrast is with *pan,* or bread, the item in question must be called *raisu,* not *gohan* or *meshi.* Even the most slyly motivated myth-monger may perhaps be forgiven for placing a potentially profound interpretation upon such richness of vocabulary and for drawing far-reaching conclusions relating to the superiority of the Japanese language over, for example, English, by reason of this richness.

But since we, unlike most modern Japanese, only wish to understand what the myth of Nihongo is all about and are not interested in becoming believers in the myth, we must first of all ask: Just what is all this about? Obviously, the Japanese language has a lot of very different words for things, ideas, and even concepts for which English, along with many other languages, gets along quite well using a simple term. The accuracy of the data cited is above question. What must be questioned instead is the interpretation that the myth of Nihongo places upon these data. And that interpretation is as demonstrably incorrect as the conclusions that the myth draws from it are misleading.

What principally leads to the mass of misleading conclusions in which the modern myth of Nihongo abounds is a very simple, and very deft, uniform agreement on the part of the mythmakers to overlook the most elementary fact of linguistic science, a fact so basic to the nature and structure of all human language that it may be termed a linguistic universal. True enough: Japanese has all these words for certain things for which English has, in each instance, a single word. But so also do a lot of other languages. At the same time, it would be equally simple to point to many other things, ideas, and concepts for each of which English as well as many other languages have a large number of words, but for which Japanese makes do with only a single term.

The linguistic universal at issue here may be paraphrased very simply, even though it is of tremendous importance for the understanding of how language works: *different languages have different ways of saying things.* Since this is always true, it immediately follows that the different ways, or the number of varied ways, in which one language expresses something does not, after all, tell us anything of significance about the nature, quality, or worth of the language as such.

When the modern myth of Nihongo focuses, as it so often does, upon this particular perversion of the first major linguistic universal, it finds itself building upon particularly strong ground. There is a real kernel of solid truth here, the basic kernel of linguistic truth just paraphrased in our simple statement of this first linguistic universal above. Actually, this is more than a kernel of truth. It is closer to being the single absolute truth that eventually explains all human language, since it follows directly from the arbitrary nature of all language that we have already stressed in chapter 1.

Language is arbitrary. This arbitrariness extends to the things that a language means, as well as to the number of different ways a language may or will select for saying things. In its decision to focus upon this particular kernel of truth, the modern myth of Nihongo has ensured itself of the availability of a substantial amount of what, at first glance, appears to be convincing evidence in favor of the special or unique nature of the Japanese language. One is well on the way toward believing that indeed the Japanese language is somehow different from all other human languages, until one realizes that what is being allegedly demonstrated is simply the restricted employment of the Japanese fragments of what is, after all, a universal linguistic feature.

If all this proves anything special about Japanese, then it could equally well be made to prove the same thing for another language as well, indeed for all languages.

Mostly, the multiplicity of terms for such things as rice or such concepts as life tells us about the culture and the society of the languages that employ them. There are so many terms for rice in Japanese because of the important role that rice has long held in the life of Japanese society. If English manages to get along with the single word rice, it is able to do this because rice is simply not all that important to most English-speaking peoples. Each language is a social phenomenon. Its distinctions and refinements reflect the needs and concerns of the society of which it is a part. Studying its details tells us much about the society, but such data cannot be used to propose far-reaching conclusions about the special or unique nature of the language itself.

Here the major methodological error of the modern myth of Nihongo is to be identified in its insistence upon locating all of this quality of the "unique," the "distinctive," and the "special" solely within Japanese itself. There is a kernel of truth here, but it is quite different from what the myth claims it to be. Japanese is unique, special, and distinctive, *but so are all other human languages.* This is the heart of the matter, as well as the key to demolishing most of the myth of Nihongo.

In other words, what we have here is simply another expression of the essentially arbitrary nature of language that has already been mentioned several times. All languages are arbitrary, arbitrary in the ways that they choose to say things, arbitrary in the things that they choose to say. Each language is unique, special, and distinctive because each language is, in this sense, essentially arbitrary. Japanese makes one set of choices, English makes another, Korean still another, Bengali still others. Japanese is unique, in this sense and in this respect; but English, Korean, Bengali, and every other language are all equally unique.

What the modern myth of Nihongo has here done, then, is to incorporate a truth-kernel that is true because it relates to universal linguistic structures and experience. But it has incorporated this kernel of truth into its mythic moil in a less than truthful fashion. Still, because the kernel itself is real enough, incorporating it into the myth immediately endows the myth with a substantial, if quite specious, patina of truth. The technique is one of employing the right thing for the wrong end. A truth-kernel that relates not only to Japanese linguistic experience but actually to all human language is taken over and presented as if it were unique to Japanese alone. Thus the myth is able to incorporate, and in the process to grow strong upon, spurious intellectual nutrients that are provided by a fairly substantial body of evidence. But the evidence itself is, to use the language of the courtroom, introduced in a fashion that must firmly be ruled out of order.

This misleading introduction of irrelevant evidence plays such an important role in the modern myth of Nihongo that it is impossible to argue too strongly against its methodology, which is erroneous, or against its conclusions, which are false. All the relevant counterarguments eventually come back to the essentially arbitrary nature of language itself. This means that these counterarguments often lack the rich variety of the myth that they must refute. Because the counterarguments generally seem less striking and less interesting than the myth they are countering, sometimes they are not as effective in refuting it as they might otherwise be. But the main reason why the necessary counterarguments may not be completely convincing at first glance has to do with the basic linguistic-science assumption of the arbitrary nature of language.

This assumption is basic, and it unquestionably is true. But it also generally runs directly counter to conventional wisdom, to the commonsense approach toward language that many otherwise well-educated persons in all countries generally grow up having. The basic assumption of the arbitrary nature of language, when its logic is followed up even a short distance, soon teaches us that the linkage between the phenomenon of language and the phenomena of the real world in which language is employed—things like rice, ideas like life, concepts like love—is itself arbitrary. No one who even knows of the existence of a single foreign language outside his or her own language would seriously argue against this assumption. Nevertheless, this assumption still runs counter to conventional common sense to an important degree. We like to think, all of us, whatever our native language may be, that our own language's words for rice or life or love are not arbitrary and that the words we use really do somehow have some meaningful connection with the things for which we use them. This is only common sense; it is the conventional wisdom of most human society; and it is wrong.

If it were not wrong, if there were something either necessary or profound, something non-arbitrary operating to link language and the real world, we could never explain why there is more than one language employed by the human race. Only the arbitrary nature of language can explain why a certain matter-of-fact object—an object plainly and easily identifiable in the real world—is called stone in one language but *Stein* in another, *pierre* in yet another, and *ishi* in Japanese.

Japanese is indeed unique and special, because it has this word for stone that is *ishi*. But so also are English and German and Korean and Turkish all equally unique: they have *stone, Stein, tol,* and *taç,* all for the same object. When the words in question seem to resemble one another somewhat, as with English *stone* and German *Stein,* we begin to suspect historical relationship (and in this case, our suspicions would be correct). But for all these languages as they stand today, and putting aside the question of their histories, their choices of linguistic signs for the same object in the real world are all quite arbitrary. All these languages are unique. Japanese is unique only because it is a language, not because it is Japanese.

In other words, the first major linguistic universal that we have been discussing teaches us that there is only one possible answer to this important "why?" question. The answer is that the relation between language and the real world consists not of rationality or morality or ethical imperatives, all of which have been suggested in certain systems of philosophy at one time or another, but rather consists of a set of arbitrary linkages. Words are used for the things they are used for, and hence words mean what they mean, simply because of the existence of sets of arbitrary agreements obtaining in the societies in which the words are used. Not only are these agreements arbitrary (which means that no ethical or moral significance can, or should, be attached to them), but they quite arbitrarily segment, or divide up, the real world (which is, give or take a few details of climate and physical geography, pretty much the same for all people everywhere at all times), into arbitrary groupings. These are the arbitrary groupings of which we have had some examples above in the various Japanese terms for life and rice.

Climate and physical geography are of course important subsidiary conditions to keep in mind in evaluating this variety of evidence for linguistic universals. If the Eskimos do not have words meaning summer heat or sandy desert, this tells us a great deal about where the Eskimos live, but next to nothing about the Eskimos' thought processes or inherent qualities, or about anything on those exalted levels. If the Hawaiian language does not have words for ice, snow, and sleet, this again tells us a great deal about the climate of Polynesia, but next to nothing about the Hawaiians. The abundance of modern Japanese words for rice tells us simply that rice has always been extremely important to the Japanese economic system, at least ever since its introduction to the islands from the Asian mainland in protohistoric times.

Actually, the abundance of these words in the language does not even tell us how much rice the Japanese have eaten throughout their history, since, for most of Japanese history, rice was something that only the very few lucky individuals on the very top of the social heap ever tasted. For the rest of the population it served instead as a rather inconvenient kind of money, something in which taxes were levied and stipends paid. Rice was extremely inconvenient to use for these purposes, because the only useful thing that really could be done with it, and the thing that really gave it its value—that is, eating it—destroyed the object itself along with its value within the society. One is reminded of the role of black-market cigarettes in postwar Germany. It was also inconvenient to use rice as money because when you hoarded it too long it would eventually spoil and then ceased to be of value to anyone. During the 1960s, when for the first time in all Japanese history there was enough rice to go around, everyone ate a lot of it. Now that too is slacking off, and the Japanese government, which still hoards rice stocks as a kind of sacramental surrogate for money, now also employs entire offices full of university graduates all busy trying to figure out ways to lure people into eating more rice. The language has a lot of words for rice; rice has been important in Japanese society since the proto-historic period; and that is about all that the language tells us in this connection.

Inherent within all this mass of pseudo-evidence that is so often cited by proponents of the myth of Nihongo, there is also to be found still another striking proof that the linguistic data concerned, while accurate enough as to their forms and meanings, actually cannot tell us anything significant about the nature of the Japanese language itself. This is the historical fact that most of the words that play a part in each of these lists purporting to demonstrate the richness of the Japanese lexical stock are, in matter of fact, not originally Japanese words at all, but are instead more often than not borrowings from foreign languages. The reader will surely already have noticed this in connection with such obvious borrowings from English as *Raifu* for *Life* magazine and *raisu* for rice, and will probably already have wondered just what such recent borrowings from a quite unrelated foreign language, English, could possibly be supposed to tell us about the unique or characteristic nature of the Japanese language. The answer is, of course, nothing.

But the question posed by borrowed words does not stop with such obvious examples as *Raifu* and *raisu*. An even more impressive number of the words most often cited by the proponents of the myth of Nihongo are also borrowings, not from English, but from Chinese. Chinese is, again, a quite different language, one that is unrelated to Japanese, and a language whose forms and words can logically be expected to tell us as little about the nature of the Japanese and of their language as English can.

In the list of words for life given above, *inochi* is the only etymologically Japanese form in the entire group. *All the other words listed are borrowed from Chinese.* So while there are, to be sure, many different words in modern Japanese that may be used to translate the English life, depending on the particular context in which the English word appears, and depending also upon which sense of the term is at issue in any given situation, if we were to restrict ourselves entirely to historically Japanese words, we would be left with only one Japanese word, *inochi,* with which we would have to render all the senses of the one English word, life.

If there is anything that is "distinctively rich" in this entire linguistic situation, the richness is to be identified in the vocabulary resources of Chinese, upon which Japanese has drawn freely for almost all of its history. Linguistic borrowings from Chinese have been particularly rampant in Japan during the past hundred years, and they are the main reason why, to express the situation in the simplest terms possible, "Japanese has so many different words for things." The richness of modern Japanese, if there is any, is actually the richness of Chinese, not of Japanese itself.

Borrowed words, or loanwords as they are often called, result when one language imitates another. The linguistic forms that result from this imitation process, like *raisu,* which is in imitation of the English word rice, or like the various Chinese borrowings in Japanese in the general sense of life. such as *seimei, jinsei,* and the like, each of which reproduces, that is, imitates to some extent, the pronunciation of an original Chinese word, are, to be sure, Japanese linguistic evidence once they become commonly used in Japanese. But the process by which such words enter the language is a part of the functioning of culture and society, not actually a part of language itself.

Borrowing the English word rice and turning it into the Japanese word *raisu* happens when the culture and the society first of all decide to imitate Western eating habits and begin to eat the item in question in Western style—typically, not from a bowl, using chopsticks, but from a plate, using a fork. The linguistic imitation that results in linguistic borrowing begins with the cultural imitation that decides to depart from inherited styles and patterns for eating rice.

Thus the introduction of such borrowed linguistic forms as *raisu* into the Japanese language tells us a great deal about modern Japanese society and culture. It can tell us next to nothing about the issues that are most stressed by the makers of the myth of Nihongo. It can throw no light at all upon such questions as whether or not Japanese is a rich language; it can tell us nothing whatsoever about whether the Japanese have "thought processes" that are unique, or about whether in some other way their language sets them apart from the rest of the human race.

Recent imitations of English words can tell us nothing along these lines, nor can imitations of Chinese, even granted the historical fact that some of these go quite far back into Japanese history. The myth purports to focus upon what is distinctively Japanese, and from such elements it attempts to show how such distinctively Japanese features set Japan and the Japanese apart from the rest of the world. When, as here, it does this with linguistic elements that are so obviously not Japanese but borrowed from the languages of other countries, it immediately refutes its own claims.

The reader will also, by this time, most likely have been struck by yet another interesting internal contradiction that is deeply inherent in this aspect of the modern myth of Nihongo. This particular contradiction looms in bold relief each and every time that the myth employs some foreign language—most often English—for the purpose of allegedly demonstrating how unique or special or distinctive the Japanese language is.

We have already seen how English is used as if it were the measure of all things in the consideration of the purported richness of Japanese in connection with such terms as life and rice. Actually, it is against the yardstick of English that the most misleading measurements of the myth are generally carried out on every level of linguistic structure. The myth sets out to tell us something uniquely and distinctively Japanese but usually ends up measuring Japanese against English. To the outsider, to anyone not directly and personally involved in the myth and its promulgation, this approach seems also to involve the tacit admission that English is somehow the measure of all things—a linguistic super-system against which other linguistic systems ought to be, and can be, measured.

There is a deep internal contradiction in all this. But once we understand that we are dealing with a myth and not with actual linguistic facts as such, we need not be as surprised by its tacit acceptance, any more than we need be unduly astonished by the tactful silence with which most Japanese writers and commentators on these subjects pass over the more striking anomalies that bedevil their approach to the Japanese language. Equally striking internal contradictions are part of many myths, perhaps part of all. Most myths find nothing contradictory in placing simultaneous emphasis upon both good and bad, angels and devils, dark and light, stressing either extreme as the circumstances demand, but always maintaining a tactful silence about the existence of the other when it would be inconvenient to notice it.

When we keep this in mind, we will be less surprised to find that even while the myth points with pride to such clusters of vocabulary items as the Japanese words for life or rice, claiming that these words are evidence for a significant or characteristic richness of the language, it does not hesitate simultaneously to plead that the language also suffers from "poverty of expression" or "inability to differentiate concepts." These two positions—boasting of "richness" on the one hand and lamenting "poverty" on the other—are of course mutually contradictory. A language can hardly exhibit both these features simultaneously, any more than a nation or an economy can.

Here again, recognizing the theoretical mechanism of a typical sustaining myth must be our first step if we are to be able to understand how the myth of Nihongo can simultaneously accommodate these two diametrically opposed themes. Until we understand that we are dealing with a modern myth, we run the risk of dismissing out of hand any system of ideas or values that so quickly and neatly contradicts itself. This would, in turn, be unfor-

tunate for our understanding of modern Japan. The myth cannot be merely
dismissed. To do so would mean closing our eyes to one of the most salient
bodies of hard evidence that we have for helping to puzzle out some of
the ways in which modern Japanese society works. But once we do understand that we have to deal here with the major sustaining myth of Japanese
society, and once we keep in mind that all myths, particularly all sustaining
myths, incorporate internal contradictions easily and effortlessly, we are
then in a position to use such apparently contradictory claims to enhance
our understanding of much of what goes on in modern Japanese life.

All myths have their emphasis on good and light, their angels and saints;
but this does not keep them from also stressing bad, evil, and dark or from
assigning important places in their systems to devils and demons. The
modern sustaining myth of Nihongo finds nothing contradictory in stressing
both the richness and also the poverty of the Japanese language, often in
simultaneous pronouncements. We must accustom ourselves to this ambi-
dexterity of analysis, this switching back and forth from the negative to
the positive, from good to evil, if we are to follow the myth to a useful understanding of what it has to tell us.

No sustaining myth, particularly no sustaining myth that displays both
the substantial dimensions as well as the remarkable stamina that characterize
the modern myth of Nihongo, can exist for long unless it genuinely fills
a real need within the society it serves. In modern Japan, many of the needs
that the sustaining myth of Nihongo caters to are close at hand and quickly
identified. They include pressing questions of national as well as of personal
identity: Who are we? Where did we come from? Where are we going?
These are the questions that modern Japanese intellectual circles generally
lump together today under the general subject of the *Nihonjin-ron,* or the
question of the Japanese people.

The expression *Nihonjin-ron* has become an all-purpose term for the deeply searching identity crisis that has arisen on every level of Japanese society
with the coming of affluence in the 1970s and also as part of the domestic
Japanese reaction to the extensive penetration of Japanese business interests
into world markets. When you go about selling TVs in Tunisia, automobiles
in Australia, and computers in Canada, eventually somebody asks you:
Who *are* you? And if your customers ask the question often enough, eventually you too begin to ask yourself the same thing. This question is essentially
what is meant by the *Nihonjin-ron.* Many of those interested in the *Nihonjin-
ron* try to find at least some of the possible answers within the myth of
Nihongo.

But it is also possible to identify yet another way in which the modern
myth of Nihongo very effectively serves Japanese society, not in spite of

the internal contradictions that the myth incorporates, but actually for the very reason that it does display these striking contradictions. The key to resolving this apparent anomaly is to be found in the internal contradictions of modern Japanese society itself. A deeply contradictory myth best serves a deeply contradictory society.

These deep social contradictions can be observed on every level of modern Japanese life; but it is not without significance to note that they are at their most striking in the lives of the newly affluent and theoretically "best-off" white-collar upper-middle-class elements of society—the same elements within Japanese society who are most steadily exposed to the bombardments of the modern myth of Nihongo in all its media manifestations.

Osamu Isokawa is twenty-seven years old. He graduated from a leading university five or six years ago. Almost every waking hour that he can remember, up until the time that he was admitted to that university, was spent in studying in order to pass the examinations that would make it possible for him to enter the university. He attended a prekindergarten cram school to help ensure that he would be admitted to a prestigious kindergarten. (Are there any other countries that, like Japan, have kindergarten alumni groups that hold annual reunions?)

After kindergarten, elementary school; then middle school, then high school, and finally the university. The four years he spent there were the happiest and most untroubled period of Isokawa's life. Few classes at a Japanese university really have to be attended, and little academic work is required of the students, who after all deserve some time off in return for the years and years they devoted to gaining university admission in the first place. But the four untroubled years at the university pass all too soon. Before he realizes it, Isokawa ends up working all day, six days a week, and often overtime until late at night, as a computer programmer in the elaborately furnished, glamorously located offices of one of the world's most powerful banks in downtown Tokyo.

But when he is finally released from his air-conditioned office at the end of a long, demanding day, what happens to Isokawa then? What does he get in return for the years of cramming to pass his university examinations? A grueling, bone-crushing ride for more than an hour in an overpacked commuter train and the return home, day after day, often near midnight, to a meal of cold rice and leftover radish pickles to be eaten on the floor of a crowded, unheated tenement room that the average West German or American unskilled laborer, with one-tenth of Isokawa's education and generally with one-half his income, would regard as unfit for human habitation. But Isokawa is not only expected to eat his cold meal and sleep in such surroundings; he will also dutifully marry and raise a family of at least two children, manage somehow to find husbands for the girls, and save enough money to pay the boys' tuition at the best prekindergarten cram school so that the entire cycle can immediately repeat itself.

Contradictions there are here, and contradictions in abundance. National affluence that can, and does, provide the hard-working, well-educated individual with so little personal comfort once he leaves his office abounds in contradictions; and a society that thrives in spite of such contradictions is plainly in need of a sustaining myth that is itself equally contradictory. Perhaps this is why the myth of Nihongo serves the society as well as it does.

But why, one is still entitled to ask, a myth of language? Why select language, out of all the other candidates available, for this important role in keeping modern Japanese society from disintegrating in response to the inherently fissionable forces that are so obviously built into it?

Several answers to this question are possible, but the most important one is also the most obvious. Language must now serve as the focus for the great sustaining myth of modern Japan for the extremely simple but important reason that every other likely candidate for the focus of such a myth has already been tried and found sadly wanting, particularly over the past four decades of Japanese history. In their selection of language as the focus of their sustaining myth, the Japanese bear eloquent witness to the long continuous history of their civilization. They also demonstrate what a profound social and intellectual toll much of that history has taken on the Japanese people. So much has been tried in the past and found wanting that only this, the most unlikely candidate of all, their language, can now serve as the focus for their sustaining myth.

When we view the question in this manner, we can begin to understand some of the reasons why the modern myth of Japanese society does not focus, for example, upon religious concepts or ideals, and also why it does not embrace anything spiritual or otherworldly at its heart, as have the sustaining myths of so many other peoples at different times and places. Historically, the Japanese have never lacked a rich repertory of distinctive views relating to religion or the other world, sometimes views that were significantly different from those entertained by most other peoples at most times in history. But whenever the Japanese have tried to use these as a sustaining force for their society, the results have not been notably successful.

During their past history, the Japanese sometimes did attempt to erect a sustaining myth on religious ideals and concepts, partly those of their own indigenous beliefs and partly those of the imported religion of Buddhism. But the former were almost always too inchoate to serve effectively in the role of the focus of the sustaining myth; only the latter—the enormously involved ethical, moral, and philosophical systematics of Far Eastern Buddhism of the Mahayana—was ever sophisticated enough to serve in this role, even briefly.

But all that was a long time ago. Today, religion of any kind plays no more of an effective role in modern Japanese life than it does in the daily life of any of the other industrially advanced countries of the world, or perhaps even less. The sustaining myth once erected on the foundations of Mahayana Buddhism had begun to lose its credibility in Japan by the latter part of the fourteenth century. It was totally swept away, as an effective force in Japanese life, during the hundred-year period of civil war that ravaged most of the settled parts of the country between 1467 and 1568. This, in many ways the Japanese equivalent of Europe's Hundred Years' War, was not really a religious struggle at all. But one of its lasting effects was to reduce almost to zero the credibility of any sustaining myth that would try to base itself upon religious concepts or ideals. After 1568, when Oda Nobunaga finally fought his way into the smouldering ruins of the city of Kyoto, very few who were not on the payroll of a temple or other religious foundation would ever again take religious ideas seriously, much less suggest that they could serve as the kernel of truth in the sustaining myth of society.

Further examples of sustaining myths that have been employed at one time or another during the long course of Japanese history, but which have proved themselves wanting and hence have had to be discarded, are much closer at hand. The nationalist-fascist dictatorship that led Japan into its ill-advised military adventures on the Asian mainland, its attempted rape of China, and its final demented challenge of the industrial powers of the West in the early hours of Sunday, December 7, 1941, in the skies over Pearl Harbor, made spectacularly effective, if extremely short-lived, use of an elaborate sustaining myth.

This myth contained so many disparate elements that it is difficult to summarize its main ingredients. By and large, it may be broken down into three equal parts. One comprised selected elements drawn out of indigenous Japanese religious beliefs; the second embraced a selection of nineteenth-century nationalistic fantasies borrowed from Western Europe, particularly from Prussia; and the third was rooted in a number of Japanese elaborations and perversions of the already quite sufficiently perverted "master race" or "superman" ideas that had by then begun to become popular in the Third Reich.

As a national sustaining myth, this unholy mixture of native and foreign materials had many elements that, for a time, worked very well. Unfortunately, as we have seen above, the acid test of a sustaining myth is whether or not it really works over a considerable period of time. The total, unconditional surrender of the Japanese military machine, the principal proponents of this particular myth, to the Allies on August 15, 1945, provided convincing evidence of the most concrete kind possible that the myth did not work —at least, that it did not and would not work after 1945.

And so, with religion per se long since ruled out of the question, with Prussian-style nationalism discredited, and with Hitlerian fantasies of racial purity apparently also no longer an effective focus for the myth, there was very little left for the Japanese to turn to: only their language was left.

The desolation of the bombed-out cities of postwar Japan was at once both the most eloquent and the most painful metaphor for the spiritual and intellectual desolation of the Japanese themselves. In city after city, nothing of all that had seemed so very substantial was left standing. What little had survived the nightly fire raids had immediately to be pulled down before it collapsed of its own damaged weight. The day the war ended, nothing of Japanese life seemed to have endured—except the language. There was nothing else to turn to that offered even the semblance of continuity with the past. And so turn to it they did, and have, with a vigor and enthusiasm that can only be appreciated when considered in the full light of the tragic historical events that led up to August 1945.

Nature is not the only thing around us that cannot long tolerate a vacuum: neither can social organization. Something had to be found to fill the gap created by the disintegration of the elements of native religious belief, nationalism, and racial superiority that had comprised the sustaining myth of Japan over the decade or so down to 1945. What was found was the language—in a word, the modern myth of Nihongo.

But, as we shall see below, it would be a dangerous oversimplification of the evidence to suggest that this contemporary myth of the Japanese language is really new in any of its essential points, or that it was simply evolved out of nothing in order to provide a workable substitute for those elements of the old nationalist-fascist myth that Japan's defeat in the Pacific War effectively rendered untenable. What happened was by no means that simple. Unless we study some of the details of what was actually a fairly complicated process of selection and elimination, we will remain unable to understand how the modern myth of Nihongo came into existence. Even more seriously, we will remain unable to understand the major reasons behind its tremendous impact upon modern Japanese thought and society.

Even though the old fascist-nationalist myth consisted, in the main, of the three major elements already listed—roughly equal portions of folk religion, European-style ultranationalism, and an emphasis on racial identity and purity aimed at establishing the innate superiority of the Japanese— this unholy trinity of perverted ideas by no means exhausted the myth's inventory of materials. The assignment of a "special role" to the Japanese language and the attempt to make of this language a "particular instrument" that somehow by its very nature gave concrete expression to the special racial identity—and hence also to the innate superiority—of the Japanese people were essential elements of the old nationalist-fascist myth in all its stages of development. Stress upon the language was part and parcel of the old nationalist-fascist myth. The only essential difference between the old, pre-1945 myth and the modern one in this connection is that in the former, language was merely one among many subsidiary, contributing elements, while in the contemporary version of the myth, it has become the central concept, the principal base upon which virtually the entire myth focuses.

How this came about becomes more comprehensible when we look in somewhat more detail at what actually happened in Japan in August 1945. When the Japanese military forces were defeated, the imperial government was forced to accept the terms of a remarkably stark, unconditional surrender to the Allies. These terms specified, among other equally harsh stipulations, that "the prerogative of the Emperor to rule the State shall be subject to the Supreme Commander of the Allied Forces of Occupation." With this single article in the instrument of surrender, most of the old myth fell apart overnight.

Elements of the inherited folk religion of pre-Buddhist Japan had played a definite if ill-defined part in the old, now-discredited myth. Dimly perceived quasi-divine figures from Japan's remote past, figures so vague and indistinct that only their names were in most cases remembered, had been invoked as gods of battle. But these indigenous gods, who were hardly very robust figures at best, could never again be taken seriously from this point on in Japanese history. If the old gods had really had any power or even importance, how would they have permitted this disaster to occur? Prussian-style ultranationalism had also played the role of a kind of antigod in the old myth. What had it brought to the Japanese except the devastation of burned-out cities and the tragedy of hundreds of thousands of deaths, both at home and overseas? It too was swiftly discredited. Nationalism, at least of the Prussian variety, had shown itself quite as impotent as the indigenous gods of Japan.

Nor were the myth's stipulations of innate racial superiority any easier to maintain in the aftermath of August 1945. Those Japanese who were lucky enough still to be alive found their cities and villages overrun by hordes of tall, strong, well-fed, and generally quite genial foreign troops. How, they asked themselves, can we have believed for a moment that we belonged to a race that was in any way superior to these great, smiling hulks of robust pink-faced lads?

Thus, very little was left of the old myth. Still less could be salvaged from it to serve in the new sustaining myth that nevertheless had to be evolved, and evolved swiftly, if Japanese society itself was to survive. Almost nothing of the old myth remained intact, *except those portions of the old myth that dealt with the Japanese language.* These segments of the myth and these alone survived the war unscathed. Nothing that happened in the war, nothing that happened during and after the defeat, nothing seen in the wilderness of bombed-out cities or experienced in the desolate cold and hunger that followed the surrender, nothing in any way compromised the portions of the old fascist-nationalist myth that had stressed the unique nature of the Japanese language. The only parts of the old myth that were still intact were those portions that focused on the Japanese language. It was to be almost entirely upon these few surviving elements of the old myth that the new sustaining myth of postwar Japan would be erected.

In fact, the tragic events of the war and the sordid aftermath of Japan's military defeat only tended to reinforce the already established mythic approach to the Japanese language that the society had earlier learned to accept from the older nationalist-fascist myth. The old, now-discredited myth had taught that one of the marks attesting to the superiority of the Japanese race was the Japanese language, with its unique features supposedly not shared by any other language on earth. And no matter how quickly the purely racial aspects of the old myth were discredited, as the GIs began to stroll up and down the fire-bombed streets of Japan's ghost cities, no one could possibly deny that the Japanese language had survived, and no one could deny that it surely was different, totally different from whatever it was that the GIs spoke, at the same time that it was the single major obstacle to any communication between them and the Japanese.

Friendly they were, by and large, and sometimes friendly to a fault, but who could make out a word that they were saying? Hardly anyone then alive in Japan could, least of all the English professors in the universities, to whom the GI language was less intelligible than the speech of Martians would probably have been. And yet, in those first hard months of defeat, how much depended upon being able to say something to these uninvited invaders! How often did simple physical survival depend upon catching the drift of what these strange beings from another world were saying!

This was no mere academic exercise, no aesthetic reverie involving Browning and Shelley and Keats. This was life in deadly earnest. With linguistic comprehension, even of the most rudimentary sort, went safety, food, and warmth; while the dangers of not understanding, or of misunderstanding, were almost as terrifying as those of the just-concluded hostilities themselves.

What had happened was that, for the third time in its history, Japanese society had found itself locked into a massive, life-and-death cultural confrontation with speakers of a foreign language. Centuries earlier, near the dawn of Japanese culture, the languages in question had been Korean and Chinese. Much later, around the turn of the sixteenth century, the confrontation had involved Portuguese, Dutch, and, to a lesser but still important extent, the English of England. Now the language was, of course, the American English of the GIs.

The tremendous stimulus afforded by this all-too-sudden contact with the virtually unknown—this daily confrontation with the frighteningly tall, healthy young men in uniform, talking loudly in an incomprehensible jargon and, for the first weeks and months at least, never letting their loaded weapons stray from convenient reach—could hardly have been experienced without producing an equally tremendous response. The principal reaction that resulted from this linguistic confrontation was the emergence of the Japanese language itself as the fetish focus for a new national sustaining myth, the modern myth of Nihongo.

The Japanese language was, in this way, the first element of Japanese culture to be restored and rehabilitated in the postwar period, long before daily life could return even to the merest semblance of its prewar conditions. What in all Japan had survived intact? Only the Japanese language. What now most often stood in the way of coping successfully with the foreign occupation forces? Only the Japanese language. What was the common possession of every Japanese alive, while at the same time the only thing that the invading Americans did not have at their command and in abundant supply? Again, the Japanese language.

Of course, just as substantial bits of rubble and debris, some large enough to be used again, still littered the streets of Japan's bombed-out cities, so also did substantial fragments of the wartime mythology survive, if only in dismembered bits and pieces. The system as a whole was completely discredited. This did not mean, however, that good use could not be made of a few of the surviving fragments as the slow, painstaking work of reconstruction began.

The old myth had been rich in elements relating to the language. These elements were prime choices when it came to this urgent work of fitting out a new myth built almost entirely around the language. And once transplanted onto the body of the new myth, some of these old elements from the now discredited myth began to achieve remarkably full, rank growth, like tropical plants suddenly removed from a hostile climate and replanted in favorable growing conditions.

But of course none of this could have been accomplished without the existence of the kernel of truth that does indeed lie at the heart of this new myth. By erroneously making the case that such features are unique or significantly distinctive to Japanese, the myth capitalizes upon linguistic universals shared by all human languages. This linguistic sleight of hand is the key technique of the mythmakers, at the same time that it is the secret of their success.

CHAPTER THREE

The Mythmakers

> It is remarkable that popular belief, the world
> over, exaggerates the effect of language in supersti-
> tious ways (magic formulae, charms, curses, name-
> tabu, and the like), but at the same time takes no
> account of its obvious and normal effects. —Leonard
> Bloomfield, *Language*, 1933

BEHIND EVERY myth there must be mythmakers.
Not even myths are an exception to the general rule that nothing can come
from nothing. Almost everything about the modern myth of Nihongo will
understandably strike the non-Japanese observer of the phenomenon as
strange and surprising. But nothing about it is likely to be nearly as strange
or quite as surprising as the identity of the people behind the myth, the
individuals most directly responsible for fitting it out in its spurious linguistic trappings and setting it up for view in the intellectual marketplace.

The outside observer of modern Japanese life will surely be struck by the
intensity with which the myth is promulgated and spread, as well as by
the peculiarly Japanese intensity with which it is believed. From the very
first, the foreigner interested in modern Japanese life and manners will probably be most astonished simply by the fact that all this intensity, and all
this effort, is being devoted to something as matter-of-fact—matter-of-fact
for the foreigner, but hardly for the Japanese—as an ordinary modern language, in common daily use by hundreds of thousands of people. But it is safe
to say that in the long run, no other single aspect of the entire modern myth
of the Japanese language will afford an outside observer as much surprise
as will the identity of the individuals who have taken upon themselves the
task of generating and propagating this remarkable set of sustaining beliefs.

41

The people most concerned with the propagation and popularization of the modern myth of Nihongo in contemporary Japan fall into two main classes. Some of them are academics, full-time faculty members at universities and colleges. The others are quasi-academics who, while maintaining some variety of relationship with educational and scholarly circles, actually devote most of their time and energy to various sorts of journalism.

Indeed, these two categories are difficult to keep separate in Japan, and perhaps keeping them apart is not really worth the effort. Few successful Japanese academics do not write essays or articles for newspapers and magazines from time to time; and few important newspapers and magazines publish nonfiction writing by authors who do not have at least some nominal association with academia. Thus the two categories tend to blend with one another quite readily. About the only clear-cut description possible for identifying the makers of the modern myth of Nihongo is that they are all academics, by one definition or another. The myth today continues to be generated in Japanese institutions of higher education; its chief practitioners and promulgators are, in a word, academics.

Again, we have here a facet of the myth that will most likely strike the non-Japanese reader as strange for at least two reasons. In the first place, the non-Japanese observer of this phenomenon will at first find it difficult to understand why academics, particularly academics whose field of specialization is often alleged to be the professional study of the Japanese language, and sometimes even the study of general linguistic science, could have allowed themselves to become involved in the highly unscientific and thoroughly unacademic manipulations of data and method that we know to be part and parcel of the Nihongo myth.

Second, once the non-Japanese observer realizes that the major effort toward promulgating and popularizing the myth is undertaken by Japanese academics, he or she will be hard put to understand, in turn, why the myth is taken as seriously as it is in contemporary Japanese society. This will be particularly difficult for an American reader to understand, since in modern American society academics are generally relegated to the lower rungs of the social ladder. No one pays the least attention to their views in any field, with the occasional exception of economics and highly technical natural-science specialties like nuclear physics and atomic power—though even in such areas the opinions of rock stars, politicians, and movie actors are far more highly regarded and more often listened to.

To be sure, even in the West, societies in which academics are expected to know something about the fields in which they specialize are not totally unknown. A modern West German, for example, will find the prestige that a Japanese academic enjoys rather easier to understand than an American will. Despite the debacles of the 1940s, West German popular culture still

pays considerable attention to academics. West German society still entertains the normal expectation that a university professor will know something
fairly difficult and rather important about the subject that he or she undertakes to study and teach.

This German-style social recognition of academic specialization provides
a good background for beginning to understand the tremendous prestige
that all academics, particularly university professors, normally and routinely enjoy in Japan. And it is only when we understand and keep in mind this
unique role of the Japanese academic vis-à-vis the Japanese reading public
that we can begin to comprehend who the Nihongo mythmakers are, and
how they are able to do their work.

Any myth, particularly in its earlier, formative stages, is only as useful
and only as impressive as the sources of authority out of which it originates.
It can only persuade and sustain its believers to the extent that they receive
it as a coherent body of beliefs and conclusions from persons or sources in
whom they have unquestioning confidence. This is turn means that in the
generation and promulgation of any sustaining myth, two distinct steps
or operations are generally essential.

Someone must, in the metaphorical sense at least, "go up to the mountain" in order to receive the myth and the revelations that its teachings will
embody from some other, still higher source of authority. No myth that
claims a totally mundane origin will be taken seriously for long. Its power
and authority must be assigned to some suprahuman sources, if only to
prevent the almost infinite proliferation of myths at every turn. If a myth
could be generated simply by ordinary human beings, with no need for
contact or communication with higher sources of authority, then anyone
could generate a myth. The more myths there would be, the less each of
them would be useful in its role as a social sustaining force.

It is only by carefully restricting the supposed source of the myth to
enormously rare (and often supposedly dangerous) contacts with otherworldly powers and authorities beyond the reach of most people in the
society that the mythmakers are able to channel their resources into sufficiently sharp focus. And it is this sharp focus that makes sure that the myth,
when it reaches the broader masses of the population, will have its desired
impact. So the first step must always be to "go up to the mountain"—in
other words, somehow to get into contact with sources of intellectual power
or authority beyond the reach of the vast run of the population.

The second essential step in mythmaking is the natural consequence of
the first. Once one has "gone up to the mountain," one must next bring
the myth down to the waiting multitudes and explain it to them. The mythmaker who ascends the mountain and simply remains there accomplishes
nothing; he or she is never heard from or seen again. Only by "coming down

from the mountain" can the authority and power of whatever he or she claimed to be in touch with up there be transmitted to the people. This round trip of "up and down the mountain," then, constitutes what might be termed the "standard operating procedure" for all mythmaking, ancient and modern alike. It is only in terms of this two-stage process that the development and propagation of the modern myth of Nihongo in contemporary Japanese intellectual life can be fully understood.

We must, if we wish to grasp how this myth has arisen, try first of all to identify the metaphorical mountain on the top of which the practitioners of this myth claim to have received their revelations and findings concerning the special, mystical qualities of the Japanese language. Next we must study their equally metaphorical, but also equally essential, "descent from the mountain"—in other words, the ways in which the newly received myth, with its authority now ostensibly derived from on high, is subsequently delivered into the hands of the population at large in forms that will make it easily comprehensible to them.

Only when these two questions have been clarified will we be in a position to identify some of the principal individuals who figure so prominently in the myth itself and to evaluate their role in modern Japanese intellectual life. Before we can usefully come to grips with the question of who the people are who manufacture the modern myth of Nihongo, we must first understand what it is that these mythmakers claim to be doing, and how they claim to be doing it.

Just what the modern mythmongers claim to be doing is generally somewhat difficult for non-Japanese to understand or appreciate, as already pointed out, mostly because there are few other countries in the modern world where academics enjoy such tremendous prestige and popular esteem as they still do in modern Japan. Essentially, the Nihongo practitioners claim to be able to bring to bear upon the nature of the Japanese language a number of special insights that they say are theirs by the right of their own membership in Japanese academic life. The problems that the non-Japanese observer will have in understanding all this mostly arise because few other countries in the world still have a privileged group of individuals whose opinions on any and all topics are respectfully heeded by the population as a whole in anything resembling the way in which the opinions of Japanese university professors and other academics are heeded.

In contemporary Japan, the university professor is listened to on almost every subject under the sun, with little concern for whether or not the subject is one about which he knows any more than anyone else. His prestige derives solely from the very fact of his employment on a university faculty, not from the specialized knowledge of some subject or other that presumably led to such employment in the first place. Once he is in his job, his opinions will be avidly sought on almost any topic concerning which he is willing to express himself—and that topic is, surprisingly frequently, the nature and role of the Japanese language.

Most Americans, in particular, will find this situation not only difficult to understand but difficult even to believe. Why should the opinions of university professors be solicited, given widespread publicity, and avidly listened to on any subjects except possibly the narrow fields of interest and specialization of the persons concerned? In American life, one will occasionally see someone from academic circles interviewed on TV, or in newspapers and magazines. But on the fairly rare occasions when this does take place, the academician in question is being interviewed because the problem at hand is one that relates directly to his or her field of academic specialization. An economist may be interviewed about problems of inflation, a nuclear scientist about possible radiation dangers from a faulty atomic power installation, a psychiatrist about the probable mental condition of an apparently psychopathic killer-at-large, and so on.

But in modern Japan, anyone who watches TV or reads Japanese newspapers and weekly magazines is immediately struck by the large number of academic figures who are featured in all these media and whose opinions are reported in considerable detail. The difference between the way this is done in Japan and the way it is done in the United States is far more significant than the mere difference in the numbers of academics involved in each case.

Japanese media not only feature academics in far greater quantity than do their American counterparts. These media also feature academics and their opinions as if these opinions were relevant to virtually any topic of the day, almost without reference to the specialized field of study of the academic in question. Particularly if the academic is glib and able to express him- or herself effectively in the TV interview or on the magazine page, his or her opinions will generally be presented almost without regard for whatever specialized information is supposed to have made the person into an academic in the first place.

Economists turn up on TV being asked for clues to foreign policy; professors of French literature are sought after for their explanations of the latest convolutions of the international petroleum market; and almost everybody in the entire Japanese academic establishment, whether specializing in nuclear physics or polymer chemistry or the history of German literature, is ipso facto a fully qualified and licensed practitioner of the modern myth of Nihongo.

To find a useful parallel, the European or American outsider who is interested in Japanese life would have to go back to the Middle Ages in Europe, when members of the clergy enjoyed both legal immunities and social status by the simple fact of their ordination, quite apart from any questions of individual ability, sanctity, or other personal accomplishments. In most countries of the West, such special privileges have long since been swept away by religious reform and intellectual enlightenment. But in other parts of the world, some Islamic sects still apparently assign comparable positions of irrational prestige and status to their clergy and so may provide a rough parallel to the modern roles enjoyed by all members of Japanese academia.

In the European church of the Middle Ages, the effectiveness of priestly functions was held to be quite separate and independent from the actual character, training, or piety of the individual clergyman in question. What a priest could do, he did as a function of his membership in the small, closed group of ordained clergy. Hence, such work could just as well be done by an indolent, slovenly, even sinful priest as by a pious, careful one. In much the same way, the revered holy men of certain modern Islamic groups apparently derive the totality of their power and prestige simply by being who they are. No one asks searching questions about just what it is that makes these holy men so holy or so much to be revered: it is enough to know that they are. The Japanese academic fits into this same picture with startling ease. He is an important, powerful figure, not because of what he knows but because of his membership in a specific group—most simply put, because of who he is. He is a Japanese academic, and when that much has been established, nothing more remains to be said.

But at the same time, we must never forget that what we refer to as Japanese academic life and Japanese academia are historically not very Japanese at all and that their essentially non-Japanese origins continue even today to confront Japanese society and intellectual life with a number of internal contradictions. For all practical purposes—and also for a large number of impractical ones—Japanese academic life begins only with the Meiji Restoration of 1868. Following that major decision to open the country to normal political and commercial intercourse with the rest of the world, a large number of subsidiary decisions had also to be made. Some were necessary simply in order to implement that prior decision. Others were required to ensure that Japan would not inevitably follow the pattern of China and other parts of Asia that already showed such alarming signs of becoming colonies of the more advanced nations of the West.

One of the most important of these secondary decisions was to introduce a modern system of education into Japan, beginning with elementary schools and fairly universal education on the lower levels but also including a number of higher-level, more specialized institutions of teaching and research for small numbers of the elite who were to be groomed for positions of leadership.

These upper-level educational facilities were mostly patterned upon German models. Within a remarkably short period of time, the Japanese authorities managed to come up with quite reasonable replicas of the *Gymnasia,* the *Hochschulen,* and even the sacrosanct *Universitäten* that were so important in, and so representative of, the peculiarly Prussian variety of German culture that the rulers of Meiji Japan admired. But unlike the situation in Meiji Japan, the society and culture of nineteenth-century Western and Middle Europe were racially diverse, multinational, and above all else polyglot. Firsthand acquaintance with half a dozen languages was a commonplace for any educated person. The professional academic took the ability to read, write, and speak in any one of a number of different languages simply as a matter of course.

These polyglot accomplishments of the European academic community deeply impressed the Meiji leaders who were directing the reproduction of Prussian educational models in a Japanese context. Remembering their own Herculean struggles to acquire a working knowledge of Dutch, or German, or English, or French, the Meiji men were quite naturally unable to contain their astonishment at the Europeans, who spoke, read, and published in any or all of these and still other languages. In the kingdom of the monolinguals, a polyglot is not only king, he can easily become a god.

The easy familiarity of European academics with foreign languages was one of the many externals of Prussian educational culture that the Meiji leaders mistakenly believed to be essential to the system they were attempting to imitate, not recognizing it for what it really was, merely a necessary concomitant of European ethnography and geography. Determined to imitate Prussian academic institutions down to the last detail, they made a certain familiarity with a limited number of foreign languages into the major accomplishment that would forever after set the Japanese academic apart from the rest of his society. And from this it has also followed that, from Meiji on, in playing out his role as one who brings the word down from the mountain, the Japanese academic has always made great capital of his supposed mastery of foreign languages, claiming to base a significant part of his tremendous authority and prestige upon this talent.

This does not actually contradict the earlier claim that, like the priest of medieval Europe or the modern Islamic holy man, the Japanese academic derives the major portion of his authority not from what he knows, but simply from the fact of what he is. Even the medieval priest had to at least pretend some knowledge of Church Latin in order to mumble through his ritual services. Even the least edifying and poorest educated of the modern Muslim holy men must pretend some acquaintance with the intricacies of the language of the Holy Koran. In both cases, these supposed linguistic accomplishments are not the real sources of the prestige and authority of the figures involved, but they are necessary trappings of the role in which such figures are involved. As such, they are also an essential part of the role-playing that in turn is actually the ultimate source of power and authority.

For the Japanese academic, almost without regard to his field of specialization, a supposed command of one or more foreign languages is the necessary ornament for successful role-playing, just as the medieval priest had to be able to mutter the text of a Latin service. Command of some foreign language is necessary for any Japanese academic, almost without regard for the field of specialization—and it is of course in connection with the academic study of the Japanese language that the important exception expressed by this "almost" becomes operative.

Everyone else on a Japanese university faculty, whether in medicine or nuclear physics or economics or philosophy, is expected to have some ability to read at least one foreign language. Being able to speak even one foreign language with any effective fluency is generally regarded as somewhat less desirable, since such ability would imply either long residence abroad or close social connections with foreigners or perhaps even both.

Either of the two, much less the combination, immediately suggests uncharacteristic un-Japanese patterns of behavior. These considerations would weigh seriously against any candidate for an academic appointment and also seriously throw into question any possibility for advancement in rank even if such an initial appointment were to be made. So even the rare Japanese academic who has somehow managed to acquire some ability in speaking a foreign language will normally be at pains to conceal this fact from his colleagues, knowing how heavily it could prejudice them against him were it to become widely known. But normally this problem does not arise, because most Japanese academics have no practical ability to speak or understand a foreign language about which any of their colleagues need be concerned.

Instead, the professor of surgery will claim to be able to read German; the professor of philosophy, either German or French; and the professor of modern English literature will admit to having read one—but surely not more than one—of the novels of Somerset Maugham or Graham Greene. (These are still the two English authors most highly regarded in contemporary Japanese university circles, for reasons that are yet fully to be explored, much less understood by anyone outside those circles.)

It is this purported ability to get to the knowledge of Europe and the West from its original sources, to read its texts in the original languages, and to obtain intellectual intelligence about the outside world at first hand that the Japanese academic claims as his special preserve. Modern Japanese society enforces the validity of this claim by universally acknowledging that the academic has an unquestioned monopoly on such sources of information and also by agreeing that what he can tell the rest of the Japanese public concerning those otherwise tightly sealed sources of enlightenment is worth knowing.

This is how the Japanese academic "goes up to the mountain": he retreats into his study, spends some hours with a German or French or English book and his dictionaries; and when he has puzzled out the text, he writes an article or monograph or popular book in Japanese and shares what he has decoded with the general reading public. To whatever he has unraveled of the original, which he generally presents not in an exact translation but in a rambling Japanese paraphrase, he also adds his own interpretations and evaluations. These carry equal weight with the original text, since in adding them he is exercising his proper function as one who "goes up to the mountain" and brings back to the common masses waiting below the wisdom and enlightenment that he alone has been privileged to encounter while up on the heights.

But what of the Japanese academic who specializes in the study of his own language? Such individuals constitute a sizable segment of the total academic community. But for all the force of their numbers, they are actually in a rather anomalous position when it comes to this question of the source of their power and prestige.

Their colleagues in other fields rely upon the charismatic operation of going up and down the mountain as we have already described it. But most of this same magic mountain is, by definition, off limits to the Japanese professor of Japanese. What could he learn up there, what could he discover from dangerous encounters with difficult foreign books high up on the mountain, what could he possibly bring down with him for the edification of the waiting faithful? The dilemma of the Japanese academic specialists in the Japanese language is that they are forced to exercise all the teaching power and exhibit all the academic prestige that go with their role in the society without being able to make overt display of this essential operation of going "up and down the mountain."

Nor is the resolution of this dilemma aided by the way in which Japanese universities tacitly force this anomalous role upon any young Japanese student who wishes to specialize in Japanese. Aspiring graduate students in Japanese universities are most often advised to enroll in programs for advanced degrees in Japanese when they prove to be more than usually ungifted in foreign languages. The rule of thumb in Japanese graduate education is that any student who can do foreign languages satisfactorily should get into some field where foreign languages are really important. For the rest, those who find foreign languages difficult or impossible, there is always Japanese literature and Japanese language. A socially comfortable solution, but it is also one that condemns the prospective Japanese scholar of the Japanese language to play out a difficult and compromising role from the very start of his or her career.

Thus, lacking the single most effective tool that exists in the arsenal of all their academic peers, the leading Japanese exponents of the myth of Nihongo are forced to set about their work of generating and embellishing this sustaining myth from a most unenviable position. The remarkable circumstances that limit and define all Japanese academic activity, particularly in the humanities, also force the mythmakers to undertake their chosen task under a severe handicap. The very content of their academic specialty—the Japanese language and its allegedly unique qualities and properties—cuts them off from the charismatic forces that are the lifeblood of all the rest of Japanese academia.

For these specialists in the myth of Nihongo, there can, in a sense, never be a going up the mountain, and hence also there can be no coming down to pass on ineffable truths. They constantly run the risk of being prophets with no mountain to take refuge upon, and the even greater risk of eventually having to admit that they alone, among Japanese academics, have no special revelation to pass on to the world that is not already the common property of everyone else.

This cul-de-sac of self-contradiction into which the majority of the Japanese specialists in the myth of Nihongo necessarily lock themselves cannot but remind the movie fan of the poignant final scenes in the classic film *The Wizard of Oz*. The wizard has long managed to make everyone in the enchanted city believe that he enjoys enormously powerful magical powers and that if he wishes to, there is nothing in this world that would be beyond his ability. But in the final scenes, Dorothy's little dog Toto unwittingly reveals the wizard for what he is: a pleasant but rather disorganized elderly man standing behind a curtain, shouting into a loudspeaker and operating a thunder machine. Few moments in the movies can equal the scene in which Frank Morgan, as the quite unwizardly wizard, frankly confesses that there is really no wizard in Oz; he only seemed to be powerful and wizardly in his magic, because everybody believed that he was. Only so long as the wizard could huddle behind his protective curtain, operating his loudspeaker and hand-cranked thunder machine, was his charismatic wizardry still potent. But as soon as Dorothy's little dog tugs away the concealing curtain, everybody can see that the Wizard of Oz really has no special powers at all.

The Japanese mythmakers who specialize in Nihongo are in much the same position as the Wizard of Oz. They themselves know that they lack special sources of power or revelation, even though society at large firmly believes that they have them. They know that they have not been up the mountain; they actually have not been privy to any special revelation of truths on the heights that are not known to everyone else in the society. And so it is always a difficult and potentially dangerous task for them to continue to act as if the opposite were true.

In order to operate successfully within this nexus of intellectual and sociolinguistic contradictions, the leading Japanese specialists in the myth of Nihongo have evolved a number of security devices, all designed to keep Toto away from the curtain for as long as possible.

Sometimes they work on the well-known principle that the best defense is always a spirited offense. They beg all questions of what supramontane authority lies behind their pronouncements by the simple but effective technique of citing no authorities for their views and analyses—a headlong approach to the issue that might best be compared with the equally effective American political technique known as "stonewalling." Implicitly admitting to themselves that they have no outside support for any of their views, they nevertheless continue to present these views with renewed stress and emphasis over and over again, correctly assuming that if the same thing is said sufficiently frequently, a lot of people will end up believing it simply because they have heard it so often.

In this particular variety of academic stonewalling, then, the Japanese specialist in the service of the myth of Nihongo does not feel any need to explain to his readers or to his TV and radio audiences what the sources are for his views and pronouncements. It is enough for them to understand that Japanese is a unique language, that it possesses a characteristic spirit or soul that other languages do not enjoy, and that it is more difficult for everyone, foreigner and native speaker alike, than any other language on earth. It is hardly ever even suggested that these allegations have behind them the kind of "down from the mountain" authority that Japanese academia normally brings into evidence in order to substantiate claims made about other subjects. In the case of Nihongo, the experts in the myth most often do not even claim to have been up on the mountain. They simply tell their audiences that these things are true because they, the experts, say that they are, and there the matter must rest.

Generally, this approach serves the myth remarkably well as a substitute for the more usual charismatic process of going up and down the mountain of academic revelation. But to employ this or any other strategic approach consistently, unrelieved by any touch of elegant variation in methodology, would be to risk exposing its built-in limitations to a dangerously wide audience. If this technique were employed exclusively, it would run the risk of familiarity; and familiarity not only breeds contempt, it is also fraught with the danger of exposing itself for what it is. To guard against this peril, the mythmakers tastefully vary their approach from time to time with two major methodological variations. The first of these variations takes a form that we might most easily predict; but the second turns out to be rather less predictable and hence somewhat more surprising.

In the first variation, the stonewalling approach is not abandoned, but it is, however, bolstered from time to time by what are supposed to be citations of evidence earlier brought down from the mountain of revelation. These purport to be quite the same as the bulk of all such evidence that normally plays a part in Japanese academic argument. Like the bulk of that evidence, it is all supposed to hinge in some way or other upon the individual scholar's putative ability to communicate with the non-Japanese world of learning through the medium of a working reading knowledge of foreign languages. But since the myth categorically denies the existence of any foreign-language scientific literature relating to the subject of the Japanese language, it is not secondary works written in foreign languages but actually these foreign languages themselves that are, by a marvelously deft feat of logical legerdemain, brought into evidence.

When the Japanese expert in the myth of Nihongo decides momentarily to forgo the usual technique of stonewalling his arguments on behalf of the unique characteristics of the Japanese language, he turns to the same source of charismatic power that is familiar to all Japanese academia but with an important difference. The specialist in any other area will come down from the mountain and pass on to his followers revealed truths that he has been able to obtain on the heights, because they are originally to be found in foreign books and journals that only he can read.

The specialist in the myth of Nihongo comes down with what are purported to be revealed truths about the Japanese language, but now the claim is not that these are to be found in foreign books or journals. Instead, the claim is that these newly revealed truths, which *sensei* (teacher or master) is now good enough to bring down from the mountain for the rest of us, are somehow to be found within the foreign languages themselves—those foreign languages that only *sensei* knows, of course, because only *sensei* know foreign languages. At the same time, the great thing about specializing in Japanese language studies in Japan, if you are a Japanese, is still the fact that this is the one Japanese academic specialty in which you do not really have to know foreign languages.

As so often in any contemplation of the myth of Nihongo and its sociolinguistic working-out in modern Japan, we begin to find ourselves propelled along on a dizzying merry-go-round of internal contradictions and mutually contrary assumptions almost before we know what has happened to us. But if we can keep a clear head amid this dizzy whirl, we will find at its heart one of the most important elements in the entire modern myth of Nihongo.

Most simply put, this first variation upon the technique of academic stonewalling works on the assumption—an assumption quite contrary to every other assumption of the myth—that all foreign languages, but particularly English, are somehow to be regarded as the measure of Nihongo, a tangible standard or yardstick of sociolinguistic norms against which the superiority of Nihongo may be measured and demonstrated. The way one does or does not say this or that in English—or, more often, the way this or that Japanese expert in the myth of Nihongo alleges that one says something in English—is held up as the measure of all things. Even the mythic entity of Nihongo is then evaluated according to how well it measures up to this wholly irrelevant foreign standard.

That this particular variation has its own built-in perils and dangers is all too apparent to any observer, even to the general Japanese reader at whom most of these mythic pronouncements are directed. Suspension of logic on the level required to tolerate this particular technique of argument is all very well and good, but it can safely be employed only on fairly rare occasions. Nevertheless, when it is trotted out of the arsenal, it can be an effective weapon for bolstering the claims of Nihongo, as we shall see in more detail below.

The second major variation on the technique of academic stonewalling is even more powerful, but at the same time it is also even more dangerous, and so must be employed even more cautiously and rarely than the first. In this second variation, the proponent of the myth of Nihongo makes as if to abandon this technique completely. He or she purports to go up to the mountain in the classical fashion of all Japanese academia, to consult there on the heights difficult foreign books and journals written in difficult foreign languages that only academics can read, and—lo and behold!—to find therein testimony from the very mouths of learned foreigners themselves that really does prove that the language is unique and distinctive, possesses a soul or spirit, and so on.

On the admittedly fairly rare occasions when this variation is the one adopted, one or the other of two additional methodological fillips is required if the technique is to be effective. If *sensei* is to come down from the mountain and share the testimony of foreign scholars with other believers in the myth, either he must come back with evidence that actually is no evidence at all, because the ostensibly scholarly sources from which he has extracted it have long since been discredited within the same foreign academic circles that produced them, or he can take an even bolder course and make up evidence that simply does not exist; in the latter circumstance, we are with one fell swoop right back to where we began, stonewalling like mad.

Each of these last two techniques is of course dangerous. To employ them is to constantly run the risk of being found out. But given the nature of Japanese academia and the limitations of most of the general Japanese reading public at whom these down-from-the-mountain revelations are aimed, both can actually be employed more frequently and rather more safely than one might think possible.

As we shall see below, it is possible in Japan today to cite evidence for this or that aspect of the myth of Nihongo from a foreign book, complete with title and author, even though the book cited actually proves upon inspection to say nothing even remotely along the lines that it is alleged to prove. The number of Japanese readers who are in a position to get out the original source and verify whether or not the foreign scholar quoted actually says what he is alleged to say is frighteningly small.

It would be easy, and instructive as well, to illustrate each of these main methods of argumentation by citing representative passages from the work of a number of the prominent Japanese exponents of the modern myth of Nihongo. But here the problem is that the possible passages that could be cited for the purposes of illustration are so extremely numerous that one hardly knows where to begin in making a selection. At the same time, since it is obviously impossible, again simply out of practical considerations of space available, to illustrate each of these methods of argumentation and their principal variations at length, one immediately runs the risk of being unfair to several of the major figures in the field by having to omit their writings from our sample. And this, of course, would never do.

Under the circumstances, the fairest course seems to be to make no attempt at a wide sampling of the enormous field represented by the modern myth of Nihongo and its major Japanese exponents. Instead, for the purposes of illustrating the techniques just summarized, we shall restrict our sampling to representative quotations and examples taken from the work of a single prominent figure, Professor Haruhiko Kindaichi. This way we cannot be accused of having been unfair to any of the others whose work is, at least in the present chapter of this book, left unnoticed.

At the same time, we have the satisfaction of knowing that the individual whose work we shall here draw upon is not a minor figure. Indeed, it would be no exaggeration to point him out as the single individual, if only one were to be identified, who by the unanimous consensus of Japanese intellectual, cultural, and academic circles is without exception and unquestionably acknowledged as the leading as well as the most creative figure in this entire sociolinguistic scene.

Haruhiko Kindaichi was born in Tokyo in 1913 and is a graduate of the Department of Japanese in the Faculty of Letters of Tokyo Imperial University—in a word, the holder of one of the most prestigious degrees in all Japanese academia. He has served on the faculties of many of the important universities in Japan, either as a regular, full-time faculty member or as a visiting lecturer, and was recently decorated by the Japanese Government for his contributions to the Japanese language. Though now far beyond the usual age for retirement in Japanese academia, he continues his busy career as Professor of Japanese at the Jesuit-operated Sophia University in Tokyo. He and his writings, as well as his numerous radio and TV performances, have dominated the Japanese sociolinguistic scene since 1957, when, only five years after the end of the Allied Occupation of Japan, he published a slim but extremely influential best-selling paperback entitled, with elegant simplicity, *Nihongo*. This book, which has accurately been described as "a classic defense of the national language," has remained immensely popular with Japanese readers ever since. It has gone through innumerable printings subsequent to its first publication, just as it has also gone through more than one generation of readers.

This particular book is an especially good choice for our present purposes, not only because it continues to serve as the basic canonical text for the modern sustaining myth of contemporary Japan but also because it has recently been published in a complete English translation under the title *The Japanese Language*. This English translation of Kindaichi's classic work is generally accurate; indeed it is often painfully faithful to the letter of the original.

With this translation now easily available, anyone in the world who can read English and who is interested in the modern myth of Nihongo may read one of the basic scriptures of the cult in an accurate, reliable rendering, even if he or she cannot manage the original Japanese text of this important book. The publication of this English edition of Kindaichi's *Nihongo* in 1978 provided still another indication that the myth of Nihongo was about to become another of Japan's export commodities. It was by no means the only such indication, but still it was probably the most important of all the signs that had yet appeared, pointing out, to those who could read the portents, some of the ways in which the myth had by the late 1970s already begun to "go international."

At any rate, with either Kindaichi's 1957 Japanese-language original or its 1978 English-language translation in hand, we are in an excellent position not only to study the heart of the canonical scriptural expression of the modern myth of Nihongo but also to select a few representative examples that will illustrate the principal varieties of the up-and-down-the-mountain schema sketched above in the abstract. Without such illustration, the general categories of theme and variations alluded to above would necessarily remain nothing more than abstract categories.

For most of his book, Kindaichi elects to employ the overall, basic approach of academic stonewalling as we have described it. He first of all sets

up a paper tiger, attempting to convince the reader that Nihongo is somehow under attack. Once this has been accomplished, he is then in a position
to come to its defense, a defense that is mounted by the classically simple
technique of adamantly denying each of the spurious leading charges that
he himself has only moments before leveled against the language. Each
paper-tiger charge is refuted by the elegantly simple technique of stonewalling. This or that is or is not so because Kindaichi says it is or is not.
But in each and every context, and no matter what the charge is that is
being refuted, the mythic case for the uniqueness of Nihongo is constantly
pushed, either explicitly or covertly.

On the one hand, we are told that "at present, many so-called intellectuals
and cultured people take every opportunity to complain that Japanese has
degenerated." "No, no!" cries Kindaichi, quick to overturn the paper tiger
that he himself has set here among the pigeons: "a careful look reveals more
instances of firmness than frailty." In support of this alleged refutation, he
gives a single item of data: when the English word Christmas is borrowed
into Japanese, it is pronounced in Japanese fashion as *Kurisumasu,* with vowels
separating the sequence of consonants that do not appear as such in Japanese
and with other regular changes in pronunciation, so that the resulting word
conforms to Japanese pronunciation habits. And this, he claims, shows
that the Japanese language is "firm," not "frail." But precisely the same
thing happens to any word borrowed into any language on earth from any
other language. No language takes over borrowings from another without
adapting them to its own pronunciation habits. The illustration Kindaichi
cites is absolutely irrelevant to the refutation of the spurious charge that
he has himself conjured up simply in order to refute it.

This wholly specious argument plays such a major part, not only in
Kindaichi's claims about the purity of the Japanese language but also in
much of the rest of the mythic literature on Nihongo, that its completely
unscientific basis must be underscored as strongly as possible. When it comes
to loanwords, every language works in precisely the same way that Japanese does. When French borrows words from English or German or any
other language, it makes them conform to French pronunciation patterns
and also to French grammar (hence, *le car, le drugstore,* and the rest of
the often-maligned "Franglais"). When we borrow French or Chinese
or Japanese words into English, we do the same thing. Anyone who
pronounces such Japanese loanwords as harakiri, sukiyaki, or shoji in the
Japanese style while speaking English will not be understood. An English
speaker who would attempt to pronounce such French borrowings as garage
or restaurant in accurate French pronunciation would risk both ridicule and
misunderstanding. Chemistry is an old loanword from Arabic; try pronouncing it in the Arabic fashion and see how far it gets you. Japanese

has absolutely no monopoly on making over foreign words into its own. This is something that every language in the world does. Of all the flimsy nonfacts that have been conjured up to support the myth of a unique, soul-endowed Nihongo, this particular argument is probably the flimsiest of all, but this does not keep it from also being one of the claims most often made on behalf of the myth.

One must resist the temptation to quote at length further examples of similar arguments from *The Japanese Language,* because once one begins, there is no place to stop. At the most conservative estimate possible, at least ninety-five percent of its argumentation is conducted along precisely this same line of approach: first the paper-tiger problem, then the claim that the charge is false, and finally the allegation that Japanese is not only in the clear on this but somehow also unique and superior by reason of being so. With the entire book in question now easily available in English, we need give no further examples; the interested reader is at liberty to identify any number for him- or herself.

This frees our time and energies to look instead at a few of the rather more interesting cases in which Kindaichi in the same book opts for one or the other of the two main variations upon the basic stonewalling technique of argumentation.

Examples of the first of these variations—the one in which the structure and resources of foreign language, particularly of English, are employed as the yardstick against which to measure the alleged superiority of Nihongo—are plentiful beyond description in the pages of *The Japanese Language,* and the reader can easily locate any number of illustrations there with no further assistance. In order to demonstrate how the evidence of foreign languages is most generally employed in his arguments in favor of the myth of Nihongo, it may be more useful to the reader to select a representative example from a more recent book by Kindaichi, his *Nihongo e no Kibō* (My Aspirations for Japanese), which has not yet been translated into English.

Much of an early chapter in this book measures Japanese grammatical and syntactic patterns against what are alleged to be their English equivalents. One quotation will suffice to display just what the English that finds a place in demonstrations of this variety is generally like. Kindaichi evaluates the Japanese construction *tachiōjō suru,* an expression that means, of a vehicle or person ordinarily or customarily in motion, "to be brought to a halt" with the implication that once the obstacle or difficulty that has caused the halt is removed or solved, normal or customary motion will be resumed. This he does by measuring it against what he says is the way one says *tachiōjō suru* in English. And how does one say this in English? "Train were being stopped," according to Kindaichi. Does one indeed?

We all know that wine suffers from traveling; apparently so do foreign languages. At least something very dismal certainly has happened to this particular specimen of English in the course of being brought down from the mountain. But how is the innocent Japanese reader to know that Nihongo is being evaluated here against a bad bottle of Algerian vinegar wine? After all, *sensei* claims that "train were being stopped" is the real thing; and who can you trust, if you can't trust *sensei?*

Still more interesting are the fairly frequent utilizations throughout all of Kindaichi's contributions to the literature of the Nihongo mythology of the second of these two variations—the one in which foreign sources and authorities are cited in evidence for the myth of a uniquely endowed Japanese language. We have noted above that one of two additional fillips is necessary with this variation. Either the ostensibly scholarly sources from which such evidence is alleged to have been extracted are totally discredited within the same foreign academic circles that long, long ago may have produced them, or else they simply do not exist, in which case we can only conclude that they have been completely fabricated.

The first of these fillips is a particularly favorite device of Kindaichi's. The pages of *The Japanese Language* provide a veritable museum of long-since-discredited views about the nature of language in general and about many of the languages of East Asia in particular. Bernhard Karlgren (1889–1978), the Swedish scholar of Chinese, is quoted as having said that Chinese is such a chaotic language and so badly organized that the Chinese themselves often have difficulty understanding what they are trying to say to one another, and so they must often resort to writing out this or that word in order to make sense of what they are trying to say.

Even though allegations of this variety against Chinese were commonplaces in Western writing about the East a century ago, one still strongly suspects that the distinguished Swedish scholar never said any such thing (no published source is cited by Kindaichi). And if Karlgren did say this, he was wrong. Western scholarship has not repeated this old canard about Chinese in a serious fashion for at least the past half-century. Trotting it out at this stage in history and attempting to pass it off as the latest informed opinion from Western scholarship is to practice deception upon the innocent Japanese reader.

But the particular point about the myth of Nihongo that Kindaichi is attempting to make by citing this thoroughly discredited slur upon the Chinese language is in itself an interesting one. It shows how each of these abuses of scholarly methodology may be turned to the immediate uses of the myth of Nihongo. Taking the alleged slur of Karlgren at face value, Kindaichi uses it to demonstrate the superiority of Nihongo. Chinese is difficult, so difficult that the Chinese themselves can hardly understand it.

But then what about Nihongo? "This is all the more true with Japanese," says Professor Kindaichi. A popular American song of a few decades ago had a refrain, "Anything you can do, I can do better." The idea of that song quite neatly sums up the employment of such evidence and the way in which it is deftly turned to the advantage of Nihongo. If anyone else is in trouble, we are in worse trouble; if anyone else is doing well, we are doing better.

In another significant passage in *The Japanese Language,* one more discredited Western linguistic authority is brought forward, this time for use as ammunition in what turns out to be an even more prolix maneuver in defense of the mythic legions of Nihongo. Here the immediate context is that of charges that Kindaichi says have been brought against the Japanese language by several Japanese intellectuals who claim that the language is weak in "theoretical elements." The charges are so vague and impressionistic that they can hardly by summarized here, any more than they can be refuted by data, since they themselves rely hardly at all on data in the first place.

But in order to refute them, Kindaichi does not search for data, turning instead to a passage from the French philosopher Lucien Lévy-Bruhl (1857–1939) to the general effect that any language of a social entity in the "prelogical" stage of development is always distinguished by an almost complete lack of terms for generalized or abstract concepts. Lévy-Bruhl is said to have claimed that such a language does have a large resource of specific terms that "depict" carefully delimited individual entities, be they persons, objects, or whatever. Kindaichi then argues that, in view of what Lévy-Bruhl says, Japanese is surely not underdeveloped, as some claim: ". . . the view that Japanese is less theoretical than the languages of Europe cannot be maintained; and though it is, to be sure, with considerable hesitation that I do this, I would recommend Japanese as being in actual point of fact rather more theoretical than those other languages, contrary to what is generally believed."

In other words, anything you can do, we can do better. If Japanese does indeed lack abstract expressions, then we must remember that this is a mark of "prelogical" languages among which Japanese is the most prelogical of all—or something to that effect. It really is impossible to follow Kindaichi's many sudden, unannounced turns of direction in the argument here. All that is really clear is that the prestige of a famous foreigner, Lévy-Bruhl, is being brought down from the mountain and used as evidence in support of the myth of Nihongo and for the edification of the Japanese readers of Kindaichi's book. What the Japanese reader is not told is that no one in the West today takes any of this whole business of a "prelogical" stage in the development of language seriously and that hardly anyone did even when Lévy-Bruhl first published his vague speculations along these lines in 1910, in a now-infamous tract entitled *Les fonctions mentales dans les sociétés inféri-eures.*

Even the title of that document shows the line of reasoning along which Lévy-Bruhl approached his chosen subject. For him, there were superior societies and inferior ones—and guess which category French society be-longed to? He considered it his business to speculate about why the inferiors were so inferior, and how they had got that way. So also for "mentality," another dangerously vague and amorphous code word that played a major part in the racist speculations of turn-of-the-century French intellectuals. Mentality was also supposed to come in at least two varieties: the good guys, who lived in places like France, and the "primitives," the great unwashed hordes out there in the other countries of the world, with their primitive mentalities.

Actually, it is much to the credit of European scholarship in general that these dangerous and absurd generalizations, and particularly their blatantly racist assumptions, were soon demolished by other more responsible think-ers. In his post-1910 writing, Lévy-Bruhl himself was eventually forced to retract much of what he had originally speculated along these really quite outrageous lines.

But none of this involved history of European scholarship is shared with the Japanese reader of Kindaichi's book—or, for that matter, with the reader of its English translation. Kindaichi goes up to the mountain and comes back with a quotation from Lévy-Bruhl's long-discredited, racist spec-ulations. That is enough for *sensei's* purposes, and indeed, more than enough.

In order to inspect a representative sample of the second fillip that may, when the occasion demands, be worked on this particular variation—the one where a quite imaginary foreign scholarly source is cited in order to embellish the myth of Nihongo—we must again embroil ourselves in the mythic moils of what is probably Kindaichi's favorite single theme within the whole enormous range of the myth: the purity of the Japanese language. Nothing is closer to Kindaichi's heart, and nothing else brings from his pen such elaborate argumentation than does the alleged purity of his native tongue. It is also true that nothing is more totally divorced from the basic concepts of linguistic science. There are no pure languages, and there is no scientific validity to any concept of purity, whether relative or absolute, in connection with language, any more than there is in connection with race. The entire question is a semantic trap, a linguistic cul-de-sac into which the average readers are likely to be trapped before they are fully aware of what is being done to them. It is also one of the issues in connection with which Kindaichi may be observed bringing his most redoubtable artillery piece into battle position, as he proceeds to bolster his arugment by simply making up foreign sources and foreign authorities out of thin air.

Nor is it difficult to explain why it is his defense of this particular theme of the purity of the Japanese language that reveals Kindaichi in what is, after all, a methodology of desperation. When no evidence exists, it must be made up. How else could he possibly cite outside sources to defend the purity of the Japanese language—a language that everyone, even the most uninformed Japanese reader, knows has over the centuries incorporated Chinese almost whole and is now consuming English day by day in ever more greedy gulps?

An American scholar of the Japanese language recently started to try and count the number of words borrowed from English used in a recent issue of the popular Japanese literary journal *Bungei Shunjū*. "I gave up counting," he reported, "after 7,000 occurrences [of such borrowings from English], or on the average of more than fifteen per page." To make a case for the purity of a language that employs an average of fifteen different recent borrowings from English in a single page of magazine-level, general-interest writing is a formidable task. To cite foreign scholarly evidence in support of this same myth of purity is more than formidable—it is impossible. All that can be done, if it is to be done at all, is to make the evidence up. Which is exactly what Kindaichi has done.

In *The Japanese Language*, when he stresses this alleged purity time and time again, Kindaichi generally employs the simple stonewalling technique. This is usually his most effective weapon in the battle in defense of purity, since all the evidence points in the opposite direction, leaving him with little or nothing to do except to repeat over and over the claim that what so obviously is true actually is not: "The Japanese language has had little contact with other languages. . . . Consequently, it is quite natural that Japanese was not influenced by other languages. It should be noted that only in its contact with Chinese did Japanese receive a great influence—especially on its vocabulary. However, it should be kept in mind that this direct influence from Chinese occurred hundreds of years ago, and that there has been no such influence since."

Not a word, of course, about the average of fifteen borrowings from English to be found on each and every page of any recent issue of *Bungei Shunjū*. Nor is Kindaichi's treatment of the historical aspect of the influence of Chinese upon Japanese any more responsible or accurate. Actually, most of the massive lexical borrowings from Chinese into Japanese are not something that "occurred hundreds of years ago." Most of them occurred in the very recent present, and they keep on occurring today at almost as vigorous a rate as do the borrowings from English.

The vast majority of the Chinese loanwords that go to make up the modern Japanese lexical stock were borrowed into Japanese—or, to put the matter a little more accurately and somewhat more technically, they were coined in Japan as neologisms made up from Chinese lexical elements—subsequent to the spread of compulsory public education in Japan in the wake of the Meiji Restoration. Kindaichi's assertion that the influence of Chinese upon Japanese "occurred hundreds of years ago, and that there has been no such influence since," is historically untrue. It is directly contradicted by the linguistic evidence on every side.

Kindaichi also goes up the mountain of books written in difficult foreign languages and returns to us with a proof-passage in vindication of his view that Japanese is not only pure, it is the purest language of them all. The foreigners have demonstrated, he alleges, that there is only one language on earth that is purer than Japanese is: "There is a tribe of people called Lati in the mountainous region deep in the Yunnan province of China. It is said that they are a community of only four hundred people. The Lati language which these people speak is even purer than modern Japanese and does not seem to have been influenced by surrounding languages."

So we are left with only two really pure languages on earth: Japanese and that other one spoken by the Lati, those four hundred poor lost souls somewhere out there in southwest China. And to prove that he really has been up on the mountain and that what he has brought back to us really is the informed opinion of foreign scholarship, the passage cited above even comes equipped with that rarest of all rarities in the Japanese literature of the myth of Nihongo—a footnote.

This footnote tells us that the information about Lati's being a pure language, "even purer than modern Japanese," is to be found in a standard reference work of linguistic science, a French volume of almost two thousand pages edited by two well-known and respected French linguistic scientists, the late Antoine Meillet and Marcel Cohen. The book in question is the well-known *Les Langues du Monde,* originally published under that title in the 1920s and reissued following the war in a greatly expanded version by the Centre National de la Recherche Scientifique (Paris, 1952). Kindaichi's original Japanese text of *Nihongo* cites the book only by title and by the first of the two editors' names, but it does not identify edition or date; his English translator specifies the 1952 edition.

The 1952 edition of *Les Langues du Monde* runs to almost two thousand pages of text, plus a handful of maps and over a hundred pages of indexes. I do not claim to have read every page in it, or to have checked every language name on each of its maps. But it is easy to put on record that the volume's comprehensive index of all languages mentioned in the text and listed on its maps contains no entry at all for the Lati language. No such language is even mentioned anywhere in *Les Langues du Monde*. Meillet and Cohen obviously do not say anywhere in their book that Lati is "even purer than modern Japanese," because they do not say anything about Lati at all.

The average Japanese reader of Kindaichi's book has, of course, no convenient way to verify the claim that *sensei* makes here. Kindaichi's English translator was in a somewhat more vulnerable position. But she, too, fails to include the necessary page number in her translation of the original reference to Meillet and Cohen for the simple reason that no such page exists in *Les Langues du Monde*. For the reader who lives abroad and who has easy access to foreign books, a trip to a library is all that is necessary to show that this alleged reference does not exist.

At any rate, all of Kindaichi's work, particularly his book *The Japanese Language,* provides us with much grist for our own mill. It demonstrates in great detail just how the academic proponents of the modern myth of Nihongo continue to go up and down their own private mountain. It shows how the classic phenomenon of personal charisma deriving from the process of "withdrawal and return" can be made into a surrogate for genuine intellectual authority, as well as into a clone for academic accomplishment. What Professor Kindaichi has to teach us in this connection is often surprising and seldom edifying; but it is always of great value if we are to understand how the myth of Nihongo arises, and if we are to comprehend some of the ways in which, once generated, this same myth manages to go on from strength to strength.

CHAPTER FOUR

The Ape of God

> ... using a variety of sounds heard around us, [I]
> gradually saw that the Japanese responses to those
> sounds by the right and left sides of the brain were
> very different from responses in other people. —Ta-
> danobu Tsunoda, *The Japan Foundation News-
> letter*, April-May 1978

ATTEMPTING to explain in scholastic terms why the Devil is as successful as he obviously is in hoodwinking good, well-meaning people, Saint Jerome long ago came up with the concept of Satan as *Simia Dei*, "The Ape of God." The Prince of Darkness, Jerome taught, has always been a consummate master at the art of disguise; and he often finds that the most effective way in which to conceal his identity is to pose as God Himself. What better way, argued Jerome, for the Devil to go about his devilish work of bewildering and befuddling the people of God and in the process tricking them into sins that surely they would not under normal circumstances ever think of, than to make them believe that sin and evil—the works of the Devil—are actually the good works of God Himself, in a word, to play the Ape of God.

Jerome's conceptualization of the Devil as the Ape of God gained wide acceptance in Christian scholastic circles to become a familiar doctrine throughout the ages of faith. It provided a convenient explanation for the commonly observed success of the powers of darkness in their continual struggle against the powers of light. It placed almost all the blame upon the Devil and very little upon the sinners whom he thus succeeded in seducing. It was a comfortable doctrine, one that people could live with.

This idea of the Ape of God was well known, for example, to Saint Francis

Xavier, the first European missionary to work effectively in Japan. When Xavier initially encountered the lights, incense, bells, and books of Japanese Buddhist religious rites, he was first of all astonished beyond words by the way these ritual observances superficially resembled the elaborate services of his own Church of Rome. But Xavier, though no scholar, had at least a rudimentary familiarity with the writings of the fathers of his church, Jerome included. He soon was able to come up with a satisfactory, and canonical, explanation for the uncanny similarities that he and his fellow European missionaries were astonished to observe between their own religious services and the rituals of the Buddhists in mid-sixteenth-century Japan.

In Japanese Buddhism with its monks, nuns, rosaries, and beautifully vested clergy, Xavier soon identified yet another instance of the phenomenon of *Simia Dei*. Here surely, Xavier argued, the Devil had once more shown himself to be the true Ape of God, manufacturing an evil counterfeit of the real thing with diabolical skill. Satan in Japan had managed to ape the externals of True Religion for the express purpose of deceiving the ignorant Japanese, who could be expected to know no better, at least until the coming of the missionaries from Europe.

In contemporary Japan, just as in all the industrially advanced nations of the modern world, the religious milieu out of which this variety of ontological and theological speculation arose has today all but disappeared. But this does not mean that the concept of *Simia Dei,* the Ape of God, is entirely without utility for understanding, if not always for explaining, certain varieties of social and cultural phenomena for which we might otherwise lack even the hint of a rational solution. One must, of course, not take the idea of the Devil too seriously or too literally in all this. Nevertheless, Saint Jerome's basic conceptualization of something at the nether end of a scale of values managing to pass itself off as something quite different, something at the most exalted end of the same scale and at the same time something as far removed from itself as the Devil is from God, cannot but be admitted to have utility. At the very least, the idea suggests an analysis for many otherwise perplexing facts and events that we observe in all societies and their daily functions.

We have already emphasized that the modern myth of Nihongo is, in all its essentials, nonscientific and antiscientific. Though it has been erected, like all myths, around a hard inner kernel of truth, its special sociolinguistic function within contemporary Japanese society is to conceal and obfuscate those same tiny elements of fact behind an elaborate facade of mythic fiction. One searches in vain throughout the myth of Nihongo for anything that will correlate with the lingistic facts of the Japanese language as it is actually spoken and used by the Japanese people. The linguist is, after all, a variety of social scientist; scientists deal only with facts and their interpretation, and, faced with most of the external manifestations of the myth of Nihongo, the linguist can usually only admit to being baffled and bewildered.

It is precisely at this moment of the linguist's maximum bafflement and bewilderment that the Ape of God enters upon the scene—this time not wearing a plumed hat and cloak to hide his horns and tail but rather assuming the drab garb of the natural sciences, specifically the guise of advanced neurophysiological research. The linguist knows all too well that there is nothing substantial in the myth of Nihongo, no genuine elements of linguistic fact that can serve as a basis for its doctrines. But linguistics is a social science, not a specific body of learning like the natural sciences. And all of us, no matter how much our individual cultural backgrounds may differ, generally share a common belief in the integrity, the utility, and the wholesale validity of the natural sciences, particularly when they happen to involve medicine and medical research.

So what more impressive area than neurophysiological research could there possibly be from which those intent upon bolstering up the modern myth of Nihongo could manage to approach the problem? Nothing could possibly serve the ends of the myth better than further elaborations of its tenuous pretensions by mythmakers passing themselves off as medical researchers.

We have all been indoctrinated to respect the methodology and conclusions of research in the natural sciences. This indoctrination is particularly effective when it comes to medical research, since at one time or another most of us must put ourselves into the hands of doctors or surgeons whose work and skills are both based upon such research. If we cannot trust our doctor or the surgeon who is about to put us under anaesthesia and cut us open—if these men and women do not have hard, genuine, indubitable science at their command—who can we trust?

And so the modern myth of Nihongo has rediscovered, in the last decades of the twentieth century, what Saint Jerome already knew very well at the end of the fourth: the most effective way that error and superstition have yet worked out for doing their work is to pose as truth and science. The Devil can ape God so effectively that sometimes it is all but impossible to tell one from the other.

The most instructive examples of the way in which practitioners of the myth of Nihongo have managed to ape the methodology and research techniques of the natural sciences, particularly those of neurophysiological research, are to be found in the truly astonishing doctrines now being widely published and circulated by a Japanese ear-nose-and-throat specialist, Dr. Tadanobu Tsunoda. Born in Tokyo in 1926, Dr. Tsunoda graduated in 1949 from the faculty of medicine of what was then the Tokyo Medical-

Dental Technical School (now Tokyo Medical-Dental University). In 1957 he was appointed lecturer in the ear-nose-and-throat faculty of the same medical-dental institution; and shortly after Dr. Tsunoda's appointment to the faculty of his alma mater, he began to conduct experiments in neuropsychiatric medicine and neurophysiology, with particular emphasis upon the way in which the Japanese brain perceives, recognizes, and deals with auditory perception of all varieties, ranging widely from the noises of the natural world (insects, musical instruments, and the like) down to and including the sounds of various human languages.

What Tsunoda now claims to have been able to demonstrate on the basis of his own medical experimentation along neuropsychiatric lines is that the brain, the physical organ itself, of the individual Japanese has in the course of time become modified in those of its functions that are pertinent to the reception of auditory activities in such a way that it is now especially arranged *in order to suit the Japanese language*. In other words, Tsunoda is trying to tell the world not only that the Japanese language is itself a special, unique vehicle for the expression of human thought—this unique nature of the Japanese language, itself one of the keystones of the modern myth of Nihongo, Tsunoda takes as a given datum in all his research work—but he is also trying to convince us that the very brain itself, that mass of nerve tissue enclosed in the Japanese cranium, is also unique and somehow different from the same mass of nerve tissue that is enclosed in a French or a German or an English cranium. And this he claims to be able to document, not in the easily demolished terms of the myth of Nihongo in its more usual manifestations, but through the allegedly rigorous methodology of natural science and medical research.

Just as every myth must have its kernel of truth, so also must the *Simia Dei* begin his desperate work of generating clever counterfeits of the truth by selecting some widely acknowledged body of more or less uncontroversial scientific evidence upon which he may base his mimicry of science. In Tsunoda's studies, this role has been assigned to a small and essentially unimportant body of medical-physiological findings mostly going back to studies originally conducted in France in the middle of the last century. These studies suggested, though they have never been able to prove, that while the right and left hemispheres of the human brain are similar in their physical formation and physiological structure, human beings may perhaps in the course of their long evolutionary history have developed a variety of division of labor as far as the normal employment of each of these two cerebral hemispheres is concerned.

Paul Broca (1824–80), a French surgeon and anthropologist (though in the middle of the last century that term hardly meant what it does today), noted that certain disorders suffered by aphasiacs seemed to be related to actual physical disruption in the left cerebral hemisphere. Subsequently, a few follow-up studies along the general line of Broca's initial findings became possible, particularly work with patients who had suffered industrial or military accidents damaging one or another portions of the brain. These studies eventually led to the view that, in the human brain, the left cerebral hemisphere is the site where linguistic functions, including the production of speech and the comprehension of auditory perceptions, as well as such logical processes as mathematical calculations, are localized. At the same time, it was believed to be the right hemisphere that controls spontaneous reflexes, handles spatial perception, and is in charge of distinguishing differences in surface configuration, such as patterns on material or facial features. This same right hemisphere, it was decided, functions analogically, in contrast to the left hemisphere, which operates as if it were handling digital functions.

So far, so good. This was all interesting information, and curious information, and possibly even of potential value to the neurosurgeon or brain specialist attempting to diagnose physiologically induced mental disorders or hoping to perform corrective surgery in this most delicate area of the human organism. But apart from these obvious medical and surgical applications, Broca's evidence concerning a possible bilateral division of labor between the two cerebral hemispheres of the human brain remained almost entirely a scientific curiosity without wider interest or implications.

Almost, one must be careful to stress. Just about a hundred years ago, an effort was indeed made to employ this small body of solid scientific evidence as the kernel of fact underlying another aping of truth, quite independent of the modern Japanese effort that we are considering here. This was the pseudoscience of phrenology, which claimed that inspection of the outer configurations of the human skull—the undulations, bumps, and knots that may be detected on the surface of any normal skull, particularly if the subject is bald—provided overt physiological indications of the personality, abilities, and talents of the subject. Phrenology was in its own day another splendid example of the entire *Simia Dei* phenomenon. Starting as a popular and harmless parlor game, it soon degenerated into a cheap system of superstition, often used for fortunetelling at carnivals and fairs. It also found its way into a number of quite serious textbooks on "linguistic psychology" and related subjects that were highly regarded at the time.

There was, of course, absolutely nothing scientific or even serious about any of this. But many people remained difficult to convince of the spurious nature of phrenology and of the nonsense behind its elaborate charts of skull patterns and brain shapes, if only because they had heard of the research done on the division of labor between the two cerebral hemispheres. They found it difficult to believe that the one, a genuine body of knowledge, was not somehow the vindication for the second, actually no more than pseudo-scientific mumbo jumbo.

Linguistic science for its part was quick to question whether Broca's research on cerebral functions even had any implications at all for our understanding of the mechanisms of human speech. What Broca was able to demonstrate in 1861 was only that damage to the third frontal convolution in the left cerebral hemisphere was accompanied by aphasia, loss or impairment of the power to use or understand speech. Such loss or impairment, in the case of the brain-damaged subjects with which he worked, was obviously the result of the physiological traumas that their brains had suffered. But linguists early noted that Broca was getting onto rather less substantial ground when he theorized from this single observed fact that it was possible to identify this or that region of the cortex as a specific center for the activity of speech.

Subsequently, linguists attempting to correlate Broca's findings with general theories of the mechanism of human speech threw considerable doubt on the propriety of drawing any conclusions regarding the employment or production of language from Broca's work: "Many injuries to the nervous system . . . will interfere with speech, and different injuries will result in different kinds of difficulty, but the points of the cortex are surely not correlated with specific socially significant features of speech, such as words or syntax. . . . The error of seeking correlations between anatomically defined parts of the nervous system and socially defined activities appears clearly when we see some physiologists looking for a 'visual word-center' which is to control reading and writing: one might as well look for a specific brain-center for telegraphy or automobile driving or the use of any modern invention." Thus did the American linguist Leonard Bloomfield, writing in 1933, dismiss the unwarranted endorsement of Broca-like applications of physiological research to the functioning of language. Bloomfield called into particularly serious question the attempts current in the 1930s to read into Broca's work implications for a generalized theory of cerebral-hemispheric locations for specific elements of linguistic operation. Dr. Tsunoda picks up the extension of Broca's theories intact from the late decades of the nineteenth century. If he is aware of the serious questions that were asked, in linguistic circles at least, about the validity of these theories in subsequent decades, he gives no evidence of it.

This, then, is where linguistic science long ago decided to leave the Broca hypothesis on the functioning of the cerebral hemispheres, at least as far as any implication for the specific location of language within a particular portion of the human brain might be concerned. It was an interesting physiological curiosity of dubious medical interpretation and of even more dubious application to any understanding of how language works. Today, one hears little of phrenology. And unless one is a brain surgeon, almost as little of the differentiation in the functions of the two cerebral hemispheres of the human brain. There the matter might have rested—but this would be to reckon without the work of Tsunoda.

All these cerebral-function conjectures might have remained just that, the exclusive property of the parlor phrenologist, entertaining neo-Victorian ladies with his charts and models of the human skull and its supposed "centers of this" and "bumps of that," had it not been for Tsunoda. Emerging from his Tokyo clinic, the doctor has now determined single-handedly to take back all this pseudoscience from the phrenologist, to ignore the methodological qualms that both linguists and physicians have for years expressed concerning the dangers of further extending Broca's hypothesis, and finally to propel the entire untidy matter boldly into the last decade of the twentieth century.

Early in his career—sometime between his graduation from medical-dental school and the time when he became a neurophysiological researcher—Tsunoda set himself the task of extending Broca's findings on the possible existence of a division of labor in the human brain into the general area of Japanese language and culture. He hoped by these studies to solve a variety of problems in this same area. He now believes that he has, and, more importantly, he has also been able to convince a large number of other people in Japan that he has.

Tsunoda claims to have done this through an experimental system that he calls his self-devised "tapping method." In this method, experiments are carried out on normal human subjects who have had no physiological brain damage and thus have afforded no opportunity for direct, scientific observation. The method has been described as one "designed to determine which hemisphere is playing the dominant role, judging this from the retardation or disruption of regularly assigned tapping on an electric key in certain tempos, which are in turn induced by the load of acoustic stimuli applied through an earphone which the subject is wearing." In other words, in Tsunoda's method the subject tests himself, and the investigator then attempts to observe and interpret the subject's totally subjective experimental evidence.

The moderately cautious observer with even a minimal concern for the scientific method would at this point begin to be extremely suspicious about any far-reaching conclusions that might be extrapolated from this quite circular process of introspection and intuitive self-experimentation. These same suspicions are immediately substantiated as soon as we study even the bare outline of the conclusions that Tsunoda seeks to draw.

From his tapping-method experiments, Tsunoda claims to have discovered that while the consonantal sounds of language are perceived by both Japanese and Westerners in their left cerebral hemispheres at the same time—and here is the critical physiological difference that he claims to have established —Westerners normally handle the vowels of language in their right cerebral hemisphere, while Japanese deal with these sounds in their left hemisphere, the same cerebral hemisphere in which they deal with the consonants.

In other words, where the normal brain of the average Westerner makes a clear-cut, and presumably also a useful, division of labor in its auditory perception and information processing of the vowels and consonants of language, the Japanese brain does not. The Japanese brain functions, in this all-important sector of human communication, in a quite different way than does the brain of any other racial group that Tsunoda has been able to experiment with. If Tsunoda is to be believed, the left cerebral hemisphere of the average, normal Japanese individual is a busy place indeed: "My tests show that the left cerebral hemisphere of the Japanese receives a wide range of sounds: not just the linguistic sounds (consonant and vowel sounds) but also such non-linguistic sounds as the utterance of human emotions, animal cries, Japanese musical instruments, the sounds of a running brook, wind, waves, and certain famous temple bells. The range of sounds [that] Westerners receive in the left hemisphere of their brains is conspicuously narrower, apparently limited to syllables made up of both consonant and vowel sounds. The same is true of Chinese, Koreans, and almost all Southeast Asian peoples."

It is particularly interesting and significant to note how extremely early in his argumentation Tsunoda lays down rigid lines of racial demarcation and also what direction these racial lines take. On one side of his racial fence are the Japanese, whose left cerebral hemispheres are busy coping with all the sounds on the face of the earth: vowels, consonants, babbling brooks, and certain famous temple bells. (Unfortunately, is it not clear why only certain famous temple bells are taken care of, but not just any old ordinary temple bells. But then, all Japanese culture is notorious for its ability to make such nice distinctions.) On the other side of the same racial barrier sit all the other peoples of the earth: the Westerners, the Chinese, the Koreans, and almost all Southeast Asian peoples, whose brains make quite a different response to all that goes on in the world about them—though one is left wondering just what these other, cerebrally less well-endowed races do about the sound of certain temple bells.

What is, however, abundantly clear in all this is that we are now being asked to believe that the Japanese brain, just like the Japanese language, is a unique phenomenon—a human organ possessing functions unknown to the brains of any other set of human beings on earth. The racist thrust of such a thesis is only too apparent. Rarely in modern times has anyone dared to put forth as unabashedly racist an approach to any issue as we confront in Tsunoda's publications. Meanwhile, this whole shocking doctrine of

Japanese organic uniqueness is said to be supported by medical-physiological experimentation and research.

Tsunoda is neither brash enough nor naive enough to claim that the actual physiological configuration of either of the hemispheres of a normal Japanese brain is any different from the configuration of the same organ as it is found in any other human racial stock or group. Such a claim could of course easily be refuted by any first-year medical student who had even minimal exposure to the subject matter involved on the tables of the autopsy room. What he claims to be different, instead, is something that cannot be refuted because it cannot be observed, except by the subject himself when he is using Tsunoda's tapping method: it is supposed to be the function of the hemispheres, not the physical configuration of the hemispheres themselves. Nor does he even suggest that this difference in function is the result of heredity. For Tsunoda, this difference is something that was determined long ago in the evolutionary history of the Japanese race. And what was it that determined it? The unique nature of the Japanese language, of course.

With this, we not only have once more come full circle, but we are also once again firmly seated on board our familiar merry-go-round of circular mythic logic. What makes the Japanese language, and the culture it operates within, so unique? The unique arrangement and functioning of the left hemisphere in the Japanese brain. Why is the Japanese brain unique in the functioning of its left hemisphere? Because of the unique nature of the language that it must process.

All that really emerges intact from this vicious circle of interconnected illogicality is the single conclusion that the Japanese are unique and hence also are somehow to be set apart in the totality of their uniqueness from all other people on earth. The sole novelty is that this time around, the all-too-familiar claim of uniqueness is ostensibly supported by scientific evidence from medical research. One does not need to go back in time to the days of Xavier to conclude, sadly but solemnly, that Saint Jerome probably had a point there, when he warned us about the clever imitative work of *Simia Dei*.

For the non-Japanese observer, the single most surprising element in Tsunoda's thesis will surely be its apparently unlimited powers of universal explanation. First, he claims—but never, as we shall see below, offers any rigorous scientific evidence in support of his claim—that the Japanese brain functions differently from the human brain as we find it in any other race on earth. Then, with no further hint of physiological, much less of any logical, connection, he launches full-sail into a veritable armada of "issues and questions that the Tsunoda research explains." The reader soon realizes that Tsunoda's research attempts to explain virtually everything that might otherwise puzzle us, or that puzzles the Japanese, about the way they think and act, as well as about the way they talk. As we shall see, it is even supposed to explain the way they do not talk.

Tsunoda claims that his research on the special functions of the left cerebral hemisphere of the Japanese brain explains so many different things, including things that to anyone outside Japanese society and culture will appear to be quite unrelated, that it is difficult to know how to begin to list them. It would probably be an easier task to list the few elements in Japanese life and society that he does not say are somehow related to the supposedly unique functioning of the Japanese brain. Even to make the attempt to present Tsunoda's claims in any rational order runs the risk of doing them more credit than they deserve; simply trying to arrange his assertions into some order, any order, may very well give them a greater semblance of rationality than they actually possess. But the attempt must be made, since it appears that Tsunoda and his theories will be with us all for some time to come.

Typical of the many all-encompassing explanations advanced by Tsunoda is the following example: "My hypothesis is that the left hemisphere, which handles the sounds signifying reason, emotion and nature, is a basic formative agent in Japan's traditional culture and the mentality of contemporary Japanese people. I call it a 'vowel-determined psychology.' . . . In this way we are beginning to formulate an approach to the hitherto elusive Japanese mentality which may render it more intelligible to us, by gradual clarification first through auditory tests and now by more scientific medical methods."

This short passage shows many attributes typical of the Tsunoda approach. In line with his basic thesis that the Japanese brain works the way it does because of the nature of the Japanese language, while at the same time the Japanese language is the way it is because of the Japanese brain, the above blanket explanation for "the hitherto elusive Japanese mentality" is also essentially circular. But by this time we are all so accustomed to the circularity that distinguishes such argumentation that this feature need not detain us for long.

Of more interest is the doctor's characterization of this mentality as "hitherto elusive." This is a splendid documentation of one of the essential points of departure for the *Nihonjin-ron,* already encountered in chapter 2. Literally, this term simply means "the question of the Japanese," but the word has become another highly sensitive and emotionally charged fetish term in modern Japanese society, where it is increasingly being used to refer to everything and anything that the Japanese feel is different or distinctive about the nation, the people, their life, and their culture. More than anything else, the *Nihonjin-ron* today is concerned with questions of national and cultural identity: Who are we Japanese? Where did we come from? Why do we act the way we do? What is eventually going to happen to us?

One heard little or nothing about the *Nihonjin-ron* and all the usually unanswered questions it asks until roughly the late 1960s. From then on, and particularly during the later part of the affluent 1970s, it soon grew to become one of the principal obsessions of Japanese intellectual life. Quite obviously, the *Nihonjin-ron* is little more than a turning inward of questions that foreigners began to put to the Japanese, once Japanese economic recovery really took off and Japanese businessmen began to dominate one after another of the world markets. But these were, and are, questions that the Japanese could not—and still cannot—answer.

The Japanese had never before asked these questions of themselves. Left on their own, the Japanese could not have cared less about "formulating an approach to the hitherto elusive Japanese mentality." They began to worry about these things only after sizable numbers of Japanese, for the first time in Japanese history, started to have occasion to come into daily contact with foreigners in the course of conducting Japan's burgeoning export trade. As Japanese automobiles began to drive the motor industry of Detroit up to the wall, more and more people—and not only people in Detroit—began to ask: Who are these people? Where do they come from? What makes them work the way they do, and what makes them so successful at landing and marketing good, serviceable automobiles that continue to undercut our own prices?

The Japanese could perhaps have begun to answer at least this last type of question, though for obvious reasons they usually preferred not to. But for the other more general questions, they had no explanations at hand. Their own Japanese mentality was as elusive to them as it was for their foreign competitors. Out of this pressing need for answers that were not forthcoming, the *Nihonjin-ron* was born. Anything that promised to provide explanations for the elusive elements in Japanese life and culture gained immediate respectability. The *Nihonjin-ron* soon became inextricably intertwined with the modern myth of Nihongo. Indeed, it is often impossible to say where the one begins and the other leaves off. And as we can see from Tsunoda's explanation quoted above, one of the special functions of his work has been to evolve an allegedly scientific basis for further mingling the specific details of these two bodies of folk fetishes.

Foreign observers may well be forgiven if, upon being told for the one-hundredth time how elusive the Japanese mentality is, they begin to lose interest in following up this or that new explanation for this particular characteristic. After all, if the Japanese find it all that difficult to explain to themselves, what point can there possibly be in the mere foreigner trying to figure all this out? But even the outside observer of the Japanese scene who has come to this rather sane conclusion will be sure to find other elements of great interest in some of the elaborations of Tsunoda's brain theories.

This is particularly true because many of these elaborations prove to involve themselves very intimately with two segments of Japanese sociolinguistics from which any serious non-Japanese observer can hardly manage to divorce his or her interests—the ability of the Japanese to learn foreign languages, and the question of foreigners learning the Japanese language. Even if we are all to agree to let the elusive Japanese mentality go about its elusive business in its own elusive way, and decide that anything all that elusive can only be of interest to the Japanese themselves, these other, outward-reaching aspects of the Tsunoda hypothesis can hardly be ignored. Tsunoda attempts, in effect, to involve his theories of brain function with the two principal avenues that are available for the Japanese in their never-ending need for communicating with the rest of the world—their learning and utilization of foreign languages, especially English, as well as the efforts that the rest of the world might possibly make toward learning Japanese. At this point, Tsunoda's theories must also necessarily become the concern of the rest of the world as well.

First of all, Tsunoda claims that his cerebral-hemisphere theories provide an explanation for one of the most persistent questions of the *Nihonjin-ron*: Why are the Japanese so poor at mastering foreign languages, especially English? It is best, again, to let Tsunoda speak for himself: "It seems that English is a problem in a category of its own. Japanese study English for years on end, giving painstaking effort, but all that study rarely produces the confidence that one can at last handle even a part of the language adequately. It may be that something about the Japanese brain makes it particularly difficult to develop English language ability. . . ."

Elsewhere in the present book we shall explore some of the facts about the way English and other foreign languages are taught in Japan. We shall see that quite adequate explanations are readily at hand for the admittedly poor performance of most Japanese in this area, explanations that have nothing to do with the way the Japanese brain functions. Most of these reasons are on a quite less involved level; by and large, they have to do with the way Japanese education functions.

The single most fascinating point about the Tsunoda explanation is that it offers not the least shred of hope for ever doing anything about this situation now or in the future. If what Tsunoda tries to suggest is even remotely true—if indeed it is the inherited mechanism of cerebral function evolved long ago by the Japanese racial stock that predisposes the entire nation toward enormous difficulties in the mastery of a foreign language, then nothing can ever be done about the situation. Indeed, Tsunoda himself not only covertly admits the utter hopelessness of the arrangement, but also appears to take considerable satisfaction in the utter bleakness of the socio-linguistic picture that he would like to paint: "Japanese themselves lose the functional usefulness of the 'creative' side of their brain as soon as they begin speaking, reading, writing, or thinking in English. Japanese who feel out of their element in English, including myself, are somehow relieved when they hear the comment, 'So many times when a person speaks really good English, he's also a real drip' [sic]."

Here we may be forgiven if at last we feel that we have got a little closer to the heart of the matter. It would appear that there are Japanese who are able to use English or other foreign languages adequately, sometimes even effectively, and also that Tsunoda is by his own admission not among their number. But what is one to say of such people, such Japanese who break the norms of the society and somehow or other manage to learn enough of a foreign language so that they are able to communicate with outsiders? Not only are they not "creative," not only have they lost "the functional usefulness" of their brains, but they are "real drips."

Readers less up to date in their command of American slang expressions than Tsunoda—or, at any rate, less up on it than his translators—might like to know that drip is defined as "any person, usually a male teenager or student, who is disliked or who is objectionable, usually because he is a bore, introverted, overly solicitous, or is not hip to the fads, fashions, and typical behavior patterns of his age group" in H. Wentworth and S. B. Flexner, *Dictionary of American Slang*. Perhaps Tsunoda's employment of this particular slang term is to be explained by the fact that its etymology involves an original medical metaphor rather too coarsely explicit to admit of fuller explanation in a book that, like the present one, is designed for the general public.

Fortunately, Tsunoda is neither modest nor reticent in telling anyone still interested in all this exactly how he arrived at this particular conclusion. Not surprisingly, it turns out to be quite unrelated to any experimentation with his tapping method, or indeed with any of his neurophysiological research: "I remember trying desperately to master the American language in the United States when I went there fifteen years ago, working literally to 'think in English.' I gradually realized that as long as I was struggling to get better in speaking and hearing English, my ability to think creatively seemed to dry up. When I returned to Japan, I stopped all effort to learn English, suspecting that 'thinking in English' was unhealthy, and then I began to produce a stream of creative original ideas. I was convinced at that time that learning a foreign language has serious demerits for Japanese."

Suddenly, many things become clear. Tsunoda has experimented with language-learning, to be sure, but he has experimented entirely upon himself. He has analyzed his own attempts to learn to speak and understand English and extended his personal reactions of frustration and difficulty to everyone else in Japan. What was true for him must necessarily, he argues, be true for all Japanese. He felt that studying English "dried up" his ability to think creatively, while stopping the study of English turned on his wellsprings of creative thought once more—the same wellsprings out of which, one must not forget to add, eventually emerged his hypothesis of the unique functioning of the cerebral hemispheres of the Japanese race. If only, one must reflect with a sigh, Tsunoda had been a little more gifted in foreign languages, how much Japan and the world might have been spared!

On the other hand, if Tsunoda had been better at English, Japanese sociolinguistics would have lost out on what has become its new universal field theory—a theory that explains everything and anything about the Japanese response to all human language, whether Japanese or foreign. Not only does it provide a putatively scientific explanation for all these responses, it also manages to make a virtue out of a number of debilities that trouble all Japanese very much, particularly out of the obvious difficulty that most Japanese have with foreign languages.

"Do you find it difficult to learn to speak English?" Tsunoda asks in effect. If you do, he replies, it is nothing to be concerned about. You need not give a moment's thought to the possibility that you experience these difficulties because the method of language instruction to which you were subjected, or are now being subjected, is incorrect or inefficient. Nor does it mean that the situation is one that might possibly be remedied in some way or another. No, Tsunoda replies, the debility in question is actually something of which you, and all of us Japanese, should be proud. We all have this trouble with foreign languages because our brains are different from those of the rest of mankind. Not only that. So intimately are our personalities tied up to these differences in our unique brains that, if by chance we happen to encounter one of our fellow countrymen who has managed to learn to speak a foreign language, we avoid him or her—there is something peculiar and potentially offensive about any such person, anyone who dares not share our common incompetence in this regard. At the very least, the good doctor reassures us, such a foreign-language-speaking Japanese is sure to be "a real drip." He or she will be a person devoid of original ideas and unable to make effective use of the Japanese brain with its uniquely functioning left cerebral hemisphere, with which nature in its wisdom originally endowed all Japanese.

Not since Albert Einstein first lit upon his epochal equation relating energy and mass has there been a single theory with as many ramifications.

Not since Archimedes has anyone come up with such a simple statement that appears to provide scientific explanations for so many diverse phenomena.

Anyone familiar with the workings of Japan's mass media, and with the ins and outs of Japan's enormous book-publishing industry, will hardly be surprised to learn that these comforting universalist theories have received a rousing reception by almost every stratum of Japanese society. They have been the subject of countless press releases, newspaper stories, and magazine articles; they have been featured on television and radio; every conceivable mass medium, with the possible exception of skywriting, has been employed to ensure their in-depth dissemination throughout Japanese life.

Nor has the publicity afforded to Tsunoda's theories, particularly to his enormously popular thesis about why the majority of the Japanese find foreign languages difficult, been by any means limited to popular media. The Japan Foundation recently commissioned an article by Tsunoda for its official Japanese-English *Newsletter*, widely distributed throughout the world. It is, in fact, from this Japan Foundation translation of Tsunoda's statements that all the quotations in the present chapter have been taken.

The Japan Foundation is an agency of the Japanese government. Funded entirely by Japanese government appropriations, the foundation is charged with responsibility for encouraging cultural and educational relations with foreign countries and with making Japan better known and better understood abroad. The foundation's higher-level administrative and executive staff is in the main career bureaucrats drawn from one or the other of two Japanese government departments—either the Ministry of Education or the Ministry of Foreign Affairs. These officials work at the Japan Foundation on temporary assignment for three or four years at a time, after which they return to their regular duties elsewhere in the government. This arrangement ensures that the view of Japan that the foundation circulates abroad will closely follow the official line established in Japanese government circles, particularly that line as it is understood by the career bureaucracy of the Ministry of Education and the Ministry of Foreign Affairs.

In their introductory note to the English-language version of Tsunoda's views, the Japan Foundation's *Newsletter* editors disclosed where the main focus of interest is located in all this, for them as well as for the Japanese reading public as a whole. They introduced the doctor and his hypothesis by asking the following question: "Does the physiology of the brain suggest the study of a foreign language diminishes the creative abilities of the Japan [*sic*] people? If this is really the case, what possibilities exist for the internationalization of Japanese culture?" And for an answer to this question, they follow with the article from which we have taken, in the present chapter, a number of representative excerpts.

Meanwhile, a hard-cover book entitled *Nihonjin no Nō* (The Japanese Brain) by Dr. Tsunoda has been enjoying extraordinary sales. First published on February 15, 1978, it had already chalked up twelve additional printings by August 1 of the same year—something of a record for a nonfiction best seller, even in Japan's notoriously volatile publishing industry. Given this impressive record of press and publicity coverage, it seems unlikely that there is any Japanese reader who has not by now been exposed to Tsunoda's views.

Still, even in Japan, there are welcome indications that Tsunoda's theories are not esteemed by everyone. It is hardly an accident that his best-selling book was published not by a responsible medical-book publisher, of which Japan has many, but by a publishing company totally outside the scientific field, a publisher that has long specialized in merchandizing books specifically related to the myth of Nihongo, as well as a profitable line of English-language textbooks and self-instruction manuals. In other words, Tsunoda's publisher now manages to have it both ways. If you want to learn English, they will sell you the books that are supposed to teach you the language. If, after trying these books out, you still find you cannot master it, then they will be happy to sell you Tsunoda's book, which will explain to you why you should not feel bad about being unable to learn English; after all, anyone who can or does is a "real drip."

Another welcome indication that not everyone in Japan has been eager to jump onto the Tsunoda bandwagon is provided by the way in which the Japanese medical research profession as a whole, like the Japanese medical publishers, has been unwilling to become involved in the entire affair. Naturally, other Japanese doctors and medical researchers have been somewhat reluctant to criticize Tsunoda and his research directly. This will hardly be surprising to anyone who has ever asked one physician for his opinion of another and has encountered the genial conspiracy of silence with which doctors have always, in all societies, managed to protect their individual reputations against suggestions of malpractice and incompetence brought by disgruntled patients. Nevertheless, at least one Japanese physician, a specialist in the physiological aspects of cognition, has gone on record to point out a few of the more serious scientific and methodological reasons why it is impossible for a neutral observer to accept either Tsunoda's experimental findings or the conclusions that he claims to draw from these findings.

This specialist argues that the Tsunoda method for detecting differentials in the functioning of the cerebral hemispheres has serious experimental flaws and that no conclusions drawn by Tsunoda ought to be taken at face value until his entire method of experimentation can be "reexamined more objectively and carefully." Most significantly, this skeptical Japanese specialist also points out that, firstly, no other physician or medical researcher in Japan, working with the published accounts of Tsunoda's experimentation and under the same experimental conditions as those described by Tsunoda, has as yet been able to obtain results identical to those reported by Tsunoda; secondly, when two non-Japanese scientists did attempt in 1975 to reproduce the experimentation described by Tsunoda, they found that the results of their experiments "did not concur with Tsunoda's findings."

No one with proper concern for the do's and don't's of medical treatment would seriously consider taking even a cold remedy that had been produced and tested using the completely self-documented, totally unverified methods that Tsunoda has used as the basis for his theories of the unique functioning of the Japanese brain. The manufacturers of Band-Aids and adhesive plasters in most industrialized nations are compelled by law to subject their products to far more rigorous test controls than Tsunoda has seen fit to extend to his basic experimentation. The Japanese medical profession has made it clear that the doctor's theories ought to be treated with the same generous caution that we would extend to any untested and potentially unsafe medical product. Unfortunately, considerations of professional courtesy have kept their voices tuned to a discouragingly low level, so low that it has hardly had any overall effect upon the strident clangor with which the Japanese media in general have welcomed Tsunoda's views. Thus, the Japanese medical profession has placed its negative testimony against Tsunoda's experimental evidence on public record, but it has done this in such a quiet, even delicate, fashion that its arguments have had little chance of being heard among the loudly orchestrated acclaim generated by those who would champion his thesis.

Among Japanese specialists in the study of language, Tsunoda's views have attracted wide attention as well as, one regrets to have to add, widespread approval. In Japanese linguistic circles, one cannot even detect the quiet voice of serious questioning that the Japanese medical profession has raised. Japanese linguistic scholars have, almost without exception, vied with one another in their eagerness to accept the thesis of specifically Japanese brain functions.

For all those in Japan who have been seeking ever new and different avenues along which to elaborate upon the modern myth of Nihongo, Tsunoda's experimentation now appears to provide a long-awaited scientific basis for views previously held for other, non-scientific reasons. At last it seems that one of the "hard" sciences—in this case, neurophysiological medical research—has provided experimental evidence for a belief that has long nestled at the very heart of the entire myth of Nihongo. That faith so long maintained in the unique nature of the language, and of the people who speak it, is now apparently vindicated by the special way in which the Japanese brain is supposed to function.

All this has been particularly unfortunate, since as a matter of fact the science of linguistics has as much or more to offer in refutation of Tsunoda's theories as does any amount of medical research. The medical specialist must note that no one else in Japan has yet been able to reproduce Tsunoda's experimental results while working under the same circumstances and conditions that the doctor describes for his own work and also that when such attempts have been made by foreign specialists, they have ended up with results that contradict, rather than confirm, the Tsunoda findings. The linguist must then put on record that Tsunoda's use of linguistic materials—which it turns out do play a major role in his work at every level—is totally without scientific basis and conducted on a level of amateurism that would not be countenanced in any serious scientific community anywhere in the world.

There are really only two elements in Tsunoda's attempts at extending his cerebral-function speculations into the area of linguistic science that are difficult to explain. The first concerns the nature of the logical or experimental link between these two different branches of his theory, which is never made clear, most likely because no such link exists. As one reads Tsunoda's accounts of his own work, the initial emphasis is entirely upon the results of his neurophysiological experimentation. Then, with no warning or theoretical preparation, the drift of his discourse suddenly shifts from neurophysiology to linguistics.

The second element that is difficult to explain concerns Tsunoda's descriptive statements relating to the Japanese language. These are uniformly either simply inaccurate or seriously misleading. Granted that his original field of specialty is not linguistics, one might still have expected that before launching into such an elaborate attempt at erecting a theoretical approach to the entire question of Japanese language, life, civilization, and culture, the doctor would at least have informed himself about the elementary linguistic facts of what is, after all, his own native language. This he has not done. Nor has he successfully grasped the difference between language, in the sense that this term is commonly employed by linguistic science, and script, or writing systems. Tsunoda consistently confuses the two very different and separate entities of language and writing, with the result that in his published work it is usually impossible to say with confidence which of the two he is talking about at any given time.

If the reader has difficulty in believing that any literate Japanese, particularly anyone with pretensions to scientific work, could or would proceed in this careless fashion, he has only to turn to any page of Tsunoda's work that mentions the Japanese language. Thus we find: "All Japanese syllables end in vowels." Absolutely untrue: not only do many Japanese words end in the final consonant -*n,* the language abounds in syllables with final consonants such as the element *hak-* in the word *hakkiri* (clear), or the *map-* in *mappira* (plainly), or the *mat-* in *mattaku* (absolutely). Tsunoda's claim that "all Japanese syllables end in vowels" is due in part to his confusion between the structure of the language and its orthographic conventions, but what he says is still inaccurate, even in orthographic terms. Equally misleading is his claim that "another characteristic of Japanese vowels is that any one of the five vowel sounds can have meaning in itself." Wrong again. Each of the five Japanese vowels can no more have meaning in itself than can any of the Japanese consonants.

Tsunoda is trying to say that there are words in Japanese—a very few, to be sure—that consist solely of a single vowel or solely of several vowels. In the first place, by the way he has expressed himself he shows that he does not understand the elementary nature of language. Secondly, by claiming that this feature is something characteristic of Japanese vowels, he shows how this prior misunderstanding is immediately thereafter employed as the basis for a secondary but equally misleading conclusion about the unique nature of Japanese. Actually, Japanese is not a whit different in this respect from any other language in the world.

Tsunoda gives as evidence for his erroneous description of Japanese vowels eight "Japanese words pronounced *i,*" but of these, only two are historically Japanese words—*i* "five" and *i* "boar." Even here, the forms that are actually found in the modern language are never the simple vowel-morphemes that Tsunoda cites but always appear with additional suffixal material, so that "five" is actually *itsutsu* and "boar" is *inoshishi.* The other five Japanese "vowel-word" forms he cites are all actually Chinese loanwords, borrowed into Japanese from Chinese in recent centuries. So he is telling us, in effect, that the unique functioning of the Japanese brain is both demonstrated by, and originally produced through, the influence of borrowed words that the Japanese have taken over from Chinese.

With this, Tsunoda's ineptness in handling linguistic evidence directly triggers yet another fatal flaw in his argument. If the existence of any special variety of words in the Japanese language actually could have had an effect on the functioning of the Japanese brain, this would have had to transpire immensely long ago, during the evolution of the human brain (evolution that he seems to assume took place separately and independently, as well as more cunningly, in Japan). But any such evolution would have had to be over and done with hundreds of thousands of years before these Chinese loanwords were borrowed into the Japanese language. Yet Tsunoda cites these same late Chinese loanwords as examples of the kind of unique Japanese linguistic feature that triggered the distinctive evolutionary process responsible for the development of the Japanese brain. His argument is a historical impossibility as well as a scientific farrago.

If there were even a shred of likelihood that the existence of linguistic forms of this or that specific configuration in any of the languages that Tsunoda attempts to treat had ever had a critical effect upon the evolution of the cerebral functions of the racial groups speaking such a language, obviously such an effect must have begun immensely long ago in the history of the language and of the racial group concerned. This is one reason why Tsunoda's citation of recent loanword borrowings from Chinese, as supposed evidence for the evolution of characteristic brain functions in the Japanese race, is so utterly absurd. We know that these borrowings all took place in the recent past.

Any attempt at refuting Tsunoda's thesis of unique cerebral hemispheric functions in the Japanese brain runs the obvious danger of giving his ideas more exposure than they deserve. Normally, the less said about claims that prove to have behind them no more of fact or substance than Tsunoda's thesis does, the better. But the avidity with which the Japanese media and more than one Japanese government-related agency have seized upon Tsunoda's ideas as more grist for the mill of the modern myth of Nihongo is far from normal. In view of the enormous exposure already given to these ideas by the Japanese media on every level, and particularly in view of the fact that they have been given dissemination through worldwide English-language publications, one probably runs an even greater danger if one elects simply to ignore them.

A generation ago in Western Europe, there were also plenty of doctors of this or that ready and willing to dish up learned nonsense purporting to demonstrate the unique role of this or that racial group. Many terrified observers knew how absurd, how unscientific, and especially how dangerous all this racist pseudoscience actually was; but in Europe of the 1930s and 1940s there were ways to enforce silence. Tsunoda's publications, and the vogue that they are enjoying both at home and abroad, show that Japan has no lack of putative doctors who stand ready to put science and medicine at the beck and call of racism. The difference is that Japan in the 1980s is not a fascist, absolutist state. People there, if they wish to, *can* speak out freely. One can only speculate about why, thus far at least, so few have done so.

CHAPTER FIVE

The Antimyth of Silence

> This does not mean that saying things in a roundabout way or obscuring things is not good in all instances. In a country like Japan with only one race, one doesn't have to say things directly to get things across to the other person, and speaking indirectly becomes a wisdom for avoiding friction. —Asahi Evening News, May 7, 1973, translating the Tensei Jingo feature column from the previous day's Asahi Shimbun

CLOSE UPON the heels of any true sustaining myth, an equally vital body of antimyth is also generally to be found. Whatever the sustaining myth teaches, whatever it holds to be essential, true, and significant, all these the antimyth denies—deriving its own vitality and purpose from the very vehemence of these denials. The antimyth is a mirror image of the myth; the one reinforces the other in such a way that the net impact of the two upon society is, in the final accounting, far in excess of the mere sum of their parts. So intimately associated with one another are myth and antimyth that most participants in a society sustained by these systems hardly ever notice that two quite separate, contradictory entities are actually involved.

If the myth were true, then the antimyth could not possibly also be true, since one is the direct opposite of the other. But this really does not matter. Nor does this in any way interfere with the effective functioning of either myth or antimyth. Logically, one necessarily rules out the other. Both myth and antimyth cannot possibly be held at the same time in any logical or rational system. But logic and rationality are, as we have already seen, both equally beside the point when it comes to the effective functioning of the sustaining myths of mankind. And they are equally beside the point in any consideration of antimyths as well.

Parallel to the modern myth of Nihongo, there is an almost equally potent mirror-image body of beliefs concerned with the Japanese language, an antimyth that one encounters throughout modern Japanese academic and intellectual life almost as frequently as one encounters the myth itself. The myth focuses on every possible overt aspect of the Japanese language—its words, their meanings, their pronunciation, the sociolinguistic behavior of its native speakers. The myth tries to make a case for the unique nature and nonpareil importance of all these aspects of the language. The antimyth simply and plainly denies all this. In point of fact, the antimyth all but denies the importance if not the very existence of the language itself. Instead, the antimyth takes as its focus the very opposite of language: silence.

The Japanese, the antimyth teaches, do not in fact use language in any important or significant fashion. What is unique and important about Japanese culture and society is the preference, whenever possible, for silence, not language. If the Japanese seem to the outsider to be actually employing language a great deal or to be making a great deal out of it, then the outsider is, as usual, misinformed. We are a nation, the antimyth teaches, not of language, but of silence. Our forte is nonverbal communication. And if you thought our language was difficult to learn and impossible to master, then how, the antimyth taunts, can you ever hope to succeed in becoming fluent in our silence?

One of the most significant elaborations of this antimyth of Japanese silence to surface in recent years is to be found in the field of modern literary criticism. One might expect that a literary critic would place major emphasis upon the overt evidence that he deals with, that is, literature. But here, as so often, the Japanese experience proves to be different and more than a little surprising.

By applying the antimyth of silence to problems in literary history and criticism, several highly regarded Japanese literary scholars have managed to evolve a school of literary appreciation in which it is not the texts they study that are important. To them, texts are valuable only because they represent "violations of silence." According to the tenets of this school of criticism, it is silence, the essence of the antimyth of the Japanese language, that is central to Japanese life and culture.

One particularly articulate practitioner of the cult of silence has even written extensively about it in English, thus making its rather remarkable conclusions easily available to anyone interested in the subject. This is Professor Masao Miyoshi of the University of California, Berkeley. His fascination with every aspect of the antimyth of silence is immediately apparent even in the title for a book he wrote in 1974 on the analysis of several modern Japanese novels: *Accomplices of Silence.* Since Miyoshi himself writes about these matters in English, his work is of particular importance for our present purposes. It may be cited in evidence with no fear that, by the process of translation, we have in any way slanted or deflected his statements on these intricate issues.

For Miyoshi, Japanese culture is distinguished, not by its language or by the use that the culture makes of it, but by what he calls "the worship of silence." He goes on to explain this in the following terms: "Perhaps more important than any other factor in this whole problem of language and style is the typical Japanese dislike of the verbal. It might be said that the culture is primarily visual, not verbal, in orientation, and social decorum provides that reticence, not eloquence, is rewarded. Similarly, in art it is not articulation but the subtle art of silence that is valued. . . . I do not believe it an overstatement to say that writing in Japanese is always something of an act of defiance. Silence not only invades and seduces all would-be speakers and writers, but is in fact a powerful compulsion throughout the whole society. To bring forth a written work to break this silence is thus often tantamount to the writer's sacrifice of himself, via defeat and exhaustion." Building upon this premise, Miyoshi then elaborates his own literary analysis of the work of several modern Japanese novelists, treating them in terms of their violation of the Japanese worship of silence.

Anyone who has lived in Japan for any period of time, whether he or she knows the language or not, will surely find all this difficult to accept. Miyoshi's basic assumptions will surely appear to run counter to most direct experience. If any single feature characterizes sociolinguistic behavior in modern Japan, it is the obvious pleasure and delight that Japanese at every level of society take in the constant and generally strident, high-decibel employment of their own language.

Where, one must ask at the outset, can one actually find the worship of silence that Miyoshi makes the cornerstone of his literary theories? Certainly not at the Kabuki theater, where crowds of fine little old ladies arrive in noisy gaggles of fours and fives, talking twelve-to-the-dozen before the curtain opens and continuing to talk to each other quite loudly throughout the entire performance, with an occasional pause in their chatter when they eat their box lunches, or sometimes—if one is very lucky—for a few precious moments during one or more particularly well-known scenes on the stage. Otherwise, the chatter in the audience at a Kabuki theater is always at least as audible as anything going on among the actors, if not louder.

Nor will one find much more evidence for this worship of silence at a bar or restaurant, at least not in an establishment operated along anything resembling traditional Japanese lines. One often finds quiet groups eating in Western-style restaurants, but a Japanese-style establishment is supposed to be, and generally is, a verbal bedlam. Shouting, not talking, is the norm for any Japanese conversation conducted under circumstances in which it is important to demonstrate that one is having a good time.

But perhaps, the foreigner may inquire, might not one find this worship of silence in the older religious and cultural centers of the country? What about all those old temples in Kyoto and Nara, is there no silence there either? Let the skeptic go and try to locate a quiet Kyoto temple enclosure, sometimes (at least in the off-tourist season) deserted except for the visitor himself, a splendid view, and a lovely rock-and-stone landscape garden. As soon as the visitor settles down to enjoy the view and to savor the quiet, a loudspeaker will erupt just at ear level with a loud tape message explaining the garden and its beauty, telling how old it is, how important it is, how beautiful it is, and so on. Wait until the tape is over; there will perhaps be a moment of silence; but Japanese technology is superb, and the tape will almost at once automatically repeat, over and over again, until the visitor finally admits defeat and heads for the exit. Here he will be assaulted, if the temple is particularly well off and well equipped, by yet another automatically repeating tape-and-loudspeaker contraption that will say: "Thank you for visiting our temple."

If the worship of silence plays a significant part in the literary criticism of Miyoshi and other modern Japanese scholars, that is their business. But the observer of the contemporary Japanese scene cannot but record, in all honesty, that such literary critics seem able to detect far more substantial quantities of this precious commodity of silence than the most diligent foreign visitor to Japan can ever verify, even on a quiet day.

At any rate, as we observe any facet of modern Japanese life and particularly as we listen to its incessant verbal din, the questions that we must always ask are: How much of what we see and observe today is genuinely Japanese, in the sense of having been inherited more or less intact from the behavior patterns of earlier generations? How much of what we see today has resulted from the superficial Westernization of Japanese life that began about a hundred years ago and that has continued ever since at an always accelerating rate of speed?

After all, no one questions that there have been major changes in Japanese public behavior over the past century, particularly in the several decades since the defeat in 1945. A century ago, give or take a few years, the Japanese were all wearing Japanese clothing, and the men were either brandishing swords or, according to rank and status, having their heads cut off with colorful gestures and disdainful impunity by the sword-brandishers. In Tokyo today, one sees almost no Japanese clothing worn and even less sword brandishing. One begins to wonder if verbal behavior too has changed radically in this lively century of active Westernization.

It is always a little risky to attempt to describe with too much confidence just how things went on in remote times in the past. Usually we can quite easily learn something about what happened in history, but it is far more difficult to be sure just how it happened—whether the Merovingians actually were loud and raucous, or whether the Anglo-Saxons really posed in Anglo-Saxon attitudes when they were happy, as Lewis Carroll claimed they did. Nevertheless, we do have a rich abundance of documentary and literary sources for earlier periods of Japanese history, and nothing that we find there inclines the even moderately careful observer toward the view that silence was any more valued, or any more observed, in ancient Japan than it is in our own day.

We are particularly well informed about the daily behavior patterns of the upper classes of Japanese society during the Heian period, thanks to the abundant literary accounts of the period that have survived, chief among them being the justly celebrated *Tale of Genji*. One searches through all these texts in vain for the least hint of a worship of silence. Indeed, one searches in vain for indications of any particularly significant stress upon the importance of nonverbal behavior or communication of any variety. Rather, the picture of early Japanese life that one can gather from reading such Heian sources as *The Tale of Genji* does not appear to be significantly different in respect to language from what one finds in Japan today. Both are sharply focused upon verbal activity; both dote upon verbal expression; both prize and encourage the use of language under every possible circumstance. There was very little silence then, any more than there is silence today.

The Heian court ladies and their lovers, to be sure, lacked loudspeakers, stereo sets, and record players (but how dearly, we can suspect, they would have loved them all!). This must have meant that the net noise level of Heian society was generally somewhat lower than the modern Japanese decibel count, which is to say, a little below the normal threshold of pain. But this is only a matter of technology and science, not actually a substantive difference.

There may have been no stereos and record players in Heian Japan, but the texts make it clear that this did not mean that there was silence, either. Instead, there was talk—constant, unending, eternal, inconclusive talk. The people from every walk of life who appear in the *Genji,* but particularly the aristocrats, are always talking, talking, talking. The talk goes on incessantly, all day long and often far into the night. They had very little else to do, to be sure. Even so, study of the texts makes it clear that they talked and talked and talked in an extraordinarily determined fashion.

Furthermore, one of the most salient linguistic features of the original Japanese of such Heian texts as the *Genji* hinges upon the society's unending fascination with talk. In Heian Japanese, reported conversation—what one character is saying to another, according to the author—is linguistically and grammatically intermingled with narrative per se—what the author is saying about the characters, the scene, and the situation—in such a complex way that these two strands of the text—conversation on the one hand and narration on the other—more often than not fuse into a single amorphous entity. In any given passage of the *Genji,* we generally know that one or more persons are talking to each other and also that the author of the text is at the same time contributing a narrative that places the conversation into the context of the work as a whole. But more often than not it is all but impossible to unravel these several strands of language. Time and time again the student of the *Genji* text must puzzle over questions of where a passage of reported conversation begins and where it ends; which fragment of the passage is actually reported conversation and which is instead the author's narrative comments and additions; and particularly the question of who it is that is supposed to be speaking at any particular moment.

Linguistically, there is no silence and surely no worship of silence in the world of Heian literature. Instead, there is never-ending, incessant talk, talk that has become so important that it now consumes all other forms of discourse, encroaching upon narrative and description until it all but obliterates both these other varieties of expression.

The evidence for the importance of talk in the monuments of Heian literature has apparently not been noticed by most Western observers of Japanese culture, just as it appears to have escaped Miyoshi's attention. One compelling reason for this oversight has to do with the way in which these texts have always been translated into English, particularly in the memorable translation of the *Genji* by Arthur Waley, and now again in the particularly fine, accurate, and complete retranslation of this same text by Professor Edward Seidensticker. Both these translators, and indeed all competent translators of Heian literature, customarily make a clear distinction between direct discourse or cited speech and indirect or reported speech and also between both of these two varieties of language and the author's expository and narrative passages.

It would be all but impossible to come up with an English translation of Heian Japanese that did not make this clear distinction. Even if one could turn the trick, the resulting English would most likely baffle any reader who lacked access to the original. The translations are excellent translations, but like all translations, on this important point at least they conceal more than they reveal. Particularly, by making their necessarily clear-cut distinction between speech, both direct and reported, and narrative exposition, they unintentionally conceal the all-important role of talk in Heian society.

When we put the English translations aside and turn instead to the Heian Japanese originals, we are never for a moment in doubt. Nor is there the least evidence of any regard for silence, no more than there is any silence in the texts. Speech, talk, incessant conversation were everything and all to the society out of which the Heian texts were created. The texts are all talk, as surely also the society was. And silence is quite out of the question— everybody is always far too busy talking.

So much for the Heian period. But what about the first few years of Japan's modern century, when earlier inherited patterns of sociolinguistic behavior may well be supposed to have survived with relatively little change? Here also we have excellent documentary sources—firsthand descriptive evidence from observers who were there and wrote carefully about what they saw. This evidence soon leads us to the conclusion that Miyoshi's worship of silence in Japanese sociolinguistic behavior was as difficult to find in Japan of the 1880s as it is impossible to locate in Japan today. It was not there a thousand years ago, and it was not there a hundred years ago. Soon one begins to suspect that it was never there.

Our principal source for these matters in the 1880s is a delightful if often overlooked book by an amazing foreign woman who traveled widely in Japan a century ago: *Unbeaten Tracks in Japan,* by Isabella Lucy Bird.

Isabella Bird was a world traveler in the pattern of the great Victorian eccentrics. She claimed to suffer from bad health. In order to cope with it, she undertook travels to unbelievably remote places, where she then saw the sights with iron strength and willful determination that would have put the most robust constitution to shame. Though the word indefatigable most easily comes to mind to describe the way Miss Bird went about her travels, it is clear from her accounts that it must only be applied to her and to her alone. Everyone with whom she came into contact, whether native or resident foreigner, was clearly fatigued beyond description just trying to keep up with her.

Arriving in Japan in 1878, only a decade after the beginning of the Meiji era, Isabella Bird undertook an all but incredible trek through the most remote parts of the country. This she did against the best advice of all the foreign colony and totally ignoring the serious warnings of the Japanese authorities themselves, who pointed out that not only was she determined to go to places where there were neither roads nor inns nor any other type of accommodations for travelers of any variety, much less for foreign ladies, but also that she was dead set on doing all this at just the worst time of

the year—the rainy season—when tiny streams would be swollen to tor-
rents and normally difficult roads would turn into impossible mud trails.

But it was no good telling Miss Bird what not to do; she did what she
wanted to, wherever she was. She managed to complete her overland trip
through the Japanese countryside under appalling conditions of weather
and facilities, a trip that would be no simple matter to retrace even today,
with modern roads, trains, and all the other conveniences that have been
added to the scene. In the preface to the book of travel accounts that she
wrote during her stay in Japan, Miss Bird noted rather dryly: "The climate
disappointed me, but, though I found the country a study rather than a
rapture, its interest exceeded my largest expectations."

Miss Bird's travel book also more than matches the "largest expectations"
that any student of Japan could entertain for it. Time and time again she
comments with impressive detail on innumerable facets of Japan a hundred
years ago, providing us in the process with important data against which
to measure our present-day observations of similar or related features. And
here is Miss Bird's account of how the Japanese linguistic behavior that
she encountered impressed her: "The people speak at the top of their voices,
and, though most words and syllables end in vowels, the general effect of
a conversation is like the discordant gabble of a farm-yard. The next room
to mine is full of storm-bound travellers, and they and the house-master
kept up what I thought was a most important argument for four hours at
the top of their voices. I supposed it must be on the new and important
ordinance granting local elective assemblies, of which I heard at Odaté, but
on inquiry found that it was possible to spend four mortal hours in discussing whether the day's journey from Odaté to Noshiro could be made
best by road or river."

Miss Bird, despite her frequent protestations of ill health, survived her
Japanese travels in excellent form. She returned to England, married, was
widowed shortly thereafter, and lived on until 1904, "devoting herself
exclusively to . . . humanistic mission work." As one reads the fascinating
accounts of her travels in the pages of *Unbeaten Tracks,* this really quite ter-
rifyingly energetic English lady comes convincingly to life—just as does
the Japanese linguistic behavior that she so vividly describes.

In Japan, it is still quite possible to "spend four mortal hours in discussing"
how to go from one place to another, even though now one eventually
goes there by train, rather than on the poor, ill-fed horses that so distressed
the tender heart of Isabella Bird. And above all, her book makes it clear
that the worship of silence was as difficult to locate in the Japan that she
knew as it is in the one that we can observe today.

Where, then, do the origins lie for this antimyth of silence that plays such a prominent part in the cultural and literary speculations of the 1980s? Obviously, it does not in any way relate to observed facts. Japan has very little silence, and, as far as we can learn, it was never characterized by silence. When we encounter any phenomenon this isolated from fact, we must try and discover to which particular source of fiction it may be traced. In this case, we soon discover that, like so much else in the myth of Nihongo proper, this antimyth of silence has its proximate origins in a single documentary source, a text still easily available to us today for study and investigation. The text is a tract entitled *Kokutai no Hongi* (Principles of Our National Polity), a creed that for over a decade fueled the fires of fascist-nationalistic fantasies in Japan of the 1930s and 1940s.

The document known as the *Kokutai no Hongi* was actually a pamphlet of 156 pages, an official publication of the Japanese Ministry of Education, first issued in March 1937 and eventually circulated in millions of copies throughout the home islands and the empire. It contained the official teaching of the Japanese state on every aspect of domestic policy, international affairs, culture, and civilization. Between 1937 and the end of the war in the Pacific, this booklet was studied in the Japanese school system at almost every level. Its turgid pages were also the object of almost constant private study, in much the same way that the Chinese masses were once reported to have taken eagerly to the full-time study and reading of the *Quotations* of Chairman Mao.

Since the *Kokutai no Hongi* consists of a discursive commentary upon various principles first supposed to have been enunciated by the Meiji emperor in his *Imperial Rescript on Education* of October 10, 1890 (another of the documentary landmarks of Japanese fascist-nationalist ideology), it was widely felt that this 1937 pamphlet shared in large measure the quasi divinity attributed to the *Rescript on Education* itself. This meant that the *Kokutai no Hongi* tract was often accorded the same worshipful honors as those that were extended to the *Rescript*. Like the *Rescript*, the *Kokutai no Hongi* pamphlet was frequently treated as a fetish object. When not actually being read or studied, it was reverently placed upon the *kamidana,* the "god shelf" of Shinto observances, a small platform in a room just above eye level where fetishes, talismans, and other important cult objects are customarily placed for safekeeping when they are not actively being employed in religious observances.

The title of the document is difficult to explain. Difficult as it is, though, the title is still the best possible guide to the pamphlet's contents. The word *kokutai* is the heart of the matter. It has generally been translated into English as national entity or national polity, and both renderings tell us something important about what *kokutai* means, even though neither translation—or even the two combined—is totally satisfactory.

The word *kokutai* was not a new coinage in Japan of the 1930s, when the *Kokutai no Hongi* was being written. It had originally been introduced into Japanese by a group of Neo-Confucian scholars who were exploring the possibilities of erecting a distinctively Japanese political ideology out of assorted intellectual bits and pieces taken over more or less intact from Chinese Confucian thought of the Sung period. For these scholars, *kokutai* meant something still rather vague and ill defined. It was more or less the Japanese "nation's body" or "national structure"; both translations happen to render the constituent parts of the compound quite literally (*koku* means state, nation, and *tai* means body, structure).

By the late 1930s, however, the term *kokutai* had begun to be used in a rather different and far more specific sense by the leaders of Japan's increasingly powerful fascist-nationalist clique. For them, *kokutai* had become a convenient term for indicating all the ways in which they believed that the Japanese nation, as a political as well as a racial entity, was simultaneously different from and superior to all other nations on earth. For the men who were busy setting Japan upon her collision course with history that terminated only in the military defeat of August 1945, *kokutai* embraced everything that was distinctively Japanese, particularly as such entities could be differentiated from their parallels in foreign countries.

The Japanese had, these men admitted, borrowed much of their culture from China. But Chinese culture, once borrowed into Japan, took on many different aspects; it was no longer the same thing that it had been in China. What explained this? It was *kokutai*. Japan was the only nation of the Far East that had managed to modernize its economic life and that had been able to get its people into a position to compete, both commercially and militarily, with the advanced nations of the West. The Chinese had not been able to do this, but the Japanese had. Why? Again, the explanation was said to be found in the Japanese *kokutai*. The Japanese had it, but of course the Chinese (by definition) did not, since no one could have *kokutai* except the Japanese.

It is interesting to note in passing that even the etymological facts of the word *kokutai* contradict the whole doctrine that was assembled behind this term. If there had ever been anything of the nature of *kokutai* in Japanese political or cultural history, one would naturally expect that there would also have been a Japanese word for it. After all, the essential quality of *kokutai* was said to be found in the fact that it was solely and entirely Japanese. No other nation had or could have *kokutai,* only Japan. But the word *kokutai* is not historically or etymologically Japanese at all. It is a Chinese loanword, a term borrowed from Chinese, and no more Japanese than are the other thousands and thousands of Chinese loans in the modern language. This simple etymological fact does not, to say the least, argue very strongly in favor of the original existence of a peculiarly Japanese *kokutai* that is supposed to have survived from remote antiquity, "unchanged through ages eternal."

If the Japanese had originally ever had or known about any such thing, they ought to have had a word for it. They do not, and did not. Professor Hisamatsu and the coauthors of the document were forced to turn to the borrowed vocabulary of a foreign language for the very term about which they centered their entire, elaborate fascist-nationalist ideology. Of all the absurd features that characterize the *Kokutai no Hongi* and its ideas, this is probably the most absurd.

At any rate, once we understand something of the enormous if quite highly specialized semantic range that this word *kokutai* had for Japanese fascist-nationalist circles by the 1930s, we are well on our way toward understanding both what the title of the *Kokutai no Hongi* meant and also what it implied. The second element in the title is a fairly simple one: *hongi* means cardinal principles, basic significance. Thus, the pamphlet was meant to explain to the Japanese people just what were the cardinal principles of their *kokutai*—always understanding that *kokutai* in this context meant the sum of the ways in which Japanese race, culture, and civilization were at the same time different from, and superior to, all other superficially parallel examples in the world.

Needless to say, the immense prestige attached to the *Kokutai no Hongi,* and the eagerness with which it was taught and studied throughout the Japanese educational system, had a tremendous impact throughout the entire population. One is easily tempted, in trying to assess the importance and role of this document, to venture an easy comparison with Adolf Hitler's *Mein Kampf,* but the analogy is a poor one and should not be pursued. Hitler's book was a private screed, the individual ravings of a single madman, already so mentally deranged at the time he wrote it that he chose this startling method for giving his own nation, and the world, fair warning of just what he and his companions had in mind, if and when they were able to put their ideas into practice.

The *Kokutai no Hongi* was totally and absolutely different. It was not the private document of a madman. It was an official document of the Ministry of Education in a modern state that was itself in the process of going mad. It did not tell what would happen if and when the author's ideas were finally implemented. Instead, it spoke from a position of absolute power and authority already achieved, and its word was already law. The *Kokutai no Hongi* spoke with all the authority of the Japanese state, it embraced the official policy that dominated all Japanese education for almost a decade, its influence on Japanese thought at all levels of society was correspondingly great, and its impact has been lasting.

Hitler's *Mein Kampf* was widely circulated throughout the world in a number of different translations. The only problem that arose in publishing these non-German versions of his book had to do with who would eventually get the royalty payments. The *Kokutai no Hongi* was, on the other hand, treated like a state secret. Few copies managed to find their way into the hands of foreigners until after the end of the war. The first translation of the document into English was originally undertaken by American intelligence officers and not completed until after Japan's defeat and surrender. The Japanese made every effort to keep the ideology and argumentation of the *Kokutai no Hongi* concealed from the rest of the world—as well they might, considering the outrageous claims, boasts, and trumperies in which it so richly abounds.

An Occupation decree issued on December 15, 1945, forbade further circulation of the *Kokutai no Hongi,* but it could hardly eradicate the deep traces that its teachings had left in the Japanese consciousness. As we now see in the exploration of the myth of Nihongo, many of these traces are quite as vivid today as they ever were.

The principal author of the *Kokutai no Hongi* was Professor Sen'ichi Hisamatsu (1894–1976), a prominent scholar of traditional Japanese literature. He completed the first draft of the document sometime before 1937. Subsequently the work was revised and redrafted at least twice by two different committees of bureaucrats and scholars.

Hisamatsu later complained that these two committees had altered the thrust and purpose of his original draft. Since his original does not survive, there is no way to verify this claim. No author enjoys having something he has written subjected to the scrutiny of an editorial committee. Many authors often feel that what they have written has suffered in the process of being edited. Whether Hisamatsu's objections were merely of this order, or whether he really had valid complaints about what was done to the substance of his work, can probably never be known. For the record, it should be noted that Hisamatsu himself served as a member on both the editorial committees in question. Whatever it was that they did to his work, he was in a position to see it being done. Under the circumstances one wonders how much he could really have objected to the final product.

A number of the scholars and bureaucrats who served on these two editorial committees responsible for the published version of the *Kokutai no Hongi* were later purged from further participation in Japanese public life by the Occupation officials, but Hisamatsu was more fortunate. He succeeded in convincing the Occupation that his part, first in writing, then in editing this infamous document had been completely innocent. He was not purged from public life or removed from the official educational system and took an active, indeed a dominant, role in Japanese literary scholarship until his death just a few years ago. He continued to specialize in the study of traditional Japanese literature, and his great number of published works in this field have done much to direct the course of such studies both in Japan and in the rest of the world.

Hisamatsu and his many disciples, both East and West, of course refrained from talking about *kokutai* after August 1945. The term, and the concept behind it, could no longer effectively serve as the focal point for an overall approach to the history and analysis of all Japanese life, civilization, and culture. Instead, a number of Japanese scholars under Hisamatsu's direction began to recycle the *kokutai* conceptualization, this time giving it new and even wider circulation under the guise of a "distinctive Japanese world view." All that was really necessary, in order to fit out the now disgraced doctrine of *kokutai* for new service in the world of postwar Japan, was to relabel some of the key terms in the system; the concepts behind the terms proved to be quite as durable as ever. The touchstone in their study of traditional Japanese literature, and their guide to the analysis of Japanese life and culture in general, soon became this newly relabeled version of the old *kokutai*. Japan was still to be viewed as unique, now not because of its *kokutai* but because of its "distinctive world view." The stage had been set for the reemployment of many of the most pernicious elements in the fascist-nationalist ideology of the *Kokutai no Hongi,* rebuilding them into the key-stones that now go to shore up the modern myth of Nihongo.

Relating the newly recycled concepts of the *Kokutai no Hongi* to Japan's new sustaining myth of Nihongo was actually a simple task. It was rendered particularly easy because the *Kokutai no Hongi* itself had placed tremendous importance upon the Japanese language. For Hisamatsu and his coauthors, the Japanese language offered some of the best evidence for the existence of *kokutai;* hence it was something that they invoked whenever the oppor-tunity presented itself. A major part of the pamphlet centers upon language, because in Hisamatsu's system the Japanese language was held to have a particularly important relationship to the Japanese *kokutai:* "Our nation has, since its founding, developed on the basis of a pure, unclouded, and contrite heart; and our language, customs, and habits all emanate from this source."

This is a representative example of the style and argumentation of the *Kokutai no Hongi.* It also illustrates well the cardinal role that the Japanese language plays throughout the muddled concatenations of aesthetic half-truths and racial self-stereotypes that constitute this tiresome tract—which, infamous and tiresome though it may be, nevertheless is the source to which we must turn if we are to understand the strange modern flourishing of this antimyth of silence.

Later in this book, in chapter 7, we shall see some of the ways in which

Hisamatsu and the other authors of the *Kokutai no Hongi* twisted and perverted the philological evidence of a number of early Japanese literary texts in order to make it appear that these texts preserved evidence for an ancient belief, on the part of the Japanese themselves, in the existence of some sort of mystical spirit of the Japanese language. This was the so-called *kotodama,* something that was supposed to make the Japanese language essentially different from all other varieties of human language. We shall see something of the way in which this spurious *kotodama* cult has continued to flourish, surviving just below the surface level of Japanese intellectual and academic life, even though the *Kokutai no Hongi* itself, together with the other trappings of the fascist-nationalist period in Japan's recent history, has been swept off into the garbage can of discarded illusions. And we shall inspect a representative sample of the ways in which the *kotodama* cult is currently in the process of an active revival in recent Japanese writing and speculation about language.

In view of all this, it will hardly come as any great surprise to learn that the antimyth of silence must also be traced back to the same infamous *Kokutai no Hongi.* And it will be even less of a surprise to discover that, just like the mischievous *kotodama* theories, so also does the antimyth of Japan as a land of mysterious, silent, nonverbal communication go back directly to a tampering with early philological evidence on the part of the late Hisamatsu and his collaborators.

Nothing in the early texts upon which these mythmakers pretended to base their mind-numbing jargon actually substantiates the antimyth of silence, any more than anything can be found there to substantiate the *kotodama* fables. It was, in both cases, possible to foist these ideas off upon an unsuspecting public only by poisoning the very sources of Japanese tradition. The pity of it all is that this fouling of the springs was carried out so effectively in the 1940s that even today the water refuses to run clean.

For substantiating their original version of this antimyth of silence, the *Kokutai no Hongi* authors relied principally upon a single Old Japanese linguistic expression and even more upon the occurrence of this expression in a single Old Japanese poem, *Man'yōshū* poem 3253. The expression at issue was Old Japanese *kötöage,* a word that means, when rendered fairly literally, "a lifting up (*age*) of words (*kötö*)," in the particular sense of a special variety of vocal prayer or invocation.

With the introduction of Buddhism into Japan, the earlier, indigenous religious beliefs and rituals that had sustained Japanese spiritual life up until that time began to fall out of fashion. Most of them were soon all but forgotten. The process was quite parallel to what happened to pre-Christian cults and beliefs in Europe. These too soon fell out of fashion and were quickly all but forgotten about, as Christianity became the state religion of the Roman Empire and then finally permeated from the upper classes deeper and deeper down into the daily religious beliefs and observances of the population at large. The same thing happened in Japan. Buddhism was at the start a new, imported religion officially supported by the ruling classes, but in time it too found its way into the living faith of most levels of the Japanese population.

In the process, much of the earlier Japanese religion was simply forgotten. There was no longer any need to carry out the ritual observances or even to remember the elaborations of ceremonial detail that had, until then, provided for the older religion's transmission and perpetuation. Much, much later in Japanese history we begin to hear of Shinto, the "Way of the Gods." Ever since this expression became current, much effort has been expended trying to pass this religious neologism off as the direct, historical continuation of the pre-Buddhist religious beliefs and practices of the Japanese people. All this is quite untrue historically, and it has led to as much sad misunderstanding as any other of the numerous tamperings with history that characterized Japanese intellectual life in the 1940s.

Pre-Buddhist Japanese religion was almost completely wiped out with the coming of Buddhism. It left even fewer traces in later Japanese life than the worship of Venus, Bacchus, and the rest of the pre-Christian pantheon in the life of Christian Europe. What later came to be called Shinto is almost entirely a deliberate fabrication in which genuinely pre-Buddhist, indigenous beliefs and elements play almost no part at all.

The few traces that survived in Japan of pre-Buddhist religious practice and belief are to be found not in the largely made-to-order Shinto cults but in a few references to the old religion scattered here and there in Old Japanese literary texts, particularly in the *Man'yōshū* poetic anthology. Since the old religion quickly became obsolete, the references to it in the surviving texts also soon became obscure. It was this obscurity upon which Hisamatsu and his *Kokutai no Hongi* coauthors capitalized when it came to erecting their almost entirely spurious ideologies of *kotodama* and the related cults of the Japanese language. Since few Japanese any longer really understood what the references in these old texts to the pre-Buddhist religion really meant, these same references could, in the unscrupulous hands into which they had fallen, be made to say almost anything.

The early text references to the Old Japanese cult practice of *kötöage* actually relate to an especially powerful kind of magical invocation that was a feature of religious life and belief in pre-Buddhist Japan. It is now the consensus of responsible Japanese literary and linguistic scholarship that in the *kötöage* cult it was believed possible to invoke the name of something or someone in such a way that the person performing this invocation would then have special control over the entity thus named.

A typical case of *kötöage* appears to have been concerned with rainfall, always of vital importance for an agricultural society like early Japan. In the pre-Buddhist religion of Japan, it was believed that drought could, under certain circumstances, be broken by the ritual invocation of rain through the solemn ritual pronouncement of the word for rain, in other words, the name of the thing sought or desired. (This was one of the religious practices that first gave way before Buddhist belief. The Buddhists professed to have an entire repertory of vastly more potent rain-making prayers, liturgies, and spells at their command—and, if we are to believe the historicity of the early notices, were able to prove that they actually did.)

The *kötöage* of the Old Japanese period thus consisted of a ritual invocation of the name of something desired, typically of rain or of safety for travelers. The few early texts in which it is mentioned also make it clear to the reader that the invocation was considered not only a very powerful magic but also a very dangerous one. It was not something that the society employed lightly or every time it wanted something trivial. It was to be strictly reserved only for last-ditch emergencies. Apparently there was some danger of the magic involved backfiring in some way or other.

At any rate, when the *kötöage* ritual is mentioned in pre-Buddhist Japanese sources at all, it is usually to remark that the ritual was not performed. Often the Old Japanese poets in effect congratulate themselves that things have worked out in such a way that it was not necessary after all to perform this dangerous and apparently dreaded ritual. In other texts, they stress the rarity of the ritual in order to emphasize the seriousness with which they are going to undertake it.

What the *Kokutai no Hongi* authors did was to take these texts, with their emphasis upon the rarity with which this ritual of name invocation was performed in pre-Buddhist Japan, and to claim that these texts proved that the early Japanese believed that their country was "a land of the deities which is free from the strife of words."

The details of this pre-Buddhist belief were obscure to the average Japanese reader of the 1940s (though the authors of the *Kokutai no Hongi* might have known better and, for that matter, probably did). What was clear from the texts was that the *kötöage* was something that was done only rarely, if at all. In the most striking of the *Man'yōshū* references to the belief in question, poem number 3253, Japan itself is characterized by the poet as a "land where the *kötöage* is not performed" (*kötöage senu kuni*). The coming together in this single text of two ideas—the idea of the rarity with which this ritual was performed and the idea that this rarity might serve as a poetic categorization of the land of Japan—provided all the raw material that the *Kokutai no Hongi* authors required.

Exploiting the idea of the rarity of the ritual and stretching its interpretation beyond all reasonable bounds, they used this text to prove that what was rare in early Japan was the use of language in order to dispute, argue, or contend. Deflecting and distorting the meaning of this particular text, Hisamatsu and his colleagues ended up with the spurious doctrine that Japan was originally "a land of the deities which is free from the strife of words," in other words, a country where people make a virtue of not expressing verbally what they feel about things. Here we have the true origins, tawdry though they may be, of the modern antimyth of the Japanese virtue of silence, or, as it is often expressed, the Japanese gift for nonverbal communication. Once more, a virtue has been made of a sad necessity.

The fascist-nationalist ideologues of the 1940s rigidly enforced this distorted view of Japanese antiquity. In the past, they taught, you Japanese took pride in not expressing yourselves verbally; therefore today also, none of you should seek verbal expression. And since it is an old custom of this, our land of the gods, you should not only stay silent, you should be proud of staying silent: silence is one of the many talents by which your ancient gods have decided to distinguish you among the nations.

Even if we did not have the help of modern, postwar Japanese scholarship in tracing the philological absurdities that underlie all this, the whole antimyth of silence would still quite clearly show itself for what it really is. But once they had passed through the hands of the *Kokutai no Hongi* ideologues, these tamperings with the texts soon became canonical authority for suppressing dissent and stifling the expression of opinion at every level of Japanese society. The old texts were cited as if to prove that the earliest period of Japanese life had put a premium upon not expressing personal views and that it had valued not verbalizing opinions. The texts were invoked to make a virtue out of silence endured in the face of conflicts, controversies, and contretemps of every variety—but particularly those of a political nature. It would be difficult to find a more blatant example of the harm that can be done by twisting innocent passages in early texts in order to make them into "proof texts" that would appear to support goals totally unrelated to their original sense.

All this might well have remained on the level of a harmless philological curiosity were it not for the amazing vitality that the antimyth of silence, like the *kotodama* cult itself, still has in our own day. It is one thing to be able to demonstrate that the *Kokutai no Hongi* taught quite spurious interpretations of several poems in the *Man'yōshū*. It is quite another when we find that these premeditated misrepresentations of the 1940s were still being echoed and cited by the *New York Times* in the 1970s, as if they provided explanations for Japanese political behavior today. When roots go this deep, one begins to wonder if any amount of scholarly exposé and correction can ever undo the original mischief.

Jerome Alan Cohen, in the lead article in the November 21, 1976, Sunday *New York Times Magazine* ("Japan's Watergate: Made in U.S.A."), first described how, in the autumn of 1974, the major Japanese newspapers and magazines resolutely printed little or nothing about the increasingly well-known scandal surrounding then Prime Minister Kakuei Tanaka and the sources of his personal fortune. He also described how, even after the disclosure of the story by the foreign press forced the Japanese news media to take official notice of the scandal, there still was almost no investigative reporting on the part of the Japanese newsmen, nor did any independent legislative inquiry develop in Japan: "By the end of 1975 . . . it was back to 'politics as usual.' Japan, it seemed, was still, as a poet described it 1200 years ago, 'the divine country whose people would not speak out.' Then came Lockheed."

Then came Lockheed—but in the meantime, what are we to make of this "divine country whose people would not speak out"? Cohen's citation is a garbled one, but it is one that may nevertheless be pinpointed with no great difficulty: it is a reference to the same *Man'yōshū* poem that we have already noted above as preserving one of the oldest references to the ritualistic performance of the dread *kötöage*—the poem that characterizes Japan as a "land where the *kötöage* is not performed."

But when this important Old Japanese poem turns up in the pages of the *New York Times,* what form does it appear in? Nothing is left of the literal, word-for-word sense of the original, nor can anything be detected here of the true meaning of *kötöage*. All that has been wiped away, concealed from view, and replaced with the twisted trumpery of the *Kokutai no Hongi*.

And so this trail of bogus philology and distorted conceptualization reaches unbroken from the pages of the *Kokutai no Hongi* into those of the *New York Times,* for all the world as if nothing at all had happened in 1945 or in the subsequent decades. The myth has once more worked its customary ahistorical magic. Time has been made to stand still. The pretensions and fantasies that by all rights ought to have burnt themselves out in the bath of fire that they brought down upon Tokyo and Osaka emerge instead like the veritable phoenix: the *Kokutai no Hongi* is alive and well in New York. One would have to look far indeed for a more convincing demonstration of the enormous power of this modern myth of Nihongo, not only to sustain Japanese society but also to sustain itself.

CHAPTER SIX

Our Language—Right or Wrong

> *Our feeling about the Japanese language is like our love for our parents; it is not proper for us to love it simply because it is a superb language. Professor Takao Suzuki wrote most eloquently, "This land of Japan is a glorious land, simply because it is the land where I was born, and for that reason alone"; and exactly the same is true of the Japanese language.*
> —Haruhiko Kindaichi, Nihongo e no Kibō (My Aspirations for Japanese), 1976

STEREOTYPED categorizations that attempt to represent this or that foreign language as somehow defective, or as somehow inadequate to the requirements of the society that it must serve, are so frequently encountered in journalism and other nonspecialized writing that we are all familiar with their allegations in one form or another. Anyone who enjoys reading travel accounts, especially descriptions of relatively distant, inaccessible, or otherwise exotic places and peoples, is often confronted with impressive allegations to the effect that this or that equally distant, inaccessible, or exotic language is decrepit or deficient in one respect or another, or somehow inadequate for effectively carrying out the usual role that one expects a language to play in a given society.

The general reader is also told that this language or that is so poorly put together or so meager in its lexical and grammatical resources that the "natives" who are forced to use it for their daily purposes of social communication—who after all, like all of us, have no other language but their own—are seriously hampered in the effective performance of daily activities simply because of these inherent flaws in their linguistic medium. The authors of such accounts often begin by making disarmingly modest claims with respect to their own command of the language that they are going to categorize in such defamatory tones. But then they immediately go on to say, in effect, that though it was possible to learn only a very little of language *x* or *y* during the short period of time spent in that remote country, even that little was quite enough to show how very inadequate the language is, how very unsatisfactory it is, and how poorly the language serves the people who, poor souls that they are, must employ it daily.

In a recent popular account of travels through the Near and Middle East, for example, an otherwise quite careful and responsible reporter first goes out of his way to tell his readers that he managed to learn only a little Arabic in the course of his travels. But this modest disclaimer is hardly out of the typewriter before the same author is launched into a wholesale categorization not only of the Arabic language of which he, by his own admission, knows only a few words, but also of the personality and character of everyone for whom Arabic is his first and native tongue. "To live in Arabic," he tells us categorically, "is to live in a labyrinth of false turns and double meanings."

Sociolinguistic stereotypes of this variety were commonplace in world-travel literature from the turn of the century and earlier periods. But it always comes as a considerable surprise to learn, as from this particular case of a book published only recently, that this kind of hackneyed categorization of distant peoples and their language apparently never loses its appeal. It survives intact even in the world of today, from which one might have thought that the inaccessible, exotic country that could be denigrated with impunity had disappeared.

At any rate, stereotypes of this language or that as inadequate, defective, or decrepit usually also manage to be uniformly denigratory of the people who employ the language in question. This may be observed in the blast leveled against the Arabic language and the society that employs it quoted above. The author of that statement is, in effect, telling us two different things and actually making two different allegations. One is linguistic, the other is sociological, and both are defamatory.

The Arabic language, he alleges, is itself, as a language and as a sociolinguistic medium for Arabic society, something that is redolent with "false turns and double meanings." In other words, simply as a language, Arabic is claimed to be worse than useless or inconvenient: it is false and deceptive. And so also, he goes on to say, is the society that employs this language, or, as he puts it, "lives in Arabic." The language is a labyrinth of false turns and double meanings; so also, he claims, is the society.

Thus these allegations that ostensibly start out as linguistic stereotypes almost always end up as defamatory racial categorizations as well. At first it is only the language of this or that group of people that is said to be im-perfect and lacking in one respect or another. But before long—or sometimes within the very sociolinguistic categorization itself, as in the example just quoted—one is being told that the people who must necessarily employ this language are themselves and by that very fact also inadequate or imper-fect, if not actually false and treacherous.

Like all irrational arguments, these stereotypes generally ignore the ques-tion of which is supposed to be the cause and which the effect. We are never told whether the society is, for example, false and treacherous because it is forced to use a false and treacherous language, or whether the language has become false and treacherous because it has so long been used for daily communication by a social group that is naturally false, treacherous, and mean. Which element is the chicken and which the egg is never made clear. But as to the uniformly denigratory intent and thrust of all such categoriza-tions, there is seldom any room for doubt or question.

It hardly need be stressed, even in passing, that this kind of stereotyping, whether it is directed toward language or toward race or toward both, is fully as unfounded in scientific fact as it is disagreeable. Linguistic science has never established any grounds upon which to distinguish between this language or that in terms of the positive or negative value judgments that such categorizations delight in employing. Quite to the contrary. Every-thing that we can learn about the wide range of human languages that have been studied to date in every part of the world shows instead that each language is adequate to serve the needs of the society in which it functions and also fully adequate for the requirements of the culture of which it is an integral element. There is no such thing as an inadequate or a false and treacherous language, any more than there are such things as inadequate or false and treacherous racial groups.

This does not mean, of course, that every language serves its own society and culture with equal efficiency throughout history. Language is a part of culture; culture is a part of history; and history is constantly in the process of change and flux, as are all the elements of culture, including language, that go to make it up. Language, like every other aspect of human culture, is constantly in a state of change, always adjusting and altering itself by this means or that in order to continue to serve as the sociolinguistic medium for the society with which it is associated.

For the importance of these changes and also for the details of the ex-tremely involved process by which these changes take place, we have the evidence of that branch of linguistic science that devotes itself particularly to questions of historical change in language. But what we do not have, from any segment of the entire science of language, is the slightest shred of evidence that would support the allegation that languages exist in any remote part of the world that are deficient or by their very nature false, corrupt, or treacherous.

The war science must wage against prejudice and superstition never ends. Linguists know that all these allegations of inadequacy or corruption, so frequently leveled against one or another of the world's languages, are misleading, stereotyped nonsense or worse. But that does not prevent them from being of perennial interest to the linguistically unsophisticated reader, any more than it detracts from their continuing popularity with editors and publishers. At best, such sociolinguistic slanders are harmless if annoying testimony to the naiveté of the writers who indulge in them. At worst, they hint at potentially dangerous bias and inflammatory prejudice.

But no matter how we choose to cope with them, all these stereotypes of a given language have one basic element in common—they are normally encountered in the form of charges leveled against a remote and little-known language by someone far removed from that language. Typically, they are undocumented charges brought by outsiders, persons who almost always lack even the slightest basis for making this kind of allegation. (Sometimes, as we have seen above, the outsider who brings these charges even goes out of his way to stress the extremely minimal knowledge that he has of the language in question, as if that too were something of which to be proud.)

Normally this is the element that such sociolinguistic categorizations all have in common. But once again, as so often in any consideration of "things Japanese," we must be prepared to discover that the Japanese experience in this area diverges strikingly from the typical. There is immediately at hand an enormous amount of writing and speculation about Japanese that follows these same stereotyped, hackneyed, and slanderous directions that we have begun the present chapter by discussing. But this important body of writing and speculation about the Japanese language, which holds the language up to criticism if not at times actual ridicule and which has as its common element the wholesale disparagement of the language as a vehicle suitable for or even adequate to the needs of the culture and society it serves, is in the case of Japanese not the product of distant outsiders trying to judge the language from afar. It is, surprisingly enough, almost entirely the work of the Japanese themselves.

This means that these claims of linguistic inadequacy cannot be understood, or excused, on the grounds that they originate with persons who know very little about the subject. Almost all of them are generated by substantial academic and intellectual figures currently active in Japanese life, figures who command serious attention throughout Japanese society. These are no mere passing travelers, learning a few words of the language from a waiter or bath attendant and then returning to Western Europe to employ this scanty knowledge as the basis for stereotyping an entire foreign culture.

These are the ultimate insiders, the leaders of an entire modern society and its sociolinguistic attitudes. They are not only at the inside of the system, they are the inside.

Furthermore, and most significantly, these are also the same individuals who elsewhere and in other contexts of writing and discourse are voluble on the subject of the strengths, glories, and ineffable beauties of the Japanese language. Yet we find the same acknowledged authorities simultaneously busy turning out hackneyed stereotypes of the Japanese language that we might tolerate—if not any more appreciate or forgive—only if they had originated with the casual foreign visitor whose experience of his subject matter was limited to several nights in an overpriced Japanese hotel room.

Our Japanese colleagues, as we know all too well from a variety of other sources, are fond to a fault of identifying elements in their society and culture that they believe to be unique. There is much in Japanese life that they would like to hold out for special attention on the grounds that this or that element is hardly if at all represented as such among any other known society or culture. Usually, such claims for the unique in Japanese life are difficult to endorse. But here one begins to suspect that those Japanese who are anxious to locate elements within their culture that are genuinely unique have actually laid hands on something worthy of their efforts.

One must seriously wonder if anything could possibly be more unique than is this spectacle of the leaders of the Japanese sociolinguistic establishment simultaneously exalting and mythologizing their language to the limits of their fertile imaginations and then in the same breath—and often on the same page of the same book—indulging a completely self-contradictory penchant for defaming that same language.

All this would be a little easier to comprehend if it turned out to be the product of two separate or somehow distinct sub-castes within the same sociolinguistic establishment. One would be no more edified, but at least one would not be quite so puzzled if, for example, some Japanese specialized in promulgating the myth of Nihongo as a unique language superior to all other languages and marvelously endowed with its own distinctive "spirit," while at the same time another separate group specialized in putting down the language, embellishing it with denigratory stereotypes designed to lower it in the esteem of the rest of the world, if not in the system of values of the native speakers unfortunate enough to be stuck with it as their only means of communication. But this is not at all the case. Absolutely no division of labor can be detected here. The denigrators are the same individuals as the mythologizers.

The variety and range of these surprisingly disparaging categorizations of Nihongo—the same language, after all, that is in other contexts held up as the cult focus of the entire modern sociolinguistic myth of contemporary Japan—are too great to permit easy or convenient arrangement under a few major types. The best that can be done, particularly in the space available, is simply to display to the reader a representative sampling of these curious materials, assuring him or her in the meantime that many, many more examples, most of them even more striking in their allegations and slanders, are easily located by even a random perusal of the enormous body of literature available in this field. What follows, then, is neither the best nor the worst of this sort of thing. But it is representative of the whole genre, and anyone interested in following up the question further can be assured that there is plenty more where this comes from.

A carefully arranged historical approach to these materials would be quite as impossible to carry off as would be any other sort of rational ordering or classification. Nevertheless, there is some merit in approaching these samples by way of an introduction to two such specimens that are not only thoroughly representative of the categorizations here under consideration but that also have more than usual sociolinguistic significance because of the way in which both may clearly be related to given historical contexts.

Both represent the ultimate in attempts to denigrate the Japanese language, since each has as its main argument the claim that Japanese is a language that is so deficient, poor, and weak in all respects that Japanese society would be better off simply to abandon its use altogether and adopt some other language in its place. Defamation of a language could hardly go further than this.

Each is also, when viewed in its historical context, part of the sociolinguistic response of Japanese society to a stark crisis situation that suddenly developed within Japanese life. The first was a response to the enormous strains put upon Japanese society by the internal forces released at the time of the Meiji Restoration. The second was a somewhat similar response to the perhaps even greater forces set into motion by Japan's defeat in the Pacific War and surrender to the Allies.

Another important factor that links these examples together is that, in each instance, the suggestion that Japanese is so inferior as a language that it ought simply to be abandoned was made by notable public figures who commanded tremendous prestige within Japanese society at the time. Reading the texts of these suggestions to replace Japanese with some other language, one's initial reaction today is to relegate both of them to the sort of fringe, crackpot suggestions with which every society, particularly in times of trouble, is generally well supplied. But that would be a misleading and historically incorrect analysis.

These suggestions were made in great seriousness by sociolinguistic leaders of tremendous authority. As a result of the prestige of their authors, they were listened to respectfully by all literate Japanese, which is to say, almost the entire population of Japan. That in both instances nothing could or would be done to implement these suggestions in no way detracts from the seriousness of their allegations or from the solemnity with which they were, each in its own time, debated within Japanese society.

The first of these suggestions for simply abolishing the Japanese language on the grounds of its alleged inability to serve the needs of Japanese society was made by one of the most important intellectual leaders of the Meiji era, Arinori Mori (1847–89). Mori was the man who, more than any other individual, was responsible for the development of the entire Japanese national education system, a surprisingly durable institution that has survived to the present with very few substantial changes from the form in which Mori originally set it up just prior to the turn of the century. Few conscious inventions of mortal man, East or West, have proved to be more durable, less susceptible to intellectual change of any variety, or more impressive in their monolithic ability to stifle the spiritual potential of an entire nation than Mori's careful adaptation of the Prussian system of tightly centralized, highly authoritarian education under which Japan still suffers.

Like many of the Meiji leaders, Mori traveled as widely in Western Europe and North America as his age and energies would permit. What he saw there inclined him more and more to doubt whether the Japanese language would ever actually be able to serve as a viable medium of instruction in the new European-style educational system that he was in the process of devising for Meiji Japan.

It is not too difficult to understand why Mori came to think along these lines. After all, the only working examples of the rigid, no-holds-barred, your-lessons-or-your-life style of education that he so admired were to be seen in the Prussian Empire or in France—and in neither of these countries did he find that the students were being taught in Japanese. Of course not; they all used German or French. From this observation it was a fairly easy step to the assumption that because Japanese was not being used in any of the educational systems that Mori admired abroad, Japanese could not be used in the Japanese system that he hoped to establish in imitation of these foreign models.

Reasoning along these lines, Mori privately reached the decision that the Japanese language would have to go if Japan was to have a strong, effective, Prussian-style educational establishment. At the same time, for reasons that are not fully clear, he began to urge that Japanese be replaced with English, even though this choice of a Western language fit in hardly at all with his strongly Prussian and Francophile ideals. At any rate, a debate of considerable dimensions was set in motion. Should Japan abandon the language of Lady Murasaki and Chikamatsu in favor of the language of Shakespeare and Dickens?

In the course of this debate—which naturally led to absolutely nothing—Mori even went to the length of entering into correspondence with Professor William Dwight Whitney at Yale University, soliciting Whitney's views on whether or not such a switch in Japan's national language would actually be advisable, and if so, how it might best be implemented. Whitney was a scholar of Sanskrit and comparative Indo-European philology, well known at the time as an authority on all sorts of linguistic questions. Mori's letter of inquiry and a copy of Whitney's reply have been preserved with the rest of Professor Whitney's papers in the Sterling Library at Yale, thus providing documentation for this strange episode from Meiji history, an episode that otherwise would be difficult to substantiate from Japanese sources.

Whitney's reply was polite and cautious but totally negative. He had never heard, he wrote to Mori, of such a feat of language switching being carried off successfully in any other country. With all due respect to Japanese inventiveness and skill, he thought it unlikely that the Japanese could manage it, even if it were thought to be in their best interests, which possibility he also strongly doubted.

So nothing came of Mori's ideas. But before too long they were to be revived within the historical context of yet another major crisis in Japanese life. In 1946, just at the very worst point in Japan's post-surrender days, the celebrated novelist Naoya Shiga (1883–1971) published a sensational article in which he too urged the total abandonment of the Japanese language. Although Shiga's argument was framed so as to fit the new and difficult circumstances out of which it grew, it nevertheless also related directly to Mori's earlier suggestion, which served Shiga as a kind of classical precedent.

To understand the sensation aroused by Shiga's broadside attack upon the Japanese language, it is necessary to keep in mind not only the circumstances under which it was launched but also Shiga's tremendous literary and intellectual prestige.

Downtown Tokyo was still a burnt-out expanse of city blocks and ruined buildings. Food of every kind was scarce and prohibitively expensive. Normal channels of distribution had virtually broken down, and what little there was to eat could usually be obtained only on the black market at enormous economic cost and also generally by becoming involved in illegal charades. Inflation was rampant. Most of the Japanese population moved about in a kind of sleepwalker's trance, still dazed by the unexpected defeat and now stripped of all sense of personal identity by the deprivations of the surrender.

Shiga, for his part, was a literary figure who attracted so much reverence and respect that he was often referred to as *shōsetsu no kamisama,* "the god of fiction," a phrase that graphically suggests the almost superhuman role that he enjoyed in Japanese intellectual circles. The story is still told of how, during Shiga's lifetime, when a film showing him happened to be included in a newsreel, a student in the audience caused a sensation by shouting out the command "Hats off!"—upon which he and his companions jumped up in the theater to stand at attention in Shiga's honor. The incident became notorious because the gesture of standing at bareheaded attention was a public honor normally extended only to the person of the emperor. But then, both the emperor and Shiga were, each in his own way, equally *kami,* incarnate deities—the one of the state, the other of literature.

With this background, then, it is not difficult to understand the tremendous impact that resulted from the publication in April 1946, in a leading Japanese journal of opinion, of an article by Shiga under the innocuous title "*Kokugo Undō*" (The National Language Movement). The article proved upon closer inspection to contain passages along the following lines: "We have been accustomed to our present national language since the days of our childhood, but we do not feel all that much in particular about it. But I am of the opinion that there is nothing as imperfect [*fukanzen*] or as inconvenient [*fuben*] as the national language of Japan. Once we realize the extent to which the development of our culture has been impeded by this, we will also see that there is a major issue that must by all means be solved on this occasion [i.e., Japan's military defeat in 1945]. It is no exaggeration to say that unless we achieve such a solution, no hope may be entertained for Japan developing into a genuinely modern nation. To document in concrete detail just how imperfect the national language of Japan really is and to show just how impractical it is, is too vexing a task, and one beyond my abilities. But this is what I have come to feel constantly and most keenly during my nearly forty years as an author."

In 1946, many suggestions were being made for "doing something about the Japanese language." But almost without exception—and up until the publication of Shiga's celebrated broadside—these had all originated with the U.S. military occupation authorities. Most of them also had to do simply with somehow reforming the traditional Japanese writing system, particularly its use of Chinese characters, and so they did not actually concern themselves with the Japanese language per se. Such suggestions and recommendations were easily brushed aside. After all, they came from the enemy; they dealt with things that were none of his concern; and at their best, or worst, they did not actually deal with the heart of the matter, the Japanese language.

But none of these convenient rationalizations could be employed to evade the impact of Shiga's resounding condemnation of his own language. He was talking about the Japanese language and not merely its writing system; he did know what he was talking about; and what he was talking about, and attacking outright, was the very language that he, as one of Japan's most revered literary masters, had helped to refine and polish so as to make it fit to serve as a consummate literary vehicle.

But Shiga is his own best commentator. The more we read of his article, the more we are impressed by the force with which he makes his arguments: "More than once during the war, I had occasion to reflect upon the suggestion made sixty years ago by Arinori Mori about adopting English as our national language. I thought about how things might have been if his suggestion had been carried out. One may imagine that Japanese culture would surely have advanced far beyond the point where it is today. It occurred to me that most likely a war of the sort we have just been through would never have taken place. And it also occurred to me that then our scholarship would have advanced more easily, and even that we would then have been able to recall our school days as having been something pleasant. We would be like our children who simply have never heard of the cumbersome old Japanese system of arbitrary weights and measures [and hence are at home with the new metric system]. We would not even know our old national language, but we would instead all be speaking English with no consciousness that it was a foreign language, and writing in English. Surely many special words for Japanese situations not to be found today in any English dictionary would have been devised; and I could even conceive of the *Man'yōshū* and *The Tale of Genji* being read by far greater numbers of persons than even look at these texts today. . . . And so I got the idea: How would it be if Japan, on this occasion [of the defeat of 1945] acted with direct and swift resolution and simply adopted the best language, the most beautiful language in the world for its national language! I think that French might very well be the best choice. ". . . I am not really at home in any foreign language, and it should not be thought that I know enough about French in concrete terms to counsel its adoption with confidence. But I have thought about French in this connection, because France is a nation with an advanced culture, and when I read French novels, it seems to me that in them there are features that the French have in common with us Japanese. Also, I have been told that French poetry has certain features in common with the spirit of Japanese *waka* and haiku, and literary specialists often claim that French is an orderly language. This is the sense in which I feel that French would be the best choice. I have gotten my idea from Arinori Mori's suggestion for the adoption of English. But I believe that my own plan is a secure one, a thoroughgoing one, and a wise one, far better than any halfhearted, halfway measures of reform that would only leave us still struggling, for years and even decades ahead, with a maimed national language. I am not at all well informed about the purely technical aspects of the question of switching from one national language to another, but I do not believe it to be all that difficult. Once the necessary teachers have been trained, I believe that the new language can simply be introduced from the first year of elementary education. . . ."

Of course, nothing whatsoever was done to implement Shiga's suggestion, any more than anything had been done to carry out Mori's idea. But this does not mean that Shiga's broadside on the language was soon forgotten, or that it has been without lasting influence in the sociolinguistic literature of Japan. While there was not the least enthusiasm for implementing his recommendations for language transplant, the charges that Shiga leveled against the Japanese language found a ready audience and continue to be popular.

Two of Shiga's major allegations concerning the character of the Japanese language as expressed in his 1946 article continue to appear in the Japanese sociolinguistic literature with surprising persistence. These are Shiga's charges that the Japanese language is *fukanzen,* at the same time that it is *fuben.* Each of these denigratory statements is important to consider in some detail, if only because each embodies important contemporary Japanese conceptualizations that will assist us in understanding much of this particular genre of the sociolinguistic literature.

The term *fukanzen* literally means imperfect, but in the contexts with which we are here concerned, it must be understood as having additional implications of incomplete, unfinished, and defective in workmanship or manufacture. The term *fuben* literally means inconvenient, but this word too has an important range of further implications, particularly in the present context of denigrating the Japanese language. Here it implies impractical, tedious, old-fashioned, and out-of-date, as for example one might say of cooking over a charcoal brazier rather than using a modern gas range, or of having to wait in the rain in order to force one's way onto an overcrowded bus or train rather than riding in the comfort of a private automobile.

These two categorizations of the Japanese language as somehow being both *fukanzen* and *fuben,* simultaneously defective in workmanship, structure, and manufacture, and also too old-fashioned and out-of-date to serve the current needs of society satisfactorily, turn up with surprising frequency in the post-Shiga literature. Soon these terms became almost canonical designations for reference to the potential "trouble spots" within the Japanese linguistic system, particularly when that system is viewed as a sociolinguistic medium necessary for a modern industrial society.

What must particularly surprise the outside observer of the Japanese linguistic scene is the seriousness with which Shiga's suggestions were initially greeted and the solemn gravity with which they have been debated over the decades following. Apparently no one in Japan has ever considered even the mere possibility that Shiga may have been having a wry joke at the expense of the badly frayed national nervous system as it existed in the dark days of 1946. No one who has commented upon the incident—and hardly a book or monograph in Japanese sociolinguistics leaves it unmentioned—ever suggests that perhaps Shiga may have been indulging in some literary figure such as irony or satire. (After all, he was a man of letters, and men of letters *have* been known to indulge in literary figures.)

To the outside observer, what Shiga wrote in 1946 seems an almost perfect burlesque of much of the other, deadly serious writing of the time. What precious little paper there was in Japan then mostly went for printing broadsides suggesting this or that ambitious program for "Building a New Japan," a utopia that would presumably rise from the ashes of the old Japan, having none of its faults and more than its share of virtues. The non-Japanese reader today is immediately tempted to interpret it as an elaborate satire—a deft burlesque of what other writers were turning out in 1946—and will also be hard put to believe that Shiga himself really took any of this at all seriously. But such an interpretation is apparently out of the question. Everyone within the society for which Shiga was writing takes every word that he published on this particular occasion perfectly literally and absolutely seriously, so presumably the outsider must return the compliment and do the same.

One inside observer of the Japanese linguistic scene who has taken Shiga in deadly earnest is Professor Kindaichi, a scholar whose seminal contributions to the myth of Nihongo have already received some notice in these pages. In fact, Kindaichi wrote his own best-known book, his *Nihongo* of 1957, with the specific purpose of refuting Shiga's charges and countering his suggestions. Kindaichi takes Shiga's allegations and recommendations seriously, and he argues against them in the opening lines of his own book: "Today, ten years after the war, the Japanese language is as alive and well as ever. The voices that once urged us to adopt French or something else have simply faded away. Today such suggestions serve only as the themes for stories that we may tell about 'the old days'—which is as it should be."

But even though Kindaichi's book was principally aimed at refuting Shiga, the tremendous impact of Shiga's infamous charges appears to have made itself as deeply felt upon Kindaichi as upon anyone else. The professor, we find, is himself not very far into his book before he is busy drawing up detailed lists of supposed deficiencies in the very language that he would at the same time defend to the hilt. Eventually he even draws up an impressive "Syllabus of Defects" for the Japanese language and further enlightens his readers with a chapter detailing "The Impracticability [*fuben*] of Japanese Word Order, in Which Attributes Must Come First, and Its Remedies." Elsewhere in the same book, Kindaichi further describes "The Impracticability of Predicates Coming Last," which to be sure they do in a Japanese sentence, though this time around he does not suggest any remedy that might alleviate the difficulty to which he has directed our attention.

Shiga was not the only major Japanese literary figure to suggest that the language he employed was unfit for the purposes to which it had to be put. The literary giant Jun'ichirō Tanizaki (1886–1965) devoted many trenchant paragraphs in his *Bunshō Tokuhon* (A Manual of Style, 1934) to detailing his own studied complaints about the language, generally along the following lines: "One of the defects of our national language is the fact that its vocabulary is limited. . . . For example, we refer to the revolving of a child's top, or of a mill wheel, or of the earth around the sun, all with the same words, *mawaru* or *meguru*. . . . This poverty of the Japanese vocabulary is evidence of the fact that our national character does not esteem light conversation."

With this particular reference to light conversation (*o-shaberi*), Tanizaki is simultaneously directing the thrust of his argument into another of the principal avenues of the myth of Nihongo, that antimyth of silence of which we have already seen something in the previous chapter.

Another major literary figure, the poet Sakutarō Hagiwara (1886–1942), had even more bitter things to say about the lexical resources of his language. His allegations hinge upon a distinction between Japanese words that are borrowings from Chinese and what are often called Yamato words. The term Yamato words simply means words that are thought to be of pure Japanese origin historically—which frequently comes down to simply meaning that these words are not suspected of being borrowings from Chinese.

Traditional Japanese poetry, with a few minor exceptions, has generally enforced the stylistic principle that in poetic diction Chinese borrowings must be shunned whenever possible and Yamato words used instead. But the poet Hagiwara found this a difficult principle to follow and accordingly complained in the following terms: "Yamato words are extremely aesthetic, but they are too feeble for occasions on which we would like to express anger, distress, jealousy, or similarly strong emotions. The Yamato words are poor in elements that might express such accents [he uses the English loanword *akusento*]. But by using Chinese words, strong accents may be expressed. Thanks to the simplicity and strength of Chinese words, we are able to give strong expression to human emotions."

Probably the most impressive as well as the most shocking of all such statements derive from the work of Kunio Yanagita (1875–1962), the all-but-sainted founder of folklore studies in Japan. Yanagita is revered as the champion and discoverer, if not actually the inventor, of almost everything that is held to be truly and essentially Japanese over an enormous range of fields, including folklore, folk art, cultural exegesis, and other manifestations of what most observers within Japanese society today would agree to be the genuine spirit and expression of Japan. But here is Yanagita on the subject of the Japanese language: "Modern Japanese has a poverty-stricken vocabulary. It has many words, but they all incline in one direction. It is also poor in the types of syntactic structures available, so that in putting together even a moderately long sentence, everyone has had the experience of not being able to come up with anything that is not simply dull and boring."

If Yanagita's attack is not as well known as Shiga's or has not caused the same sensation, it is only because it is shorter and perhaps also because it appeared in a less widely read publication. In its own way, it represents an even more devastating attack upon the intellectual idol that is normally enshrined within the very holy of holies of the modern cult of Nihongo.

Shiga was, to be sure, notorious for the way students honored him as the deity of fiction, even according him near-imperial honors in public places. But all the honors paid Shiga, either during or after his lifetime, can hardly hold a candle to those still accorded to Yanagita. If Shiga was a Japanese-style, *kami*-like deity, Yanagita and his enormous prestige can only be expressed in terms of some more powerful godlike figure from the Hellenistic or even the Judeo-Christian tradition.

Even today, more than one Japanese academic bases his career and his entire scholarly reputation upon the mere fact of once having spent a day or two in Yanagita's sainted presence. The number of books published annually about Yanagita, or dealing with Yanagita, or in some way or another capitalizing upon Yanagita's fame simply by getting the words Kunio Yanagita onto the cover of the publication, is literally beyond calculation. Most Western societies lack figures with anything even resembling the prestige that Shiga and Yanagita represent in Japan. Anyone who has not experienced firsthand the reverence that such men still command in Japan will find it more than a little difficult to imagine, much less to believe.

But simply being at once *fukanzen* and *fuben* are not the only charges that this particular segment of the sociolinguistic literature routinely levels against the same language that it is otherwise intent upon honoring. There is also much evidence at hand showing that this segment of the literature frequently categorizes the Japanese language as being fragile and easily betrayed. It is spoken of as being particularly susceptible to falling apart under the stress and strain of contacts with foreign languages, or even when its speakers simply come into contact with such languages.

In one particularly significant expression of these fears, an author reports that mere residence abroad appears to be enough to bring the Japanese language to its feet and to rob it of most of its effectiveness, not only for literary purposes but even for ordinary communication: "I had often heard

tales of how difficult it is to compose haiku when one is in a foreign country . . . but I actually learned firsthand on my recent trip to Europe when
I personally ran up against a thick wall different even from what I had been
led to expect from the stories I had heard about this problem. . . . This wall
had to do with the fact that when I was in Europe and using the language
they have over there [*achira no kotoba*] every day, I found that when I tried
to use Japanese and write a haiku, what do you suppose happened? I myself
was startled to find that my Japanese had begun to show signs of becoming
disordered or of what one might call "foreign-language-style craziness"
[*achiragoshiki na kurui*]. I was startled to find that my Japanese language *as
Japanese* had lost its potency. And this was not only for writing haiku, but
even for using Japanese in conversation with other Japanese. . . . When you
live in a foreign country, your own Japanese language begins to run wild.
For conversation, English will get you by anywhere. My own English conversation is a rather bogus thing. I just line up nouns and here and there
insert a modifier, nothing more than that. But even so, when I tried to
switch back to Japanese and write a haiku, I found that the balance [English
in the original: *baransu*] of my Japanese had collapsed. All I could bring off
was a simple reportage of events in 5–7–5 syllables with no savor of a poem
about it at all. Truly, the Japanese language is a mysterious thing."

Professor Hajime Nakamura, professor emeritus of Indian and Buddhist
philosophy at Tokyo University and one of Japan's most distinguished philosophers and intellectuals, is a frequent if unexpected contributor to the
literature of this particular genre of sociolinguistics. A well-known partici-
pant in many international conferences, where his ability to speak and
understand English well make him particularly welcome, Nakamura vigorously continues a busy academic career even after retirement, and, despite
his original training in Indological fields, he does not hesitate to share with
audiences around the world his own view of the Japanese language and its
defects.

At an "East-West Philosophers' Conference" held in Honolulu in 1964,
for example, Nakamura lit into the Japanese language along the following
lines: "Concerning logical thinking, we can say that, although the mass of
Japanese people have been limited to a language that was rather deficient as
a tool of logical exactness, philosophic thinking did develop among Japan's
educated classes through the use of Chinese. Logic can be disseminated and
developed among the Japanese people, if they endeavor seriously in a right
way. . . . It is important for the Japanese people as a nation to develop the
habits and language tools of logically exact thinking."

But if we are to believe Nakamura, no matter how important all this
is, it still cannot be done if the Japanese persist in using the Japanese language:
"In short, the Japanese language, so far, has had a structure rather unfit for

expressing logical conceptions. . . . It is difficult to make derivatives representing abstract nouns. . . . When we step into the realm of syntax from that of word construction, the Japanese language manifests its nonlogical character all the more clearly. The language lacks the relative pronoun 'which,' standing for the antecedent, that helps develop the process of thought. We find it inconvenient, therefore, to advance closely knit thinking in Japanese. . . . Because of these defects, Japanese presents difficulties for logical expression . . . its nonlogical character naturally handicaps the development of ability in logical thinking among the Japanese people."

We began the present chapter quoting a modern journalist who claimed that "to live in Arabic is to live in a labyrinth of false turns and double meanings." If we are to believe Nakamura, to live in Japanese is to live in a labyrinth of illogic and inconvenience. Very little separates one set of allegations from the other, except for the obvious fact that Nakamura unarguably does know the Japanese language—indeed, he can employ it if he so wishes to level his charges of illogicality and inconvenience against the language itself—while the journalist quoted did not even claim to know more than a few words of Arabic.

The surprising facility with which all such sociolinguistic allegations shade off into racial and ethnic slurs is also easily documented from the Japanese sources. In fact, deft shadings from the one to the other may be detected in the quotations from Nakamura's pronouncements given above. But they show themselves even more clearly in the following quotation, which once again comes from a rather surprising source—Professor Hideki Yukawa. Yukawa, who died in 1981, was a physicist and the first Japanese to win a Nobel Prize for research in the natural sciences, awarded to him in 1949 for his work in nuclear physics.

Speaking at the same "East-West" conference in 1964, Yukawa elaborated upon Nakamura's strictures in a very harsh fashion. To hear Yukawa tell it: "The Japanese mentality is, in most cases, unfit for abstract thinking and takes interest merely in tangible things. This is the origin of the Japanese excellence in technical art and the fine arts. The unconscious recognition of their own defect in abstraction seems to drive the Japanese to the uncritical adoration and the unconditional adoption of the religious and philosophical systems brought in from the outside. Such a task is relatively easy for the high-level Japanese intellect."

But the wholesale categorizations of Japanese life and culture that we find in such allegations are not always as upbeat and hopeful as they are in Yukawa's pronouncement. Sometimes they take surprising turns, so that one wonders if their authors intended that all the implications of some of these attacks be followed up literally by the outsider.

A striking example may be cited from the work of Dr. Keigo Okonogi, who, in addition to writing about the myth of Nihongo, specializes in the practice of neuropsychiatric medicine at the Keio University Medical School. In a recent article in the influential journal of opinion *Chūō Kōron,* which was quickly selected by the editors of the *Japan Echo* for translation into English and worldwide distribution, Okonogi shared the following rather startling insight into Japanese sociolinguistic behavior with his readers: "In day-to-day living we Japanese . . . are accustomed to putting ourselves in the place of others and directing our behavior in line with others' feelings. This psychological tendency is evident in our way of addressing others by putting ourselves in their place. . . . For instance, I refer to myself as 'papa' when talking to my daughter, by the informal first-person pronoun *boku* to my wife, by my personal name, Keigo, to my parents, and by the neutral first-person pronoun *watakushi* to hospital and university staff. We have an unusually developed ability to adjust our own condition to accord with time and place. . . . Instead of enjoying ourselves alone we tend to enjoy the feeling of unity that comes from sharing the pleasures of others. Association among men illustrates this well; indeed, to Western eyes Japan appears to be an unusually homosexual society."

The practice of medicine in Japan is a highly respected and well-paying profession. The entrance examinations for the pre-med courses in Japanese universities are among the most difficult of all the complex rites of passage that the society has evolved. Especially in view of these circumstances, it is all the more difficult to understand why so many qualified doctors, once having gone through this difficult and expensive training and preparation, seem so eager to abandon the practice of medicine in order to dabble in the myth of Nihongo.

In chapter 4 we saw some of the results of this process of professional switchover, as we followed Dr. Tsunoda's peregrinations first from medicine to neurosurgery and then on to linguistics. Here, in a somewhat different context, we are able to observe what happens when a neuropsychiatrist similarly begins to climb aboard the sociolinguistic bandwagon. As far as Okonogi's categorization of Japan as an "unusually homosexual society" is concerned, about all one can say is that this certainly appears to be a pretty serious charge to bring simply upon the evidence of Japanese pronoun usage. Even more perplexingly, Okonogi does not say that it is actually such a society, he only says that it appears to be so "to Western eyes."

The reader whose attention has not been atrophied by this melancholy recital of baseless slanders by the Japanese of their own language, society, and culture will by this time have noticed that several of the passages cited, particularly those for which we are indebted to Nakamura, Yukawa, and Okonogi, more or less manage to have it both ways. At the same time that they profess to identify some defect in the way that the Japanese language serves Japanese society, they simultaneously manage to make this feature out to be either a plus or at least something that the Japanese "do better than anyone else."

Frequently the thrust of the argument is clearly along elitist lines. We are told that "the mass of the Japanese people" are inflicted with this or that deficiency in their thinking or conduct as a result of the language that they are saddled with. At the same time, it is claimed that a few of them, "the educated classes"—which of course always includes the expert being quoted—do manage to fight their way out of this sociolinguistic impasse to go on to better and greater things as a result. The thin line that separates self-blame from self-praise thus becomes more and more blurred; in the sociolinguistic literature of love and hate, it soon disappears altogether.

Particularly deft in this delicate technique of turning hate into love—of deflecting the cutting edge of an allegation of incompleteness and impracticality so that it becomes a paean of praise—is Haruhiko Kindaichi. Here, as in every other range of the sociolinguistic scene, the dexterity with which he is able to wield his highly polished, double-edged blade would do credit to the most celebrated swordsmen in Japanese cinema history.

The careful student of Kindaichi's oeuvre may even identify several stages in his mastery of this particular technique. In his 1957 book, *Nihongo*, Kindaichi was still very much on the defensive. Here his sword work was deployed in a serious but relatively unspectacular manner and almost entirely in self-defense—defending Nihongo against the attacks of Naoya Shiga and against the charges of everyone else who had ever suggested that it might not possibly be the ultimate in the human linguistic condition. But by 1976, in his book *Nihongo e no Kibō* (My Aspirations for Japanese), Kindaichi had realized that there is more than one way to defend one's own thing against an enemy, whether real or imaginary. In this book, he refined the technique of simultaneous slander and elitist self-adulation. Partly because his discourse has now become so elaborate and highly honed, it is almost impossible to select individual passages for brief citation from the 1976 book. We must content ourselves with a brief paraphrase of what has become his principal dialectic device.

In this book, Kindaichi develops quite a regular pattern for his argumentation, even though he is, as usual, difficult to come to terms with because of his skill in presenting the reader with a rapidly moving target. On point after point, he begins by suggesting that Nihongo is defective or deficient in some respect or other—its pronunciation, its grammar, its lexical resources, any other linguistic category that can come to mind. First he whets the reader's appetite with a mock-serious recital of the supposed defects of "our language" for a good number of pages. But then, with almost no warning and before any but the most careful reader will have noticed, what begins as blame swiftly shifts to praise.

Yes, he says in effect, Nihongo is truly and lamentably poor, weak, and deficient in this or that quality or element. But lo and behold! We are still very fortunate to have this language, and, if you will bear with me for a moment, I will be able to demonstrate how this defect really works to our advantage. Finally, a genial coda is appended to each of these praise-from-blame transformations to the effect that if you want to see a language that is really defective, you should take a look at Chinese or Korean, both of which Kindaichi categorizes as being "sick languages." Japanese, it goes without saying, is a healthy language.

Love and hate—praise and blame—adulation and denigration, each so deftly intertwined with the other that it is generally impossible to say where the first leaves off and the second starts. There is a mighty ambivalence here, a shifting back and forth of point of view that transpires at bewildering speed. It concerns, of course, mainly the Japanese authorities who generate it, but we, for our part, must ask just what the outside observer of the Japanese sociolinguistic scene is supposed to make of this magnificent ambivalence. Any human phenomenon this paradoxical cries out for some kind of explanation. One wishes to feel that there must necessarily be some logical, rational connecting link that somehow brings together these two extremes—something that explains how it is possible to extol the mystic virtues of the Japanese language on the one hand while simultaneously slandering it on the other. But if such a link, or indeed any rational explanation for the coexistence of these two radically divergent approaches to the same subject, often taken by the same writers and observers at one and the same time, actually does exist, what might it possibly be?

Just as we approach the point of despair in our attempts to make order out of this segment of the modern myth of Nihongo, we are fortunate enough to be provided substantial assistance in the form of the insights of a Japanese colleague, Professor Takao Suzuki of Keio University. Nor will this prove to be the only time we will have occasion to avail ourselves of Suzuki's help; he and his writing will be coming to our assistance many times during the remainder of our investigation.

As befits one of the most prolific writers and innovative observers concerned with contemporary Japanese sociolinguistics, Suzuki has a personal background somewhat unusual for anyone in Japan professionally engaged in writing and teaching about these subjects. He not only has the usual Japanese academic credentials, but he has also taught—and, we are told, studied as well—in both Canada and the United States. In addition, he has traveled extensively in the Middle East.

Suzuki is currently a professor in Keio University's Institute for the Study of Language and Culture. This means that he holds a fairly important academic post and also helps ensure that his views will be listened to respectfully by almost everyone in Japan who comes into contact with them. It also means that, since Keio is a private university, he himself is not fully bound by all the intellectual constraints and academic shibboleths that would necessarily accompany a more prestigious position within Japanese academia, as for example a post at one of the national universities. Perhaps this too helps to explain Suzuki's unusual determination to approach his subject in a search for new insights rather than simply plowing already well-turned furrows.

In the present context, Suzuki comes to our aid only after first indulging in a representative specimen of the same variety of sociolinguistic denigration. This he begins by reminding his Japanese readers of the well-known French maxim *ce qui n'est pas clair n'est pas français*. This is a genial equation of limpidity in literary expression with the French language itself—a summation of the belief, devoutly held by most French speakers and even by a number of French writers, that clarity is an inherent quality of any idea or concept fortunate enough to find itself expressed in the French language.

But in the case of Japanese, Suzuki suggests, quite the opposite is true: "I must say that the great majority of the writing by Japan's famous authors and scholars—I am not speaking here of literary works as such—seems to be done as if to ensure that it will provide indirect contradiction to the clarity of French as set forth with such conviction by [this French maxim]. Time and time again the reasons and premises for an author's statements are not made clear, and sentences dissolve into vapidity. [Japanese authors] dislike clarification and full explanation of their views; instead, they like giving dark hints and attempt to drop nuances. But what we must not lose sight of in this connection is that in Japan this is exactly the type of prose that gets the highest praise from readers. Indeed, because readers seek just this kind of writing, and because they enjoy coming into contact with it, one suspects that this type of prose is, as a result, written more or less intentionally. . . . I think one might very well conclude that, rather than turning away from such writing, [Japanese] readers instead have a tendency to anticipate with pleasure the opportunities that it will offer them to savor this particular variety of 'mystification through language.' "

Suzuki then documents his opinions by citing at some length a passage in Japanese from a recent book published by a celebrated Japanese scholar of English literature, an author who is also a well-known and widely read Japanese novelist. The passage that Suzuki cites is beyond any question a fair stylistic specimen of modern Japanese literary criticism. It touches upon

Tennyson, Meredith, Browning, Carlyle, and Conrad, but unfortunately it is quite impossible to reproduce it in translation here, since, as Suzuki himself testifies, the entire passage makes almost no sense at all in Japanese, no matter how often one reads through it.

Its nonstop sentences and almost equally lengthy sentence fragments move smoothly along, held together by a rich variety of syntactic connective tissue. It seems to be language, and it appears to be a continuous text. As such, it ought to be subject to the normal expectation that anything that occurs in one language can always at least be approximated in another, i.e., translated. But here this normal expectation proves to be false. No matter how often one reads and rereads the passage, it simply refuses to yield up any sense that could be rendered, even approximated, in any other language, even though we are told that it communicates something to the Japanese reader—indeed, it impresses the Japanese reader with its erudition and importance.

As Suzuki puts it: "As I read through this, attempting to understand what the author is saying, I find myself increasingly puzzled. There is simply too much here that cannot be understood. The passage abounds in expressions that may be taken in any number of meanings, and the relation of sentence after sentence to what goes before or comes after is anything but clear. . . . Since I do not myself pretend to any special literary training, I showed the passage to a friend who is a literary scholar and asked him to read it and tell me what he thought of it. I did not reveal the author's name to him but just asked his opinion about the passage. He was not far beyond the first line of the text when he had already arrived at three different opinions about what the author was trying to say."

With this testimony in hand we might be forgiven for simply writing off the entire episode as nothing more than an example of extraordinarily bad writing—the kind of thing that happens from time to time in all literary cultures. It might be surprising, perhaps, to find such bad writing in a book by a person of great literary and scholarly reputation, but even in that case, the incident would be without further significance for the purposes of our present study. That easy solution, however, proves to be impossible.

As Suzuki goes on to point out in convincing detail, writing of this variety—writing that since it does not communicate to the reader anything at all specific about what the author is trying to say and hence violates the most elementary functional definition of language as the medium of social interrelationships—is not only prized by many Japanese scholars and intellectuals; the techniques for its generation are actually quite carefully cultivated. Moreover, such writing is widely felt to have a strange, mysterious, but very real power and strength. In a word, this kind of prose too is a part of the ineffable process of mystic ecsasy through which modern Japanese sociolinguistic culture enjoys viewing its own language. We all know that there is great potential power in the unknown. What Suzuki is suggesting here is that an equal or perhaps even a greater power resides in the unintelligible.

But the importance of Suzuki's analysis of this particular passage lies in his concluding suggestion about why Japanese readers, and for that matter Suzuki himself as a representative Japanese reader, find this variety of prose not only tolerable but desirable: "There is a mysterious power in this indecipherable passage. As one reads it over and over, one begins to pick up a hint here and a clue there as to what the author was driving at, until suddenly and before one realizes it, one can grasp the entire text: how inexplicable [*fushigi*] all this is! . . . In difficulty of this variety, there is something that may be thought of as the covert pleasure that we all feel in pain, and this is what drags the reader along."

Here at long last we glimpse, though far away and perhaps even beyond the end of a long, dark tunnel, some semblance of the answer that we have been looking for. Our hopes for eventually understanding all of this a little better are suddenly kindled anew as we read Suzuki's surprisingly frank reference to "the covert pleasure that we all feel in pain." And even if we are perhaps reluctant to be included without comment or protest in the generous embrace represented by Suzuki's genial "all"—if here and there we must have to reckon with individual holdouts who stubbornly insist that no, they do not actually feel any pleasure at all, covert or otherwise, in pain—that in no way detracts from the usefulness of the insight that our Japanese mentor has given us.

Suzuki has been good enough to describe his own psychological response to involute, all-but-meaningless Japanese prose with utter candor. It pains him, but nevertheless he enjoys it. Reading it, even though he cannot puzzle out any single connected idea or train of thought, he nevertheless experiences pleasure—"the covert pleasure that we all feel in pain." Frankness on this personal a level of psychological analysis may often be the source of considerable embarrassment to the outside observer. But it would be highly regrettable if we allowed such very natural embarrassment to get in the way of our appreciation of Suzuki's inner emotional responses. With this perceptive comment, Suzuki has, in fact, directed our attention toward a whole new and extremely productive analytic approach.

At first glance, of course, one is mostly impressed by the plain appeal that Suzuki makes to masochistic tendencies in the "typical Japanese reader," of whom he offers himself as a working example. That considerations of masochism do play an important role on every level of Japanese society is hardly a proposition that anyone at all familiar with Japanese life and culture would wish to question for a moment. But that masochism also provides a useful analytic approach to the characteristic sociolinguistic response exhibited by Japanese readers toward certain varieties of Japanese prose style opens many new avenues for future study. Regrettably, these questions have almost nothing to do with linguistic science, and so they must be left to the attentions of other specialists, those more qualified to deal with such delicate matters and those who can usefully discuss such specialized delights.

But even the linguist, while admitting that he or she is unqualified to become involved in questions of masochism and other aspects of the "covert pleasure that we all feel in pain," may perhaps be forgiven for at least mentioning yet another possible psychological interpretation for Suzuki's remarkably candid admission. Without in any way detracting from the masochistic explanation that the professor offers, we might at the same time suggest that much of this also fits in rather well with yet another psychological phenomenon, the cluster of reactions that is often referred to in the West by its original German designation of *Schadenfreude,* and which has been defined as "those well-known feelings of joy and relief that we all experience upon hearing of the misfortunes of others."

The cluster of psychological reactions and reflexes that is summed up in the term *Schadenfreude* is probably familiar enough to all of us, even though the term itself may not be. Which of us, on hearing of disasters or difficulties experienced by our dearest friends, does not first of all enjoy a fleeting reaction of relief closely allied with pleasure—relief that is hardly to be separated from the gratitude we feel upon learning that these disasters have not happened to ourselves? The airplane crashes, the boat sinks, the building burns; which of us, upon learning of these disasters, is not immediately relieved simply to know that it was not *our* plane, *our* boat, *our* building?

Of course, Suzuki's insight into the psychological reaction that he, as the typical Japanese reader, has when confronted with prose of this variety is not solely restricted to the plane of the phenomenon of *Schadenfreude.* Much of what he suggests is in fact closer to masochism; actually the two elements are so closely intertwined in his response that it is difficult to unravel them.

Suzuki's reaction upon being confronted with turgid, inchoate Japanese prose is initially and essentially masochistic. As he himself tells us, this kind of language causes him pain, and he enjoys it for that reason. But there are also strong elements of *Schadenfreude* in this same cluster of reaction patterns. Suzuki's own prose is everything that the incomprehensible example he cites is not. Suzuki writes clearly, directly, and effectively. One need not always agree with what he is saying, but one must admit that he says it very well. He himself writes Japanese of remarkable clarity and directness, Japanese prose that could well serve as a stylistic model for many academics and journalists of lesser gifts. May not the masochistic pleasure he experiences in reading the muddled pages of many of his colleagues derive also in part from the *Schadenfreude* feelings of joy and relief that he experiences at the moment when he realizes that he himself does not write this way? It is, at the very least, another possible explanation.

Love and hate—pleasure and pain—our sincere concern for our friends and the unmistakable joy we nevertheless feel upon learning that some disaster has overtaken them and not us—each is only one side of a thin, thin spectrum of behavioral experience, and each makes but little sense if we insist upon attempting to view it in isolation from its partner. Perhaps that is the best that can be made out of the paradox of all these mutually contradictory claims and allegations concerning the Japanese language, a few of which we have been exploring in the present chapter. The essence of the modern myth of Nihongo is that the language is worthy of honor and love and respect, but this is only one side of the coin. Always present and immediately available on an adjacent, intimately accessible dimension is the direct opposite: love is countered by hate, pleasure by pain, affection and concern by *Schadenfreude*.

Meanwhile, our continuing suspicion that none of this, for all its superficial ambivalence, ever really departs very far from the essential dimensions of the modern sustaining myth of Japanese society is enhanced when we observe that, here also, myth may be observed in the process of generating antimyth, particularly among those who are relegated to the role of outside observers of this entire sociolinguistic scene. If Japanese authorities alone could be cited in support of this highly complex pattern of love-and-hate reactions, we might wonder if the phenomenon were really generalized enough to merit inclusion within the dimensions of the myth. But when we find evidence for an equally vigorous antimyth of parallel configuration also current among non-Japanese, our overall confidence in the essential accuracy of our analysis is confirmed.

A young French musician recently shared with the world his own poignant testimony to the proliferation of this particular antimyth of love and hate in the pages of *PHP*, the widely distributed English-language moral-uplift house organ of the Matsushita Electric Company. In an article entitled "My 'Adopted' Country, or, The Immigration Blues," Claude Ciari told of his surprise that, after living in Japan for six years, learning to speak the language, and marrying a Japanese woman, he was still not permitted even to apply for Japanese citizenship. This is not a case of any particular discrimination against Ciari. Japanese law does make provision for the naturalization of foreigners, but the actual procedures under which the provisions of the law are implemented allow an extraordinary degree of administrative selectivity. In most countries, the longtime foreign resident is expected to assume citizenship, with its duties and responsibilities; in Japan, to be permitted to do so remains an exception concerning which the bureaucracy continues to exercise great care. In effect, working-level officialdom is left free to pick and choose the fortunate few who will be allowed the privilege of naturalization. Ciari would have been better advised to have acquainted himself with this ever-present if subtle distinction between the letter of the law and its administrative implementation before he embarked upon his quest for Japanese citizenship.

Ciari appears, at least in the optimistic pages of *PHP,* to be undaunted by his experiences. Indeed, he is actually beginning to enjoy the whole thing, rather in the same way that Suzuki enjoys reading unintelligible Japanese prose. As our young French friend expresses it: "Because the laws are so strict, yet the Japanese are so warmhearted, many people have been doing their best to find a loophole in the law—an exception to the rules—to allow me to become a Japanese citizen. This duality—the rules-are-rules toughness combined with a very romantic softness—is what I find so appealing about the Japanese."

Earlier in a moving account of his struggles to apply for Japanese citizenship, Ciari tells us of the efforts that he made to learn to speak Japanese "a little better than I speak English." He does not tell us whether or not he has attempted to learn to read and write Japanese in addition to speaking and understanding the language. If he has studied the written language as well, then Ciari is in a position to do the study of sociolinguistics a considerable favor. He would appear to be uniquely qualified to pursue the investigation of all these problems into areas where linguistic science can hardly follow—love and hate, the covert pleasure one feels in pain, the delight we take in the misfortunes of our dearest friends. All this is clearly the domain of someone other than the linguistic scientist, and, from what he tells us of his own reactions to the rebuff at the hands of Japanese law and officialdom, Ciari might well be the very man for the job.

If he has actually mastered written Japanese as well as the spoken language, Ciari has still another treat in store for himself. Anyone who finds the Japanese refusal to grant his heart's desire of becoming a Japanese citizen "so appealing" ought by all means to get in touch with Suzuki, busy somewhere at this very moment reading turgid examples of Japanese prose and experiencing the covert pleasure he feels in the pain they cause him. Each of these gentlemen surely has much to teach the other. For the rest of us, it is time to admit that we have already tarried too long in these murky corridors of the mind, and time also to return to what must inevitably seem, by comparison, our rather routine linguistic concerns.

CHAPTER SEVEN

"The Spirit of the Language"

> *Some people hold that Japanese should be made an official language of the UN too.... If a language has real power which nobody can disregard and is closely associated with a charming and profound culture, many people will study that language without being asked to do so.* —Daily Yomiuri, November 1, 1974, translating an article from the previous day's *Yomiuri Shimbun*

SURVEYING contemporary Japanese speculation about the Japanese language, we cannot help but notice how one particular expression looms in lonely splendor far above the generally unrelieved intellectual wasteland that constitutes the bulk of this field. The expression is one that continues to be introduced into all discussions of the language so frequently and usually also in such a strident fashion that it would be impossible to ignore it even if one wished to do so. This is the *kotodama,* and no consideration of the modern myth of Nihongo can advance very far without coming to grips with this term.

The Japanese expression *kotodama,* when considered simply as a lexical item in the modern language, is easy enough to explain and equally easy to translate. It means "the spirit of the language." Its constituent parts are *koto,* meaning language, speech, words, and *dama,* which is the form that the word *tama,* meaning spirit, soul, has in certain compounds where its initial *t* automatically changes to *d.* Thus, on the surface at least, *kotodama* is a simple expression for an ostensibly simple concept: it is the "spirit" or the "soul" of the Japanese language.

But as a matter of fact, no other single term or expression in the entire technical vocabulary of the modern myth of Nihongo is of greater importance for understanding the myth and for grasping some of the ways in which it operates than is this superficially simple expression *kotodama*. The further we delve into this term and in particular the more that we learn about its history, the more we discover about the myth of Nihongo as well as about how that myth is being remade today into a new body of sustaining beliefs for contemporary Japanese society.

The whole concept of *kotodama* is, as we shall see, simply a fable, and not even an innocent fable, but this does not mean that it can be ignored. So important is this term, in fact, that it is dangerous to content ourselves with the straightforward though quite accurate analysis and translation of the word and its constituent elements given above. At least two further elements of clarification are necessary, even for a preliminary understanding of this expression and its importance in the modern myth of Nihongo.

The first of these two points requiring clarification concerns the first part of the compound, the noun *koto*. What is important about the element *koto* in this term *kotodama* is less what it says than what it implies and the covert way in which it makes this implication. The Japanese word *koto* lexically means language, speech, or, in certain contexts, words. In the modern language it has this last sense in particular, as in the most common expression for words or a word: *kotoba*—but this in turn is a term that also very often means language, which tends to bring us full circle again to our original topic of discussion.

The point that must be stressed here is not simply or solely that *koto* in *kotodama* means language or even words, but that in the cult employment of the term in the modern myth of Nihongo, *koto* is currently taken as being exactly equivalent in meaning to the Japanese language or the word (for anything) in Japanese. Thus the undifferentiated concept of *koto,* meaning language, words, is deftly particularized as soon as the term enters into the compound *kotodama,* where it then becomes a specific term referring only to the Japanese language and to Japanese words but without overtly indicating that it has been so specialized and particularized.

It hardly need be pointed out at any further length how important as well as how subtle this lexical particularization is, or how beautifully it serves the ends of the modern myth of Nihongo. Without any overt identification of the entity under discussion as being Japanese, it is now nevertheless understood as meaning, and equally importantly as being equivalent to, Japanese. Something that is entirely general—language, words, speech—is now identified with the particular, in this case with the Japanese language, with its words, with its manner of speaking. The linguistic universe has become a linguistic microcosm. And all this has happened implicitly, by common but unverbalized consent.

The heart of every myth must dwell in darkness at once inaccessible and invisible to the believers, if they are to continue to be faithful to the tenets that cluster around the core in question. To label the *kotodama* overtly as having to do with the Japanese language would be, in effect, to begin to strip away a sizable portion of the protective darkness that makes the myth function. Here the identification of the general (language, speech, words) with the particular (Japan, the Japanese language) not only functions all the better because of its unspoken nature, but in that very fact it finds its most effective resources of mythic strength.

To say *Nihongo no kotodama* (the spirit of the Japanese language) would not only be a solecism but also a sacrilege. It would mean stripping away the veil of obscurity that provides the identification of the word *koto,* the most general term possible for language, speech, words, with the most particularized identification possible, i.e., with Japan. This would immediately destroy the identification implicit in the expression, and this in turn would necessarily give rise to doubt in the minds of the believers concerning the efficacy of the entire myth, since so much of the mythic power depends upon this same identification, spurious though it is.

One might very well compare the process with what would happen if one insisted on opening and looking into one of the small fetish cases that are the center of most Shinto shrines. One of the great modernizers and forward-looking intellectuals of the Meiji era, Yukichi Fukuzawa (1835–1901), describes in his autobiography how in his childhood he once did just that. Being quite skeptical even at an early age of the efficacy of the worship of the fox deity, he decided to test his theories on the subject with a definitive if rather devastating experiment. Fukuzawa tells us in his autobiography how, shortly before one of the regular monthly celebrations in honor of the fox deity, he forced the small tabernaclelike strongbox that formed the center of the shrine. Initially his interest was simply to see what there was that was kept with such reverence within the shrine. He found that it was simply a rather ordinary, if somewhat phallic-shaped, piece of stone. Having satisfied his curiosity on this matter, he then proceeded to replace this stone, which had most likely been the unseen center of the shrine and its cult for generations if not for centuries, with another perfectly ordinary stone that he found lying on the ground in the vicinity of the shrine. Relocking the door to the innermost shrine enclosure, where his new and quite unmiraculous stone now replaced the ancient cult object, he waited to see what effect this replacement of the sacred by the profane would have upon the cult. As he expected, it had no effect whatsoever, for the simple but profound reason that no one but he knew what had been done—and he was not a believer in the first place.

The rest of the community gathered to honor the fox deity on the appointed day, presenting the same offerings to the carefully concealed cult object and getting the same benefits, both spiritual and material, from their observances. It all worked just as well as ever, because no one knew what had happened. But of course this would hardly have been the case if Fukuzawa had gone out of his way to announce to everyone concerned what he had done, making it clear that they were now not only bowing down to wood and stone but in point of fact to a particularly undistinguished bit of stone, one he had himself only the day before picked up from the ground.

In the essential obscurity of the cult object and in the practical impossibility of identifying it because of its covert nature are to be found the principal elements of its power. For the cult of the fox deity Inari-sama, the operative element of obscurity is real and literal, provided by the strongbox of the inner shrine in which the fetish object is normally concealed. For the cult of Nihongo and for the manifestation of its modern myth, the operative obscurity is not literal but no less real. It is to be located precisely in the linguistic identification of the general with the particular as just described and in the process by means of which *koto* in the key cult-term *kotodama* has been transmuted from meaning simply and generally language, words, speech to specifically the Japanese language—together with everything else about the Japanese language that might possibly be singled out as capable of serving in the proliferation of the modern myth of Nihongo.

The second element in the compound *kotodama* is equally important, though its role in the functioning of the modern myth is less subtle than is that of the first. The Japanese word *tama,* which becomes -*dama* in the compound *kotodama* "the spirit of (the Japanese) language," is generally translated as spirit or soul. Unfortunately, neither of these two English equivalents does very well by this significant Japanese term, nor does either give a fully adequate idea of the implication of the word *tama* in the expression *kotodama*. To understand correctly what the *tama* of *kotodama* really signifies and in order to build upon such understanding toward comprehending the fetish role that this term plays in the modern myth of Nihongo, we must realize that Japanese *tama* refers to something much more positive and energetic than either of the English words spirit or soul normally does.

Japanese *tama* above all else refers to an active concept, one that embodies elements of creative energy, infusing new, vigorous life and activity into its receptacle or vehicle—and in this case, the vehicle of this marvelously energetic *tama* is of course *koto,* now understood as meaning the Japanese language.

An important clue to the correct understanding of the element *tama* in the compound *kotodama* can also be gathered from recalling that this is the same word *tama* that was part of the expression *Yamatodamashii,* the "spirit of Yamato," the official rallying cry for the Japanese armed forces in World

War II. It was in order to comply with the stern demands of *Yamatodamashii* that teenage Japanese pilots allowed themselves to be strapped into suicide-mission airplanes loaded with high explosives. No other guidance or direction was provided to them except a vague indication of the quarter of the horizon at which the enemy might be found; *Yamatodamashii* would do the rest. The *tama* in the word *Yamatodamashii* was conceptualized as a vital, positive source of energy, something capable of fueling the Japanese military advance throughout the Far East.

For a country absolutely dependent upon foreign supplies for all petro-chemical sources of energy, such a concept obviously had much to recommend it—apart from the obvious drawback that it did not work very well. When the 40,000-ton Yamato, the last superbattleship the world was ever to know, was sunk by U.S. planes off the east coast of Kyushu on the morning of April 6, 1945, she not only had the last gallons of fuel to be found in Japan; several of her bunkers had at the last moment been filled with edible vegetable oils in a desperate attempt to fit her for her fatal sortie. But battle-ships, even Japanese battleships, proved difficult to get out of port and into battle when their bunkers were empty, no matter how much *tama* the captain and crew were able to muster above and below decks.

Once we understand this, we begin to see why such words as English spirit or soul can only mislead us when we use them to translate *tama* in such an expression as *kotodama*. These English words are too pale, shy, and retiring to do the Japanese term full justice. Something quite the opposite is needed. Perhaps the German *Geist* comes a little closer. Or in certain cases a useful equivalent might be the French *élan,* which is perhaps the closest of all, at least in suggesting a forward thrust or drive. But finally we must conclude that nothing in any commonly used European language, including English, really does justice to Japanese *tama*. The spirit, soul, *Geist,* or *élan* to which the Japanese term has reference, whether it is the *tama* of *Yamato-damashii* or the *tama* of *kotodama,* is a vital and active entity that plays no part in any usual Western-language imagery or expression. We have no such word, and we make use of no imagery capitalizing upon the concepts that it employs; but the Japanese have, and they do.

When modern Japanese writers write of *kotodama,* "the spirit of the language," then, they are making overt reference to the single most important fetish term in the entire modern myth of Nihongo, and they are employing this term in order to indicate the entire range of the core belief of the cult. These beliefs are widespread in their application and far-reaching in their implications, but what they have in common is the way in which they all center about the central idea that the Japanese language (*koto*) has abiding within it a distinctive spirit (*tama*). At the same time it is this spirit that imparts to the language a character or inner essence that ends up making it radically different from any other language on earth, ancient or modern, living or dead.

The implications of this *kotodama* belief are so momentous that anyone not well acquainted with the currently fashionable elaborations of the modern myth of Nihongo may be forgiven for finding them difficult to follow—or for finding it difficult even to believe that such irrational ideas are seriously taught and advocated by people in important educational, academic, and intellectual positions in modern Japan. Indeed, one would like to disbelieve all this, but facts must be faced.

Among the least believable of all the facts and one of the most difficult for many foreign observers to deal with is that the *kotodama* cult has again begun to be promulgated in certain official Japanese circles under the guise of providing "correct and accurate information about Japan" to the rest of the world. The anomaly that is presented by such official promulgation of the *kotodama* cult becomes all the more complicated and if anything all the more difficult for most foreign observers to find credible when we note how closely many of the contemporary, officially sanctioned pronouncements on this issue reproduce the rhetoric and expression of the *kotodama* cult as it was originally found in Japan's notorious fascist-nationalist document of World War II vintage, the *Kokutai no Hongi*.

We have already seen something of the history and significance of this particular document in chapter 5, when we considered the antimyth of silence and learned how this curious approach to the Japanese language can only be understood in terms of the *Kokutai no Hongi's* philological perversions of Japanese antiquity. We also noted in the same connection the great importance that Sen'ichi Hisamatsu, the principal author of this document, attributed to the Japanese language in its role as a part of his fantastic system: indeed, midway in this document he gives it first place in enumerating the virtually sacred trinity of Japanese language, customs, and habits upon which the document focuses.

But while a special role for the Japanese language was assumed throughout the *Kokutai no Hongi,* the *kotodama* cult in particular was intrinsic to the ideological framework of this charter of 1930s Japanese fascist-nationalism. We find that the canonical exposition of the *kotodama* doctrine surfaces early in book I, chapter IV of the text in a section that carries the almost mockingly deceptive subtitle "Harmony and Truth." Here Hisamatsu and his coauthors begin by telling how "when we trace the marks of the facts of the founding of our country and the progress of our history, what we always find there is the spirit of harmony. . . . Herein indeed lies the reason why the ideologies of our nation are different from those of the nations of the West."

From this it is only a short, quick step to "The Martial Spirit: War . . .

is not by any means intended for the destruction, overpowering, or sub-jugation of others; and it should be a thing for the bringing about of great harmony." Now the authors are ready to go on to teach how "Sovereign and Subjects In One" offers to the fortunate beholder "an unadulterated manifestation of the supreme harmony." They eventually also quote the Meiji emperor's *Rescript Granted to the Army and Navy* on the "Five Virtues" that are to be encouraged among military men: fealty, etiquette, chivalry, fidelity, and frugality. But all these five virtues, we are told, may be summed up under the single rubric of *makoto,* "sincerity." And it is as a further elaboration upon this word *makoto* as it appeared in this all-but-sacred context of the Meiji *Rescript* to the armed forces that the 1930s version of the *kotodama* cult received its most authoritative expression.

Thus not only does the *Kokutai no Hongi* provide the best possible evidence for the central role that *kotodama* was forced to play in the nationalistic political philosophy that came to dominate Japanese life in the late 1930s, but also the very fact that this document treats *kotodama* under no less important a heading than *makoto* demonstrates just how important this term and the concept held to lie behind it were considered to be in the entire fascist-nationalist ideology for which the *Kokutai no Hongi* text served as the principal blueprint.

Nor must it be overlooked that this same document employs *kotodama* as the chief hermeneutic gloss for the most august context imaginable—the very *locus classicus* for the term *makoto* as employed by the Meiji emperor himself. The Meiji emperor had summed up the five articles of his *Rescript* under the single term *makoto,* and the *Kokutai no Hongi* authors chose to illustrate this same association of *makoto* with *kotodama.* One could hardly ask for a more striking documentation of the importance that the architects of the fascist-nationalism of the 1930s attached to the term with which we are here concerned.

The immediately relevant passage from the *Kokutai no Hongi* may be translated along the following lines, taking it up after its citation of the Meiji emperor's epitome of his own *Five Articles* as being summed up in the single word *makoto:* "Furthermore, it is particularly and solely deeds that possess sincerity that are true deeds. True words most often become true deeds. It is particularly those words and solely those that are liable to be put into practice that are true words. Our nation's ideology of *kotodama* has its basis in this fact; words that are not liable to be put into practice are shunned and not uttered. This is the sincerity of the human heart. *Kotodama* means language that is filled with sincerity, and such language possesses mighty movement. In other words, it possesses limitless power and is comprehensible everywhere without limitation. This is what is meant in the *Man'yōshū* by 'a land to which *kotodama* brings good fortune.' Once anything is verbalized, it must necessarily be carried out; consequently, words having reference to anything that cannot be carried out are not lightly uttered. Further, once anything has been verbalized, it must necessarily be carried out; nay, the word that possesses sincerity, by reason of *kotodama,* must inevitably be carried out. Thus, sincerity is found in the fundamental principle of the word able to become the deed. There is no room for self in sincerity. All of oneself must be cast aside in speech, for it is in the deed and in the deed alone that sincerity is to be found, and there only that sincerity shines forth."

The *Kokutai no Hongi* is always a difficult, as well as a tedious, document to read. This is true no matter what the content of any specific portion of the text may be. But when Hisamatsu and his coauthors turned their attention to the Japanese language, they really outdid themselves in jargon-clotted rhetoric. The passages that deal with the Japanese language are all so extremely involved and so filled with purposeful obscurities of terminology and expression that many of them quite understandably baffled translators who first undertook to render the *Kokutai no Hongi* into English in 1949. These translators, whose work we generally rely upon elsewhere throughout the present discussion for citations of the *Kokutai no Hongi,* were generally adept in tracing their way through the terminological thickets of this text. But the authors of the original document intertwined so many unwarranted assumptions and unsubstantiated conclusions about the Japanese language and its putative *kotodama* that they ended in simply obscuring the point of much of the passage cited above, so much so that the 1949 translators were confounded by this entire section. That is why it has had to be retranslated here in order to make clear what is actually at issue in this portion of the document.

Almost anyone who reads and rereads the repetitions and incantations of the *Kokutai no Hongi,* either in the cliché-besotted Japanese of the original or in literal translation as above, will almost surely be seized with a strong, indeed an overpowering desire to put all this behind and to forget about such perversions of language and sense as soon as possible. At the same time, the reader will also quite likely be hard put to believe that anyone ever took any of this seriously—which might, if true, be all the more justification for putting all this behind us once and for all.

Unfortunately, neither of these courses of action is possible. We cannot put all this *Kokutai no Hongi* nonsense behind us because influential elements in contemporary Japanese intellectual and academic circles will not let us do so. Nor can we console ourselves with the argument that no one in Japan ever really took any of this seriously. Not only do we know that they did in the past, but we are now faced daily with the most melancholy evidence that many Japanese still take it seriously—and, even more ominously, that many are actively trying to persuade others to do the same. There is today abundant evidence for a revival of the *kotodama* cult in terms so close to those originally found in the *Kokutai no Hongi* that virtually all possibility either of coincidence or of independent invention must be ruled out.

Before inspecting something of how this new revival of the *Kokutai no Hongi* cult of the *kotodama* is being carried out in modern Japan and before investigating some of the ways in which it fits into the larger picture of the cult of Nihongo as a modern sustaining myth in contemporary Japanese society, it is important to reassure ourselves that all this is just nonsense. In point of fact, it is worse than nonsense. The cult of *kotodama* as it appears in the *Kokutai no Hongi* represents nothing more or less than a conscious distortion of several different strains of early Japanese indigenous folk religion in order to make these quite innocent materials from Japanese antiquity serve the twisted purposes of the authors of the document in question.

The *Kokutai no Hongi* coauthors, most of whom were, like their leader Hisamatsu, specialists in the study of traditional Japanese literature, naturally drew most of their materials from their own field of study. This explains why we find numerous references to the *Man'yōshū,* the earliest anthology of Japanese poetry, scattered through the document. Capitalizing upon the general ignorance of the Japanese public with regard to the precise meaning of most of these difficult early texts, the authors of the *Kokutai no Hongi* proceeded to twist and pervert out of all historical shape what are, in the original *Man'yōshū* poems, extremely innocent and quite uncomplicated references to a set of early Japanese folk beliefs. In chapter 5, we have already seen how this was done to distort the idea of *kötöage* into a cult of silence. The story is much the same for *kotodama,* except that here even greater violence had to be done to the truth of the matter.

Early Japanese society, like many other early societies, held the belief that a certain amount of magic lurked within the name for anything. This meant that to know a name, whether of a person, a place, or a thing, was equivalent to having a certain amount of power that could be brought to bear toward controlling the entity thus named. The entire set of beliefs in question is only a subvariety of what cultural anthropologists have sometimes called sympathetic magic. In their quest for a means of controlling the environment in which they were struggling to survive, early humans often hit upon the idea of manipulating some token of the larger entity with which they were concerned. The hope was that the larger entity would as a result somehow follow suit and thus be forced to act in magical conformity with the desires of society.

Thus, in its search for a way to make rain, an early society often performed ceremonies involving the ceremonial manipulation of a small amount of water. The idea, of course, was that the larger entity—rain—would somehow put itself under the society's control by reason of these rituals with a small quantity of water, since rain was indubitably in its essence water. It was hoped that the whole would respond in sympathy with the part, hence the term sympathetic magic.

The cult of the name represented a somewhat more advanced refinement of this general sympathetic-magic approach. Rather than try to turn the trick by manipulating a small quantity of an analogous substance—water for rain, a small portion of rice for the food supply, etc.—the name of the larger entity was invoked. Thus the belief was gradually evolved that by ritually pronouncing the "correct name" of something, that something would be placed under one's power and eventual control. Judaism, even at its most advanced stage of theological and intellectual development, retained extremely interesting and significant traces of this variety of sympathetic magic. The Old Testament is full of examples in which "knowing the name" of a person or place gives an individual effective control over the person or place in question. When Jacob wrestled with the angel, his learning the angel's name, and the angel's learning his, were the chief issues at stake. And nothing was more momentous in the classical Judaic religion than the annual ritual occasion when the high priest solemnly, and secretly, pronounced the word Yahweh. For this was believed to be the ineffable name of God, too sacred ever to be written out in full even in the holy texts and still today never uttered by observant Jews. Christianity, in its turn, inherited a full helping of this cult of the name from its Judaic origins. Any Western reader will be able to supply numerous examples of the ways in which the entire idea, while still retaining its ultimate roots in sympathetic magic, survives in countless ways throughout the culture of this, our own post-Christian age.

All this means that identification of the name of something with the thing itself and the belief that a name, once known and mastered, might be employed in magical practices that would place the thing thus named under the power or within the control of the person uttering that name are surely not unique to early Japan. Nor is any particular wonder to be attached to the fact that references both to the belief and to a number of fairly formalized rituals of naming as an overt magical rite are to be found in such repositories of early Japanese poetic art as the *Man'yōshū*.

With the introduction of Buddhist religion and culture to Japan from the middle of the sixth century on, early folk beliefs of the indigenous Japanese cults, such as the practice of sympathetic magic, were gradually replaced or forgotten. This happened mostly because the folk beliefs were generally too simple and too naive to remain attractive when they were confronted with the intellectual competition represented by the sophisticated philosophy of the new, imported religion.

What happened in Japan in this connection was much the same as what happened to the older pagan cults of Europe with the coming of Christianity. And by and large it happened in both places for much the same reasons. But in the case of Japan, the pre-Buddhist beliefs did not offer the same evidence of vitality that much of the religion of pre-Christian Europe did. In Japan, pre-Buddhist beliefs such as the belief in the power of names or words—the same pre-Buddhist elements of folk belief upon which the *Kokutai no Hongi* authors erected their tissue of misrepresentation and twisted half-truths— soon became nothing more than philological curiosities. The beliefs survived if at all only in a few chance mentions in the earlier texts. In much the same fashion and for many of the same reasons, the supposedly indigenous Japanese religion known as Shinto does not, in most instances, represent a direct inheritance from pre-Buddhist beliefs. It too is a largely artificial concoction of recent times, combining carefully assembled elements of disparate origins; but that story, important though it is for an understanding of modern Japanese life, cannot be told here.

What the authors of the *Kokutai no Hongi* did, then, was to extract from the *Man'yōshū* several of the more striking references to this older belief in the magical power of names as it existed in early Japanese religious life and then to twist the significance of these texts in such a way as to make it appear that these early texts showed that the ancient Japanese had had a belief in a mystical power or spirit, the so-called *kotodama,* that somehow distinguished the Japanese language from all other human languages, at the same time that it made Japanese social life and organization superior to all other forms of human society and national groups.

Again, the *Kokutai no Hongi* authors had no particular monopoly on the subtle perversion of philology. We need look no further for a perfect if chilling parallel than the excesses of some of the German linguists and philologists, who similarly attempted to make the data concerning the interrelationships between the Indo-European languages serve the racist goals of National Socialism and to validate Nazi claims for the superiority of an Aryan race, culture, and linguistic stock. Both represented wholesale and conscious distortions of truth, and history can only record that the practitioners of both sets of lies were equally culpable, even though the superiority of German technology tempted the National Socialists to extremes to which the Japanese were not able to aspire.

So much for the recent origins of the *kotodama* cult: it is sufficient to understand that it begins with the *Kokutai no Hongi* and that it is all utter nonsense, nonsense that would be risible if it did not so easily lend itself to such perverse ends. And there the matter might mercifully be permitted to rest undisturbed, were it not for the inescapable evidence now at hand for a significant effort in certain Japanese circles to revive the whole shoddy structure.

A significant landmark in the progress of this current revival of the myth of *kotodama* may be identified in the publication of an English translation in the *Japan Echo* (Winter 1974) of an article by Professor Shōichi Watanabe, originally published in Japanese in the popular and enterprising monthly magazine *Shokun* in August of the same year. This latest official revival of the myth ought probably to be dated from the publication of this English version of Watanabe's article in the *Japan Echo* rather than from the appearance of its original Japanese text in *Shokun,* because this was the first issue of the *Japan Echo* to receive worldwide distribution from Japanese embassies and consulates throughout the English-reading world. It is also difficult to believe that the appearance of Watanabe's article under the title "On the Japanese Language" in the first issue of the *Japan Echo* to receive such official distribution by the Ministry of Foreign Affairs was a total coincidence.

Watanabe is a member of the faculty of Sophia University in Tokyo, a Jesuit institution of higher education founded by and originally under the direction of the German Province of that order. He is a specialist in German language and literature who also teaches and writes widely about English. He demonstrates his impressive familiarity with both languages in the opening passage of his *kotodama* article, where he compares German and Japanese, which he believes are examples of "living languages" (in the very special sense in which that term was used by the German patriot-philosopher Johann Gottlieb Fichte [1762–1814]), with French and the other Romance languages, which for Fichte—and now apparently for Watanabe also—are examples of "dead" languages: "After pondering his statements, it is probably safe to conclude that what Fichte called a 'living' language is, in the Japanese style of expression, a language with 'spirit,' and a 'dead' language, one without it. Having made such a definition, we are compelled to examine what is widely known in Japanese as *koto-dama* (the spirit of language), whose substance, however, remains very much in obscurity."

Watanabe continues his discussion with an attempt at demonstrating, originally for his Japanese readers but then also in the *Japan Echo* for foreign readers as well, just what this obscure concept of the *kotodama* consists of and how it distinguishes the Japanese language—the language that, as he most concretely puts it, "goes to the root of Japanese national identity." For the purpose of this demonstration he employs what may be considered to be a variation of the comparative method—he contrasts a translation into doggerel English by a certain J. Tsunashima, otherwise unknown, of *Man'-yōshū* poem 2 with the "This royal throne of kings, this sceptered isle . . ." speech from Shakespeare's *Richard II.*

It will come as no great surprise to learn that when, in this fashion, one of Shakespeare's most stately passages is pitted against a childish English version of an early *Man'yōshū* poem, Shakespeare wins. What is surprising, however, is the interpretation that Watanabe puts upon the outcome of this clearly unequal match: "When rendered into their own language, foreigners will be able to fully appreciate the meaning, as well as grasp the dynamism, of [Shakespeare's] lines. [But] seen rhetorically, or in terms of its superficial, semantic contents, (which may be communicable to foreigners in translation), this unsophisticated poem [*Man'yōshū* 2] is almost equal in quality to a scribble a middle-school child on a school excursion might make on a post card for home. Nevertheless, this much is almost enough for Japanese to have their soul stirred. The only possible explanation is that in the emperor's poem [*Man'yōshū* 2 is attributed to the emperor Jomei], there is *koto-dama* at work, which is warrantable among the Japanese people as a whole. It is neither a question of the transfer of logical ideas nor that of intellectual comprehension, but one which concerns something quite close to the 'mental capacity for the formation of genius,' as referred to by Kant in his *The Critique of Judgment*."

Even leaving aside the suggested implication of Kant (the reference to his *Kritik der Urteilskraft* of 1790) and the question of what possible relevance he might have in this case, Watanabe's essential point is clear enough. According to him, Japanese differs from foreign languages; and, in particular, Japanese poetic expression differs from foreign poetic expression by the fact of the existence of a palpable quality present in the former but lacking in the latter. It is the existence of this quality that makes Japanese poetry in particular and Japanese literature in general uncommunicative in translation. Shakespeare lacks this, whatever it is, and so Shakespeare may be translated, and his text will still communicate what he had to say to the intellect and emotions of the reader of that translation. But the *Man'yōshū* does have it, which means that when we translate the *Man'yōshū* for foreigners, they find nothing in it for their intellect and virtually nothing for their emotions (though to the Japanese it still speaks to both). At the same time, this very untranslatability is the principal mark of the internal existence of this special linguistic quality, what Shakespeare lacks but what the *Man'yōshū* has in abundance. And while Watanabe and all the other Japanese critics have a difficult time categorizing or further identifying it, what they do not lack is a name: it is *kotodama*.

In point of fact, by introducing Shakespeare in this fashion into his already heavily weighted argument and comparison, Watanabe tells us more about his own academic background and training than he does about anything related to Japanese language or literature. What we have to deal with here is, among many other things, essentially a twentieth-century Japanese reflex of the *Shakespearomanie* that swept through German scholarship in the nineteenth century (the term itself dates from 1827). Those German poets and scholars who found Shakespeare to be "more than anyone else the Creativity of life itself made man" (*wie kein anderer das menschgewordene Schopfertum des Lebens selbst*) were the very same who claimed that the "inmost destiny" (*innerstes Schicksal*) of the German language was to be found in translation and, above all else, in translation of Shakespeare. Watanabe has, either intentionally or unconsciously, taken over the bulk of the assumptions and argumentation of the *Shakespearomanie,* substituting Japanese for German, *mutatis mutandis.* All this is very much, to quote Goethe, *Shakespeare und kein Ende.* The entire issue of the influence of German scholarship from the previous century upon present-day Japanese work on Japanese language and literature is one that would take us too far afield, but it deserves serious attention in another place. In the meantime, a brilliant introduction to the overall scientific problem of translation as treated in German scholarship and to the German cult of Shakespeare translation in particular is available in George Steiner's *After Babel: Aspects of Language and Translation.*

Now we understand something of the way in which the *kotodama* cult of the 1930s is currently being revived for popular consumption, and we have identified something of the implications that attach to its proximate source in the *Kokutai no Hongi.* But the discovery that official sources, including Japanese embassies and consulates abroad, are actively involved in giving public circulation to these newly revived ideas has naturally caused a certain stir.

I had occasion to call the attention of readers particularly interested in questions of modern Japanese society and culture to this curious state of affairs in mid-1977 in an article in the *Journal of Japanese Studies* that for the first time discussed this new revival of the *kotodama* cult and at the same time provided philological evidence of a rather technical nature demonstrating the main ways in which the *Kokutai no Hongi* authors had managed to distort the materials they found in the early Japanese texts in order to come up with their spurious tenets.

The publication of this article, as was only to be expected, caused quite a storm in Japanese teacups; a foreign cat had at last been set among the *kotodama* pigeons. Shortly after the piece appeared, I was accosted during a lunch at the Embassy of Japan in Washington, D.C., by a visiting Japanese professor, also—by one of those strange coincidences—a guest at the same affair. He began the conversation by telling me that I knew nothing about Japan or the Japanese and understood nothing about the Japanese language. He went on to argue that it was only further evidence of my total ignorance of his country, his countrymen, and their language for me even to suspect that Professor Watanabe, or the Ministry of Foreign Affairs, or anyone else in this world or the next was trying to revive the *kotodama* cult.

Soon thereafter I began to receive a good deal of mail from various Japanese sources interested in the same problem, almost all of it unpleasant in the extreme. The publishers of the *Japan Echo* wrote to tell me that I was quite incorrect in suggesting that their publication in any way represented the official or unofficial views of the Japanese government or of the Ministry of Foreign Affairs. Their journal, I was to understand, was simply the work of a lot of well-meaning people with a lifetime supply of glossy coated stock and unlimited access to a six-color high-speed rotary press; and it was distributed free to the world at large through Japanese embassies and consulates just for the sheer fun of the whole thing.

Watanabe wrote to tell me I had misunderstood everything, and several other people not then or now readily identifiable also wrote, over a period of months, to tell me much the same thing. Fortunately no one suggested taking me to the International Court at the Hague, but just about everything else in the way of sanctions and restrictions on my future activities along these lines was brought up by one or another of these correspondents. Finally, I noted that in subsequent issues of the *Japan Echo* (which despite all the fuss continues to arrive from the consulate on time) the notice under the publication's masthead that earlier had authorized free and unrestricted republication of all the articles printed in the magazine now was changed to read that "nothing in this publication may be reprinted without express permission of the publisher."

But institutions, like individuals, have conveniently short memories. The publishers of *Japan Echo* have proved to be no exception to this old saw. Close on the heels of their strident denials that there was the least hint of official sponsorship or guidance behind the glossy pages of their publication, the managing editor of the *Japan Echo,* Takeshi Mochida, published an article describing the *Echo,* its history, and its mission in *The Japan Foundation Newsletter* (August–September 1978). His piece, which carries the subtitle "A Journal of Opinion to Bridge the Communication Gap," describes the *Japan Echo* and its auspices as follows: "*Japan Echo* . . . had its beginnings in response to suggestions by friends in the Ministry of Foreign Affairs and elsewhere, concerned over the pervasive misunderstanding of Japan among foreigners and particularly critical of journalists for sending distorted news reports overseas. . . . I remember that when I was covering the Japan–U.S. textile negotiations . . . I was astonished by the highly misleading stories on Japan's stand, both government and private, being disseminated from Tokyo by foreign media. This and similar experiences prompted frequent debates among journalists and friends in the Foreign Ministry as to how best to help people overseas see Japan as it really is. Out of these discussions came the idea of translating significant articles from leading Japanese magazines in *Japan Echo.* . . . With four years of experience under our belts, we feel that we are winning the battle but we are also aware that it is a battle with no real end. . . . Two reasons seem to account for the growing popularity of *Japan Echo:* the timeliness of the topics chosen and the scrupulousness with which the editors select articles that faithfully reflect a spectrum of responsible and informed Japanese opinion."

So now at last we know. How grateful we should all be to everyone concerned for having cleared up this little matter of who is behind the *Japan Echo* and who is responsible for using its pages for reviving the spectral shades of *kotodama* and all that this term implies. Just a few of what would in American political life be called "the good old boys"—or, as Mochida expresses it so neatly, "friends in the Ministry of Foreign Affairs and elsewhere." They sit around, presumably at the Foreign Ministry "and elsewhere," and worry night and day about "how best to help people overseas see Japan as it really is," pausing from these concerns only long enough to be "astonished by the highly misleading stories . . . disseminated from Tokyo by foreign media."

This help, it would appear, they believe to be best provided by reaching back into the darkest days of Japan's past to serve up a reseasoned stew bringing together every fetid ingredient that poisoned the wells of Japanese intellectual, spiritual, and moral life a generation ago. Confident that few of their foreign readers will recognize the source of their "clarifications," they turn to the half-forgotten pages of the *Kokutai no Hongi* to help people "see Japan as it really is." Theirs sounds like a busy and rewarding life; one can only ask how they make a living at it and, for that matter, where the "elsewhere" is that features so prominently in their game plan.

Once we understand where this modern revival of the *kotodama* cult actually originates, and once we learn something of the way in which its materials are drawn directly from the *Kokutai no Hongi*—the document that originally distorted the facts of early Japanese folk religion in an attempt to document Hisamatsu's nationalistic fantasies—we can see just how nonsensical all this business of a special, unique "spirit of the Japanese language" really is. It also becomes clear that any modern revival of this cult is potentially dangerous for contemporary Japanese cultural and intellectual life.

Nonsense is not necessarily harmless simply because it is nonsense. Hitler's concept of racial purity was also nonsense, but the fact that it was nonsense did not prevent it from doing untold damage. Hundreds of thousands of innocent people died terrible deaths in Europe of the 1940s because of erudite German academic nonsense in high places. The *Kokutai no Hongi's* perverted vision of a unique, intrinsically superior Japanese state, civilization, and language was nonsense too, but hundreds of thousands of Japanese died fiery deaths in the aftermath of this vision.

The Japanese language has no spirit that distinguishes it in any manner, shape, or form from any other language. It has no particular power, no unique gift that sets it apart from other varieties of the human linguistic experience. To claim, with the editors of the *Japan Echo*, that it does is nonsense—and worse. It is worse than nonsense because, when such claims are circulated throughout the world "in response to suggestions by friends in the Ministry of Foreign Affairs and elsewhere," someone somewhere must point out the potential danger that lurks in all of this, even at the risk of appearing to be rude or of being called ignorant. It is easy to understand why Japanese scholars and critics are less than pleased by the spectacle of foreign observers stridently pointing out to the world jest how absurd and how dangerous all this is; but if the sight does indeed disturb them so, then their best course of action might well be to begin to contradict some of this official nonsense themselves. And this, for one reason or another, they have been remarkably slow to do.

CHAPTER EIGHT

Race and Language:
Language and Race

> To be a Japanese, at the same time that it means
> being a member of the Japanese race, also means
> speaking the Japanese language. —Takao Suzuki,
> lecture of March 18, 1978, on "Why Teach
> Nihongo to the Foreigners?"

THE ANTIMYTH of silence and the cult of *koto-dama*, the "spirit of the Japanese language," are by no means the only ideas from the *Kokutai no Hongi* ideology to survive to the present day; would that they were. The unfortunate inheritance of several other equally non-sensical notions, all going back directly to the exaggerated nationalism of Hisamatsu and his colleagues, runs like a vivid, disfiguring stain throughout the otherwise generally drab fabric of much contemporary Japanese intellectual life. And among all these inheritances from the 1940s, none is probably of more serious long-range consequence for Japan in its new role as a member of the world community than the *Kokutai no Hongi* teaching that Japanese race is exactly equivalent to Japanese language. At the same time, no other single concept from the 1940s has proven more difficult to eradicate.

We have already seen something of the substantial efforts currently under way in certain Japanese circles, aiming at a formal revival of the *kotodama* nonsense as taught in the *Kokutai no Hongi*. The best—and at the same time the worst—that can be said of that document's equation of race with language is that, unlike the somewhat more sophisticated *kotodama* cult, this identification of Japanese race with the Japanese language does not appear to stand in need of any modern revival. This particular idea from the 1940s has never shown the least sign of passing away, not even for a moment. There is no need to revive it; it is still quite as alive and well as it ever was.

Nor can one report, as much as one would like to, that contemporary Japanese academic and intellectual circles appear to be doing anything to loosen, or even to relax slightly, the strangling effects that this pernicious and totally false equation of disparate entities exercises over all areas of Japanese life and culture. To the contrary, they give every evidence of doing their best to tighten even further the grip that this equation of race and language continues to hold on Japanese life.

In a pluralistic society such as that of the United States, or indeed in the societies of most modern industrial nations, even those like West Germany, France, or Italy that have a large amount of racial homogeneity, most people are quite accustomed to making the necessary distinction between race and language. Indeed, most non-Japanese will not be in the least puzzled either by the distinction, nor by the necessity for making it. All that will probably puzzle them in this connection is the way in which modern Japanese life and culture customarily confuse these two quite separate entities.

After all, in the United States almost everyone is accustomed to living together with people of different races. At the same time, again without significant exception, everyone generally comes into frequent contact with people who either can or perhaps customarily do speak a language different from one's own. Of course, all this is particularly true of the American cities, and less the case in the hinterland of so-called Middle America or even in the northwestern sections of the country. But despite these apparent exceptions—which are really only exceptions that prove the rule—most people in the United States are hardly likely to equate language and race, even though their parents or grandparents may have done so.

To take another example, even though the population of West Germany is far more homogeneous than is that of the United States, every German city of any size today has a large (and potentially difficult and problematic) resident population of "guest workers." This alone is enough to make it unlikely that most citizens of the Federal Republic will equate language with race. The children of the "guest workers" from Turkey, the Balkans, and other places grow up speaking German to a greater or lesser extent. Providing ways for both them and their parents to gain a working command of the German language sufficient for effective functioning in the society in which they apparently are going to continue to live is one of the major problems of secondary education in West Germany today. Even in the recent past, when the National Socialists carried out their inhuman implementation of

Hitler's racist theories, there was no confusion between language and race in Germany. German Jews were slaughtered simply because they were Jews; no one cared that most of them spoke only German.

All this means that for most non-Japanese observers today, the identification of race with language, and the confusion of one with the other, plays so little part in contemporary thought that they will generally find Japanese discussion along these lines, based as almost all of it is on the assumption of a total identification of one with the other, all but impossible to follow. Often we react negatively to a discussion that we can neither follow nor understand. This means that the customary Japanese equation of race and language also provides one of the most serious sources of misunderstanding between Japanese and foreigners. Most foreigners are simply unprepared, either intellectually or by previous experience, for their first encounter with the rampant Japanese racism that results from this essential confusion between language and race. This confusion is thus not only internally destructive for Japanese society; it also contains within itself the potential for continuing mistrust between Japan and the rest of the world.

There is a great danger inherent in all this, a danger that carries with it the genuine possibility for the most serious misunderstandings between the Japanese and outsiders to their society and culture. When most non-Japanese encounter the usual manifestations of this habitual Japanese equation of language with race, there is the great danger that they will doubt the good faith—or if not the good faith, perhaps the good sense—of the Japanese who persist in perpetuating this confusion. For the person outside Japanese society who becomes interested in this question, the principal problem is keeping in mind that the Japanese are quite sincere about all this, and also that when they insist that language and race are one and the same they are not consciously attempting to deceive either themselves or others, i.e., they are keeping perfectly good faith. But they are also seriously misled on this topic. They were misled by the *Kokutai no Hongi,* and they have been misled ever since.

After all, keeping race separate and distinct from language really ought to be the simplest thing in the world. And the best reason for thus keeping them apart also happens to be the most obvious one: everyone knows that you can change your language, because many people have done so and still frequently do; but everyone also knows that you cannot change your race. The point is so simple that it hardly requires further elaboration. What must be done instead is to emphasize that most modern Japanese on almost every level of the society, including intellectual and academic circles where all this is to be the least expected, simply do not make a distinction between race and language, basic though this differentiation appears to be to almost everyone else in the modern world.

One must first put oneself into the frame of mind that is rooted in this erroneous identification of race with language, before one will be in a position to comprehend any of the all too numerous subsidiary errors that arise from this basic blunder. It is neither necessary nor possible to approve of this confusion or to condone it; but it is important to realize how deeply and sincerely most modern Japanese believe in it, if we are to make progress in understanding what most modern Japanese believe—both about themselves and about us.

Once we make this attempt, we are first of all struck by the fact that confusing the Japanese language with the Japanese race lands us, along with the modern Japanese, squarely in the middle of a tightly enclosed circular maze from which it is then all but impossible to extract ourselves—or them. This is the same sociolinguistic maze that Hisamatsu and his *Kokutai no Hongi* colleagues so carefully constructed in the 1930s, and it has survived in excellent repair down to the present day. Once one enters its confines, around and merrily around one goes in any and all directions except out, for there is no escape from the circularity of its logic.

Japanese race consists in using the Japanese language. But how does one become a member of the Japanese race? By being born into it, of course, just as one becomes a member of any other race. Can one acquire Japanese race except by being born a Japanese? Hardly. Can anyone not already born into the Japanese race learn the Japanese language? Hardly; no more than anyone can arrange to be born again as a Japanese. But what if someone not a Japanese by right of race or a member of that race by right of birth does manage to acquire some proficiency in the Japanese language? Well, in that case, the system literally makes no intellectual provision at all for his or her very existence. Such a person is a nonperson within the terms and definitions of Japanese social order; and a nonperson can only have a shadowy and most unsatisfactory nonexistence.

This nonperson's nonexistence is predicated upon the society's assumption that the Japanese-speaking foreigner is for some unknown reason involved in working out serious logical contradictions in his or her life. What this reason may be is unknown, and the unknown is always potentially dangerous and a source of fear. Why any outsider would wish to behave in such an illogical manner can only be guessed; all the possible guesses only multiply the suspected dangers, while at the same time they magnify the inchoate fears. He or she had better be watched pretty carefully; obviously something is seriously amiss somewhere, otherwise why would this foreigner be speaking Japanese?

The problem is not great so long as the foreigner's command of the Japanese language remains on a rudimentary level. But once it gets too close to the real thing for the comfort of Japanese sociolinguistic sentiments, then he or she is in real trouble. After all, race is language and language is race. Race cannot be acquired or learned, and so by logical extension, neither can the Japanese language; you have to be born to the one as to the other. A merry-go-round indeed—except that the implications of this racial-linguistic maze for modern Japanese life and for the lives of foreigners who find themselves in contact with modern Japanese life turn out more often than not to be anything but merry.

Japanese social custom tends to be hospitable and convivial in its treatment of guests and foreigners. This was true even in the dark days following the war, when there was not much to eat and drink for anyone, much less for guests. Today, when food, whiskey, and money are all equally plentiful, Japanese hospitality can often be as overwhelming as it is warm. This long-standing, deeply implanted tradition of hospitality toward visitors renders the shock afforded by the ultimate realization of Japanese racism, particularly as it results from the identification of race with language, all the more severe.

On the one hand, the foreign visitor to Japan, whether he or she is there for a long or short time, cannot but be favorably impressed by the genuine concern, the solicitude for personal welfare, and the warm hospitality that will be extended on every hand, as often as the occasion presents itself—and sometimes oftener. But on the other hand, there is the ultimate refusal to admit the foreigner, the outsider, the non-Japanese—who is non-Japanese in race and hence non-Japanese in language, or similarly, non-Japanese in language because non-Japanese in race—to the genuine, inner circles of the society. Eat and drink your fill, enjoy our hospitality, watch our dances and listen to our curious musical instruments. But do not try to understand us. Do not try to join us within our society in any significant way. You may not because you cannot—and you cannot because you may not. These ideas survived the fire raids of the 1940s, so there is little reason to suppose that they cannot also survive the affluence of today.

Concrete implementation of this language-equals-race-equals-language maze is offered on every hand by the provisions of Japanese law, as well as by the customary limits within which Japanese law is applied and enforced. (The non-Japanese reader must note that these two, i.e., Japanese law on the one hand and the customary limits within which such law is applied and enforced on the other, are seldom identical or seldom even exhibit the same rough outlines or dimensions. What the Japanese law codes say is, as in any modern state, naturally important; but in Japan the selective ways in which those codes may or may not be enforced and applied to any particular case in question are of equal, sometimes of greater, and always of rather surprising importance.)

No one would attempt to deny, of course, that the relatively high degree of racial uniformity in modern Japan plays its part in perpetuating the linguistic-racial identification. Most people who live in Japan today are Japanese; and since all of them who have learned to talk do indeed speak the Japanese language, the association of language with race does have its obvious correlation with the facts of the real world. This does not make it correct; it only makes it easier to believe. At the same time, it is important to point out, if only briefly, two important exceptions that again prove the rule in this connection. The first has to do with the status of the large resident population of Koreans in modern Japan. The second concerns the historical background of Japan's presently highly homogeneous racial makeup.

The situation in which the resident Koreans find themselves in modern Japan illustrates in a most striking and disagreeable fashion the ultimate hopelessness of anyone trying to escape from the language-equals-race maze. Most of these Korean residents either came to Japan themselves during the period of Japanese colonial rule over Korea or they are the children of Koreans who did so.

During that period of history, Korea was a colony totally subject to Japan. This meant that the Koreans who came to Japan—and most of them were brought under force to serve as laborers in a variety of war-related industries—were Japanese subjects, but they were seldom Japanese citizens. (The distinction between subjects and citizens will be unfamiliar to many Americans, but English readers will recognize what it means, since the distinction is still made in British colonies, as for example in Hong Kong, where all resident Chinese are British subjects, but only a select few are permitted to become British citizens.)

Following the surrender of Japan to the Allies in World War II, Korea of course ceased to be an integral part of the Japanese state and once more became an independent country. Some of the Korean residents in Japan returned, or were forced to return, to the Korean peninsula. But at least as many stayed on in Japan, where they or their children still are today. Their situation since then has continued to be as anomalous legally as it is ideologically. Legally, they were never Japanese citizens, only Japanese subjects; but this in turn meant that following the war, when Japan was no longer permitted to have colonies, their status as subjects apparently evaporated without their receiving compensatory status as citizens. Under postwar Japanese law, they have remained resident aliens and must register with government immigration authorities at regular intervals as aliens, even though most of them have never been outside Japan in their lives.

This large population of Korean resident aliens in modern Japan presents a number of important phenomena to the student of contemporary Japanese society and culture. The many kinds of discrimination to which these persons continue to be subjected, particularly with respect to opportunities for education and employment, are striking. So also is the adamant refusal of Japanese society to let them pass as Japanese, even when they themselves try to conceal their ethnic identity by such methods as changing their Korean surnames (such as Kim, Yi, Pak, and the like) to ostensibly Japanese names. Physically, few of the Korean resident aliens in Japan can easily be distinguished from Japanese. If a Kim becomes a Kaneda or a Kanezawa, there ought to be no easy way to continue to discriminate against him or her in school admissions, employment applications, and the like. There ought not to be—and yet there is.

The method used is the so-called *koseki shōhon*. This is an official, notarized transcript of the individual's complete vital-statistics dossier, kept permanently on file in a local government office somewhere in Japan. This dossier is an accumulative record of every detail concerning the life of an individual. It begins with the official record of birth, including names and birthplaces of both parents, followed by a complete listing of all changes in residence, any changes of name, marriages, adoptions, births of children, and so on.

When a transcript of this record is submitted, as by law and custom it must be, together with an application for a job or for admission to an educational institution, it unquestionably identifies the individual in question along racial lines. It makes racial passing out of the question. A person of Korean racial origin in modern Japan can change names, look Japanese, speak Japanese, and act Japanese, and yet he or she will be identified as Korean the moment the official transcript of this *koseki shōhon* is submitted.

The entire system of racially discriminatory treatment that hinges upon the necessity for submitting a transcript of this document is surprisingly thoroughgoing and effective on every level of Japanese society today. The document must be obtained from a local government office and submitted together with almost every one of the hundreds of different kinds of applications that figure so prominently in daily Japanese life on every level. The child who is to be entered in a kindergarten or preschool must present a copy of the *koseki shōhon*. He or she will need it again when applying for university examinations, or a driver's license, or for a position with a company, or for getting married—or for obtaining a passport or travel card. Every time the Korean resident alien in Japan has to present this *koseki shōhon,* he or she is unmistakably identified as a Korean.

The system is quite as invidious, and probably much more thoroughgoing, than any system of passbooks or identification papers used by other modern racist states such as South Africa or the USSR in enforcing their own particular varieties of apartheid and racism. It does the same thing that these other systems do, but it does it under the guise of submitting a supposedly harmless document.

It is, of course, only the linguistic component of this entire discriminatory structure with which we are primarily concerned here. At the same time that this structure of rigid discriminatory treatment for the Korean resident aliens in Japan is perpetuated by the confusion between race and culture, it also neatly gives the lie to the confusion that meanwhile it perpetuates. If this seems quite without logic, that is because, like most of the related patterns in contemporary Japanese sociolinguistic approaches to language, it is precisely that—illogical in the extreme. But its towering illogicality does not in the least impair its effectiveness as a medium for the social repression of the Koreans in Japan—or indeed of any other minority not ethnically Japanese.

All this is especially illogical because the Korean residents in Japan all either speak Japanese with native fluency or, in the case of the second generation, do not know or use or have effective control over any other language *except* Japanese. If the sociolinguistic attitudes that contemporary Japanese society has inherited from the *Kokutai no Hongi* equation of race and language were literally and logically enforced, these people would all be Japanese, not Koreans. But they are not. Why? Because they are Koreans. One seeks in vain for logical structuring in any pattern of racial discrimination and repression, but rarely is it as conspicuous by its absence as in the continued official insistence upon the alien status of the Korean resident population in Japan.

One cannot help but be struck by the selective fashion in which the equation between language and race is enforced in modern Japan. When it can be evoked in order to demonstrate or document the non-Japanese quality of any individual or group, it is. But when invoking it would in fact document the Japanese quality of an individual or group, then it may be conveniently forgotten about. That such selectivity of application should mark this particular pattern of racial discrimination is hardly surprising; after all, selectivity is what any system of discrimination is all about.

Archaeology is one of the fields of humanistic studies that might very well be assumed to be above the moil of mixed-up logic that our investigation of contemporary Japanese sociolinguistic attitudes toward race and language has revealed. Our surprise is therefore all the greater when we find that even otherwise quite responsible and respected archaeologists become embroiled in the same un-logic, when faced with such an ostensibly simple matter as defining what they mean by "Japanese" in such an expression as "Japanese archaeology." When we find such scholars entangled in the rat's-maze cross-identification of race with language and vice versa, we cannot but remark upon the evidence that this provides for just how widespread and all-pervading the confusion between these two entities is on every level of modern Japanese academic and intellectual endeavor.

One example must suffice. Professor Yoshio Higuchi begins his article

on Japanese archaeology, published in a standard reference-book series, with
an attempt toward defining and delimiting the area that his specialty studies.
Such attempt at definition is a normal and indeed a thoroughly laudable
academic technique, or at least it is until we see the problems that Higuchi
soon lets himself become involved in.

Archaeologists deal with physical sites and material finds. Why not define
his field in terms of where the things he studies are or are likely to be found?
Instead, so all-permeating is the identification of Japanese language with
Japanese race that we find him initially attempting to define his field of study
along these lines: Japanese archaeology is the study of the archaeological
remains of the Japanese, and the Japanese are—we could have guessed it
by now!—those who speak Japanese. But having written this, Higuchi reflects
a little reluctantly and also a little surprisingly that there are plenty of foreigners who speak Japanese, and so he proceeds to reframe his definition
of the Japanese whose archaeology he studies along the following lines:
"...they are those who in childhood mastered Japanese as a language of
daily use in Japanese society."

At first glance, it might look as though Higuchi had slipped up and
allowed the Koreans resident in Japan to enter into his definition through
the back door. After all, Koreans in Japan also "master Japanese as a language
of daily use in childhood." But a more careful reading of his statement
clears this up. He gets the Korean minority out of the question with his
caveat that they must also have done all this "in Japanese society." The
Korean resident minority is effectively prevented from functioning within
Japanese society, thanks to such systems as the *koseki shōhon* and other formal
documentary controls upon their identity. So even though they "master
Japanese as a language of daily use in childhood," they do not do this "in
Japanese society." After all, they are Koreans.

It should probably also be mentioned, even if only in passing, that on the
historical level all this makes even less sense. During the formative period
of Japanese culture and civilization, Korean immigrants played a major role
in the development of the society. A close parallel exists in the role of the
Norman French in English life and cultural history. Like the Korean immigrants to early Japan, the Norman French brought to England a sophisticated continental culture embodied in a highly developed world religion—
Christianity in the case of the Normans, Mahayana Buddhism in the case
of the early Korean immigrants. In both instances, together with the religion
came an almost endless list of related cultural innovations—literary art,
sculpture, architecture, music, dress, etiquette, and many other skills, all of
which were to persist long after much of the religion that originally fostered
them had retreated into the background of society.

Much of early Japanese history is distinguished by fraudulent attempts on the part of totally Japanese familial lines to establish alleged genealogical ties with the highly prestigious Korean immigrant lines. Now an equal amount of bureaucratic effort is expended on making sure that no Korean immigrants are able to pass themselves off as Japanese.

Early Japan was racially pluralistic. The Korean immigrant group was the largest, but to them must also be added significant numbers of Chinese, along with Indians and other South Asians from many different places. The consecration of the Great Buddha image in the Tōdai-ji temple at Nara in A.D. 752 brought together an international cross-section of Asia. Buddhist clerical figures resident in Japan but originally coming from half a dozen Mahayana countries across all Asia participated in the elaborate ceremonies held at that time.

Not the least of the ironic historical fabrications of the *Kokutai no Hongi* was the deft way in which the authors managed to appear to extol Japanese antiquity on the one hand, while on the other they neatly swept out of sight all the evidence that the early historical record preserves for the multinational, pluralistic character of the formative period of Japanese culture and civilization. If it's old and Japanese, they taught in effect, it's good. But in order to combine this approach with their fascist-nationalistic presumptions, they were first of all forced to conceal by any means, fair or foul, the evidence that remains in the record for the way in which many things in Japanese culture are both old and good, but are not ethnically Japanese. The only way to cut through this anomaly was to obscure and falsify the historical record, which they did with great zest.

But our principal concern here is with language and with the linguistic dimensions of the false equation of race with language that contemporary Japan has inherited from its fascist past. So many different facets of sociolinguistic attitudes and approaches in modern Japan must, in the final analysis, be traced back to this fallacious equation that it is difficult to draw up a fairly comprehensive list of the major ones, much less discuss each of the items in detail. And even though we may speak and think of these as different facets of the question, in point of fact their differences from one another are almost always superficial and, in every sense of the expression, far more apparent than real. The further we pursue the matter, the more we become convinced that we are dealing here simply with different manifestations of one major, underlying, and quite undifferentiated intellectual blight.

A number of the more striking of these superficially different facets of the question have, as we might expect, to do with foreigners and their employment of the Japanese language. We have already discussed briefly a rather special case, that having to do with the Korean minority in Japan. Next our concern is with non-Korean foreigners in Japan and principally with foreigners of Caucasian racial extraction.

Once we follow through with the implementation of the Nihongo myth and its cult, an enormous range of secondary conclusions follows in a natural order, each more irrational than the one before. The most striking of these secondary conclusions, which are the necessary fallout of the false identification of race with language, has to do with the view that contemporary Japanese society holds of foreigners who manage to learn and use the Japanese language to a greater or lesser extent.

In most cultures, a foreigner who makes the attempt to learn the language of the society in question is thought, by the members of that society and by the native speakers of that language, to be providing a significant indication of the high esteem in which he or she holds both the society and the language. The gesture of learning a foreign language is consequently usually interpreted elsewhere in the world as one respecting, if not actually honoring, both the society and the language in question. Put more simply, the members of most societies are pleased when a foreigner tries to learn and use their language, and they reward such a foreigner with approval in direct proportion to the degree of success achieved with the same.

Thus, it always comes as a particularly rude awakening when the foreigner who is resident in Japan for any length of time finally realizes that Japanese society behaves in a fashion that is directly contrary to this general rule. Japanese society usually distrusts and dislikes any attempt by a foreigner to learn and use the Japanese language. The distrust and dislike grow stronger, and show themselves more and more stridently, the more the foreigner gains fluency in understanding and using the language.

This state of affairs is a direct consequence of the thoroughgoing confusion between language and race that we have been discussing here. If the Japanese language is equivalent to the Japanese race—and we have seen how firmly, if erroneously, contemporary Japanese academic and intellectual circles continue to hold that this equation is true—then any attempt to learn and use the language by a foreigner can only be interpreted as an attempt by that same foreigner to acquire Japanese racial identity and to enter Japanese society. Since both these attempts must, it goes without saying, be resisted by all means, so also must learning and use of the language be resisted. It is the fatal equation of race with language that triggers this sociolinguistic defensive mechanism. The mechanism in turn tries to repulse the supposed invader of racial integrity.

The end result is that far too many otherwise quite sensible and unemotional Japanese continue to display amazingly strong reactions to a foreigner understanding and speaking their language, even though they may otherwise be quite accustomed to everyday dealings with foreigners in considerable numbers. That the foreigner in question may very well have gone to the trouble of learning to speak the language for no more sinister motive than the simple and quite uncomplicated wish to communicate with Japanese individuals—and particularly that he or she may not harbor even the smallest intent or desire to become a Japanese or in any other way invade the Japanese racial entity—never seems to occur to these same people, so threatened do they feel when confronted by a Japanese-speaking, Japanese-understanding, or, worst of all, Japanese-reading-and-writing foreigner.

That many Japanese have an unexpectedly negative reaction to the spectacle of foreigners learning, using, and speaking the Japanese language was documented as early as the first part of the present century. Basil Hall Chamberlain (1850–1935), a pioneer student of the Japanese language and a trenchant observer of "things Japanese," put it in the following way: ". . . seeing that you speak Japanese, they will wag their heads and smile condescendingly, and admit to each other that you are really quite intelligent, —much as we might do in the presence of the learned pig or an ape of somewhat unusual attainments."

Apart from employment situations where, because of the nature of the work involved, foreigners are expected to be able to conduct business in Japanese, little has changed in this connection since Chamberlain's day. Effective employment of the Japanese language in Japan today by anyone who because of his physical characteristics is obviously not of Japanese racial origin still usually elicits exactly the same constellation of reactions that the pioneer English traveler and scholar described so well.

But it will not do simply to document and record these surprising Japanese reactions to the use of their language by others; we must also address ourselves to the question that has occurred to everyone who has, for the simple reason of having a command of the Japanese language, been compared to "the learned pig or an ape of somewhat unusual accomplishments." The question is, in a word, why?

Non-Japanese are not the only ones who have noticed this phenomenon. Professor Suzuki of Keio University, whom we met earlier in the course of chapter 6, has devoted a considerable amount of thought and speculation to the problem of why this happens; and while he does not answer all the questions that arise in this area of Japanese sociolinguistic behavior, his comments on the question can be used as a point of departure for any further analysis of our own. (Nor is this the last time that we shall have occasion to receive assistance from Suzuki; we shall meet him again in chapter 9 as the world's sole living champion of the innate superiority of the Japanese writing system and most impressively of all in chapter 12, where he will try to set us straight on a number of the important if quite unexpected implications of the myth of Nihongo for all of us foreigners who live in the rest of the world.)

Meanwhile, Suzuki suggests that it is useful to approach this particular problem—the question of why the Japanese react as they do to the spectacle of foreigners speaking and using the Japanese language—as nothing more than a special case within his larger hypothesis of the existence of an overall love-hate relationship between Japanese society and its language in general. This hypothesis has already been explored, in somewhat expanded terms of reference, in chapter 6.

Suzuki believes that the largely negative reaction to the spectacle of foreigners speaking and using the Japanese language originates among those relatively few individuals who have themselves had such a firsthand confrontation as part of their personal experience, but that this reaction is soon thereafter propagated through every level of Japanese life and society, where it has become a generalized phenomenon in each successive generation. The speed and thoroughness with which such dissemination of the psychosis is carried out in successive periods of time will surprise no one who is accustomed to the rapid rate at which fashions, fads, and crazes of all sorts circulate throughout modern Japanese life.

Taking a leaf from Suzuki's book, we might even wish to formulate a technical description of the entire range of sociolinguistic behavior with which every non-Japanese who becomes involved in using the Japanese language must inevitably contend. This could be dubbed the "Law of Inverse Returns" and runs to the effect that the better you get at the language, the less credit you are given for your accomplishments; the more fluently you speak it, the less your hard-won skills will do for you in the way of making friends and impressing people. But by the same token (and this is what makes it an "inverse law"), the less you can do with the language, the more you will be praised and encouraged by Japanese society in general and by your Japanese friends in particular.

This curious Law of Inverse Returns applies only, it must be emphasized, to Europeans and Americans, to employ the usual Japanese euphemism for what we equally delicately term Caucasians, i.e., whites. Koreans, Chinese, Southeast Asians, even Indians are exempt from the curiously involute provisions of the law. All nonwhites are expected to know the Japanese language if they live or work in Japan. And it is surely no accident that for several decades following World War II, the only Japanese language-training program for non-Japanese sponsored by the Japanese government was a small language school attached to Chiba University, which specialized exclusively in teaching the language to Southeast Asians and other nonwhites.

As soon as one understands the basic postulates of this Law of Inverse Returns, much of the otherwise quite inexplicable sociolinguistic behavior that every foreigner in Japan has confronted quickly falls into place. What happens may still be as inexplicable as ever, but it is no longer surprising, since it all follows the "Law." The white foreigner who learns a few words of the Japanese language may easily be forgiven for gaining the impression that he has mastered the entire language in a matter of minutes. He has only to say a few daily greetings in anything approaching recognizable pronunciation to be told that he "speaks Japanese better than we do ourselves." If he actually manages to generate a complete sentence, his Japanese friends and drinking companions will all but fall from their barstools in unabashed admiration for his polyglot gifts. Such successes naturally tempt anyone to further experiments, and since one learns any foreign language best by actually using it, in the natural course of events the foreigner in Japan does in most cases get better and better at the language—very slowly and even perhaps very painfully, but eventually he does make real progress.

But it is when the foreigner really begins making progress in control of the spoken language that he first notices the Japanese reaction cooling down. He now hears less and less about how "skillful" (jōzu) he is in Japanese, to the point where he could be forgiven for wondering if he is even communicating successfully, though it is obvious from the extralinguistic evidence available to him that he is. The telephoned order for sushi is delivered; requests for directions to an obscure address are answered. He is obviously able to use the language increasingly well to satisfy his daily needs—in other words, he is now speaking Japanese quite well and effectively. But now there is no mention of how jōzu he is.

The moment of truth, as well as a striking indication that the "Law" is operating, comes when the foreigner happens to be on the scene and in a position to overhear a relative newcomer to the country get the "how skillful you are with Japanese; you speak better than we do ourselves!" treatment that he has apparently outgrown. He can hear for himself how halting and stumbling the newcomer's Japanese really is, and he can hear his Japanese friends on every side telling each other how well the newcomer speaks. The Law of Inverse Returns is at work.

In addition to his many other contributions to the study of this entire field, Suzuki has been particularly active in the analysis of the operation of this Law of Inverse Returns, even though he does not formulate the statement of the law as such. But he has, in several of his recent books, drawn attention to the operation of the law and has also attempted to account for its existence in contemporary Japanese sociolinguistic behavior. He assigns the enduring vitality of the law to the existence of a belief, which he claims is generally held among Japanese, that "foreigners properly ought not to understand Japanese at all" —Gaikokujin ni wa Nihongo ga wakaru hazu ga nai is the way he puts it in Japanese. This locution, for all the difficulties of translation it poses, is quite the usual way of saying what Suzuki is trying to say. The only difficult term to translate here is the noun *hazu,* a word that has semantic adumbrations of normality, regularity, and natural order and other nuances that extend, depending upon the context, into the spheres of ethical and moral conduct. It is this *hazu,* this natural expectation of ethical, moral normality and regularity, this standard of natural order, that is violated when foreigners give evidence that they understand the Japanese language by using it and speaking it. (Any parallel linguistic operation other than the actual use of the language can more easily be forgiven, since no one can ever be sure just how much anyone knows of a foreign language unless he says something in it himself. Otherwise, in the case of mere passive understanding, how do we know for sure he is not just pretending to understand what we say?) "Foreigners properly ought not to understand Japanese at all." When they do, something is ethically, even morally out of joint somewhere in the universe. They ought not to understand and should not understand. When or if they do, then things are in a bad way. Something is out of kilter in the natural order, and caution is necessary on the part of all.

It would be somewhat unfair to Suzuki's theorizing to underestimate the importance of his point, simply because what he has to say in this connection is so deeply cloaked in what might be termed the nontechnical technical language of modern Japanese intellectual dialectic. Such expressions as his phrase *hazu ga nai* (where in addition to the word *hazu,* already discussed, the *ga nai* is simply the subject-marker *ga* followed by the negative-copula "is/has not") are perfectly acceptable Japanese usage in the context of such discussions. They are widely employed by Japanese academics as key terms in the development of their argumentation on a wide variety of topics, language and sociolinguistic behavior included. If we, for our part, happen to find such phrases abstract, difficult to pin down semantically, and prone to crumble into ashes of all-but-total meaninglessness at the merest gesture toward clarification, these are problems involved with our understanding of the Japanese language and of the Japanese mentality that finds its expression in that language, but hardly problems of proper concern for the Japanese themselves.

That does not mean that the problems presented by such turns of phrase, and by their ready adoption by Japanese writers on these subjects, are any less real—for us at least, if not for them. All that we can do in such a case is to abandon the chimera of translation as soon as possible. Instead we must make the attempt to arrive, by paraphrase and our own analysis, at what we hope will eventually be somewhat the same area of semantic confrontation that the Japanese are involved with when they use such terms. In other words, our concern is less with what the Japanese mean when they say *hazu ga nai,* and less with what Suzuki meant when he wrote it, than how, in this particular context, they feel when they use the expression.

Suzuki comes at least partially to our aid as we struggle with the analysis of his expression *hazu ga nai* in this particular context, i.e., the mastery and utilization of the Japanese language by foreigners, and by Caucasian foreigners in particular, by making it clear that for him at least it implies an upset of the natural order of things and also that these implications of upset carry strong secondary adumbrations of the unnatural, even at times of unethical and immoral activities. Clearly the expression refers to things that can only, in the normal course of events, be expected to result in escalating social disorder and sociolinguistic disaster. A foreigner speaking Japanese amounts to the public performance of an unnatural act. The better he speaks it, the more unnatural the act. And such flouting of the natural order can only result in natural retribution. Hence any sensible person shuns direct identification with such dangerous episodes, not to mention the foreigners who openly carry on in this outrageous fashion. Only the fool challenges nature to take its revenge.

The television and other Japanese mass media necessarily stay in close touch with the thinking of the greatest number of the Japanese people; they would not be in business long if they did not. When we find that the media, and TV in particular, have begun to capitalize upon the humorous possibilities of a certain stereotype figure, we have little reason to doubt that this same stereotype is one that large numbers of Japanese at every level of life both recognize and approve of.

Japanese TV frequently gives prominent display to a stereotype figure who is closely tied up with the entire syndrome of negative reactions that Japanese society in general entertains on the subject of foreigners using the Japanese language. The picture that the Japanese media have to offer us of the Japanese-speaking foreigner is not a pleasant one, but it has a great deal to tell us about how Japanese society feels on this particular issue.

The media stereotype involved here is that of a foreigner who is unexpectedly able to use and understand the Japanese language. The media dub such a person a *hen na gaijin*. Even this term itself is highly significant of how Japanese society feels about an outsider who can employ the Japanese language effectively. The word *gaijin* means foreigner. It is never a compliment, but for that matter, it is not actually a put-down either; it is just the way you say foreigner in Japanese. The crux of the matter is rather in the adjective that in this particular expression modifies *gaijin*.

Kenkyusha's *Japanese-English Dictionary* is a reliable guide in matters of this sort. In it, we will find just what *hen na* means, in unmistakably clear terms: it means "strange, queer, odd, crackbrained," according to the Kenkyusha, and the Kenkyusha is not at all far from the mark. Indeed, the semantic spectrum described by this range of terms precisely sums up what the general Japanese reaction is to any foreigner who can understand and speak the Japanese language. The term *hen na* is not complimentary; neither is the attitude behind it.

One can hardly watch any popular Japanese TV program, whether a game show, a situation comedy, or whatever, without one of these *hen na gaijin* coming onto the scene. When one appears it is immediately clear that what makes the particular foreigner in question so strange, queer, odd, and crackbrained is the fact that the foreigner knows and uses the Japanese language.

Most often the *hen na gaijin* on TV is played by a Japanese actor specializing in such representations of foreigners; there is also a small resident stable of genuine foreigners in Tokyo who play such roles. Many of this group, in point of fact, only look like foreigners; actually quite a few are the survivors of a small colony of Turks who fled to Japan in order to escape from racial pogroms in the Near East between the two world wars. They have lived in Japan ever since, growing up to speak no language but Japanese, attending Japanese schools, and otherwise living entirely Japanese lives. But of course, they are not Japanese, because they are foreigners. Since they speak Japanese with native-speaker fluency, they must be taught to imitate the less-than-native speech patterns of a "typical foreigner" in order to do their TV work. One cannot but be reminded of the black American singers who in the 1950s were forced to disguise their normal command of standard English in order to "sound like Negroes" in such musicals as *Porgy and Bess* or *Carmen Jones*. At any rate, and whether the actor playing the *hen na gaijin* is really a non-Japanese or not, the comic or dramatic situations in which he appears make it clear that what is strange, queer, odd, and crackbrained about the person is his command of the Japanese language.

In a typical scene, a Japanese person collides with the *hen na gaijin* in a crowded subway passage. The Japanese tries to apologize to the foreigner in halting English ("*aimu soo saarii*"). The foreigner politely says, in understandable if perhaps not letter-perfect Japanese, that he is sorry too, it was as much his fault as it was the fault of the Japanese, and so on. The Japanese, who had just picked himself up off the floor, falls down again, thunderstruck. The foreigner is speaking Japanese! Unbelievable! Incredible! Unnatural! And rendered effectively dumb by the concatenation of so much wonder and awesome mystery, the Japanese person can only lie prone and mutter, over and over, *hen na gaijin! hen na gaijin!*

As soon as this magic phrase is uttered, the studio audience (or the canned laughter, in more cases) responds with gales of approving laughter. They have all had the same experience or would like to pretend that they have; they too have encountered such strange, queer, odd, and crackbrained persons; they too have collided with a *hen na gaijin* in the subway and have lived to tell the hilarious story. The strange foreigner who can speak Japanese then swiftly disappears from the scene (his is always a small part and soon over), and the comedy or drama, such as it is, goes on to deal with real, normal people.

The *hen na gaijin* is also a feature of many of the quiz or game shows that Japanese TV so faithfully and shamelessly imitates from the American originals. Again, just as in the dramatic programs, these alleged foreigners are most often played by Japanese actors who specialize in such roles. The quiz master or master of ceremonies asks various questions, to which the *hen na gaijin* responds in Japanese just accurate enough to be understood by the audience but not close enough to the real article to be suspect of being fraudulent, which as a matter of fact it usually is, since the actor involved almost always handles the language with native-speaker fluency.

Finally the actor who is impersonating a foreigner is made to say something mildly outrageous, or somewhat surprising, or possibly even something humorous, at which point the quiz master shouts triumphantly, *hen na gaijin!* This is the cue for the audience to dissolve in helpless gales of laughter. It is considered particularly funny if the pseudo-foreigner in such a TV program is made to express a liking for or even a toleration of some item of traditional Japanese food such as raw fish, fermented soybeans, or even simple white rice. "Do you, by any chance," the quiz master slyly asks, "happen to be able to eat . . . radish pickles?" "Yes," the pseudo-foreigner replies. "*Hen na gaijin!*" followed by thunderous laughter and applause from all sides.

One of the major advances over the past several generations in our understanding of human behavior has resulted from the work of what is generally called the structural school of cultural anthropology. Most briefly put, this school's approach to human culture teaches that any individual act, behavior pattern, or cultural trait actually has meaning or significance only when it is understood in terms of the part that it plays in the overall structure, in other words, in the larger cultural complex of which it is a part. In this system of viewing cultural appraisal, no specific item or entity has an absolute value of or on its own. Culture is an arbitrary phenomenon. It assigns abstract values to different entities, and we cannot guess or predict how any given culture will evaluate any given factor until we study that culture.

Naturally, much of the approach of cultural structuralism grew out of the observation of linguistic systems. As we have already stressed, language is one of the most involved facets in all of human culture; but at the same time, the value that each linguistic element has in each individual language follows no overall plan or rule. Each separate language must be learned independently, just as each culture must, if we are to understand what either "means."

For example, many cultures admire and encourage straight white teeth. We ourselves may find them desirable and more attractive than, for example, the blackened stumps of decayed teeth. If that is so, then our particular culture has made an arbitrary structural judgment in deciding that straight white teeth are good or beautiful. We may be so very familiar with this feature of our culture that we believe it to be a universal feature, or even something that is morally right. But actually it is nothing more than a selection from among many possibilities, arbitrarily made and arbitrarily honored by our own particular culture. In such a case, straight white teeth are prized in our culture because our culture prizes them, not because they are intrinsically good, useful, desirable, or beautiful.

Other cultures may, at the same time, prize blackened teeth so highly that their members even discolor perfectly healthy teeth in order to make them conform to this cultural norm. Actually, this happened to be the case with the aristocratic culture of Heian Japan, and the vogue continued throughout most of Japanese history. Until modern times, any respectable married woman of the Japanese upper classes would as willingly have appeared in public unclothed as to have displayed a full set of strong white teeth. If she happened to have them, she carefully disguised the fact by applying an iron-oxide dye that blackened healthy teeth. Each culture decides what it will esteem, and it is the business of those participating in the culture to acquire what the culture esteems.

Without the theoretical work of the structural anthropologists, we would be hard put indeed to explain the carryings-on of these Japanese TV programs. Why is a foreigner who can speak Japanese so strange that he is a sure-fire comic bit under any and all circumstances? It might seem only logical that a society would honor a foreigner who went to the trouble to learn the society's language well enough to understand and speak it, rather than make him a figure of fun and the butt of jokes.

True, many societies do reward such linguistic behavior by foreigners. But we forget the lessons of cultural structuralism if from this we assume that all societies do so, or that because some societies do and because it seems logical to us that they should, it is therefore reasonable to expect that every society will, or should, do so.

Japanese society is being neither cruel nor illogical when it chooses to make jokes about the odd foreigners who go to the trouble of learning to speak and understand the Japanese language. It is simply exercising its cultural prerogative; it is making an arbitrary choice about what it will and

will not consider to be conduct worthy of approbation. Like the purposely
discolored teeth of a samurai wife a century ago, this phenomenon too can
be understood only when viewed from the perspective of cultural structuralism.

In the case of this characteristic Japanese delight in crackbrained foreigners
who can speak Japanese, the key to understanding the cultural structuralism
involved is provided by the identification by the culture as a whole of
language with race. This is at the heart of the matter. It is scientifically
incorrect, but it is still the key to understanding all the subordinate cultural
structures that descend from it, including that of the comic *hen na gaijin*.

Foreign newspapermen stationed in Tokyo often have occasion to recall
the legend of a Reuter correspondent named Cox. He was arrested by the
Japanese secret police in 1939, along with a number of other British nationals
rounded up at that time on suspicion of espionage. The affair appears to
have been instigated by a pro-Nazi element active within the Japanese
Foreign Ministry at the time. Their aim was so to enrage Britain by mistreat-
ing British subjects, and particularly by lodging transparently absurd charges
of spying, that Britain would declare war against Japan.

At any rate, the part of the Cox legend that is significant for our present
purposes has to do with the sad end he met. According to what is told
about him in foreign-news circles in Tokyo to this day, Cox had the bad
sense, during his interrogation by the Japanese secret police, to answer
their questions in Japanese. His interrogators had of course planned on conducting the proceedings, as was normal then and now, through their own
interpreters, whom they had thoughtfully provided for the convenience of
the accused spy. The police would ask the questions in Japanese; the
interpreter would render this into English; the suspected spy would reply
in English; this would be translated into Japanese by the official interpreter,
and so on.

But Cox apparently understood and spoke Japanese perfectly well. He
understood the questions when they were put in Japanese, and he immediately replied to them in Japanese. What is particularly remembered within
the foreign correspondents' colony in Tokyo is what happened to Cox for
displaying his linguistic abilities: the secret police were so outraged that
they threw him out the window to his death.

It is, alas, impossible to document this legend of the defenestration of
Cox. As with any legend, the more time elapses, the more the various
strands of the oral tradition begin to diverge from one another. Some
sources now claim that Cox jumped out the window of his own volition.
Some even wonder if his command of Japanese was sufficiently good to
have allowed the macabre scene to have been played out.

Documentation is unfortunately lacking for the entire episode—unfortunately, but not surprisingly. The only parties involved who could or would have kept a record were the Japanese secret police. They went out of business (at least as a formal organization of the Japanese state) in August 1945. Most such police records were destroyed at that time by Japanese officials in their preparations for the first waves of the occupation forces. The fragments that survived these hurried burnings were confiscated by the American forces, expensively shipped to Washington, D.C., for study and analysis, and then promptly lost to history somewhere in the hopelessly inefficient and impossibly overloaded documentary archives of the U.S. government—to the considerable relief, it must be added, of the same Japanese officials, who could themselves hardly have done a better job of getting all this incriminating evidence safely out of sight.

Nevertheless, one thing is without question: Cox did leave through the window, and he was quite dead by the time anyone got down to the street to pick him up. Most of the resident foreign colony in Tokyo, if they know of Cox at all, still believe today that he was flung out of the window because he was stupid enough to let the police find out that he understood them when they spoke Japanese, and even more stupid to reply to their questions in the same language.

Everything that one learns and experiences about the contemporary Japanese response to the employment of their language by foreigners inclines one to believe that the Cox legend is no legend, only a plain and quite painfully accurate account of what actually happened. And even if it is not, it still is a good example of what the Italians mean when they say of similar stories, *se non è vero è ben trovato*—"if it isn't true, it certainly ought to be."

CHAPTER NINE

What Do You Mean, Difficult?

> *"Japanese is an impossible language"* is a remark
> heard frequently. With this in mind, the author put
> together these alphabetically arranged, simple reading-
> aids, containing as many expressions as possible that
> are difficult, if not impossible. —Publisher's blurb
> advertising a new book entitled *A Handbook of
> Modern Japanese Grammar*, September 1980

THE PRACTITIONERS of the modern myth of
Nihongo are necessarily committed to a never-ending battle against common sense, reason, and intellect. If the mythmaking forces were ever to
relax their vigilance for a single day, someone somewhere in Japan would
surely begin to see through their tissue of false assumptions and misleading
linguistic premises. This would be the beginning of the end for all concerned.
The mythmakers must always be on the defensive.

Meanwhile, in the entire arsenal of semantically loaded terms and catch-
words that the myth employs for this all-important purpose of its own
constant self-defense, no single term or concept appears to be more potent,
or is more often trotted out by the advocates of the myth, than is the idea
that the Japanese language is difficult—not simply difficult as we all know
any language is difficult, in one sense or another, for someone somewhere
sometime, but always and forever difficult for everyone everywhere all the
time—and even difficult for the Japanese in Japan.

Moreover, the myth teaches, this difficulty of the Japanese language is
itself something extraordinary and significant. Japanese, the myth holds, is
difficult in a special way and exists on a particular level of difficulty, a level

that in and of itself is sufficient reason for setting Nihongo apart from all other languages.

The outside observer of the myth, already likely to be fairly bemused by the mystical trappings in which the myth always seeks to envelop the Japanese language, can surely be forgiven if he or she finds these constant references to the difficulty of the Japanese language to be among the most puzzling manifestations of the entire cult of Nihongo. The repeated assertions about how difficult Japanese is for everyone, Japanese and foreigner alike, are certainly very puzzling. But, as so often with the myth of Nihongo, there is more to all this than at first meets the eye. This oft-repeated emphasis on the difficulty of Japanese is more than something to bewilder the outside observer. Behind this emphasis on difficulty lurks an entire constellation of sociolinguistic attitudes and concepts, all of which are deeply involved in one way or another with the functioning of contemporary Japanese social and intellectual life.

We cannot hope to clarify every element and dimension of the extremely involved sociolinguistic constellation that centers around the idea that Japanese is particularly, and somehow also significantly, a difficult language. But the more of this constellation of ideas that we can pin down, the closer we will approach a useful understanding of some of the ways in which the modern myth of Nihongo plays its role in contemporary Japanese life.

The myth employs this all-powerful weapon of the supposed difficulty of the language in so many different senses that merely to draw up a list of the major semantic categories in which it uses this concept is no small task. At the same time, even the attempt to draw up such a list carries its own danger. By so doing we risk deflecting attention away from our target, since the principal reason why the myth finds this concept of Japanese as a particularly difficult language to be such a powerful tool lies in the very fact that the myth does not distinguish among the many different kinds of linguistic difficulty that may be involved. By lumping them all together, the myth ends up with a defensive weapon that is far stronger, in the sum of its genially undifferentiated parts, than any carefully defined list of separate categories of difficulty would be if they were taken individually. By attempting to dignify this sector of the myth with our own analysis, we risk obliterating the very thing that we are trying to study.

Nevertheless, if we set about the task of reading representative samples of the myth's allegations concerning the difficulty of Japanese without making at least a preliminary effort toward first defining some of the possible varieties of difficulty, we will find ourselves fully as helpless in the myth's moils of misunderstanding on this issue as the most avid mythmaker could possibly wish us to be. So the attempt must be made. We must first of all consider what some of the possible categories of difficulty might actually be, as this term and the concept behind it relate to human language.

The best way to begin is probably to stress at the outset of the discussion what the word difficult cannot reasonably imply in the context of a language. In studying and evaluating the myth's allegations concerning the difficulty of the Japanese language, we must always keep firmly in mind that, as far as the science of linguistics is concerned, and also as far as linguistics is able to measure in any scientific fashion: (a) no language is difficult for its native speakers, and (b) no language is more difficult than any other.

One or the other of these two extremely elementary postulates of linguistic science will effectively serve to defuse almost every allegation of the myth of Nihongo concerning a special or significant difficulty of Japanese. The two propositions together are sufficient to render meaningless almost every claim of the myth in this entire area. Each of these two postulates of linguistic science, therefore, deserves brief discussion if we are to place ourselves in a position to cope with the claims that the myth makes concerning the special difficulty of Japanese.

The first of these general propositions will probably be the less surprising of the two to a reader who is relatively unfamiliar with the assumptions and methodology of linguistic science. Linguistics assumes that no language is inherently difficult for its native speakers, largely because such an assumption is an essential part of the way linguistics views language, which is to say, as a set of arbitrary vocal signs by means of which the members of a social entity cooperate with one another.

More than an empty, theoretical assumption is involved here. Practical experience and scientific field observation both teach us that every native speaker in a natural sociolinguistic entity who does not suffer from some mental or physical handicap—such as brain damage, psychological retardation, oral or aural malformation, or the like—has achieved completely effective control over his or her own language by the early teens at the latest. In the sense of this effective control over one's own native language, control that is achieved in the normal course of events by daily participation in the sociolinguistic entity that employs the language in question, difficulty is simply not a concept that, as far as linguistics can establish by any objective scientific tests or evidence, ever enters upon the scene.

To assert that no language is difficult for its native speakers is not, it must at the same time be stressed, to claim that all native speakers of a language control it with equal effectiveness. Such a claim would be absurd and easily refuted from daily personal experience by members of any sociolinguistic entity. What is at issue here is not the degree of effectiveness or skill with which a native speaker controls his or her own language but instead the quite separate concept of what linguists term competence.

Competence in a linguistic context refers to the ability of a native speaker to speak and to be understood, as well as to understand what is said by others, on a level that makes possible satisfactory cooperation in the ongoing activities of the society in question. As in any other social activity—singing, dancing, politics, sexual relationships, etc.—individual variation will always be observed in the degree of skill and effectiveness with which a given person in the society employs language. Some members of any social group will always be better at dancing than others; some will be more successful in carrying on love affairs than others; some will also use language more effectively than others. But while everyone cannot dance well enough to make a living at it, everyone fortunate enough to have normal motor reflexes and the necessary unimpaired bodily functions can go through the physical movements that the dancer employs. Everyone who is not somehow handicapped has the physical and emotional potential for the wide span of human sexual relationships, even though not everyone will, in a normal statistical sampling of a given society, be able to arrange the opportunities necessary to make full employment of that potential (while still others may consciously reject the opportunities that come their way). The essential distinction here is one that must be made between skill or effectiveness, and competence. As far as competence is concerned, all native speakers are equally competent in their own language, and the question of any difficulty of the language in which they are thus competent simply does not enter into it.

Dr. Tsunoda, the cerebral-hemisphere specialist whose work we saw something of in chapter 4, would probably express this by saying "Some people are drips," meaning that some people are less successful than others in functioning within their social groups—or in making others like or admire the way in which they function within those groups, which often amounts to much the same thing. In this sense, Tsunoda is—for once—quite right. Everyone will agree that some of the people one comes into social contact with are indeed drips, even if one might generally choose a somewhat less inelegant metaphor to express the failure of such individuals to perform at a desirable standard of social behavior. But even drips perform without difficulty. They have no difficulty with their language or even with their society. The difference between a drip and the rest of us is that drips are not very good at what they do. But they can do it, and they do do it, without any particular difficulty.

The second of the two assertions will probably raise more questions than the first. All of us, even if we are fortunate enough to have been totally isolated from the literature of the myth of Nihongo, have heard often enough that this or that foreign language is somehow more difficult than another or more difficult than our own. American student culture has generated its own quite substantial body of linguistic myth in this connection. This myth finds eloquent, if confused, expression in the kinds of remarks one often hears from students trying to decide what foreign-language course they ought to enroll in: "I'd like to take German, but I don't know. German is so difficult, I think I'll take Spanish instead; everybody knows Spanish is easy."

It is no accident that such well-meaning statements, embodying value judgments on the relative difficulty of this or that language, are almost always expressed in terms of the supposed difficulty of learning one or another foreign language. No native speaker, as we have already seen, has any difficulty in the scientific sense of the term in learning to speak and understand his or her own language. But when it comes to learning a second or a third or some other language—a foreign language—we are almost always faced with learning an entirely new set of involuntary sociolinguistic responses. This is always a task of enormous difficulty for anyone who tries it.

Learning a foreign language is difficult for several reasons. Involuntary responses, such as constitute the bulk of linguistic activity, are the most difficult of all human behavior patterns to learn to control; that is, after all, why they are called involuntary. Another major reason for the genuine difficulty experienced in all foreign-language learning is that we are almost always forced to try and compress the whole process into a tiny time span—a matter of a few years or even a few months. But in real life the normal language-learning process occupies a native speaker full time for at least the first twelve or more years of life. One hardly need be surprised when such extreme compression of the available time span leads to the experience of enormous difficulties.

These are not, of course, the only reasons why learning a foreign language is always a difficult task, but they are the major ones, and understanding them is enough to document the difficulty we all experience in learning a new language, particularly when we are adults. Being an adult generally means that all our learning processes have already noticeably slowed down from their childhood and early-teen pace. Adults also generally have less free time and energy to devote to such problems as language learning. None of these limiting factors tends to make the task any easier. All in all, learning a foreign language is difficult for everyone.

And yet we do know, either from our own experience or from what others have told us, that some foreign languages are easier to learn than others, even for adults and even under less than ideal circumstances like the classroom. We all know English-speaking people who have studied only a little Spanish and who manage to survive in a Spanish-speaking situation fairly well. At the same time, we know people—or perhaps we have had the experience ourselves—who study Japanese or Chinese or Russian for years and find that they are still at a loss when called upon to employ the language. And this is not to mention the thousands and thousands of Japanese who study English almost all their lives, only to end up unable to speak or understand a single word of the language, try as they will. What is all this about? Is one language—Japanese, for example—actually more difficult than another—Spanish, for example?

Here linguistic science has a simple but straightforward answer. Some foreign languages appear to be, and indeed probably are, easier for a given individual to learn than others. But this is only because the ones that seem easier to learn are more similar to the learner's native language than are the ones that seem more difficult.

Effective language learning makes it necessary to acquire a new set of involuntary linguistic reflexes. This task will obviously be the most difficult when all the new habits that must be acquired are totally different from the ones that the learner already has available—whether they are the ones of the learner's native language or of a second foreign language already well acquired. On the other hand, the task will be facilitated when, as it often happens, the new involuntary linguistic habits—including those involving pronunciation, grammar, syntax, and all the other elements of a language— happen to be somewhat similar to corresponding features in the learner's own language.

Learning a whole raft of totally new habits is always going to be more difficult than learning only a few. In any language-learning situation, this is the variable that affects the ease or difficulty of the task—the degree to which the language being learned resembles or does not resemble the learner's first language. It is never a question of the new language that must be learned being intrinsically more difficult than any other. If one already knows German or French or Bantu, then German or French or Bantu is the easiest language in the world; but for such a person, English could well be extremely difficult—until he or she managed to learn it.

In other words, linguistic science has never yet been able to devise any rigorous method or procedure for setting standards of absolute difficulty that would serve as a valid measure for any language. It may very well seem to us, when we set about trying to learn a language like Russian with its numerous cases, declensions, and gender agreements that must be memorized somehow or other, that Russian is intrinsically more difficult than a language without these features. But how are we to measure such intrinsic difficulty? How, for example, are we to decide whether having cases for nouns and gender for adjectives is really any more difficult than having tones, like Chinese, or some other linguistic or structural feature unknown to Russian but common in yet another language? One always ends up trying to equate lemons with apples. The features that would have to be compared in trying to make any scientifically valid measurement of linguistic difficulty simply cannot be compared with one another.

Who can say—and on what basis—whether having tense as a category in the verb (like English) is more or less difficult, in the abstract, than having gender in the article (like German *der, die,* and *das*), or that either of these features is more or less difficult than having aspect in the verb (like Russian, which thereby distinguishes whether an action is completed or continuing, rather than, like English, being concerned about when the action took place)? The Chinese have no trouble pronouncing their tones. For anybody else to learn to do it correctly is a difficult matter requiring many hours of practice and much patience. What this comes down to is that any language is difficult until we learn it; and no language is difficult when we know it.

What most of us have in mind when we talk about the difficulty of this or that language—and what is also generally at issue when we speak or write about the difficulty of our own language, whatever that language may be—are almost always factors that are actually extralinguistic. This means that we are really talking about sociolinguistic factors or considerations that are not an integral part of language itself; they are a part of the way in which the society that uses the language functions. And what we most often mean when we talk about a language being difficult is the problem of learning to employ the written forms of the language effectively—learning to read and to write, to spell correctly, and to write elegantly or pleasingly, or at least in a style that does not cause offense.

Every society that makes use of writing—which today means every advanced industrial society, and most of the third-world societies as well—has standards of performance as well as requirements of competence. In all such societies, reading and writing, and all the literary techniques and skills that are tied up with reading and writing, plainly exhibit a wide range of difficulty; of that there can be no question. It is difficult for the American or English schoolchild to learn to read and particularly to spell English in its customary written form. It is not as difficult for a Spanish or Mexican schoolchild to learn to read and not nearly as difficult for him or her to learn to spell Spanish, because the Spanish system of spelling bears a regular, one-on-one relationship to the language itself and to the way in which it is pronounced. The system of Spanish orthography is not absolutely regular in terms of the Spanish language—there are some irregular spellings that children must learn and that hence teachers must teach—but these are very few in number, particularly when contrasted with the enormous number of arbitrary, irrational spellings for hundreds and hundreds of English words that the rest of us must master (threw and through, might and mite, sight and site, and the whole enormous spectrum of similar English orthographic absurdities). What is generally spoken of and thought of as difficulty in this or that language usually turns out, on closer inspection, to refer to the way the language is written, not to the language itself.

To say that Japanese today employs a difficult, complex writing system is to risk the most sweeping understatement possible. Modern Japanese is written using approximately two thousand individual Chinese characters, each of which must be separately memorized not only for its written form but also in terms of the several different words or parts of different words that it is used to write in the Japanese writing system. Together with these thousands of graphic symbols borrowed from China, the Japanese today make simultaneous use in their writing system of two different sets of syllabic phonetic symbols, each set consisting of just under fifty symbols each. Unlike the Chinese characters that are employed in the Japanese writing system, the symbols that belong to each of these two syllabic writing systems do not go with specific words or parts of words in the language. Instead, they are used phonetically for writing a certain limited number of words or parts of words, but always in conjunction with the Chinese characters.

The entire Japanese writing system is a tremendous burden on the memory and an even greater burden upon technology. The Japanese, always highly skilled at adapting to their own ends the most modern innovations from the West, have recently developed electronic script-processing systems that now enable their writing system to be employed in modern high-speed communications on every level. This has been done at great and quite unnecessary cost, both to the industrial system and to the society of the country, but it has been done, and that is what is important. Japanese technology has managed to cope with the script; so also must every Japanese schoolchild and nearly every Japanese adult. And the script is indeed difficult; one cannot question that.

One might expect that when the modern Nihongo mythmakers go on and on about how difficult Japanese is, they are mostly talking about the Japanese writing system. It turns out that sometimes they are, but only occasionally. More often than not, when they reiterate the alleged superior difficulty of the language, they are not concerned with the script at all. In fact, they usually avoid mixing the two levels of language and writing when arguing in this connection. Again we can only remind ourselves that the essential element of a myth is always to be identified, in part at least, in the way in which it unabashedly takes on, indeed revels in, the irrational and the unreal. Far from stressing the difficulty of the Japanese script, an area where it would have its work cut out for it, the myth of Nihongo usually turns the tables on us when the subject of the Japanese writing system is raised. From the standpoint of the modern myth of Nihongo, the Japanese script is not what makes the language difficult. It even turns out that the script, difficult and cumbersome as we all know it to be, is for the myth-makers one of the superior features of Nihongo—one of the things that makes the language more desirable as a medium of human communication than any other variety of human linguistic behavior.

What, then, are some of the elements that are commonly cited by the modern myth of Nihongo when it sounds its clarion call concerning difficulty of the language? As we inspect a few of them we must first of all be certain to keep firmly in mind the two assumptions of linguistic science discussed previously. The myth works upon propositions that run directly counter to each of these assumptions, and so it is necessary to keep these facts firmly in mind. The other general caution that is necessary before anyone plunges into these turgid materials is that it is folly to look for reason or order in the argumentation. Reason and logical order are missing, of course, from every dimension of the entire myth of Nihongo—otherwise it would be no true myth. But it is in surveying this particular segment of the evidence that we find the most striking illustration of the chaotic approach that is the hallmark of the myth.

What the authors of the myth and its materials mean by difficult and difficulty is never discussed or defined. To do so would immediately remove the entire concept from serious consideration in the terms along which the myth is interested, for its own ends, in presenting it. We must be prepared to find the same word often being used in several different meanings within the same sentence, with no warning that the sense has suddenly shifted. All in all, when the myth begins to try and exploit the alleged difficulty of the Japanese language, we must be prepared for heavy seas.

The most eloquent contemporary advocate of the difficulty of Japanese is, without question, Professor Haruhiko Kindaichi. Since we have already seen some representative excerpts from his writings cited in earlier chapters, this news will hardly come as a surprise. Even so, the reader should probably be warned. Kindaichi is particularly gifted in writing about the mystical qualities that for him, and for the many others who are members of his particular school, distinguish the Japanese language. He is more than usually eloquent in tugging at the Japanese reader's heartstrings in his melodramatic accounts of "our language, right or wrong," with their vivid descriptions of the self-flagellatory delights and joys that one is supposed to find in the failures and shortcomings of "this language of ours—the only one we have." Nevertheless, Kindaichi manages to put all these triumphs firmly behind him when he sets about to describe what is for him the single most important quality of the Japanese language—its difficulty.

Everything else that Kindaichi has written about the myth of Nihongo pales into genuine insignificance when compared with the lapidary quality of his passages extolling the difficulty of the cult's chief fetish object. Here, like the true literary artist that he is, Kindaichi manages to make his own written style exactly serve his expository and expressive ends. His point, after all, is that Japanese is involute, complex, difficult to an extent probably unsurpassed and surely never equaled by any other human language. And to give concrete examples of this same involution, complexity, and difficulty as he goes along, he almost always manages to phrase his own comments on this particular aspect of the myth in prose that is surely involute and complex enough for the taste of anyone who appreciates those qualities in writing. Gilbert and Sullivan imagined a Japan in which the punishment fitted the crime; how they would have enjoyed Kindaichi, whose prose so deftly fits its theme.

Most of Kindaichi's many significant contributions to the making of the myth of Nihongo are, as we have already noted, brought conveniently together in the pages of his extremely popular paperback entitled *Nihongo*. He does not apparently have a very high regard for his readers' attention span. Rather like the American TV writers who know that it is necessary to grab the viewers' attention in the first five seconds of a new program or they will turn away to another channel, Kindaichi also assumes that he must grab them in the first few seconds that he has available. So he wastes no time in launching into the theme of how difficult the Japanese language is, even before the book itself begins. In the first lines of his introduction, he writes: "Some people may think that there is nothing at all to writing about the Japanese language. After all, they might feel, we have lived all our lives using the Japanese language ever since our births, and so, they might conclude, we ought to be able to write anything and everything about the language. But once we really consider the question, actually there is nothing as difficult as to write about the Japanese language. It is very difficult for us Japanese to find out anything about languages other than Japanese; that being the case, how much more difficult for us, then, is coming to grips with such problems as the question of what is the true essence of the Japanese language, and the question of what does constitute its 'unique character.' What kind of language, then, is Japanese? This question is a theme concerning which, despite all its difficulty, we cannot but have great interest."

This is not only the way the introduction begins, it is also the way his entire *Nihongo* book begins; and the reader who finds this rather rough going must be warned that it never really gets much better. Even in this short, purely introductory passage, one hardly knows how to deal with the lightning leaps of illogic that apparently tie the extract's various parts together—until one recalls rather gratefully that one need not actually make the effort to cope after all, since logic has nothing to do with any of this. Once we remind ourselves of this important constant, our task becomes somewhat easier. We still do not understand any better than before why Kindaichi is presenting his ideas in the order and progression in which he has decided to offer them, but at least we are now somewhat less troubled by his remarkable gift for the non sequitur, a stylistic technique that his little book *Nihongo* manages to elevate to the level of a major literary device.

One of the most brilliant non-sequitur passages that Kindaichi has ever managed to carry off is, as it happens, found in this same introduction. Why, the reader will surely feel it necessary to ask, does Kindaichi, of all people, take the fact that the Japanese find it "difficult . . . to find out anything about languages other than Japanese" as a point of departure for his argument about the enormous difficulty of Japanese? And what in the world can he mean by the difficulty of writing about Japanese, which after all is precisely what he himself is about to do for several hundred closely printed pages? What does the proverbial Japanese difficulty when it comes to foreign languages—which no one for a moment would wish to question—have to do with the whole matter under discussion? And in particular, what role can it possibly play as a logical kingpin for introducing a book that seeks to tell us about "the true essence of the Japanese language, and the question of what does constitute its 'unique character' "?

The answer to this essential question is that the two things really do not have anything to do with one another. Kindaichi simply brings together, in the same line of his introduction, the Japanese command of foreign languages and the difficulty of Japanese. If we are not careful, he will end up making us assume that simply because he thus confronts these two separate entities, they must have some logical connection, even if that connection is not immediately apparent to us.

It is all a little like the case of the emperor's new clothes. The emperor, we should remember, really didn't have anything on at all, much less any new clothes. There is really no connection at all between the two ideas that Kindaichi juxtaposes in this deft fashion and that he would make to serve as the keystone of his entire book and its argumentation, apart from the fact that he has written them so closely on the same part of the page, one following fast upon the other.

With these preliminaries mercifully out of the way, Kindaichi finally gets into the body of *Nihongo* and proceeds to elaborate upon this same theme of the difficulty of the Japanese language. Now we begin to catch more of the true drift of his argument, even though any logical connection of one idea with another is still generally difficult to grasp, largely because such connections do not exist. Still writing about difficulty, he now deftly begins to employ that term in quite a different sense, thus changing the thrust of his argument suddenly and without warning. Since he still purports to be talking about difficulty, the reader must have all his wits about him.

It will help if the reader is well experienced in coping with the sort of automobile driver who changes lanes suddenly and without any warning.

Not wholly accidentally, Kindaichi soon chooses a few trenchant lines from a sociolinguistic tract going back to the days of World War II as his transition paragraph for carrying us along on his next roller-coaster flight of linguistic fancy: " 'Our language is at this very moment expanding overseas, in the wake of the extension of our national destiny, with extraordinary vigor. This is, of course, an expected consequence of the progress of the Japanese race; nevertheless, and particularly because the one is following directly upon the other in this fashion, it is desirable that the national language of Japan be still more lucid, and yet more correct. We are profoundly struck today by the fact that our language is all too chaotic.' "

The wartime author whose views Kindaichi is citing in support of his own thesis concerning the difficulty of the Japanese language was really talking about something quite different. He was dwelling upon another favorite theme of the myth of Nihongo, quite as dear to the mythmakers in the 1930s and 1940s as it still is today, to the effect that at the same time that the Japanese language is unique and superior, it is also in a great state of disrepair and somehow always threatening to come apart at the seams. We are already familiar with most of the spectrum of contradictory love-and-hate reaction patterns that this variety of sociolinguistic approach involves from our consideration of these questions in chapter 6. Here we have yet another manifestation of the same sociolinguistic syndrome, the only difference being that this time around, the love-hate constellation is trotted out in support of the myth of difficulty. It is folly to expect even the least warning, even the slightest signal, when these fast-moving writers of the myth of Nihongo suddenly decide to shift from one line of argumentation to another. All that the reader can do is keep a safe distance away and hope for the best.

The World War II author cited by Kindaichi is saying, in effect, that even though, "as is well known," our language is a poor thing and chaotic even while at the same time it is glorious and unique, we still have the problem of teaching it to the foreigners whose countries we are currently in the process of invading and occupying. All this naturally raises certain unsolved questions. Teach it we will, and teach it we must; but oh, if only we had something better to teach than what we do have!

With this, Professor Kindaichi is again off and running: "But actually, when I talk about the 'difficulty of Japanese' in the true sense of that expression, I do not have in mind this 'difficulty in teaching the Japanese language to foreigners.' In Europe, it is an accepted fact that the Basque language is a difficult language. Basque is the language of a racial minority found on the boundary between France and Spain.... When the Basque language is said to be difficult, this is because the Basque language is very much isolated from the other European languages. This is why Basque is difficult for Europeans. In other words, we really ought to discount the actual difficulty of Basque. And if Japanese were difficult only in the same way that Basque is difficult, in other words, if its difficulty consisted only in the fact that it is difficult for foreigners, then we could not really claim that Japanese is truly a 'difficult language.' But the fact of the matter is that the difficulty of Japanese is not simply something involved with the difficulties that foreigners have learning our language. Japanese is quite equally as difficult for the Japanese themselves to learn. In Europe, school children spend different periods of time mastering their native languages. In Italy only two years, and in Germany only three years are needed for this purpose. Even in England, where the most time is spent on this, a child masters reading and writing in five years. But in Japan, even after six years in elementary school and three years in middle school, a student still cannot read a newspaper satisfactorily. And we all agree that even when a student has graduated from high school, he or she will not be able to write Japanese prose that correctly makes use of the phonetic syllabaries and Chinese characters."

More rapid changes in direction, again quite without warning—the same words are suddenly used to mean quite different things, as the meaning, along with the professor's logic, goes careening down the page. Suddenly Kindaichi is talking not about the Japanese language at all, but about the way the Japanese language is written—not about language, but about script and writing systems.

The quick shift in the topic of the discourse from Basque to Japanese is particularly impressive. With Basque, there is no question of writing or script, since the Basque language is not normally employed as a formal written or literary language. When people talk about the difficulty of Basque, they are really talking about the difficulty of the Basque language. But Basque, Kindaichi argues, is not really difficult; it only seems that way because it is "isolated" from the other European languages familiar to the speakers who try to learn some Basque. The term "isolated" as used here is vague and impressionistic, but if we try to understand it as meaning "different in structure from," his argument is for once fairly easy to follow. But soon we are again propelled down a quite different lane of the highway and always at breakneck speed.

The "Japanese learning Japanese" is of course a reference to learning reading and writing skills of the sort described above. This is difficult for everyone, and it is particularly difficult when the society, like Japanese society, insists upon employing a perversely involved writing system for its language. So without warning us that he has stopped talking about language and is now talking instead about writing, Kindaichi unfolds another of his glorious generalizations before our eyes. Ah! he says, see how difficult Japanese and Japanese alone really is! We cannot even learn it ourselves. Other difficult languages you may have heard about, like Basque, are not really difficult at all; we have the corner on difficulty, we and this language that we love because it is so difficult and that we hate for the same reason.

Kindaichi is so consummately adept at carrying out these sudden, unsignaled changes in his argument that even though our intelligence may be insulted at the implications of what he has to say, we can hardly begrudge him the admiration due his unquestioned dexterity in doing what it is that he does. Without a single word of warning, he has managed to get all of us involved in what turns out to be the Japanese version of a sociolinguistic complaint that will be all too familiar to any American reader. This is the situation that reflects parents' proverbial dissatisfaction with the ability of the elementary and secondary school system to teach children the elements of reading and writing effectively. It is usually expressed, in the United States at least, as the problem of "Why Can't Johnny Read?" In America the answer implicit in this question is almost always, "because the teachers in the schools aren't doing their job properly."

Here we encounter, thanks to Kindaichi, the Japanese version of this same sociolinguistic confrontation. Immediately we note how differently things are ordered in Japan. In Japan it is the teachers, not the parents, who bring the subject up. And when the teachers in Japan bring up this subject, it is not to complain about it or to suggest that anything be done to correct it—it is to make it an occasion of pride and the basis of a claim for linguistic superiority over the rest of the world.

In America, parents confront the teachers of their children, angrily claiming that Johnny can't read and noisily demanding that the teachers mend their ways, do something about the situation in the schools, and figure out some way so that Johnny can learn to read. But in Japan it is the teachers who proudly point to Tarō's inability to read even a simple daily newspaper after years and years of schooling. (Kindaichi is a school teacher, though to be sure he probably has not had to teach schoolchildren how to write for a good many years.) For Japanese teachers, the alleged failure of their school system to teach elementary literacy is something they point out with pride— when they are not claiming that Japan has the highest literacy standards in the world, that is. And when they call attention to this situation, there is not the least hint of anything being wrong in the way in which they do their teaching; in fact, there is not the least hint of anything at all being out of joint anywhere in the entire Japanese sociolinguistic situation.

Far from anything being wrong, the teachers in Japan tell parents in effect that if Tarō can't read, this is something we should all be proud of.

See how difficult our unique, special language must be, if this is true (and it is true, because we, the professors and teachers, say it is true). The question, then, in the Japanese version of the "Johnny Can't Read" syndrome, is not what is to be done about it. The question is how we can manage to live up to the glory and demands placed upon our nation and our race by the sheer possession of this enormously difficult and unique language that is ours.

Regretfully, we cannot allow ourselves the luxury of pursuing further some of the larger implications of the passage upon which we have been commenting. To do so would be to run the risk of not being able to keep pace with Kindaichi, who does not even have to pause to catch his breath before he is off and running fast, carrying his argument into yet another unexpected direction. Immediately following the passage translated above, he returns to what we soon learn to recognize is one of his favorite proving grounds for almost anything he proposes about the special qualities of the Japanese language—Japan's activities in World War II and particularly her experiences following the military defeat:

"Once the war was over, there were those who argued that one of the reasons why Japan had been defeated was to be found in the complications of the Japanese language. Commander Bruance,* whose offensive strategy smashed the Japanese Combined Fleet in the naval Battle of Midway, is said to have confessed that, 'Since Japanese is a language that is lacking in accuracy and precision, I launched this attack, believing that we would be sure to bring about confusion in the enemy's communication of orders for immediate execution.' A reporter for the *Asahi Shimbun* assigned to cover the International War Crimes Tribunal commented upon how deeply he was moved by the spectacle of the irritating slowness of the Japanese lan-

---

*This must be a reference to Rear Admiral Raymond A. Spruance, demoted in rank to Commander and with his last name garbled to become Bruance. (English seems to have its own difficulties, along with Japanese.) Whether Admiral Spruance, here Bruance, ever said anything along these lines is not on record. One suspects that Kindaichi made up his views on Japanese at the same time that he garbled his name. As far as American military historians are concerned, the alleged inability of the Japanese to understand their own language played no part in the Battle of Midway. Instead, they attribute the American success in the engagement to the fact that American aircraft were able to sink all four of the Japanese heavy cruisers that constituted the most important striking element of the Japanese fleet. If language played any part at all, it was because "the Americans were still reading the Japanese coded radio messages," and hence "had the advantage of surprise" in their assault on the Japanese Combined Fleet commanded by Admiral Isoroku Yamamoto. See T. N. Dupuy, Col., USA, Ret., *The Naval War in the Pacific: On to Tokyo,* vol. 12 in The Military History of World War II (New York: Franklin Watts, Inc., 1963), pp. 3–5.

guage; just as he had expected would be the case, he observed that Japanese was absolutely no match for foreign languages, as he listened both to the Japanese-language speeches of the defense lawyers and to the speeches of the other side, who were using English."

Thus, the experiences of World War II can be and are invoked with equal authority on every possible side of every possible facet of the myth of Nihongo. The experiences of Japanese occupation groups trying to teach subject peoples to use Japanese simultaneously carried a lesson about the tremendous difficulty of the language and also about its imminent danger of coming apart at the seams. The language was so difficult that we could not use it effectively ourselves, and so it helped to lose the war. Or is Kindaichi saying that the language alone lost Japan the war or at least the Battle of Midway? If so, this certainly is a pretty serious indictment. Apparently, it not only lost us the war, it also lost us the first years of peace, since if it had not been for this terrible, difficult, unique, but wonderful language of ours, the Japanese war criminals would all have been let off scot-free.

The question of the content of what the defense and the prosecution were saying—the problem of what the Japanese war-crimes defendants were accused of having done to cause them to be brought to trial for crimes against humanity—is never mentioned. Kindaichi's assumption is that content always counts for nothing, only the way in which something is said can possibly matter. We lost the war and the war-crimes trials not because of what anyone did or did not do, but because the Japanese language is so difficult, concludes Kindaichi. And now, writing in 1957, more than a decade after both the defeat and the war-crimes trials, what does he propose doing about all this? We can hardly wait to read on: "We must recognize the difficulty of the Japanese language; but it will not do for us to continue to be in grief because we have inherited this tedious and troublesome tongue. A national language is something that is fashioned. In modern German and French, there are a great many elements that have been artificially fashioned. ... We must seek to discover just where the defects are in the Japanese language, and learn what may be done to remedy them."

At first glance, one wonders if Kindaichi has not perhaps decided to redirect his emphasis toward what today is sometimes called language planning. Language planning involves trying to set rules and standards for linguistic usage, particularly in the case of literary and other forms of written expression. But language planning is almost entirely a sociolinguistic concern of newly developing third-world countries, most of whom lack wide-scale literacy and have no long tradition of employing writing for everyday purposes. Obviously neither of these conditions is in the least relevant to Japan, any more than the whole concept of language planning is. Again, Kindaichi has genially counted upon our momentary inattention and has assumed that no one will be quick enough to notice that he has suddenly redirected the line of his argument.

Language planning plays no part in modern Japanese life. The entire concept of language planning is quite irrelevant to the role of language in Japan today, where—unlike most of Asia and especially many of the newly developing third-world countries—a uniform, accepted national standard of both spoken and written language has been in existence for over a century and where not the slightest possibility exists to "discover just where the defects are in the Japanese language," any more than to "learn what may be done to remedy them."

Two different interpretations for the passage cited above are possible. Either Kindaichi assumes that the entire concept of language planning, which is what he is actually calling for, will be so obscure to his readers that they will not realize that what he is saying represents nothing more than yet another ninety-degree veering away of his line of argument. Or—and this is equally possible—perhaps Kindaichi himself is so unfamiliar with what language planning consists of and knows so little of its relationship to the growth of national societies in newly developed countries that he really believes that what he suggests here is somehow relevant to the sociolinguistic role of Japanese in Japan.

Either way, what he has given his readers comes off as a stirring call to arms, the kind of appeal to the heart and soul that hardly anyone, with the possible exception of a competent linguistic scientist, will find easy to resist. It seems not only difficult but actually mean and spiteful to be against what Kindaichi proposes. Improving the Japanese language, making it a better one, making it more like French and German—who could resist such a call to do good for one's country? Ardor will probably cool off at the point where the reader, his fervor aroused by this strident summons to action, discovers that neither in this particular passage, nor indeed in the 224 pages of the book that follow, does Kindaichi ever give the least hint of just what it is that the reader is actually expected to do in order to bring all this about. We are never actually told how French and German were "artificially fashioned," nor are we told how the lessons to be drawn from that mysterious operation are to be applied to Japanese. But this hardly matters. Long before the reader notices that no specific instructions are ever given, and long after his call to arms has been sounded, Kindaichi will have changed directions so many times and so rapidly that the reader will find it difficult just to locate the professor, much less to complain to him about his unfulfilled promises.

The first of these mind-boggling changes in direction takes place immediately following the passage just cited, in a single short sentence with which we must reluctantly bid a sad farewell to Kindaichi and his theories of the difficulty of Japanese. Having just told us that Japanese is in dire need of improvement and having assured us that "something can be done about it," he then goes on to share with us his idea about what that something is: "In order to make Japanese a better language, what is essential is that we clearly understand what the special nature of the Japanese language is."

And just what this special nature of the Japanese language is, Kindaichi is prepared to tell us in the over two hundred pages that follow these introductory passages or indeed in all of his many other contributions to the literature of the myth of Nihongo. Once more, we find that we have been placed aboard a swiftly revolving merry-go-round of illogical and largely unconnected argumentation. But before our heads begin to spin too mercilessly, a moment spent trying to paraphrase the disconnected steps by which Kindaichi got us into all this will prove to be a good investment of time.

Remember that we began with elaborate claims for the difficulty of the Japanese language: difficult for foreigners, difficult even for the Japanese, so difficult in fact that it made the Japanese lose the war, and even worse, later got substantial numbers of Japan's wartime leaders convicted and executed as war criminals. Could any language be more difficult than that? But should we sit around and complain because we have this terribly difficult language, which makes us lose wars and gets our leaders convicted as criminals against humanity? Heavens, no! No language is perfect, and if there seem to be flaws in our own, not to worry. They can be remedied.

How can they be remedied? By further contemplation of the special nature of the Japanese language. Remember also that all this began with an invocation of the special nature of the Japanese language, that special nature that is most strikingly illustrated by its astonishing difficulty—the same difficulty that is claimed to be one of the major reasons behind the language's special status among all other languages. The language, we have been told, is special; it is special because it is difficult; it is difficult because it is special.

In other words, the entire argument itself as well as its strong emotional appeal to the reader are both perfectly circular. The snake continues to grasp its own tail firmly to form a perfect circle from which, once one enters its bounds, there can be no escape. This is the same quality of inherent circularity that is, for example, so well exemplified by the classic Indic myths of the creation and destruction of the cosmos. In these myths the world is pictured as continually undergoing innumerable separate creations, each followed by total destruction, out of which another cosmos always arises—only to be destroyed in its turn.

If a myth is to be a lasting, ongoing enterprise, it must somehow manage to incorporate this element of circularity, otherwise it will eventually find its mythic powers of explanation fading away. Of that at least, Kindaichi need have no fear. The circle of his argumentation is perfectly enclosed, and once set in motion, it need never come to a halt. For him, as for all the Nihongo mythmakers, the Japanese language is special; it is especially special because it is so difficult; and it is so difficult because it is so special. If we should ever wish to know more about any particular portion of the endless circle that all this involves, Kindaichi stands ready, willing, and more than able to tell us. After all, telling people what they want to know, particularly if they do not already know it, is what professors do best.

It is best now to disengage ourselves from this web of circularity. We know that the Japanese language is difficult, but only in the very general sense that any and every language is difficult until one learns it. We also know that the difficulty of the Japanese language cannot be documented or substantiated as a possible scientific criterion for any special or unique nature of the language. To the contrary, its difficulty—once we understand what the actual, scientific implications of difficulty in the case of language actually are—is simply another of the innumerable features that Japanese has in common with all other human languages. The difficulty of Japanese does not set it apart or make it special; to the contrary, it helps to demonstrate that it is just another language among thousands of others.

We have seen in chapter 5 how the whole modern myth of Nihongo itself has generated an impressive antimyth of silence. We will probably, therefore, not be too surprised to learn that the myth of its difficulty has, in much the same way, also given rise to a substantial number of related antimyths, two of which in particular are encountered frequently enough to require some mention here.

The first of these two antimyths that revolve around the difficulty thesis is the less important of the pair, but it deserves mention in first place because it is so very unexpected. The myth teaches that Japanese is the world's most difficult language, difficult for the Japanese themselves and even more difficult for foreigners; but in the same breath, it can often be detected simultaneously teaching that it is the world's easiest language—and most surprising of all, the world's easiest language for foreigners!

This antimyth was most impressively documented in the early 1970s by a writer in the Sunday *New York Times Magazine,* telling about his experiences in trying to learn a little Japanese in preparation for his first visit to Japan. He found that "the Yamaguchis [had] moved in recently to an apartment in our building—a quiet, modest and hardworking family who run a gift shop nearby." So he asked them for help in learning a few words and expressions in Japanese, enough to help him and his wife get over the rough spots that any tourist expects when visiting a new country with a totally unfamiliar language for the first time.

Some place or other the writer had previously been told that when the Japanese borrow an English word, they change it to conform to Japanese pronunciation patterns, and also that these changes follow a relatively small number of quite regular rules: *l* for *r*, *b* for *v*, and sequences of two or more consonants broken up by adding vowels between them, as well as at the end of the word, so that English strike becomes *su-to-ra-i-ki*, life becomes *ra-i-fu*, and virus, *bii-ru-su* (to be carefully distinguished from *bii-ru*, which is beer, and *biru*, which is short for *building*), etc.

Applying these rules of phonetic substitution to an apparently random list of English vocabulary items, the writer then tried out his homemade Japanese on the Yamaguchis. The effect was instantaneous and sensationally effective: "They all heard me out patiently and politely while I ran through my list of nouns for them. Then Mr. Yamaguchi, after a whispered consultation with his son and his wife and his daughter, spoke for all the family. In a strongly accented, but gentle voice, he agreed that my plan for going to Japan on our own was excellent, and that the list of Japanese words would be more than adequate for communication in his country." And, he might have added, certainly more than adequate to document his article on the whole experience for the Sunday *New York Times,* where it appeared under the engaging title, "I Can Teach You All the Japanese You'll Ever Need to Know."

Here the myth has managed to reverse itself totally, as the Yamaguchis faced up to the task of trying to say something that was neither rude nor unkind to this strange New York neighbor of theirs, who thought that he was speaking Japanese simply by making English words sound funny. The Yamaguchis were surely well aware of the myth and its teaching that the language is so difficult as to be practically impossible for anyone, Japanese and foreigner alike. Yet here is this apparently serious, well-meaning foreign neighbor at their door, making funny noises like *ra-i-fu* and *su-to-ra-i-ki* and asking them if they understand. Will the Japanese understand this if I and my wife go to Tokyo?

What can they say? The Yamaguchis understand, of course; their own English pronunciation is probably not so far from their diligent neighbor's attempts to mangle English *à la japonaise*; of course they understand. And if the neighbor and his wife are lucky enough to meet Japanese in Japan who have also studied some English, they too may very well understand. Better to seek solace, not to mention safety, in the antimyth: Yes, you speak very good Japanese; everyone will understand you; that's all you need to know—and you see, it wasn't difficult at all; anybody can learn to do it in an hour or so! With this, the Yamaguchis probably managed to get their curious neighbor to go home and themselves retired for the night, making a note, like the good, sensible New York residents they are, to put another double bolt and chain on the front door as soon as possible. One never knows what will turn up when the doorbell rings in this strange, dangerous city.

The second of the antimyths that has been generated out of the heart of the difficulty myth is somewhat more subtle than "All the Japanese You Need to Know in an Hour." But of the two, it is also by far the more important and the more dangerous, since its potential for adding to the serious misunderstanding of Japanese life and culture on the part of outsiders is enormous.

This particular antimyth concerns the Japanese writing system. As we have already seen, when the Japanese make references to how difficult their language is or to how their language enjoys a degree of particular difficulty that somehow sets it above the other languages of the world, they are often actually talking about the way in which Japanese is written, not about the language itself at all. And as we have also noted briefly, in this one particular, it is difficult not to grant the myth its point (while insisting, of course, on keeping language separate and distinct from writing, which the myth seldom does). The Japanese writing system is indeed complex; it is a considerable feat for the memory and a burden for the schoolchild; it is in fact difficult.

The antimyth that is generated in response to this really genuine difficulty of the Japanese writing system attempts to make a virtue of the many obvious defects of that system, especially its needless prolixity, complication, and intricacy. It claims that while the Japanese writing system is indeed difficult, this very difficulty means in turn that the writing system is the best in the world—better than any other writing system in common use for any other language and a writing system that serves the Japanese nation well in many subtle ways—in a word, part and parcel of the modern myth of Nihongo itself.

The blatant liabilities of the Japanese writing system are thus made out to be virtues, particularly the system's most complex and burdensome feature—the way in which it employs at least two thousand Chinese characters borrowed from another quite foreign language and culture for its own orthographic ends. This continued use of the Chinese script within the Japanese writing system remains the height of orthographic folly, a major foolishness not to be observed in any other modern industrialized society. Even the country where these characters were invented and first used, China, has now made fitful starts in the implementation of a national policy in which the use of the characters will slowly be phased out in favor of the roman alphabet, as part of the overall modernization of Chinese life, culture, and society in the People's Republic.

The durable and intrepidly outspoken Chinese political leader Deng Xiaoping astonished a visiting delegation of Japanese in June 1977 by commenting frankly upon what leadership circles in the People's Republic think of the Chinese script. The Japanese delegation began their meeting with Deng by a ceremonial apology for the damage and destruction that

Japan inflicted upon Chinese life and property during World War II. Deng replied, in his characteristically sharp and frank fashion, that no apologies were in order. China, he said, had itself done far more wrong to Japan during the years of their historical association than Japan had ever done to China. The visiting Japanese delegation reacted with astonishment and through the interpreter asked Deng what he meant. Deng replied: "In years gone by, we managed to inflict upon your nation two of the greatest burdens known to mankind—Confucianism and the Chinese writing system. Now we in China have got rid of the first and are on our way to getting rid of the second. But it seems that you Japanese are to suffer the consequences of both for the rest of your history. This is a crime that China can never be forgiven for."

At any rate, the problem of how Chinese is to be written, and in what kind of script, is far from being an important issue in China. The People's Republic, by the free admission of its leaders as well as the evidence of any visitor, is still generations from becoming a modern industrialized society. Even though literacy has risen dramatically in the decades since the establishment of the present government, the percentage of literate persons in the Chinese population as a whole is still so very low that the question of how such reading or writing is to be done, or through the medium of what kind of script, hardly matters.

But Japan of course is quite different from China, in this way as well as in so many others. Japan is an economic superpower, one of the most modern, most advanced of the world's industrial giants. It has an admirably high literacy rate. No one knows just what that rate is, and it cannot be as high as Japanese educational and official circles claim when they suggest that 94.7 percent of the Japanese population is literate. No country anywhere in the world could possibly have such a high literacy rate for the simple reason that in any normal population sample, the number of adult individuals whose mental development is sufficiently advanced to permit them to learn to read and write anything, even the simplest, most efficient writing system known, does not come anywhere near the official figure quoted for Japanese literacy. But literacy in Japan is certainly high, quite apart from these inflated official claims. It is reasonable to suppose that almost every adult Japanese who is not mentally incompetent or otherwise unable to learn to read and write has been taught to do so, well enough at least to handle the two phonetic syllabaries and, in almost every case, also well enough to read written material of an average level of difficulty. (Kindaichi's absurd claim that even after graduation from high school most Japanese cannot read the daily newspaper is patent nonsense, a prime example of the myth shamelessly employing exaggeration to make statements that anyone who has spent even a day in Japan will know to be untrue. If they cannot read those newspapers, then why in the world are all those people on the subways holding them up before their faces, hour after crowded hour?)

In attempting to make a virtue out of the modern Japanese writing system, and not only to justify its existence (which is quite difficult enough), but actually to present it as a superior way of doing things, something of which the Japanese ought to be proud, the myth has its work cut out for it, to say the least. Such a task clearly calls for new, strong hands, as well as a fresh approach to the work of mythmaking. And as luck would have it, all these qualities and more have suddenly become available from the mid-1970s on in the person of Professor Takao Suzuki of Keio University—already no stranger to these pages and currently the world's unrivaled champion of the innate superiority and efficiency of the Japanese writing system.

Even to formulate a simple defense of the existence of the Japanese writing system—an *apologia pro vita sua,* as it were—is something that would drive most minds, no matter how innovative, to the brink of imbalance. To go the enormous step further and attempt to prove that the system not only has a right to exist, but is actually superior to any other known system of writing would, in most cases, simply provide the final push. The task involved might roughly be compared with that of persuading a population suffering from a long-standing epidemic infestation by a virulent, debilitating disease that they are not only in perfect health, but that actually they are all in better health than anyone who lives in the countries surrounding them, countries where this epidemic disease from which they all suffer is unknown. Only a thoroughgoing, perfectly structured sustaining myth could pull this off with a straight face. The fact that the modern myth of Nihongo not only attempts this tremendous feat of sociolinguistic deception, but actually has considerable success in selling it in certain quarters, only provides additional impressive evidence for the enormous mythic powers of the Nihongo cult in contemporary Japan.

Suzuki and the other scholars who specialize in this strange subdivision of the myth not only end by claiming that they have made a virtue out of something that is clearly an enormous social and cultural liability, they generally cannot resist the temptation to twist the knife an extra turn. Most often their arguments on behalf of the Japanese writing system end with yet another triumphal shout: You see, they exclaim in effect, not only is our writing better than yours, but this also means that we understand our language—this difficult, difficult language of ours—better than you understand your own far easier one! A triumph, indeed—if any of this were true.

Suzuki has devoted an important section of one of the several books that he published in 1975 on Japanese sociolinguistic problems to his own innovative theories about why the Japanese writing system is superior to any other script in the world. Few Japanese publications in this entire field of sociolinguistics are at all easy to summarize, as we have seen, but in this respect Suzuki's work is somewhat out of the ordinary. His views are generally presented with uncommon rigor and candor, so that it is relatively easy to summarize what he is saying on most subjects, this one included.

On the topic of the script and its putative superiority, Suzuki argues more or less along the following lines. He begins with a kernel of fact, as usual. This kernel is his statement, correct and above question, that when Chinese characters are employed in the Japanese writing system, they often serve as discrete symbols for writing the individual parts of compound words—the individual parts of words that linguists usually call morphemes. As is usual with many sciences, linguistics included, calling them this is little more than using a difficult or unfamiliar term for a rather simple entity. The morpheme, or part of the word that is written with an individual Chinese character in the Japanese writing system, is equivalent in English-language terms to such parts of words as the elements "man" and "kind" in the English word mankind, or to the elements "half," "heart," "-ed," and "-ly" in a word like halfheartedly. Japanese has many long compound words of this same sort. Some of them are native Japanese words, but most are borrowings from Chinese. In either instance—but particularly in the case of the long compound words that have been borrowed from Chinese—the Japanese writing system uses a different Chinese character to write each separate part of the whole word.

It is in this particular feature of the writing system that we find Suzuki prepared to take his stand in arguing for the innate superiority of the entire system. He claims that when such long compound words in a Japanese text are written with a number of different Chinese characters—one for each morpheme, or for each separate part going to make up the word—these words are more easily understood by "the common reader" in Japan than similarly long compounds in English are likely to be understood by an equivalent "common reader" of equal educational background in North America or England—particularly, he further argues, when the long compound words in English are those based upon Greek or Latin borrowings. After all, English has many compound words that incorporate borrowings from Greek and Latin, sometimes borrowings from both languages in the same word. Such terms—words like anthropology, geophysics, and traumatic—play roughly the same role in the historical formation of the English vocabulary and its resources as do the equally numerous Chinese loanwords in Japanese. We have all from time to time certainly had to look into a dictionary to see what this or that unfamiliar English word based on a borrowing from one of the classical languages really means. Returning from a visit to the doctor, who has not had to look up this or that neologistic medical term to see what the diagnosis really was?

So if this sort of borrowed, potentially unfamiliar vocabulary item is really easier for the average Japanese reader than its English equivalent, and if that ease of understanding is to be explained by the nature of the Japanese writing system, with its liberal use of nearly two thousand individual Chinese characters that must be learned by rote, one is initially tempted to agree with Suzuki. It may at first glance appear that there is in fact something to what the Keio University professor has to say about this. Or is there? As it happens, the one specific example that Suzuki provides in his 1975 book, as putative proof for just how this peculiarity of the Japanese writing system really makes it superior to the English alphabetic script, collapses of its own weight as soon as we take it in hand for even moderately careful scrutiny.

Suzuki cites and examines the theoretical case of a British typist "of no particular educational accomplishments." He suggests that she might very well not understand just what the English word anthropology means when she encounters it in something that has been given to her to type up. But the Japanese equivalent of such a person, he argues, i.e., a Japanese typist "of no particular educational background," would do far better with the Japanese word for anthropology, which happens to be the borrowed compound *jinruigaku*. Moreover, he also claims, she would be better off with this Japanese word because of the very nature of the Japanese writing system, which means here the borrowed Chinese-character orthography in which a word like *jinruigaku* is normally written in a modern Japanese text.

By simply looking at the word *jinruigaku* and at the way in which it is written in the Japanese text set before her for copying, Suzuki argues, the Japanese typist will be able to guess what the word means, even if she does not already know. This, he suggests in turn, means that Japanese orthography, far from being the cumbersome, costly, troublesome burden upon the mind and memory that we may have heard it called, is actually far superior to the way in which the modern languages of Europe are written. Once again, as so often in the writings of the myth of Nihongo, before we notice what has happened, Japan has suddenly turned out to be "Number One."

There are so many specious elements in Suzuki's argument about the superiority of the Japanese writing system that one hardly knows where to begin in criticizing it. One useful place is the Japanese word *jinruigaku* (anthropology) itself, if only because it is always with the word that any linguistic discussion, including any treatment of sociolinguistic problems, must always begin. So what can we say about this word *jinruigaku*?

The modern Japanese word *jinruigaku* is a neologism. This means that it is a fairly new word, coined in Japan by putting together borrowed Chinese roots, much in the same way that English words like anthropology are themselves neologisms coined by putting together Greek roots. The Greeks never had a word for anthropology, any more than the Chinese ever had an original term for the equivalent of *jinruigaku*. A modern Greek knowing only the classical Greek language, or a Chinese trained only in traditional Chinese literature, would each be equally and totally puzzled by such newly coined terms as anthropology and *jinruigaku*. They would in each case recognize the individual parts, but they would not know what the words mean. The individual parts of the words, the borrowed roots that are put together to make them up, are what we mean by etymology. Etymology is a useful and important branch of linguistics, but etymology is not the same thing as meaning. Etymology tells where a word came from, not what it means. To know what it means, you have to know the language, and moreover, you have to know the word.

Suzuki, we must stress again, bases his argument for the superiority of the Japanese writing system on his thesis that an uneducated Japanese typist (by the way—is there such a thing?) would immediately be able to grasp what the word *jinruigaku* means, in the sense of effectively understanding just what the academic discipline and science to which this word refers are all about. Not for her the rigors of lectures on anthropology or the labor of reading a paperback introduction to the subject; she is spared all this and also put head and shoulders above her ill-equipped British or American sister—all thanks to the marvels of the Japanese writing system.

This, he argues, is because the Japanese writing system writes the first morpheme of this word, *jin,* with the Chinese character for a word meaning man, the second morpheme *rui* with the character for another Chinese word meaning category, and the last morpheme *gaku* with yet a third Chinese character, one going with a Chinese word meaning study. From all this, the Japanese typist is supposed to be able to understand what the discipline known as anthropology is and what it studies.

First, it is just as well to begin by clearing the decks for criticism of the Suzuki thesis on the superiority of the script by mentioning a few salient difficulties that distinguish his data, but to which Suzuki never alludes. First of all, he neglects to mention that the British typist who so greatly excites his sympathy is able to type her English-language, alphabetic text on a modern electric machine with only some forty-five keys. The Japanese typist must do her work hovering over an enormous Rube Goldberg contraption that can only be described as a manually operated typesetting machine.

A Japanese typewriter is a very large machine that covers the better part of the top of an average-size office desk. It is built to hold upward of two thousand individual pieces of type. The typist must operate it by manually positioning a floating unit over the body of the machine so that a kind of iron-claw mechanism can pick up each piece of type, print it on the paper, and then redeposit it into the bed of the machine—and so on, over and over, one slow piece of type at a time. It is physically hard, desperately slow work. The unfortunate young ladies who must do it hour after hour in Japanese offices would probably have something of their own to say on the subject of the superiority of the Japanese writing system, had Suzuki ever thought to ask them. As it is, the process of typing in Japanese is so slow and so costly that it is used only under special circumstances, usually restricted to official or legal documents. All other written texts, as for example the manuscripts for Suzuki's many books, must be entirely handwritten, as he knows very well, since it is usually the author who must write them out.

So much for the sheer mechanics of the two writing systems, that of English and that of Japanese. Suzuki neglects this aspect of the question entirely; all his attention focuses instead on how much the typist understands of what she is given to type. But even granting, for the sake of his argument, that this is an important consideration in evaluating a writing system, we find that this aspect of his argument also breaks down as soon as we subject it to scrutiny.

The fact of the matter is that the Japanese typist—supposing that she is not too exhausted even to care by the time she has located the three Chinese characters involved and propelled the mechanism that picks them up, prints them, and redeposits them in her machine—will no more be able to put together the etymology of the constituent morphemes of the word she is typing, and from this etymology arrive at the meaning of the word in question, than could the British or American typist, if she happened to be of Greek ancestry and knew the Greek language but did not know what the word anthropology meant.

A string of individual morphemes of the order of man plus category plus study will tell the Japanese typist as little about what anthropology means as will a sequence of morphemes of the order of man plus study, which after all is the etymology of the borrowed Greek roots in English anthropology. All that the borrowed Chinese characters as they are used in modern Japanese writing can do is to remind the reader, or in this case the typist, of the etymology of a given word. This is always interesting, but it is not the same thing as the meaning of the word, nor does it provide a useful or functional guide to the usage of the word.

Actually, the Japanese typist looking at the written word *jinruigaku* could make several different guesses as to what the word means. If she takes the first two elements *jinrui* in their usual sense of mankind, where *rui* (category) becomes a kind of class-plural, she will end up with "the science or study of mankind." If she takes this same *rui* element more literally as category, she will end up with "the science or study that categorizes or classifies men." Either way, she will understand very little about what *jinruigaku* (anthropology) really means or about how it is used in the language. The only help that the Japanese writing system would provide in all this would be to clue her in as to the etymology of the word; but the etymology can only lead her away from, rather than toward, its actual meaning. How much quicker and better simply to look in a dictionary when you want to know what a word means, no matter what the language or how it happens to be written.

To point out further flaws in Suzuki's argument for the superiority of the Japanese writing system would be to run the risk, as so often in these pages, of bestowing a dignity upon claims that they clearly do not deserve, and so we will resist the temptation to point out additional areas where his ideas collapse, except for the following point, which can hardly be neglected.

Consistently, Suzuki argues that it is the *Japanese* writing system that is superior. But when he gives examples in explaining what it is that he finds to be superior, it always turns out to be the way in which this writing system uses Chinese characters—which were, of course, as their name indicates, borrowed by the Japanese from China. So if there really were anything superior in the whole business, it would in no way reflect upon Japan, nor would it be a clue to the special variety of Japanese superiority that Suzuki is trying to demonstrate. All that his evidence could ever possibly prove is that *Chinese* writing is superior. And we have already seen what the Chinese today think of that argument in our quotation from Deng Xiaoping.

Given the cumbersome, costly, and highly involved system of writing in common daily use in Japan, one might reasonably ask if there is any likelihood that it will be changed or reformed in any significant respect in our lifetimes. The answer appears to be no. The script is firmly entrenched within both the society and the culture. Perhaps it is their covert realization that nothing is likely to be done about the burden that the script places upon Japanese life at every level that leads such scholars as Suzuki into their ill-advised attempts to make a virtue out of what appears to be a culturally and socially determined necessity. Suggestions for radical script reform in modern Japan are sometimes heard, but they come only from what are very obviously fringe groups outside the mainstream of the society, groups that may in all fairness be compared with the proponents elsewhere of flat-earth theories or advocates of the single tax.

One reason for suspecting that Japanese society will continue to resist all attempts at significant script reform as long as possible derives from a quick survey of Japanese history. Japanese society has already encountered and survived three major historical catastrophes. Each of these shook it to its foundations, and each was also involved with the question of Chinese characters and their employment to write Japanese. Each time, serious questions arose in connection with the use of the Chinese script in Japan—the first time, whether to use it; in the other two instances, whether to continue to employ it.

The first of these catastrophes, the so-called Taika Reforms of the late seventh century, spelled the end of domination of Japanese life by the descendants of the earliest territorial rulers and the eventual concentration of political power into the hands of a single extended family. It also set the course of the society toward the importation of many new ideas and political forms from the Asian continent. Among these, an important place was held by the Chinese script, the imported orthographic elements of which still form the heart of the Japanese writing system.

The question of whether or not to abandon these borrowed Chinese characters arose during each of the two subsequent catastrophes that again altered the face of Japanese society—the Meiji Restoration of the late 1860s and Japan's defeat in World War II. Each time the answer was strongly against abandoning the system.

Deng Xiaoping may very well be correct in his outspoken comments on the use of the Chinese script in Japan. Having already survived so many forces for change in the past, there seems to be little reason to imagine that the script will prove any more vulnerable in the future—always, of course, barring a fourth major historical catastrophe of even greater magnitude. The Chinese seem determined to rid themselves of their own invention, the Chinese characters, and to eliminate the costly burden on time, memory, and labor that the characters represent, long before the Japanese do.

Meanwhile, as the mythmakers continue to generate their specious arguments that attempt to justify the continued use of the Chinese script in writing Japanese, the technocrats, for their part, play into their hands by developing the high-level technological innovations that make it possible to continue to employ this cumbersome writing system in a modern industrial society like Japan. One can, in truth, detect few if any signs of hope on this whole horizon.

Two more subsidiary antimyths, both also intimately related to the overall hypothesis that Japanese is a specially difficult language, deserve our attention, if only because they are frequently encountered in accounts of modern Japan written by foreigners, among whom these particular antimyths have apparently taken deep root.

A typical expression of the first of these antimyths is found in Jack Seward's book *The Japanese,* advertised by its publisher as a book that will tell "what everyone needs to know about the 'inscrutable' Japanese today—from bed to business, their customs and attitudes, public and private."

Seward claims that in the thirty years during which he has "had a deep interest in American students of things Japanese," he can recall having met only five Caucasian Americans who are really able to use the Japanese language effectively. "I believe," he adds, "that the five mentioned . . . must constitute a large percentage of the genuine experts to be found in either the United States or Japan." He also flatly asserts that "of more than one thousand U.S. businessmen in Tokyo, perhaps three are fluent enough to make an impromptu speech in Japanese."

It would not be difficult to cite many other passages from popular or journalistic writing about Japan by foreigners, particularly Americans, where equal stress is laid upon the near impossibility of any "Caucasian American" or other non-Japanese ever becoming fluent enough in reading, writing, and speaking Japanese to employ the language in an effective fashion. The myth of difficulty has done its work well. It has managed to extend this particular antimyth of nonlearnability into the sociolinguistic reaction patterns of foreigners, who then in turn disseminate it all over the world.

These and similar accounts purporting to document the "five or ten Caucasian Americans who know the Japanese language" or "the three fluent enough to make an impromptu speech in Japanese" are of course misleading nonsense. They could simply be dismissed out of hand were they not such a significant expression of the antimyth of difficulty, this time turned against non-Japanese by a non-Japanese observer himself.

It simply is not true to say that only three or four or five Americans, whether businessmen or not, who live and work in Tokyo know the language well, or well enough to make an impromptu speech; it is not even near the truth. Anyone who has ever lived in Tokyo for any period at all during the postwar decades can think of the names of many individuals who can carry off such a feat perfectly well. Tokyo has plenty of foreigners who speak, read, and understand Japanese very well indeed, surely quite well enough to meet Seward's standards. Seward, in a word, grossly underestimates the number of foreigners who can handle the Japanese language effectively. By his misleading account of their numbers he helps to give further credence to the mythic view of the enormous difficulty of Japanese, a mythic view that he himself appears to have swallowed whole.

But for every sociolinguistic phenomenon there is an explanation, if we can only locate it. What is the explanation for Seward's misleading estimates about the number of foreigners, particularly Americans, who can handle the Japanese language effectively? Several reasons suggest themselves; but without knowing more of Seward than the writer does, it is impossible to suggest which may be the correct one.

Perhaps Seward himself simply happens to be one of those individuals—and they turn up in any random population sample—who has enormous difficulty in learning a foreign language and who as a result never got far with the task of learning Japanese. Such individuals are often prone to generalize upon the basis of their own experience; perhaps that is what Seward is doing. Perhaps he assumes that no one, or almost no one, has ever learned Japanese effectively as a foreign language because he himself has never managed to do so. At one point in his book, in close proximity to one of these misleading estimates of the small number of foreigners who have learned to use Japanese effectively, Seward does, for that matter, make a somewhat laconic reference to "the six Japanese language schools that I attended." Perhaps this is a clue to at least part of the problem. No one who encounters only the normal amount of difficulty in learning Japanese, or any other foreign language, has to attend six different language schools.

Another possible reason may well hinge on the fact that Seward is an American. Perhaps because of this, he tends to generalize upon the basis of Americans whom he knows in the American Embassy and its consular service in Japan. If one were to generalize about the ability of foreigners to learn the Japanese language effectively on the sole basis of acquaintanceship with persons from the U.S. State Department and the American Foreign Service employed at the Tokyo embassy and the various consulates throughout Japan, one would most likely end up with an estimate along the spartan lines of Seward's remarks.

In striking contrast to the personnel of the other major foreign diplomatic posts in Japan, the Americans at the embassy in Tokyo and elsewhere throughout the country, particularly since the mid-1950s, have made almost a cult of not being able to employ the Japanese language, no matter how long they live and work in Japan. Someone else will have to write another book about another body of linguistic mythology in order to explain this most curious phenomenon, but anyone wishing to verify it need only have a Japanese friend stop by at one of the American diplomatic establishments in Japan and try to conduct even the most trivial business with one of the American staff members stationed there.

The chances of a Japanese visitor to such an establishment ever seeing an American are, in the first place, remote in the extreme. The Americans are all locked up somewhere upstairs in safety, while the daily business of the place is always conducted below decks by locally recruited Japanese employees. But should a Japanese-speaking client eventually manage to have an interview with one of the Americans, a local interpreter will have to be employed, with only the rarest of exceptions. The figures that Seward cites are actually pretty close to the facts for this extremely limited segment of the foreign community in Tokyo. But fortunately the American diplomatic establishment in Japan is no more representative of that community than it is of the United States. If Seward has indeed had in mind his knowledge of the linguistic skills that distinguish American diplomatic personnel in Japan by their conspicuous absence, he has erred only in generalizing them to categorize all foreigners in Japan, to whom emphatically they do not apply. Any average day of any average week, the sub-assistant chauffeur at the Soviet Embassy in Tokyo is certain to be far more fluent in Japanese than either the American or the Soviet ambassador; but then, he has to be.

These misleading accounts of how extremely few foreigners have ever been able to become fluent in the Japanese language arise for a variety of reasons. But none of the reasons have anything to do with the nature of the Japanese language, any more than they reflect the actual state of competence in the Japanese language among foreigners resident and employed in Japan.

Most often at fault is the tendency of a few Americans to generalize upon the experience of themselves and a few other Americans. Americans living and working abroad, everywhere in the world, still generally resist learning the necessary foreign languages. Because they resist the task, they are generally not very good at it. Since they are generally not very good at it, they assume that the same is true of everyone else in their position, which hardly follows. Partly also these baseless accounts reflect a subsidiary antimyth growing out of the same myth of difficulty that we have been considering in this chapter. The antimyth reasons, if the Japanese themselves find their language difficult and impossible to learn, how could a foreigner ever manage to do it? And so it concludes that no foreigners ever do.

The second of these subsidiary antimyths builds upon the first. It attempts to explain the failure of American business to capture a greater share of Japan's import trade by the difficulty of the Japanese language—which difficulty is, of course, supposed in turn to explain the inability and hence also the failure, of any Americans to learn to use Japanese effectively. Once more, the myth functions here in its classic role of providing face-saving explanations for what are, in matter of cold fact, rather unpleasant truths.

It is certainly true that American manufactured products have not been bought in large quantities by Japan and have not been sold widely in Japan during the past decade of affluence. Hardly a month goes by when the balance of payments between Japan and the United States is not heavily in Japan's favor. Meetings are held; high-level conferences are called; and regularly, the decision reached by both sides is announced to the world press: Japan is willing to import another six cases of American grapefruit, provided that the United States will promise to buy another six thousand automobiles in the same month. This is called adjusting the balance of payments, and it usually does not work very well.

One reason it does not work very well is that the Japanese do not like grapefruit very much; another reason is, whenever the famous additional six cases of grapefruit are due to be unloaded from the ship at Yokohama, the Japanese Ministry of Agriculture can almost always be depended upon to confiscate them on the general grounds that they may possibly contain some as yet unidentified poisonous substance. Why the Americans should be so disagreeable as to ship over poisonous grapefruit is never explained, nor is any explanation forthcoming for why the Americans appear to eat the same dangerous fruit with no ill effects. The newspaper headlines scream, "Suspicion of Poison on Grapefruit in Yokohama, Authorities to Destroy Entire Shipment." Once more, the balance of payments resists balancing.

The sociolinguistic difficulty myth then takes this whole situation in hand and comes up with a face-saving answer, one that saves as many faces in Japan as it does in America. The answer is, Japanese do not buy American goods because Americans are poor at speaking Japanese. If Americans could learn to speak Japanese, they could peddle their grapefruit from every corner in Japan, and the Japanese would buy a lot of them; the poison they contain would be magically neutralized, and the balance-of-payments problem would be solved. But of course the Americans cannot do this. They cannot do it because the Japanese language is impossibly difficult, even for the Japanese, and even more so for Americans. So there is nothing to do about the whole untidy situation other than confiscate another shipment of grapefruit at the docks and send the Americans another load of automobiles.

American goods and products sell poorly, if at all, in Japan. There are many reasons for this. Sometimes it is because they are inferior to competing Japanese goods. Sometimes it is because they are things the Japanese neither want nor can use, like enormous gas-guzzling automobiles. But mostly it is because the Japanese Government, in collusion with Japanese business interests, makes it all but impossible for Americans or anyone else to land their goods and get them onto the market. The Japanese Government's permanent civil service has thousands and thousands of full-time employees whose only function is to devise an ever-increasing panoply of regulations, rules, and rituals, all with the common end of making it practically impossible for foreign manufactured products to reach the Japanese customer.

There are things made in America and in other places in the industrialized West that the Japanese would welcome if they could get their hands on them at anything resembling a fair price. One has only to observe the shopping sprees of Japanese tourists on the loose in any foreign city to realize how true this is. One can also imagine the problems it would cause for Japan's domestic producers of the same or similar goods. Why, it might even lead to a slightly sluggish domestic economy, or—heaven forfend—unemployment in certain home industries! Japan sensibly prefers to export unemployment, rather than to suffer its effects at home, and so long as the rest of the industrial world permits it this luxury, why not?

Meanwhile, the subsidiary antimyth, to the effect that the inability of foreigners to learn and to speak the Japanese language somehow has something to do with all this, provides a convenient, if totally misleading, cover story—as convenient for many indolent American businessmen as it is face-saving for most Japanese. Under the circumstances, no wonder this particular antimyth is now so widely disseminated.

And widely disseminated it is, in all its various permutations. In May 1979, Robert S. Strauss, then serving as the United States Special Representative for Trade Negotiations in charge of U.S. participation in the then-current negotiations among ninety-nine nations of the world and of guiding the results of those talks through the U.S. Congress, was quoted in press reports as follows: "We have a thirty-billion-dollar trade deficit in this country. Now, that shouldn't be. This country has the know-how. This country has the technological capacity. We've been lazy. My gosh, I'll bet there are one thousand two hundred and fifty Japanese people in New York today knocking on doors and selling products, and they can speak English as good as you. And I'll bet there aren't but thirty Americans over there in Japan and there aren't but two of them who can speak Japanese."

By now, we have seen enough of the myth and its extensions to be able to pinpoint the sources for every one of Strauss's categorical assumptions. His homespun rhetoric only makes the exotic wellsprings of what he is really saying stand out all the more clearly; the surface expressions may be those of the New York marketplace, but the message is unmistakably labeled "Made in Japan." The myth is as vigorously pushed on the export market—and is as avidly sought out by the American consumer, in this case, Ambassador Strauss—as any other useful, durable, competitively priced Japanese product. Business is booming.

The ultimate test for any genuine myth always involves its powers of explanation. Is it able to provide plausible explanations for what would otherwise strike the uninformed observer as unexpected or irrational elements in the world around us? The meteorologist today knows the simple, geophysical explanation for a flash of lightning in the sky overhead, followed by a frightening clap of thunder. But before this rational explanation was worked out by science, only myth could satisfy man's questions about what was happening. And the more elaborate, the more striking, the more colorful the mythic explanation, the greater its explanatory powers.

A bearded king of the gods hurling his adamantine thunderbolt through the skies in divine anger was a splendid mythic explanation for the observed phenomena, particularly splendid because it was elaborate, striking, and colorful. To provide a rational, scientific explanation for what is so often called the difficulty of the Japanese language is, as we have seen, quite within the competence of linguistic science. But the matter-of-fact treatment of this question by linguistics will never be as striking or as inventive as the pseudo-explanations provided by the myth of Nihongo.

For some, that will always seem to be a weakness of linguistic science. And there will also always be those who prefer to find a bearded king of the gods behind every bolt of lightning, rather than simply a matter-of-fact discharge of atmospheric electricity.

CHAPTER TEN

How Did It All Happen?

> The reasons why Japanese is an expression of national thought and sentiment and is at the same time its plasmic product shall be explained. —Ministry of Education Order No. 2, March 25, 1943

THE MORE one confronts the copious evidence available at every level of contemporary Japanese life for the all-embracing importance of the modern myth of Nihongo, the more puzzled one becomes. How are we to explain the tenacious hold that this myth continues to exercise over the minds of the Japanese public, particularly over the minds of otherwise intelligent, sophisticated individuals who are, in many cases, products of one of the world's most elaborate, advanced, and costly systems of higher education? Even more difficult is understanding how the myth has managed to survive, and indeed today appears to be growing stronger than ever, in the context of one of the world's most highly technological and industrialized societies.

Everyone in the world, particularly those of us who live in the other industrially advanced countries, has had firsthand experience with the level of Japanese scientific achievements. The worldwide distribution of Japanese manufactured products has shown us all, in the most concrete fashion possible, the exceptionally high level of technology that Japanese society has achieved in the three decades following the end of the Pacific War. We drive Japanese automobiles, use Japanese cameras, choose Japanese TVs, radios, and electronic equipment whenever possible, because we know that Japanese society produces all these items at levels of technical competence generally unsurpassed anywhere else in the world, particularly when the often lower prices of the Japanese products are taken into consideration.

All this evidence for Japanese technological and scientific advancement cannot simply be dismissed in the consideration of any question relating to contemporary Japanese life.

How, then, are we to understand, and how are we to explain the enormous paradox that becomes so striking to an observer of the Japanese scene who attempts to reconcile all this evidence for a highly advanced, Western-style technological civilization with the equally plentiful evidence for the permeation and enduring importance of the modern sustaining myth of Nihongo? The two seem strangely out of step with one another; and the more one studies both sides of this bewilderingly unbalanced confrontation, the more puzzling an anomaly it all becomes. No serious consideration of the modern myth of Nihongo as it operates within contemporary Japanese society can avoid a confrontation with this particular paradox. Eventually we must ask ourselves just how all this came about, if we are to make any progress at all in resolving this conundrum, this sociolinguistic anomaly with which modern Japanese life confronts us.

Not very surprisingly, as soon as we undertake the task of trying to identify possible or probable historical explanations for the persistence of this modern myth of Nihongo within contemporary Japanese society, we learn that there is no one simple answer. No single historical factor or cause can easily be identified as providing a universal explanation for the almost unlimited forms that the myth takes in modern Japanese life. If we persist in attempting to identify some such easily categorized, simple answer, we will only be disappointed. What we find instead is a broad spectrum of interrelated contributory causes and historical issues. None of them operates alone or independently of the others; but all of them, taken together, do go a long way toward making clear to the interested observer some of the most likely explanations for this astonishing persistence of a mythic approach to the Japanese language, despite the enormous advances toward modernization and rationality that have been achieved in other areas of contemporary Japanese life.

Here too—as so often in any consideration of contemporary Japanese sociolinguistic conceptualizations—we are able to identify a fairly proximate point of departure for our historical explanations in the infamous *Kokutai no Hongi* document from the fascist-nationalist period of the 1930s and 1940s. We have already seen in some detail how a number of the most striking elements in the contemporary myth of Nihongo, often in the very form in which these same elements are now being remade to serve the sociolinguistic needs of the newly affluent Japan of the 1980s, can be directly traced back to the ideology of the *Kokutai no Hongi* authors. Particularly striking in this connection are the antimyth of silence and the nefarious doctrine of the *kotodama,* the "spirit of the Japanese language." We have already explored some of the ways in which these spurious sociolinguistic concepts were first formulated by Hisamatsu and his coauthors, who falsified and twisted the quite innocent and irrelevant philological evidence of early texts before finally incorporating these concepts into the *Kokutai no Hongi*. We have also seen some of the important ways in which fascist-nationalist perversions of Japanese literary antiquities have been enjoying a revival in our own time, often under official auspices and under the guise of apparently serious academic discourse.

But even after we have considered these particular varieties of evidence, we still find ourselves confronted with the question that concerns us in the present chapter: How did all this happen, and indeed, how does it all continue to happen? How does Japanese society manage to carry off the successful exploitation of its high-level, rational, Western-style technology on the one hand, simultaneously combining it with the totally unscientific, irrational myth of Nihongo on the other? And immediately following upon that particular question, we are confronted by yet another, if anything more pressing issue: How are we to explain the survival and the contemporary revival today of these nefarious sociolinguistic elements from the *Kokutai no Hongi* ideology of the 1940s, particularly in view of the wholesale bankruptcy that the entire fascist-nationalist ideology sustained in the defeat of 1945? How can anyone in modern Japan take seriously the revival of such obviously *Kokutai no Hongi*-related concepts as the antimyth of silence or the "spirit of the Japanese language," in view of the total discredit that Japan's military defeat cast upon all other related ideas of the same period?

The answer lies, once again, squarely within the Japanese educational system and in its curious, self-imposed limitations. Modern Japan has left itself open to once more being victimized by such concepts as the antimyth of silence or the "spirit of the Japanese language" because ever since 1945, it has failed to provide genuinely responsible educational guidance for the Japanese people concerning the history of the Pacific War or concerning Japan's part in that debacle. Despite all the years that the average Japanese person now spends in the classroom, he or she learns too little of a substantive nature about Japanese history of any period and far too little about the history of the period immediately leading up to and including the tragic war that ended in 1945.

Today, well over half of the population of Japan was born after the conclusion of the Pacific War. These younger people have no firsthand knowledge of what happened in the 1940s. Most Japanese living today simply do not know anything about World War II as it affected Japan; they have never heard of the *Kokutai no Hongi*; they do not know any of the history of how people like Hisamatsu and his colleagues twisted and betrayed Japanese literature and history in order to come up with the disastrous ideology of the 1940s.

Santayana taught that those who do not learn from history may too often be doomed to repeat it. One reason for that is surely because those who do not learn their own history are unable to recognize it when they see it threatening them again. Not having studied the past, they may very well mistake what has already been tried and found sadly lacking for something new and promising.

The modern Japanese mythmakers, particularly those who specialize in the sustaining myth of Nihongo, are thus able to go back time and time again to the mother lode of philological quackery represented by such totally discredited documents as the *Kokutai no Hongi*. They can search here and there in the rank conceptualizations of these now all-but-forgotten sources of the old fascist-nationalist ideology, confident that when they emerge from their labors of textual excavation, hardly anyone in modern Japanese society will ever realize just where they have been digging.

So effectively has modern Japan managed to isolate itself from any and all firsthand recollections of the war and its aftermath that for most Japanese readers such tired, thoroughly discredited ideas as the antimyth of silence or the "spirit of the Japanese language" or the entire range of closely related 1940s sociolinguistic quackery now too often seems bright, new, and credible. Most Japanese readers today do not realize that these are all old ideas that long ago were tried and failed. Not knowing their own history, they are unable to recognize it when it is about to be recycled and served up to them once more.

Of all the self-imposed limitations by which the Japanese educational system hampers itself, this inadequate instruction in Japanese history is surely among the most serious. Japanese university students graduate and go out into the world with only the vaguest idea of the names and sequence of the principal periods in Japanese history and with even less of an idea of just what happened during any one of them. Depending upon their interests and the content of certain courses that they may have followed with more than the usual amount of attention, such students often have a surprisingly detailed acquaintance with Western history or with the history of China. But when it comes to the history of Japan, their minds are almost without exception left a total blank.

The main responsibility for this appalling vacuum in modern Japanese education must be assigned to an ideological conflict that arose within Japanese academic circles at the time of Japan's military defeat in 1945 and which has yet to be resolved. When the war ended, it was obviously not immediately possible to resume education in Japanese history using the same texts and along the same lines that had been current up to 1945. New textbooks had to be prepared in almost every educational field, textbooks that would free Japanese schools from the ideological limitations that had been imposed during the years of fascist-nationalist domination. Specialists in each field set about this long-overdue task with enthusiasm.

But in the field of Japanese history, this same enthusiasm soon ran aground on another somewhat unexpected ideological barrier reef. Obviously, no one in Japanese education believed that it was any longer possible or desirable to continue to teach the warped view of Japanese history that had been evolved by Hisamatsu and his colleagues and enforced by the authorities down to August 1945. All this must now be replaced: the question became, replaced by what?

Instead of these suddenly discredited fascist-nationalist fantasies of non-history, what would the Japanese schools now tell their students about Japanese history? Would they present the subject in conventional, Western bourgeois historiographic terms—or would they offer it along the inter-pretive lines of Marxist historical dialectic? Both these rival approaches to Japanese history had been outlawed from Japanese academic life until 1945. Now with the surrender and with the occupation forces' guarantee of academic freedom, they became strident rivals, clamoring for the attention of the Japanese student.

The full story of the sterile standoff that resulted from the postwar con-frontation of these two possible approaches to Japanese history would take us too far afield. We can only point out that the rigid confrontation of these two approaches to history has continued and that it has yet to be resolved within Japanese educational circles. The principal result of this continued confrontation has been that not enough is taught about Japanese history in the normal course of the Japanese educational system, simply because the educational authorities have yet to reach an agreement among themselves upon which approach—the bourgeois or the Marxist—is to be favored. Most Japanese classroom teachers—or at least, most of the leaders of the Japanese teachers' unions—will hear of nothing but the Marxist approach to history. Most Japanese school administrators, as well as the enduring bureaucracy of the national educational establishment—still hewing closely to the ideals of Arinori Mori and his Franco-Prussian models—cannot countenance any departure from the Western bourgeois interpretation. And so long as neither side in this power struggle, not labor on the one hand nor management on the other, is willing to risk the all-out confronta-tion that would be necessary to achieve a clear-cut victory, the result is that not much can be taught about the whole subject of history.

This sterile standoff has seriously inhibited the teaching of Japanese history of all periods on every level of the national school system. Scholars representing each of the two major rival factions are still busy writing textbooks that stress one or the other of these two opposed views of history. The educational bureaucracy for its part is just as busy playing one group off against the other, if only to ensure that neither party manages to become dominant. All this has meant that when it comes to modern history, particularly the years leading up to the Pacific War and the circumstances of Japan's military defeat in 1945, the educational blackout has been almost total through the postwar decades.

Since most Japanese now alive have no direct, personal experience of the war years, and since most of them were not taught anything about the war and its origins while they were in the school system, they have been left in a dangerous intellectual vacuum on all these issues. This is the vacuum into which the mythmakers are quick to intrude, and also the vacuum in which they find that their sly revivals of *Kokutai no Hongi*-related concepts dealing with the Japanese language, such as the antimyth of silence and the "spirit of the language," are gratifyingly easy to cultivate.

One cannot but compare this situation with what has happened in West Germany. The educational authorities of the Federal Republic have admittedly had their own special problems in ensuring that the West German educational system would not permit its people ever to lose sight of the tragedy of the war or of the utterly degrading events that disfigured every sphere of German life during the war years. But the Germans have been determined not to run the risk of repeating their recent history. They have taken substantial, eminently responsible steps to make sure that their educational establishment does what an educational establishment is supposed to do in this and every other circumstance—in a word, make sure that it educates. The Germans have not shirked the extremely unpleasant task of continuing to teach new generations of children what happened to their country in the recent past, in the hope of preventing a repetition of that tragedy.

Any attempt today, within the borders of the Federal Republic, to refurbish and recirculate the ideological conceptualizations of *Mein Kampf* or the other discredited screeds of National Socialism would be met with undisguised contempt, as well as with severe legal countermeasures. It would be greeted with undisguised contempt because German educational authorities have not shrunk from their responsibility to educate the postwar generations about what happened in history. It would also be met with severe legal action because such things are against the law in the Federal Republic. But neither is the case in Japan, where few remember the recent past, and no revival of recent folly is illegal. And so the sociolinguistic deceptions multiply apace, as unchecked by education as by law.

Only one significant exception may be identified in this general blackout on the teaching of recent Japanese history. The atomic bombings of

Hiroshima and Nagasaki are mentioned frequently, and no one is allowed to forget them. But they are taught and talked about in a historical vacuum. Both are always described in isolation, divorced from the context of the events that led up to them. These two events are of course quite terrible enough even when they are viewed in full historical context. But when they are presented, as they always are in modern Japan, with no mention of any of the things that led up to them, they appear particularly terrible and coldblooded. Most Japanese today simply do not realize that, terrible as Hiroshima and Nagasaki both were, neither would ever have happened without there first having been a rape of Nanking or a bombing of Pearl Harbor.

The *Asahi Journal,* a generally responsible weekly magazine of news and opinion, recently published an article about International Christian University, a large, privately operated institution in the Tokyo suburbs. In attempting to describe how and why this particular school was founded shortly after the end of the war, the magazine unconsciously provided striking documentation of just how completely every event of the 1930s and 1940s has been forgotten in contemporary Japan—with the single exception of Hiroshima and Nagasaki.

The International Christian University was begun by American Protestant missionaries, and their goal was an extremely modest one. More than anything else, they wished to build a church somewhere in the greater Tokyo area that would be bigger and have a higher tower than the church of Saint Ignatius at the Jesuit-operated Sophia University in downtown Tokyo.

As the U.S. occupation forces settled in and began to get about their business, many of the Protestants among them began to feel that the soaring bell tower of the Jesuit church at Sophia University was as offensive as it was ostentatious. Still, having just told the Japanese that Japan must now permit freedom for all religious groups, they could hardly go and simply tear the thing down. Instead they settled upon the next best thing—to build a bigger, taller tower for a larger, even more ostentatious church themselves. The result was an enormous cement church with a soaring bell tower (minus, however, any bells) and eventually even a small university complex out in Mitaka, at the edge of the Tokyo suburban area. The church and bell tower dwarfed their Jesuit model in scale and size, if not in durability; the initial construction was undertaken so hastily that a few years later everything had to be torn down and rebuilt even more expensively—which was promptly done, money at the time being of course no object.

At any rate, all this architectural *folie de foi* had been well forgotten by 1978, when the *Asahi Journal* reporter was assigned to write an account of the International Christian University and tried in the course of his visit there to find out how and why the university had been established. While on the campus, he put his question to a number of the students he met there, and they were equally puzzled. Finally one of them came up with the answer: the money for the university was contributed by Americans who were anxious to make an offering in order to get God to absolve them from their sin in dropping the atomic bombs.

Followers of the dour doctrines of Calvin, Wesley, and John Knox in the U.S. contributed so much of the money involved that the reformers must really have turned in the grave at this. The university apparently does quite as poor a job of teaching its own hard-line Protestant theology—a system in which buying absolution from sin with money is hardly supposed to play a major role—as it does in reminding its students of the major events in the recent history of their own country.

Against this background of educational neglect and irresponsibility, the reader will probably not even be surprised to learn that there is an important segment of contemporary Japanese intellectual opinion that now argues to the effect that Japan did not, in actual fact, lose the war, and that also claims Japan did not actually surrender to the Allies in August 1945. When education fails as utterly in its duties and elementary responsibilities as Japanese schools have done in this connection, no practical limits can apparently be set upon the fantasies that can be generated. Black quite easily can be made out to be white; up becomes down; and yes is no. Since entire generations of young Japanese have been taught nothing about what happened to their country prior to 1945, it eventually even becomes possible to convince at least some of them that, in fact, nothing happened in 1945.

The principal exponent of this particular myth of "no defeat, no surrender" is Professor Jun Etō of the Tokyo Institute of Technology. Which particular variety of technological science is the subject of Professor Etō's research remains obscure, but apparently it is not too demanding a specialty, since most of his time is divided between lecturing abroad on literary and cultural subjects and publishing acerbic accounts in Japan of the horrors and perils of academic life in the West, showing in detail how poorly it compares with the more abundant creature comforts, as well as with the intellectual riches, of life in Japan.

Etō has recently attracted a good deal of attention in the United States with a lecture in which he argues that Japan did not actually surrender to the Allies in August 1945. As a result, everything that was done in Japan during the period of American occupation—such as, for example, outlawing the *Kokutai no Hongi* or carrying out rural land reforms—was totally illegal and quite unfair and ought now to be apologized for or, better yet, undone.

Etō bases this novel view of recent history on a memorandum allegedly prepared in January 1946 by a disgruntled employee of the Japanese Foreign

Office named Ryōichi Taoka, who was serving at the time as director of the Japanese Foreign Office's Treaty Bureau. Since in 1946 Japan had almost no valid treaties still in effect with any foreign countries, the post of director of the Treaty Bureau can at the time hardly have been a very taxing position at best; and apparently it left Taoka with a good deal of time on his hands. This leisure Taoka employed in a meticulous study and restudy of the texts of the Potsdam Declaration, which called for the unconditional surrender of Japan to the Allies, as well as the texts of the Japanese communiques that accepted this declaration and of course also the Japanese texts of the Instrument of Surrender.

The thesis that Taoka eventually evolved from all this careful study, and that Etō is now championing on his foreign lecture tours, holds that Japan never actually surrendered. Only the Japanese armed forces surrendered, claims Etō. And since everyone knows that the Japanese armed forces were soon thereafter abolished and ceased to exist shortly after August 15, 1945—shortly after whatever it was that did happen in August 1945—nothing really happened at all. Japan was never defeated; Japan never surrendered. It is impossible to fault Etō on his logic; one can only ask where Gilbert and Sullivan are now, when we could really use them.

Poetry has been defined as emotion recollected in moments of tranquility. In its own way, this Taoka-Etō theory of no defeat, no surrender has a poignant, poetic quality—perhaps because it too incorporates generous portions of emotions recollected in moments of a variety of tranquility. Be that as it may, when Taoka originally announced his idea in January 1946, he was promptly dismissed from his position in the Foreign Office; there were simply too many others still around who remembered only too well what had really happened in history. But now Etō is able to revive the Taoka thesis and is listened to in full seriousness.

All this is very ominous; it seems to be fraught with serious trouble for Japan's future, and it probably is. Fortunately, however, the picture is not all this black. There are a few other, less frightening aspects to this same issue. We can also identify a few other probable explanations for the successful revival and apparently enduring popularity of the sociolinguistic myth of Nihongo that will be neither quite as terrifying nor quite as fantastic as those just alluded to.

Many of these more or less benign explanations for the perennial flourishing of mythic elements in Japanese sociolinguistic life are now increasingly easy to identify and understand, thanks in large measure to the timely publication of Edward W. Said's *Orientalism*. This book is a wide-ranging study of what happens in terms of intellectual history when one culture or tradition creates an image of different cultures or traditions as being the

"Other." The author, a Palestinian Arab who is now professor of English and Comparative Literature at Columbia University, uses the term that is also his book's title, *Orientalism,* as a technical expression for what he calls "a way of coming to terms with the Orient that is based on the Orient's special place in European Western experience." In these terms, he manages to subject to brilliant scrutiny most of the "deepest and most recurring images of the Other" that Europe has consistently employed when encountering any cultural or intellectual confrontation with other parts of the world, but especially with the Near and Middle East.

The Near and Middle East, and the role of Orientalism as he understands and uses this term in the treatment of those parts of the world by Western European and American scholarship, are Said's major preoccupation. His book does not deal with Japan or other parts of the Far East in any detail. Nevertheless, this concept of Orientalism as a specific, critical stage or technique in the processes of intellectual history soon shows itself to have important implications for modern Japanese sociolinguistic life as well. In particular, it helps to explain—along with the vacuum in historical education discussed above—some of the most important reasons for the continuing popularity of the modern myth of Nihongo.

For Said, Orientalism is a shorthand term for the entire, wide-ranging complex of views with which Europe and North America have traditionally come to terms with the Near and Middle East—coming to terms with these different traditions and cultural systems by agreeing, either overtly or implicitly, to relegate these entities to the realm of the Other.

In its own rather special way, the ideology of sociolinguistic exclusiveness that we find running like a bright, connecting thread throughout so much of the modern myth of Nihongo might very well be categorized as a special kind of reverse Orientalism. It is rather as if the Japanese were, in this instance at least, determined to do it to themselves and to their own culture before others can do it for and to them—the "doing" in both instances being the creation of an image in terms of which other cultures or traditions will consist of something radically different—what Said calls establishing the Other. Orientalism, as the term has now been given currency by Said, is always what someone else does to yet another culture. But in the case of Japan, we have to deal instead with the rare spectacle of a culture vigorously determined to Orientalize itself.

By insisting that the Japanese language is unique, distinct among human languages, and endowed with a spirit that sets it apart from other varieties of human speech, Japanese sociolinguistic culture has taken a major step toward its own Orientalization. It is then in a position to employ this same attitude of the Other—the attitude that is at the heart of all Orientalism—as a convenient way for coming to terms with the West—not only with the West itself, conceptualized as a conglomeration of cultural, social, and political entities, but also with the West as a sociolinguistic phenomenon.

As we have seen, not the least of the operations of the modern myth of Nihongo are the many ways in which it interferes with the learning of foreign languages by the Japanese. At the same time, the myth provides a convenient if totally spurious methodology for coming to terms with many of the problems that arise from the very necessity for learning foreign languages. If followed through to its illogical conclusion, the myth seems not only to explain why the Japanese find foreign languages difficult, it can also be manipulated so as to appear to make a virtue out of this same difficulty. So also for the Japanese writing system, where the myth can be used to bestow quite spurious but seriously entertained notions of superiority upon what is clearly, by any independent standard of measurement, one of the world's most cumbersome cultural artifacts.

This same convenient concept of reverse Orientalism also provides a number of useful insights even into the ultimate motivation of such earlier manifestations of Japanese exclusivity as the *Kokutai no Hongi* document itself. It helps explain the exaggerated claims of such texts, as well as the continued popularity of their ideas when they are revived under transparent modern guise decades later, even though of course it does not excuse their conscious tampering with fact or their distortions of philological truth.

Viewed in this way, such ideological screeds as the *Kokutai no Hongi* are themselves nothing more or less than textual manifestations of this same inner urge toward self-imposed reverse Orientalism on the part of Japanese academic circles. By setting up Japanese life and culture as somehow unique and by taking every possible step to ensure that both should remain the exclusive preserve and domain of a small closed group, a group to which an individual can gain admission only by circumstances of birth, these leaders were early determined to practice cultural and social Orientalism upon themselves, before others could practice it upon them.

This was particularly true during the period of the Meiji Restoration, when the spectacle of a prostrate China being picked to bits by the predatory Western powers was understandably a matter of concern for all informed Japanese. The West had Orientalized China with a vengeance. First it had done the job intellectually and academically; now the Orientalism inherent in the abstract and ostensibly harmless games of chinoiserie had come home to roost in the terrifying spectacle of the physical dismemberment of the Chinese state. The Western-led rape of China represented an international catastrophe in which the Japanese for their part were only too willing to participate; and participate they did, right down until 1945. But at the same time that they were busy picking the bones of the recumbent giant, they could hardly refrain from asking themselves how all this had come about and what the Chinese had done to allow themselves and their country to fall into this ignominious position.

One answer was clear, perhaps clearer than any other. The Chinese had permitted themselves to be Orientalized by the West. They had allowed, permitted, even perhaps at times encouraged the West to take them as the Other, as representing the kind of separate, unrelated cultural and social expression that one could rob, steal, and trample upon with impunity. If this was what happened when one permitted oneself to be Orientalized, the Japanese ideological leaders reasoned, the best thing was obviously not to be Orientalized. And the best way to avoid being Orientalized by others was to do it to oneself, before anyone could beat you to the draw.

The claims for cultural, social, and national exclusivity that are made so stridently in such documents as the *Kokutai no Hongi* represent the epitome of Orientalism—but it is a particularly Japanese brand of the phenomenon: an internal, reverse, self-Orientalism directed against a society by itself as a kind of desperate, last-ditch measure of self-defense against everything that threatens to pour in from the outside. The same is true, and even more strikingly so, of the sociolinguistic aspects of this same *Kokutai no Hongi* mentality. Just like the exclusive claims of *kokutai,* that fictive Japanese national entity or identity, so also do the exclusive claims made on behalf of the Japanese language provide a measure of self-defense by invoking the prerogatives of Orientalism on behalf of the society itself.

Anywhere else in the world and at any other time in world history, Orientalism has characteristically been something that one society, or a group of societies, does to others. In adapting the technique of Orientalization to the internal ends of their own society, the Japanese have pulled off a coup. Japanese claims to be unique in this or that area are, as we have seen, universally suspect and never more suspect than when these claims relate to the Japanese language. But there is indeed one element that is distinctive about all this. Orientalism, as a defensive technique employed by a society against itself, probably must be regarded as something truly unique, a genuine innovation of Japanese society and culture.

In tracing the interlocking courses of the often tortuous historical strands involved with the generation and perpetuation of the modern myth of Nihongo, our task is at least rendered somewhat more feasible by the existence of an abundance of Japanese sources for study. Much of what we have already learned about how important segments of this myth relate to the doctrines of the *Kokutai no Hongi* and the fascist-nationalistic school that this document exemplified would remain obscure if we did not have the text of the *Kokutai no Hongi* available for study and verification. Fortunately we do. In much the same way, it would be extremely difficult to understand how a modern, industrialized society could continue to preserve within its intellectual and academic life the full spectrum of an outmoded and totally discredited inheritance from the 1930s and 1940s, if it were not for the independent evidence that we have concerning the critical lack of instruction in the elementary facts of recent Japanese history throughout the Japanese educational establishment. In identifying all these mechanisms for the perpetuation of the myth, we have the assistance of substantial Japanese materials, which can supplement the evidence gained from our own knowledge of Japanese society, education, and culture.

But there are other, probably equally important areas of this same question where this variety of assistance is not readily forthcoming from Japanese sources. In several other dimensions of our inquiry, we must resign ourselves to working with a dearth of materials. There are also areas in which, for a number of different reasons, our Japanese colleagues have produced little or nothing in the way of study or analysis that will help us in our task.

Often this is because these areas have never struck Japanese observers of sociolinguistic phenomena as particularly significant or worthy of study. But that fact alone does not mean that these problems can safely be ignored. It may instead tell us only that these areas are so very central to the overall issue and so intimately related to its fundamental questions that the Japanese whose observations have been so helpful to us elsewhere in the present study have tended to overlook them simply because they are so basic, so essential, and so massive. It is often a case of the Japanese observer not being able to see the forest for the trees; focusing too much attention on the visible tip of the iceberg is a good way to overlook the rest of the monster that lies hidden beneath the water.

Pursuing our own studies into these areas is a difficult business. Here we must navigate without the help of Japanese guides and largely without the assistance of Japanese documentary materials. But the risk of missing out on some of the most important elements that go to explain the persistence of the modern myth of Nihongo is an even greater one.

Actually, we are not totally without guidance in this particular area, even though this guidance does not derive directly from the work of our Japanese colleagues. Professor Edward Seidensticker of Columbia University is not only a translator of genius and a notable scholar of Japanese literature, he is also an acute observer of the Japanese sociolinguistic scene. He is able to bring to his analysis of Japanese linguistic behavior the highly specialized expertise that can only be gained by a superb command of the language combined with long periods of residence, study, and work in Japan over several decades. When someone of Seidensticker's gifts and unique qualifications suggests one or more underlying reasons for the persistence of the myth of Nihongo, anyone interested in the subject will surely wish to take note of his views. Nor will we be disappointed when we do, since Seidensticker's analysis proves to open new vistas of insight that none of the available Japanese sources and materials even hint at.

Most Japanese sources make an attempt, at one time or another in their analysis of Japanese sociolinguistic behavior, to relate the various aspects of the overall phenomenon to the richness of Japanese social culture. Seidensticker takes a different tack. He suggests instead that one might more accurately interpret much that is striking in Japanese linguistic behavior as "evidence of social ineptness and awkwardness."

This important and original observation he then goes on to explain along the following lines: "There are subjects on which the Japanese can be extremely voluble, but one is soon struck at how very parochial they are. Eavesdropping on this or that conversation singled out from the enormous gabble of a drinking place, one notices of how little interest the contents are to the outsider and to the world in general. They are all about how Nakamura-kun behaved in a manner which the speaker finds at odds with the warm fellow-feeling that ought to prevail, and how the *kachō* took approving notice of a little coup on the speaker's part, and how the bonus this summer is likely to be a disappointment to everyone. It is all shop talk."

Napoleon is said to have described the English as a nation of shopkeepers; Seidensticker appears to be describing the Japanese as a nation of shop talkers; and there is at least as much to be said in favor of the latter view as of the former. In fact, if we pursue the theme that Seidensticker has placed before us and expand it to cover a range of sociolinguistic behavior somewhat wider than that of the office-workers' pub to which he initially relates his analysis, the concept of Japanese sociolinguistic behavior as being essentially a phenomenon of shop talk par excellence not only rings very true; it also contains within itself many new insights that will aid in our further understanding of the persistence of the modern myth of Nihongo. Properly exploited, it can represent a whole new approach to our understanding of the basic question of how things got to be the way they are, at least in this particular segment of Japanese life and culture.

The all-pervading shop talk to which Seidensticker directs our attention is, however, only a sociolinguistic symptom. Behind it one must be prepared to recognize how it ultimately relates to the high degree of specialization that distinguishes every level of Japanese social activity. The university professor of English literature in Japan does not simply specialize in English or in English literature; he specializes in one or two books by a single foreign author. The lavishly successful achievements of Japanese technology are intimately tied up with an equally high degree of specialization. Seidensticker's observation that much, perhaps most, of ordinary Japanese conversation is something that might on one level or another be described as shop talk is a particularly valuable insight, because of the way in which it permits us to associate the persistence of the myth of Nihongo with the otherwise apparently contradictory advances of Japanese technology and industrialization.

Having specialized intensively in this or that small segment of knowledge and activity from early youth, the Japanese office worker or company employee or university professor comes into adulthood with very, very little to talk about, except for shop talk—the necessarily involved talk of the specialty to which his or her life is devoted, culminating several decades of specialized education and training all designed to prepare him or her for a lifetime of further specialization.

Nevertheless, opportunities for talk do present themselves. There are the parties, the company outings, the nightly rounds of drinks in the tiny bars on the way home. Conversation implies a common ground of interests and experience, a common ground that the extreme degree of specialization that is a hallmark of modern Japanese life has all but destroyed. So long as the participants in the conversation group are all members of the same "shop," then shop talk will fill the bill. But as soon as anyone who is not a member of the shop joins in, there will be next to nothing to say. The one thing—perhaps the only thing—that may still be assumed to be common social and cultural property under such circumstances, and that may be depended upon to bridge the gap between the shop talk of this shop and the shop talk of another shop, generally turns out to be Nihongo.

So many otherwise anomalous and disparate strands of contemporary Japanese society and of its characteristic linguistic behavior are brought into meaningful relationship with one another here that the analysis implied must surely reflect a large proportion of reality. Only the language itself—and now, in particular, the language as mythified and mystified by the cult of Nihongo—can serve as a common sociolinguistic bond that will make intershop communication possible, despite the high degree of specialization that is necessary for the continued successful existence of modern Japan. There is, at best, little enough to talk about; take away the myth of Nihongo, and there would be next to nothing.

What has been said so far relates essentially to the sociolinguistic behavior of Japanese functioning totally within Japanese society and takes no notice of how the system described might be disturbed by the introduction of foreign elements. As such, it is both a useful as well as a provocative analysis, one that takes us far toward evolving a cogent theory for the persistence of the myth of Nihongo in the midst of modern Japanese industrialization.

Seidensticker also throws additional light upon the entire mechanism by considering next what happens when this already highly involved sociolinguistic behavioral pattern is disturbed by the introduction of a non-Japanese observer—when a foreigner enters upon the scene—typically, a *hen na gaijin* who, like Seidensticker himself, can both understand and speak the Japanese language: "When for a moment [this variety of shop-talk conversation] is expanded to include the outsider, there is nothing, really, to say. Language itself is an ideal subject for someone who does not wish to talk about anything at all, because when language becomes the burden and not the vehicle, communication ceases." Again the analysis rings so very true that any question of its accuracy and validity is ruled out. The introduction of the outsider into the closed circle of shop talk—in other words, the introduction of a foreigner into any genuinely Japanese conversation—provides us with the specific case that conveniently serves to verify the more general, typical experience of the society.

What happens to such a conversation when the *hen na gaijin* enters it is not essentially different from what takes place when he or she is absent; only the details change. The isolating barriers of shop talk and specialized interests that make Japanese conversation among Japanese difficult at best and that lead in turn to perpetuation of the myth of Nihongo as an always convenient substitute for genuine discourse become totally impregnable once a foreigner enters the conversation group. He or she cannot, by definition as well as by universal social agreement, be an active participating member of any recognized shop-talk sector of the society. If there is to be any discourse with such a person at all, it must be about something that stands clearly outside of the shop talk of Japanese life and society—this, the ultimate of all shops—in a word, it must be Nihongo.

But before we are too critical of Japanese behavior in this connection, we might each of us ask ourselves what we and our friends would choose to talk about if a Martian suddenly appeared at our neighborhood bar and grill, demanding a glass of beer and a ham on rye. He—or it?—would place us and our conversational avenues of escape roughly in the same situation that a *hen na gaijin* does every time he or she confronts Japanese sociolinguistic behavior. Little wonder, then, that it is almost always Nihongo, and only the mythic Nihongo, that can fill the bill in such circumstances.

One further likely reason may be advanced for the overwhelming prevalence of the mythic Nihongo as a topic for conversation in a wide variety of Japanese social situations. We have already stressed the lack of formal education about the events of recent history throughout the Japanese educational establishment and have suggested that the information vacuum that has resulted from this conscious neglect goes far to explain how the society is able to tolerate the periodic revival of ideas and concepts that would surely be regarded as absurd or illegal if the bulk of the public confronted with these outmoded concepts were somewhat better informed. In this same context, however, one further important consideration deserves mention.

The Japanese today may not know much about their own history, and they certainly do not study it in their schools to any useful extent; but economics is another matter. One could almost suspect that the hours the educational system saves by its neglect of Japanese history are all relegated instead to the study of Japan's economic position vis-à-vis the rest of the world and to ensuring that every Japanese who makes it through the school system is effectively aware of the delicate economic tightrope that modern Japan must manage to walk if the country is to continue in its present role as a major industrialized economic power.

The same Japanese university student who will be stumped if you ask him whether the Heian period came before or after Kamakura, often knows that Japan must import from abroad 92.3 percent of the iron ore necessary for its vital automobile export industry and just a little less of the copper and tin that it requires for the same business, while 100 percent of its bauxite and nickel requirements must also be obtained from foreign sources. Often he or she will not know that the town that used to be called Edo is the same place that is now called Tokyo or that when political historians talk about the Edo period, they are talking about the same part of Japanese history that art historians generally call the Tokugawa period; but he will often be able to quote the average FOB discount customary in landing a shipment of cameras or TV components in Tacoma or Abu Dhabi.

What such a product of the Japanese school system has learned is only a mass of discrete details, but they are details that illustrate the same point; and that point is that Japan has only two totally indigenous, completely renewable natural resources—its people and its language. Everything else that Japan requires for daily survival, not to mention continued industrial growth, must be purchased from foreign countries and then transported to Japan over enormous distances. The people themselves and the language they speak are the only self-sufficient, home-grown resources that Japan has.

Even if this were the whole story, the language would clearly emerge as an object of exceptional interest for the society at large. But this is not, as we have seen in chapter 8, by any means all that there is to it. The modern sustaining myth of Nihongo identifies race and language as being nothing more than two phenomenological variants of the same inner reality. For the myth, Japanese race and nationality are Nihongo, and Nihongo is Japanese race and nationality.

Captive within the confines of this myth, the individual Japanese with no special training in these matters may surely be forgiven for taking over this ready-made identification and for concluding in turn that actually Japan has only a single totally self-sufficient, totally renewable resource: it is the

Japanese language, which is the same as the Japanese people. Thus does Nihongo, to coin a phrase, soon become the only game in town, as most Japanese conversations volubly—if not necessarily eloquently—testify.

But in all of this, the more questions we answer, the more there remain to be asked. Seidensticker has not only advanced our overall understanding of some of the important reasons why Japanese sociolinguistic behavior has developed along the lines that it has taken; he has also not hesitated to ask additional, extremely hard questions that deserve answers. The following is a particularly important example: "Why is it, for instance, that *all* Japanese say to the stammering, stumbling *gaijin*: 'You speak Japanese better than we do'? How and where did they all learn that it is the thing to say? Do mothers advise and caution their little ones: 'My dear, we all of course hope that it will not happen, but still you must be prepared. Some day a strange, ugly creature known as a *gaijin* may come slouching up. You must tell it that it speaks Japanese better than we Japanese do. That will please it, and soften its erratic impulses.' Or is the lesson slipped somewhere into *kokugo* [Japanese] classes, or the more insidious *shakaika* [Social Studies]? Or has NHK taken advantage of its enormous power and indoctrinated all those eager followers of its educational programs? The Japanese are among the most conformist of peoples, but some of their conforming ways seem rather eccentric, and inquiry into the processes of eccentric conformity would be more interesting than a great many of the things that occupy social scientists."

Seidensticker has not only greatly advanced our understanding of some of the ways in which the myth of Nihongo has come to take the enduring form that it has; here he also shows us how very much more remains to be discovered about this entire phenomenon, and how very far we still are from understanding all of its implications for contemporary Japanese society. We have, to be sure, made some modest advance in our task of identifying and understanding a few of the principal ways in which all this came about. But as Seidensticker warns us in the passage quoted above, all such analysis is still only the beginning.

What is needed now, and what must follow closely upon the analysis of the causes and origins behind the cult, is an equally careful study of how the cult itself is handed down within the society. What are the mechanisms that Japanese society has evolved for ensuring that the myth of Nihongo is passed on from generation to generation? Precisely where in the society does this take place, under whose auspices, and under whose direction? Who is in charge of this variety of cultural transmission, and how do they monitor the process?

This is only a sample of the broad spectrum of vital questions raised by Seidensticker's trenchant observations. But the sad fact of the matter is that for most of these incisive queries there are, at the present time at least, no answers readily forthcoming. We have made some small headway in understanding a few of the ways in which all this came about; but we still understand next to nothing about how, and under what particular social circumstances or constraints, this complex body of sociolinguistic beliefs is transmitted across history and down through Japanese society. Learning more about that process is one of the many tasks that remain for the future.

CHAPTER ELEVEN

Inside Looking Out

> *Nobody (except the Japanese, who will surely discover convenient linguistic difficulties) will ever again be able to say that he thought it was alright to kill, steal or bear false customs valuations against his neighbor's trade.* —The Economist of London, commenting on the Tokyo Round of the GATT Negotiations, April 21, 1979

IF THE MODERN myth of Nihongo were something solely involved with the private lives of the Japanese in Japan, then it might be possible—even better, perhaps—for the outsider to ignore the entire phenomenon completely, curious though it is. The myth then would be a purely internal matter, something of no valid concern to anyone outside Japanese society, and none of their business at best.

To be sure, even if the mystical, magical approach to the Japanese language that we have here identified as the myth of Nihongo actually did affect only the Japanese in Japan, it would still be a sociolinguistic phenomenon of great academic interest. It would surely still draw the attention of linguistic scholars in all parts of the world interested in such matters; and it would also still have much to tell us and to teach us about some of the reasons why Japanese society behaves in the ways that it does.

But the sad fact of the matter is that this modern myth of the Japanese language cannot be all this easily ignored by the rest of us. It is not, unfortunately, a sociolinguistic phenomenon that solely affects the Japanese in Japan. It is not a purely internal matter, a domestic issue for the Japanese and for them alone. The more we study it, the more we are impressed with the many different ways in which this modern mythic view of the Japanese language has, in area after area, managed to make its impact felt upon the ways in which the Japanese view other languages as well—particularly upon the way in which they view the English language.

The modern makers of this new sustaining myth of Nihongo have not been content to restrict the scope of their activities to the Japanese language. Rather, they have habitually generalized upon many of the arcane aspects of the myth, and then in turn they have applied the same generalizations to foreign languages as well, and particularly to English—generalizations that even in their original form, and when they dealt solely with Japanese, were almost always quite devoid of any basis in linguistic fact.

With this larger, generalized application to other languages, the myth of Nihongo comes, as it were, full circle. What began as a totally domestic phenomenon, an entirely at-home explanation for an entirely at-home situation, is suddenly transformed into an all-embracing sociolinguistic theory of bewilderingly vast proportions. And once this has been accomplished—once the major assumptions and premises of the myth of Nihongo have been taken over wholesale and transferred to other languages, particularly to a language such as English, which played no part in the original generation of the myth—the myth ceases to be a purely internal Japanese question. No longer can it be regarded simply as something that affects the lives of the Japanese in Japan; now it must be of concern to everyone without exception.

This is because, by affecting the way in which the Japanese approach other languages as well—and particularly by significantly affecting the way in which they approach English—the modern myth of Nihongo has managed to elevate itself to a dominant sociolinguistic position from which it now controls almost all of the channels through which the Japanese reach out for contact and communication with the rest of the world.

Japan is, after all, an island nation. Modern communications and jet travel often make us forget this important fact of the sheer geographical isolation of Japanese culture and society; but the Japanese themselves never forget it for a moment. Rapid means of travel and modern methods of communication do much to alleviate the difficulties of Japan's geographical isolation; the problem arises when we allow these marvelous devices to lull us into the mistaken idea that by alleviating many of the practical problems brought about by Japan's isolation, they have at the same time ended or destroyed that isolation.

The Japanese know this is not so. They are always conscious of their own isolation, as well as of their need to look out at the rest of the world from where they live, out from inside their island nation. They are, in this sense, a society and a culture that are inside trying to look out. Most of the time this looking out must necessarily be done through the medium of a foreign language. The most sophisticated overseas telephone circuitry imaginable will be of no use if, when the person in London or Abu Dhabi picks up the receiver, the person at the other end of the line in Tokyo or Osaka is still saying, "*Moshi, moshi....*" Japan must look out at the rest of the world; Japan must and does reach out of its islands for contacts with the outside through its use of foreign languages. And most often today, that foreign language is English.

The myth of Nihongo, as we shall see in this chapter, constantly manages to take a terrible toll of English-language teaching and English-language learning as they are conducted in Japan. Both these activities are vital parts of the Japanese effort to look out from inside. The role of the modern myth of Nihongo in strangling at their source many of the efforts that the Japanese are making to learn and teach English would, quite alone, be sufficient reason for the phenomenon to be of concern to the rest of the world. But the teaching and learning of English, important as they are, are not all that is at issue here.

Just as in the overall Japanese sociolinguistic response to the Japanese language and its use, so also are there numerous elements in the Japanese sociolinguistic response to English and its use that will appear totally baffling and apparently illogical to the observer outside Japanese society. Such elements in the Japanese attitude toward foreign languages—particularly in the Japanese attitude toward English—will remain a serious source of misunderstanding between Japan and the rest of the world until they can be understood; and they can be understood only by referring them back to the bedrock out of which they originally sprang—which is, in almost every instance, the myth of Nihongo.

Thus, the myth manages to make itself felt in a surprisingly wide range of fields, fields that at first glance would seem to have little or nothing to do with the Japanese language proper. It has managed to elevate itself into a controlling position. It now plays a major role in determining most of the ways by which and also the degree of success with which the Japanese are able to look out from inside their still very isolated and closed society at the rest of the world. And because it does this, it cannot simply be written off as a domestic concern of the Japanese themselves—as simply another internal problem of Japanese society, with which foreigners neither are nor should be concerned. Now it has become everybody's business.

Learning English in Japan is never an easy job. Indeed, for a Japanese in Japan to learn any foreign language well enough to make effective use of it for communicating with outsiders is, under any and all circumstances, a task of tremendous difficulty—even though English is probably the one foreign language that is, for all the difficulties, the easiest to acquire in Japan.

At the outset of the discussion, it will never do to underestimate the difficulties that face a Japanese, any Japanese, who decides to try and learn to speak or even to read and write English.

The difficulties are tremendous. And the fact that these difficulties are sometimes so largely overcome—the fact that some Japanese in Japan actually do sometimes manage to acquire enough English, or sometimes even enough of some other foreign language, to permit them to communicate effectively with foreigners using that language, speaks for tremendous dedication, hard work, and unstinting personal sacrifice and effort. It is no accident that these are the same remarkable qualities that Japanese society has been able, in so many instances, to bring to bear upon Japan's economic life. Tremendous dedication, hard work, and unstinting personal sacrifice and effort were the secret of Japan's postwar economic recovery; they remain, to a considerable extent, the secret of Japan's rousing success in the competition among the advanced industrial nations for a share of the world's markets; and they also explain the only way anyone ever acquires a foreign language while living in Japan.

These are facts of Japanese life, easily observable and simple to verify; no one would seriously question them. The possibility for different interpretations of these facts arises, however, when we begin to try and explain why this should be so. Why should studying and learning foreign languages, particularly studying and learning English, be such a tremendously difficult feat for the Japanese? Why should it require such tremendous dedication, hard work, and unstinting personal sacrifice and effort simply to become passably fluent in a foreign language? Here opinions begin to diverge. More than one analysis becomes possible, and different theoretical systems may be elaborated, depending upon which variety of explanation is favored over another.

It is also at this point that the modern myth of Nihongo enters upon the scene, even though the issue at hand actually has nothing at all to do with the Japanese language; after all, the question under discussion is why do the Japanese in Japan have such tremendous difficulties learning foreign languages. But the modern myth of Nihongo is not simply a set of approaches to the Japanese language, not merely a system for viewing and thinking about the Japanese language. As we have seen, it is a modern sustaining myth of Japanese society that has extended its tentacles until now they reach deeply into every nook and cranny of Japanese social behavior. As a result of this elaboration and extension, the myth itself in turn leaps to the fore whenever the society with which it is thus elaborately entwined begins to display unusual stress or difficulty.

Learning a foreign language is difficult for anyone, anywhere, any place in the world. Much of what constitutes a language takes place by means of involuntary reflexes. Learning a new language is a difficult matter, because in the process we are asked to bring involuntary behavior patterns that are more or less on the level of breathing or blinking our eyes up to the level of conscious, voluntary control—and this is no easy task for anyone.

The myth of Nihongo, however, begins its intrusion into the problems of Japanese language learning by completely ignoring these basic linguistic considerations. In effect, it ignores the well-established fact that language learning is a difficult, tedious, and laborious activity for anyone and everyone, particularly for any adult. Actually, it does not so much ignore this universal difficulty of the activity as place a false and misleading construction upon the significance of this difficulty.

Here, once more, we are confronted with the phenomenon of the kernel of truth existing behind the myth, a phenomenon that we have earlier seen to be of great importance for our understanding of the modern myth of Nihongo and how it operates in contemporary Japanese society. This time, when questions of foreign-language learning are concerned, there is also a solid kernel of truth behind the approach that the myth takes to the problem. This time the kernel of truth is, in effect, the very real difficulty that any adult anywhere in the world has in learning another language well enough to employ it for practical purposes of communication. What the myth does is once again to seize upon this kernel of truth and then to twist it to the myth's own special interests and ends.

The construction that the myth places upon this kernel of truth, the universal experience of difficulty that we all have in learning a foreign language, is that the Japanese experience this difficulty to a greater extent than anyone else because they are Japanese. At the same time, since the myth also makes the absolute equation between Japanese race and Japanese language that we have earlier explored, it simultaneously teaches that the Japanese experience this extraordinary degree of difficulty with foreign languages because their own language is Japanese—which is the same thing, within the system of the myth, as saying that the difficulties experienced in learning foreign languages happen because they, the Japanese, are Japanese. And since no one could possibly disagree with this last part of the formulation—the Japanese, after all, are Japanese, and no one would wish to argue with that—the society by and large also accepts the earlier, quite preposterous stages of argument that have led it into this quite illogical coda.

So much for the kernel—the very minute kernel, it must be stressed—of hard linguistic fact that can actually be detected somewhere near the heart of this particular extension of Japan's modern myth. But it is also obvious that this kernel, even though it is true, is simply another linguistic universal. It is the same factor of difficulty experienced by everyone, everywhere in the world, when it comes to learning any foreign language. As such, its impact can hardly be great enough of a consideration to explain how the myth is able to focus so stridently upon this single feature of language learning.

There must be other factors of difficulty that the Japanese experience in their attempts at foreign-language learning, factors that are not part and parcel of the universal human linguistic experience. There must be some things that the Japanese in Japan experience when they go about learning a foreign language that make their task more difficult for them than the comparable task would normally be for, let us say, a European or an American making the same attempt. There must be, and indeed there are. Furthermore, one of these factors does in fact have a direct relation to the nature and structure of the Japanese language, although not at all in the way in which the modern myth of Nihongo would attempt to relate the two problems.

This is the phonetic structure of the Japanese language, a factor that interposes itself in all attempts by Japanese to learn foreign languages and one that renders those attempts more difficult than most comparable attempts by non-Japanese to learn Japanese. As luck would have it, the sounds of which the Japanese language consists are arranged in a relatively small number of rather rigidly fixed patterns. It is the existence of these patterns in the Japanese language that more than anything else leads to the generally extraordinary difficulties that Japanese speakers have with learning to speak— and also with learning to understand—all foreign languages.

It is also this rigid patterning and structuring of the sounds that are found in the Japanese language that mainly make learning a foreign language and its pronunciation so difficult for most Japanese, rather than the actual inventory of the Japanese sounds themselves. This does not mean, of course, that a Japanese speaker approaches the learning of a foreign language without finding it necessary to learn to pronounce and to recognize sounds that are new for him or her, in the sense that these sounds do not exist in Japanese and hence are not familiar ones on the level of the speaker's involuntary linguistic response system.

Each human language has only a limited inventory of sounds, but the nature and content of that inventory is always different in the case of each language. French does not use exactly the same number of sounds or the same actual sounds as English does; nor does German or Italian or Hungarian or Japanese. Every time anyone learns a new foreign language, he or she is sure to encounter certain individual sounds in the new language being learned that play no significant part in the learner's own language; or if these sounds do appear in the learner's own language, they have such a minor role there that for practical purposes the language learner must learn all over again how to give these sounds a significant role in the new foreign language now being studied.

There are some varieties of spoken Chinese that have no *r*-like sounds; speakers of such Chinese languages faced with learning a foreign language like English which has both *l* and *r* sounds will at first experience considerable difficulty in learning to distinguish between the two, and even greater difficulty in learning to make the distinction correctly when speaking the new language. Most Japanese speakers have at their command several varieties of *r*-like consonant sounds, but their language has nothing that sounds very much like any of the several varieties of *l*-like sounds necessary for an effective command of English. This means that the problems of any Japanese learning English, or any one of the many other foreign languages that employs both *r* and *l* in its linguistic system, will be considerable. What is true of consonants is also of course equally true of vowels. Japanese has no vowel that is pronounced anything like the vowel in the English words man or can, or like the vowel in words like bird or heard. A Japanese learning English must practice very hard and for a considerable amount of time before he or she will be able to pronounce these vowel sounds correctly enough to be understood by a native speaker of English.

But this variety of foreign-language learning difficulty is, in a sense, still only a special case of a linguistic universal. The details of the problem will differ depending upon the learner's native language and also upon the phonetic inventory of the language being studied, but the overall problem remains the same. New sounds, in the sense of sounds that are not found in the learner's own language, must be learnt when they occur as significant units in the new language. This learning process is always difficult for everyone.

But as we have already indicated, the particular difficulty that occurs for Japanese speakers when they go about learning any other language generally has less to do with the factor of phonetic inventory than it does with the way in which the sounds of Japanese arrange themselves into rigidly structured patterns. In English, for example, several consonants can, and often do, come together, one after another, with no intervening vowels. English has words like street or strike, where no vowel separates the *s* from the *t* or the *t* from the *r*. Other languages, as for example Polish, have much longer, and much more involved, combinations of consonants.

Japanese lacks this feature almost entirely. In Japanese, the usual patterning of the sounds of the language places them in a regular alternation of consonant followed by vowel. Combinations of more than two consonants without a vowel between them are unknown, and even combinations of two consonants are limited. Language-learning studies teach us that learning to break away from the involuntary-response patterning that is represented by such regular sound systems as the alternation of consonants and vowels in Japanese is even more difficult than is the admittedly quite difficult task of learning to cope with new sounds themselves.

This means that when a Japanese learning English, for example, attempts to learn to speak, understand, and use such a word as sleep, he or she is immediately faced with two separate sets of problems. First there is the problem of the consonant *l*. This consonant does not exist as a significant individual unit in Japanese pronunciation, and so it must be learned anew. This is very difficult. But even when this difficult task is mastered, another, even more difficult one still lies ahead. Japanese has no combinations of consonants comparable to the *sl-* combination of sleep, nor do any Japanese words end in the consonant *p* not followed by a vowel.

The Japanese speaker will at first, even after learning to cope with the *l* sound, continue to experience great difficulty with a word such as sleep, because it is even more difficult to learn to depart from the rigid sound patterns of his or her own language. These sound patterns insist that some vowel be inserted between the *s* and the *l,* and that some vowel be added after the final *p,* since Japanese only has words built up along such patterns. And it is this last step in the language-learning process, this ability to depart from the rigid sound patterns of the Japanese linguistic structure, that always proves to be the most difficult single factor encountered in foreign-language learning by Japanese.

Again, in a sense we here approach another kernel of truth. Here there really is something that is special about the Japanese language, in the sense of making it extraordinarily difficult for Japanese speakers to learn most foreign languages—at least, more difficult than the same task would probably be for the speakers of some other language that does not have these same rigidly arranged sound patterns.

This problem is a matter of fact. It is a difficult one; and little can be done about it, except by diligent practice and hard work. A Japanese speaker can learn to distinguish *l* and *r;* a Japanese speaker can eventually manage to pronounce sequences of consonants one after the other, like the *str* in street, without inserting vowels between the *s* and the *t* and between the *t* and the *r;* he or she can, with much practice, learn to pronounce a simple consonant like *p* at the end of a word like sleep without adding a vowel to the end of the word. But all this takes time, patience, and a reliable model upon which the speaker may pattern him- or herself.

But the principal problems that arise when the Japanese in Japan today go about learning a foreign language, particularly English, are actually of yet another order. These are the problems that arise, not on the matter-of-fact level that is involved with the structure of Japanese or with the linguistic facts of English, but rather with the overall thrust of the sociolinguistic attitudes that prevail in contemporary Japanese society.

These sociolinguistic attitudes, sets of assumptions and a priori conclusions about the nature and role of language in general and about the questions of English-language learning in particular, interpose far more difficulties into the path of a foreign-language learner in Japan than do any specific features of the languages themselves. And most of them are nothing more—or less— than the illogical extension into the area of foreign languages of some of the essential elements of the modern myth of Nihongo. Here again, we find that this modern myth has come full circle. No longer is it simply a body of beliefs that relate to the Japanese language. Now it becomes a body of assumptions that end up inhibiting, when they do not actually strangle at birth, any effective attempts that most Japanese might ever make to learn another language, particularly a language such as English with which they would finally be in a position to look out from inside their isolated, insular civilization.

A comprehensive listing of all the levels upon which the myth of Nihongo manages to intrude itself into problems of foreign-language learning and foreign-language teaching in Japan would be almost literally endless. Here we will make an attempt to limit our discussion to three main problems from among the far too many that could easily be identified.

First place in any such listing, whether it is a list that only attempts to give a few of the major problems or whether it is an attempt at a comprehensive catalogue of these inhibiting factors, must always go to the assumption that is universal throughout Japanese academic circles, on every level, to the effect that only the Japanese themselves are ever really and throughly qualified to teach foreign languages in Japan. This assumption is, naturally enough, never verbalized, since even to put it into words immediately demonstrates how utterly absurd it is. But unverbalized though it remains, this same assumption is nevertheless firmly held without question or hesitation on every level of Japanese society. Its universal acceptance throughout the society is reflected in the policies and administrative practices of the whole Japanese academic establishment, from the enormously powerful Ministry of Education itself down to the smallest local Board of Education directing the work of the most insignificant neighborhood elementary school.

This assumption is essentially a racist one. It makes membership in a closed racial group—Japanese, in this case—the ultimate, unwavering qualification that must always take precedence over any and all other considerations. Japanese law specifically bars any person not of Japanese nationality from ever being appointed as a tenured professor on the faculty of any Japanese national university. Since Japanese nationality

is normally only acquired by birth, one must first arrange to be born
as a Japanese if one is ever to aspire to the faculty of a national university.
Again, one must look to South Africa for an example of any other social
system that has arranged its affairs along such resolutely racist lines; but
even in that instance the parallel breaks down, because South Africa is
not a modern industrialized superpower like Japan.

All racism is, as most of the world has by this time already learned, ultimately self-defeating. Japan's particularly stringent variety of academic
racism is particularly so. At the very least, it almost always defeats the
efforts of the Japanese to learn foreign languages well enough to make
practical use of them. For it is this essentially racist assumption of Japanese
academic circles that, more than any other single factor, renders the task
encountered by the average, hard-working, intelligent Japanese individual
who undertakes to learn a foreign language difficult beyond all reason—
when it does not indeed make it downright impossible.

One can see immediately how this first assumption of Japanese foreign-
language teaching is involved with the myth of Nihongo. Behind this
particular extension of the myth into the teaching and learning of foreign
languages there lies, it must be pointed out, yet another generally accepted
though equally unverbalized assumption to the effect that "language
teaching is language teaching, and language learning is language learning,
whatever the language involved may be."

When the language being taught in a Japanese school or university is
Japanese, it goes without saying that only Japanese are qualified and competent to carry out such instruction. This is beyond question or debate
but it is also the point at which the myth of Nihongo enters upon the scene,
as well as the tiny opening in the argument into which it is able to insert
its mythic adumbrations. If Japanese works this way—if only Japanese are
qualified and competent to teach Japanese to the Japanese—then, the myth
suggests, the same must be true of any language: only the Japanese are
qualified and competent to teach English, or French, or German, etc., so
long as the people being taught are Japanese.

The consequences of this extension of the myth into foreign-language
teaching are obviously disastrous. Foreign-language learning is almost
entirely a matter of the imitation of accurate models. Only native speakers
of the language being studied or others who have managed to acquire
native-speaker competence in the language can provide such models. But
even in the case of English, the single foreign language most widely studied
by the Japanese and most widely employed by them in their communication with the outside world, there are very, very few Japanese who have
the necessary linguistic skills in English to serve as competent models of
the language. Only a very few Japanese have a native-speaker command

of English or anything approaching such a command; and the skills of such individuals are in far too great demand by business, industry, and international trade to make it even remotely worth their time to teach English to others.

The result is that the average, intelligent, hard-working Japanese student of English, who with proper guidance and instruction could eventually learn English satisfactorily, despite all the difficulties that Japanese sound patterns place in the way of his or her learning any foreign language, generally does not. He or she generally does not because he or she hardly ever is provided with a satisfactory model of English as a language. Most teachers that the student encounters, during what often amounts to between ten and fifteen years of studying English throughout the Japanese educational system, will be Japanese. And it is unlikely in the extreme that any single one of these Japanese teachers of English will be able to provide the student with a model for imitation that is even remotely close to the real thing.

The student will never learn to pronounce the *str* in street because few of the teachers who teach the student will be able to pronounce it. No one, no matter how hard-working or diligent, can ever learn to make the distinction between *r* and *l* from a teacher who has never learned to make it—and there are not more than a handful of teachers of English anywhere in any educational institution in Japan, no matter how famous or important, who can make the distinction.

The foreign reader unacquainted with the facts of Japanese education may suspect that the above account has elements of exaggeration. Surely, such a reader may ask, one has heard of many Americans and Englishmen who make good livings in Japan today teaching English. If what is said above is true, then what are all those people doing?

The answer is that they are all, to be sure, teaching English in one way or another. But they are all doing it outside, rather than within, the Japanese educational establishment. And it is the national educational establishment, from the Ministry of Education on down, that implements this racist assumption concerning who is and who is not competent to conduct English and other foreign-language teaching in Japan. It is the national educational establishment that has decided that every student in Japan without exception will study English for four or five years; if a student is to go on for a university degree, then he or she must study English for many additional years. But at the same time, the educational establishment decrees that at no point during this entire career of English study will the student, as a student in an official school, ever be taught for "credit" by anyone who is not a Japanese by race and hence also by nationality.

There are, to be sure, generally a few exceptions to this arrangement, but closer study of the system shows that they are clearly cases of the canonical "exception that proves the rule"; in other words, they are not really exceptions at all. Many native speakers of English, some of them competent and effective teachers of the language, are employed throughout Japan in a variety of private schools and language-teaching facilities. These range all the way from rather informal·conversation classes at which housewives gather to learn a few words of daily greetings up to intensive, deadly serious programs by means of which businessmen may acquire the linguistic skills necessary for effectively carrying on Japan's highly competitive foreign trade.

In one way or another, all these private language-teaching activities are commercial, in the sense that they are all conducted by a proprietor—some person or organization that organizes and sponsors the classes or instructional program in question—for a profit. The proprietor pays the foreign teachers; the students pay the proprietor. The other thing that all these activities have in common is that they are not part of the national, official educational system; people pay for them and engage in them solely in order to learn, not in order to get credits or degrees.

The workings of the myth of Nihongo and the absurd results of the prior assumption that only Japanese are qualified and competent to teach foreign languages to Japanese students on any level are all demonstrated with particular clarity when one inspects how the foreign-language departments of any Japanese college or university, whether private or national, are organized. Here especially one finds that "exception that proves the rule" operating at its most effective level. In these affluent days, when a foreigner can often cost less to employ than a Japanese, every college or university will have a few foreigners around. But before leaping to the conclusion that their presence makes even a dent in the thoroughgoing racism of the entire Japanese educational system, the observer will be well advised to check a little more closely into what the official status of these foreign teachers actually is within the system that employs them and also to find out what it is that these foreigners really do. Such a check will reveal that the foreigners employed by the language departments of Japanese institutions of higher education are supernumerary window dressing. They are employees, not faculty members; and it is pointless to inquire about their official status, because they do not have any. They play no part in determining educational policy or content. Especially, they play no part at all in the formal, official training of any students in the state-operated, government-funded elite schools, because it is from among the graduates of these schools that the leaders of government and business in Japan of tomorrow are to be culled. And it would simply fly in the face of all reason to subject Japan's future leaders, during their impressionable student days, to the ministrations of non-Japanese foreigners, even in such areas as mastering the pronunciation and grammar of foreign languages.

As to what they do, these foreign teachers teach something called "conversation." On the face of it, even that sounds reasonable enough, until one discovers that this arcane subject is always taught to upwards of fifty or more students at the same time, with the foreign teacher alone at the far end of an enormous lecture hall, often finding it necessary to rely upon electronic amplification simply to make his or her voice carry to the back rows of seats.

But whatever they are called and however they are taught, none of the classes conducted by the foreigners employed as non-faculty supernumeraries in any Japanese college or university are ever credit courses. This means that they never count toward the student's graduation. If the student wishes to attend them, fine; if the student does not wish to, that is fine also. The student needs a certain number of credits to graduate, and only courses taught by Japanese teachers carry credits. One can imagine how diligently under these circumstances most students attend any college or university course taught by foreigners.

Most of the teachers who become involved in this charade of language instruction in Japanese colleges and universities are native speakers of the language they try to teach, but few of them are qualified language teachers. This is not their fault; indeed, most of them do not even claim to be qualified language teachers. It is the fault of the Japanese educational system, which is quite unconcerned about the qualifications of such persons, since they are only window dressing and are not meant to play a real part in the educational scheme in the first place.

It would be a contradiction on several levels for a Japanese college or university to employ a genuinely qualified person to teach English to Japanese students. If the person were qualified, then surely students in such classes should receive academic credit for the work done. But they do not, and they will not, receive such credit. So it is simpler and more logical, and incidentally a lot cheaper, to employ someone who will be grateful for the work and not interfere with the "real" language teaching, which is done almost totally in Japanese by the Japanese faculty.

The Japanese Ministry of Education must under Japanese law charter all Japanese educational institutions, including the many private ones that do not rely to any great extent upon public funds. This chartering process involves an evaluation of the faculty, programs, facilities, and other factors relevant to the work that the institution proposes to do. Once the charter is granted, periodic reevaluations are carried out to ensure that standards are maintained.

In all such charter evaluations, the Ministry of Education consistently refuses to count any persons not of Japanese nationality—i.e., not of Japanese race—as faculty members or teachers in any department or area of learning. A college that submitted to the ministry a plan for a language department that included seven foreign college professors, each with first-class credentials and years of experience in teaching English to foreigners, plus one Japanese professor of English, would be recognized by the ministry as having only one professor in its language department—the Japanese. For the ministry, all foreigners, no matter what their qualifications, simply do not exist; they are nonpersons, not even considered in the chartering evaluations. The best that can be said is that the ministry does not hold their presence against a given institution—always provided, of course, that there are enough Japanese professors on the books to make up the difference. If there are not, no charter.

Most of what has been said above relates directly to the situation on the college and university level for Japanese English-teaching. The only way in which the problem on lower levels in the Japanese educational system differs from that on the higher levels is that on the lower ones it is even worse and even more self-defeating. On the college level, a student may at least sometimes have the opportunity to attend a class taught by a native speaker of the language being studied. The class will generally be enormous, the native speaker a single isolated figure at the remote end of a vast room, and it will not really matter very much since the class will not carry academic credit— but at least the chance, for whatever it may represent, does sometimes exist. On lower levels of the system, even this slim opportunity is hardly ever provided. Most Japanese study English for half their lives without ever once coming face to face with a competent speaker of the language.

This is tragic, since of course it is during the earlier years of the educational process that foreign-language learning is particularly effective. A grade-school child can learn with relative ease to make the always difficult adjustments in involuntary behavior patterns that are necessary in learning another language. With competently directed instruction, and above all with the models of native-speaking teachers available, almost any mentally competent child will make rapid progress in speaking and understanding a foreign language.

Unfortunately, the ability to make these adjustments in our involuntary behavior patterns rapidly slopes off during adolescence and the teens. By the time a young man or woman reaches college age, it is in a sense almost too late for genuinely effective foreign-language learning. College is a good time to do advanced work with a foreign language in which a student has already managed to get a good foundation in earlier school years. But if that earlier good foundation is missing or nonexistent, then college is really too late for the whole difficult process.

Pronunciation habits in particular are set very early in language learning; the late teens and the college years are simply too late. And since Japanese schoolchildren have even less opportunity to be taught by competent, qualified native speakers of foreign languages than do their college-age brothers and sisters, almost all of them, despite their years of hard work on English, come into college and eventually into adulthood unable to make any of the sounds of the language, unable to understand it when they hear it spoken, and unable to speak it themselves. What are potentially the most valuable years for foreign-language learning are totally wasted in the course of hour after dreary hour in the English classroom with Japanese teachers, most of whom drone away in Japanese explaining the grammar and pronunciation of a language that they themselves have rarely even heard and certainly cannot speak.

The spectacle of teachers busily engaged in attempting to teach youngsters what they themselves do not know—the charade of English education that goes on most of the day, six days a week, throughout all Japanese elementary and secondary foreign-language education—does not appear to strike either Japanese educators or even most Japanese parents as ludicrous or even very illogical. The foreign visitor will find it extraordinary, but for most Japanese it is the only way that things have ever been and the only possible way they ought to be. Whenever cultural attitudes differ this strikingly, it is always a safe bet that there is something within one of the two conflicting cultural systems that helps to explain the wide divergence in views—something that will explain, even though it can never excuse, the waste and misdirection of educational potential that are involved here.

In this particular case, we must therefore seriously look for some underlying cultural or sociological explanation for the fact that most Japanese parents and educators find nothing in the least strange, for example, in the spectacle of school teachers, who cannot themselves make the distinction between *r* and *l*, lecturing endlessly in Japanese to children about how this distinction is to be made. The necessary explanation more likely than not is to be sought in Japan's inheritance of Zen monastic and devotional practices.

Like all other forms of religion, Zen Buddhism long ago ceased to be a matter of any importance in Japanese life, at least as far as its genuinely religious elements are concerned. Throughout their long history the Japanese have generally been remarkably avid in adopting foreign religions. First Buddhism, then Christianity were taken up devoutly and sincerely by considerable numbers of the population. Each was practiced for a while and then—each in its turn—just as quickly cast aside. Unlike Christianity, however, Buddhism was kept around long enough for many of its nonreligious, purely cultural attributes to make a fairly serious impact upon Japanese life. Many of these cultural attributes survive in Japanese society even today, where foreigners often mistake them for the Buddhist religion, with which however they actually have almost no connection.

Several of the most durable of these cultural inheritances that modern Japanese society has kept alive from its past centuries of Buddhist faith go back to the Zen sect or school of Buddhism. Zen was at one time a powerful force in Japanese intellectual and spiritual life—never, perhaps, as powerful as some of the contemporary Western Zen fans would like to imagine, but nevertheless for some centuries it was a force to be reckoned with in any historical account of the development of Japanese culture.

The rule and order of the Zen cloister have left many traces in present-day Japanese life and thought; and among these cultural inheritances from the Zen sect of Buddhism, it is not difficult to identify several elements that go far to explain why the Japanese not only tolerate but often actually encourage the blundering attempts of the average Japanese foreign-language teacher who every day of his life attempts to do the impossible—to teach others what he himself obviously does not know.

This all comes about, in large measure, because of one of the ways in which the Zen variety of Buddhism differed from the many other forms that the religion took in early Japan. Most Buddhist sects stressed study, instruction, and teaching. It was always necessary for the believer to learn a great many involved things about this extremely involved imported religion, and the only way to do this was to study, and read texts, and above all to work constantly at learning about the faith under the direction of older teachers who themselves were the products of similar intensive teaching and instruction.

Members of the Zen sect or school took sharp issue with all this. In their view, little that was really important about religion could be gained by studying texts or even by receiving direct instruction, in the form of lectures or sermons, from older, better-trained teachers. Instead, the Zen monastic tradition set great store by the possibilities of communication between teacher and disciple over and beyond mere verbal exchange. The Zen school of Buddhism taught that all written scriptures were extremely limited in their usefulness as well as in their doctrinal content. Zen held that there was a great amount of religious truth that had actually never been written down. It had never been written down because it was too profound for verbal expression. This body of truth could only be communicated from master to student by indirect means, such as sudden blows to the head or shoulders, shouts, cries, gestures, and similar irrational, or at least nonintellectual, means.

Indeed, the Zen teacher typically did not himself claim to know any more than the student. He did not profess to have any specific knowledge that he could communicate verbally to the student. He did not specifically teach anything; he only directed the student in a routine of inherited monastic practices. Both student and teacher thus believed that in the doctrine of Zen there was much that remained beyond both of them, as much beyond the comprehension of the teacher as it was beyond the comprehension of the student; and both also believed that they were somehow approaching this ultimate but inexpressible something together.

For Zen, this undoubtedly works. The Zen master may very well be able to communicate with shouts, blows, and manual gestures something that he himself does not actually grasp very well, some ultimate truth that he himself cannot verbalize. If the Zen disciples believe that the system works, that is their business. But as one observes how the prestige of this Zen method of instruction has been carried over into modern foreign-language education in Japan, one must be a little less tolerant. It clearly does *not* work in foreign-language education. There, at least, no teacher, no matter how motivated or diligent or famous, can possibly teach students to have a useful command of a language that the teacher himself has not even begun to master adequately.

Foreign-language teaching in Japan today has more than one such inheritance from the pedagogical traditions of the Zen monastery. Another important area of similarity between the two may be pointed out in the area of net results. All the instruction and monastic practices of the Zen school were carried out only as means toward an overall end—the attainment of enlightenment, defined (more or less) as the liberation of the spirit from the bonds of the material. This enlightenment, this liberation, was the ultimate goal toward which all the hours of meditation, all the endless hours, days, and years of monastic discipline, all the curious rituals of shouts, blows about the head or shoulders, and the like were directed. All these were supposed, in one way or another, to lead the seeker toward his ultimate enlightenment. There is no doubt that these methods accomplished precisely what they were supposed to do in many, many cases. But the catch is that, on the question of whether of not they worked, we always have only the word of the seeker involved. No other, external, independent check or verification is ever possible.

In other words, the only way to verify whether or not Zen instructional methodology has worked has always been to ask the subject who has undergone it. Only the individual concerned can ultimately answer the question of whether or not all this carrying-on has done anything to advance his spirit toward liberation and enlightenment. Here another of the striking similarities between Zen monastic practice and the bulk of the foreign-language education now carried on in Japan reveals itself with particularly striking clarity.

Since most of those teaching foreign languages in Japan do not themselves control the languages being taught well enough to verify whether or not their students are making any genuine progress toward the mastery of the language, they too—quite like the Zen masters—can do little or nothing to check on whether or not their work is effective or even useful. And since no outside verification of progress is possible, the whole system, like the Zen monastery, must eventually fall back upon self-introspection and self-examination.

For the Zen master, it would be spiritual presumption of the worst sort to attempt to determine whether or not a disciple has progressed toward the ultimate spiritual goal of illuminatory liberation. He, the master, must himself constantly be equally engaged in this same quest, and he is consequently in no position to ask hard questions of his students. Everyone in the Zen cloister, regardless of rank or status, is involved in the same quest; one can sometimes try to help another to direct his efforts along the correct path, but one can never be sure that the other has succeeded. This is something that each individual can only verify for himself, about himself.

But what works for the monastery, and for measuring progress in spiritual life, hardly is effective for evaluating progress in foreign-language instruction. When the teacher cannot usefully evaluate the student, the student has no way of knowing if he or she really is making any progress in learning the language in question. Usually, given the quality of instruction and the essential incompetence of most foreign-language teachers in Japan, no progress is actually being made. Normally, this would serve as a check upon the entire system. A student of swimming who discovers that he is still sinking beneath the surface of the water every time he enters the pool will eventually conclude that something is wrong with the way he is being taught to swim. But this built-in system for automatically verifying the effectiveness of instruction does not operate in most foreign-language teaching in Japan; and that the system is allowed to continue, despite this limitation, can only be explained by the still impressive inheritance of Zen pedagogical traditions, reaching far back as they do into Japan's once devoutly religious past.

With this identification of some of the major Zen inheritances that persist to plague modern Japanese foreign-language instruction—inheritances that account for much of the failure of that instruction, at the same time they explain why the society that is the unwitting victim of such obviously ineffective instruction accepts it so passively—we have once more come pretty well full circle, back to yet another confrontation with the impact of the modern myth of Nihongo in contemporary Japanese life.

We have already noted how, at the heart of the failure of much foreign-language education in Japan, there is to be found the essential racist assumption that teaching (and learning) a foreign language in the classroom in Japan is and must be the same as teaching (and learning) Japanese in the same classroom. No one not qualified to conduct the second type of instruction— to teach Japanese to the Japanese—is considered qualified to conduct the first—to teach foreign languages to the Japanese. And with this, we are immediately propelled directly onto the old Zen merry-go-round just discussed. So long as the Japanese teacher of Japanese to the Japanese in Japan remains the racist norm for all language instruction, including instruction in foreign languages, Japanese foreign-language instruction and Japanese foreign-language learning will both continue to be as ineffective and inefficient as they demonstrably are today.

The reason behind this cul-de-sac of ineffective instruction is hardly difficult to identify, particularly so long as we keep in mind that in all these matters, it is always the Japanese teacher of Japanese who remains the role model. But what does the teacher of Japanese to Japanese students in the Japanese educational establishment really do? He or she is not teaching them the Japanese language; all the students know that before they ever set foot in the classroom. Any mentally competent person has a satisfactory functional command of his or her native language by age ten. No native speaker requires instruction in his or her native language.

What does in fact go on under the description of Japanese-language instruction for Japanese students in Japanese schools is something quite different from language learning; it is learning the writing system. Japanese students know Japanese already; what they must now learn is how to read and write it. But they do not already know English, or French, or German, or any other foreign language. And this means that when instruction in any of these second languages is carried out along the same lines and in terms of the same assumptions concerning methods and goals that are implemented in the Japanese-language classroom, nothing much useful will, or can ever, be accomplished.

Again, Zen methodology steps in to save the teachers' reputations and jobs. The work of the Japanese teacher of Japanese to the Japanese can never seriously be evaluated; the students in question know Japanese when they enter the classroom, and they still know it when they leave. The Japanese teacher of Japanese to the Japanese may be effective in teaching what he teaches, or he may be incompetent and ineffective; either way, he or she and the work being done are in no danger of evaluation. No hard questions are asked, any more than the Zen cloister asked hard questions about whether or not anyone had really advanced toward enlightenment. The students' command of their native language is not essentially altered in any way by whatever it is that they have done to them in their Japanese-language classrooms; they emerge in the same shape in which they went in, and if their teachers are ineffective or incompetent, there is little or no danger of their being shown up for what they are.

But in the case of the products of the foreign-language classroom, the showing-up happens all too soon. It happens every time the student tries to communicate with a foreigner using the language that he or she has studied so hard and, to all apparent academic evidence, so successfully, for so many years. Most often, no communication at all is possible; but by the time the student discovers this, it is too late. School is over.

In this way, we begin to understand some of the motivation, as well as some of the major implications, that lie behind the almost exclusive employment of Japanese teachers for foreign languages, particularly for English, in Japanese academia. Economic considerations are often cited as the reason behind this phenomenon. Questions of money of course played a role in the matter during the decade or so immediately following Japan's defeat in World War II. One could hardly have expected the educational system of a nation still struggling to feed and clothe itself to spend very much of its then extremely limited financial resources in order to employ competent teachers of foreign languages for its children, even though ironically enough it was the turmoil of the postwar years that brought home to everyone, as it had never been brought home before, the great and immediate necessity for such language work in the Japanese school system.

But what began as an immediate economic necessity was soon thereafter to become an end in itself. With the 1970s came growing affluence. Today Japanese education can afford anything that it wants. The Japanese Government spends enormous amounts of its enormous financial resources on education at every level. Japanese parents, eager to push their children ahead ever more rapidly in the race for advancement in an overcrowded, immensely competitive society, willingly add to this already lavish national expenditure for public education by making their own enormous personal investments for special tutoring, cram schools, and every other conceivable private educational arrangement.

Today, money is absolutely no object at any stage of the educational process in Japan. The society resolutely refuses to let fiscal considerations stand in its way when education is at issue, any more than it is willing to consider for a moment the appalling physical and mental costs that the whole system extracts from those tiny, sad-faced, listless boys and girls who may be observed every morning fighting for their own tiny places on overcrowded commuter trains and subways, their tiny backs weighted down with backpacks overflowing with dictionaries, pocket calculators, and notebooks. A society so willing to sacrifice its own children's health and happiness to "getting ahead" is quite obviously not going to quibble about anything so minor as money.

If Japanese society really wanted to expose its children to competent foreign teachers of foreign languages, the money involved would be no object. In fact, such teachers would probably cost less than employing the incompetent Japanese teachers who now carry the burden of the system. The real reasons are not economic; they are sociolinguistic, and they run deep into the structure of the society. And not the least of the results of this entire system of assumptions and a priori conclusions concerning the conduct of foreign-language instruction in Japan is that foreign-language learning—the one academic exercise that might otherwise be expected to lead society in the direction of internationalism and racial pluralism—has instead become one of the major factors perpetuating the essentially racist nature of contemporary Japanese society. Like so many of the other traces of the myth of Nihongo in Japanese life, this particular development is not only extremely ironic, it is also extremely destructive.

The second major category of sociolinguistic phenomena by means of which the Nihongo mythology inhibits the learning of foreign languages by the Japanese—and thus also strangles off at the source most strivings to peer out at what lies beyond the limits of their own society—is involved with the goals set for foreign-language learning. We have already seen how that most obvious goal for all foreign-language instruction—the ability to communicate in the language in question with a native speaker of that language—is ruled out by the exclusive employment of Japanese teachers for foreign languages in the national educational system. When most of the teachers could never pass such a test, it of course follows that no such test will ever be set for their students; and it also follows that this, the simplest and most effective goal for any and all foreign-language instruction, is also ruled out by the same merry-go-round of illogic.

Thus the goal of the whole complicated and immensely expensive enterprise of foreign-language learning and instruction in Japan has become to pass examinations, rather than to make actual or effective use of the languages taught. Passing examinations is a terrible, crucial necessity encountered at every stage of the slow advancement that takes the individual up the rungs in Japanese society. Kindergarten children whose families can afford the expense are tutored after school hours to help ensure that they will be able to pass the examinations necessary if they are to be admitted to a prestigious elementary school. Stories about middle-school children who commit suicide upon failing examinations for high-school entrance are a tragic commonplace in Japanese newspapers. Students seeking admission to an important national university—particularly to Tokyo University, the most prestigious institution in the entire Japanese educational system—

consider it a worthwhile investment of their lives (and of their parents' money) to spend three, four, or even five years following high-school graduation taking and retaking and taking yet once more the formidable Tokyo University entrance examinations, each successive attempt preceded by a full year of intensive night-and-day cramming.

Each year well over half of the class entering Tokyo University is made up of such delayed entrants, each of whom has spent three or four years with an unsuccessful attempt each year at fighting his way into the system ("his," because girls are rarely encouraged to try more than once; this horrible rite of passage in Japanese society is almost entirely a male prerogative). And at every stage of this progress through what the Japanese themselves call the examination hell, and particularly at that last, most crucial stage—the university entrance examinations—testing in a foreign language, which means in this context almost always English, plays a crucial role.

No matter what the prospective university student plans to study, no matter what his career goals may be, an important part of the entrance examination that he will be forced to complete successfully will deal with English. The goal is to pass the examination. To pass the examination, one must be able to do successfully the parts of the examinations dealing with English. And just how abstract, and how utterly divorced from reality, the entire English-language examination operation has become in modern Japan can easily be verified by glancing at any of the typical examinations in question.

This is quite simple to do. The entrance examinations for all major Japanese universities are published regularly, often in the daily newspapers, so great is public interest in this whole matter. The entrance examinations administered by Tokyo University of course set the level for the rest of the nation in this matter as well as in every other field. Each year, the English-language portions of the Tokyo University entrance examinations have in common the following: they could not possibly be answered successfully by anyone who is simply a native speaker of English, no matter how literate or experienced in using the language he or she may happen to be. Only someone who has "studied English" throughout the manifold mazes of the Japanese academic jungle can even begin to pass the tests successfully. It is also generally doubtful whether anyone genuinely competent in the English language could ever learn to do so, no matter how long he or she studied to prepare for this arcane task.

These extraordinary English-language examinations do not test the student's knowledge or command of English. What they do exhaustively examine instead is how well the student has managed to conform to the rigors of the officially set English curriculum uniformly enforced by the

Japanese Ministry of Education throughout the entire educational establishment. The student is not actually being tested on English at all, but on his or her willingness to conform. The conformers pass. Those who either are unwilling to conform, or would desperately like to conform but cannot manage to do so, either because they are not bright enough or not lucky enough, fail.

The stakes in all this are frighteningly high. Passing the university examinations automatically admits the successful candidate to the upper levels of the Japanese white-collar middle class. Little or no academic work is expected of the university student once admitted—which seems only fair, after all that he or she has been subjected to during the examination procedures. Four years later, equally automatic admission to the nine-to-five ranks of the white-collar office worker will follow for these fortunates. Such jobs are the undisputed life goal of the vast majority of Japanese society; they all require a university degree, and a university degree requires passing the examinations for admission to a university—examinations in which questions involving the English language always play a major part. The stakes are truly high. Failure to obtain university admission means failure to obtain a university degree. Failure to obtain a degree means that the student must give up forever all dreams of a nine-to-five office job and make a living instead as a manual laborer or perhaps on the assembly line of a factory or in the service industries.

The Japanese university examinations are the ultimate, the most frightening rite of passage known to any modern society. Little wonder, then, that they are a matter of such seriousness, and little wonder also that English, which plays such a major role in all these examinations, is also a matter of such deep concern to the society.

But what kind of English is it? Since the teachers who set the examinations almost never have a working command of the language, none of the questions that they write for the English-language portions of the examinations really have anything at all to do with testing the student's ability to employ the language as a means that one human being might possibly employ in order to communicate with another.

Testing the student's ability to understand the language when spoken by a native speaker, for example, or the student's ability to reply in English to questions posed in English, would all be ways in which to estimate whether or not the student being examined had any effective working command of the language. But such matter-of-fact testing of course plays no part in the English-language portions of Japanese university examinations or indeed in English-language testing at any stage of the Japanese educational process, largely because the teachers themselves would in almost every case be unable to pass such tests with anything resembling satisfactory scores.

Another reason why such testing is never done takes us back to the intense racism inherent in all Japanese educational institutions. The only significant testing that is possible for all foreign-language competence and performance involves the student's ability to understand and to speak understandably to native speakers of the language in question. But to involve native speakers of a foreign language in the examination procedures would mean involving foreigners in these, the most hallowed rites of passage of Japanese society. It would mean admitting non-Japanese into the very heart of one of the society's most important secret rituals. Most serious of all, it would mean allowing foreigners to have a significant role in the operation of a completely monolithic, simplistically racist society, something that is of course by definition impossible. So Japanese teachers, and Japanese teachers alone, always decide the English and other foreign-language portions of examinations, especially those in the all-important national universities.

And what kind of examinations in English, then, do the Japanese teachers set? They cannot actually test foreign-language competence or performance, since their own competence and performance in the foreign language involved are uniformly unsatisfactory. Failing this, they end up testing social conformity, as measured by the ability and willingness of each student to commit to memory long passages of prepared foreign-language text, selected fragments of which the student is expected to be able to regurgitate by rote in the course of the examination. The successful regurgitators pass; the unsuccessful ones fail.

Well in advance of the dread day of the university examinations—and all previous English-language instruction throughout the entire school system is designed solely to prepare the student for this final, most important, and most awful stage of the entire process—a large number of prose passages from modern English authors are set for the student to memorize. These passages are usually extracted from a few modern British novelists particularly well known in Japan, especially from the work of Somerset Maugham and Graham Greene. The popularity of these two British authors for use in Japanese university entrance examinations does not in any way reflect upon their popularity as authors in Japan, any more than it indicates that Maugham and Greene are read widely in the original in Japan. They are not read widely in Japan—no foreign-language author ever is—but they are well known, mostly because of the large number of successful films that have been made from their work.

Because of the popularity of such movies as *The Letter* and *The Third Man*, Japanese translations of the original novels upon which these and similar films were based have also sold uniformly well in Japan. The upshot of all this is that Maugham and Greene pretty well represent modern

English literature, as well as the English language, in Japanese academic circles. (School teachers go to the movies, too.)

At any rate, when it comes time to set the English-language portion of a university examination, the teacher in charge takes from his shelf a well-worn copy of a Maugham or Greene novel, opens it pretty well at random, and selects a page or two as the raw material of the test that he will now compose. To do this, the teacher first copies out the passage he has selected—which will be in the middle of the story, so that once it is extracted from its larger context it will carry very little indication of what comes before or follows it in the narrative—and then carefully blocks out certain key words in the passage, replacing them with blanks.

Thus, a passage that read as follows in the original will be selected: "There is a point of no return unremarked at the time in most lives. Neither Jones nor I knew of it when it came, although, like the pilots of the old pre-jet air-liners, we should have been trained by the nature of our two careers to better observance."

Such a passage, once chosen for use in the test, will turn up in the English-language section of a Japanese university entrance examination in the following form: "There is ____ point of ____ return unremarked at ____ time in most lives. Neither Jones ____ I knew of it when it came, although, ____ ____ pilots of ____ old pre-jet air-liners, we ____ ____ ____ trained by the nature of our two careers to better observance."

The problem that the student is presented with is a deceptively simple one: Fill in the blanks with the correct English words. Deceptively simple, because in a fill-in-the-blanks riddle of this variety, a native speaker will in almost every instance be able to make perfectly good sense and perfectly acceptable English grammar and syntax out of the passage by filling in one of several different English words at almost every blank. But for the purposes of this sort of examination as it is used in the Japanese educational system, only one answer is correct for each blank: the word that was in Maugham's or Greene's original.

In the case of the example just given, for example, the first blank might equally well be filled in with "the" as with "a," even though only "a" is the correct answer because "a" is what appears in the Graham Greene original from which this passage is extracted. For the second blank, "no" is the only correct answer that the examination would allow. A native English speaker could, of course, think of any number of other words that would fit in equally well with the passage: "There is the point of easy return . . . ," "There is the point of quick return . . . ," "There is the point of simple return . . . ," and so on.

The reader will probably have tired of this fill-in-the-blanks game by now, but if he or she is willing to try and work out the entire passage, it will soon be seen how numerous are the correct possibilities that exist for almost every blank in the problem. Indeed, the blank following the name "Jones" is probably the only one in the example that unambiguously demands a single, clear-cut answer, since the "Neither" that comes before "Jones" pretty well determines that the word "nor" must follow "Jones" and precede "I." Apart from this single case, however, almost every blank in the example has a number of equally correct answers for anyone with native-speaker competency in English—but not, of course, for the poor Japanese teenager whose ability to come up with the correct answers for all the blanks will play a major role in determining whether he spends the rest of his life in a nine-to-five white-collar office job or putting together economy-size automobiles on an assembly line.

Obviously, this type of English test cannot be successfully passed simply by knowing English. In fact, as the reader has already seen demonstrated, a practical working knowledge of English can only get in the way of solving it. But large numbers of Japanese youngsters do manage to get substantial numbers of these blanks filled in with the acceptable correct answers. How do they do it?

The answer is complicated, as one might suspect, but it is not too difficult to describe. Some of the students who take this sort of examination come up with surprisingly high scores, scores high enough to qualify them for entrance to the Japanese university system. They do this through a regimen of almost unbelievable hard work, carried on in conjunction with a system of only partially disguised fraud and cheating. The hard work is very real and very hard. It involves the rote memorization of page after page of English text, often with little or no idea of what the English sentences being memorized really mean. But equally real are the elements of fraud and cheating that are now also a necessary part of the entire process.

No matter how diligently any student has managed to memorize English texts by rote, he or she could not possibly hope to hit the right one and fill in the blanks correctly when it came to an examination if the possible range of English texts likely to appear on any given examination were actually unlimited. Such feats of memory would be impossible even if, for example, the examination range were to be limited to a single author. And in theory, even this limit is removed; in theory, the student is supposed to be able to fill in the blanks correctly in a passage selected from any author in the entire field of modern English literature—an obvious and transparent impossibility. The only possible way in which any student, no matter how diligent at rote memory or how devoted to the goal of passing the university examinations he or she may be, can ever get a sufficiently large number of the blanks in such a problem filled in correctly is to have some prior information about which passage is likely to turn up in a given examination, so that that particular passage, with the blanks correctly filled in, may be memorized completely and perfectly. Without such prior information, it would be impossible for any of the students who take the examinations to get passing marks. The number of different but still completely satisfactory answers—satisfactory when viewed simply as filling in the blanks so that the completed passage both makes sense and represents normal, grammatical usage—is always enormous. The actual number of linguistically correct answers is always far too great to permit anyone taking the test to arrive at the one, the only correct answer—which means reproducing intact the exact form the passage has in the original book from which it was taken— unless he or she has been tipped off in one way or another about which passage or passages it would be well to memorize with particular care before the examination.

The human memory can perform tremendous feats, when sufficiently motivated. No one would deny that the serious social implications of the Japanese university examination system provide motivation sufficient for almost any accomplishment. But even this tremendous motivation does not make it possible for students to memorize the entire body of modern English literature word for word. The field must be narrowed down; the odds must somehow be reduced. And it is in the final stages of this all-important process of narrowing down, of reducing the odds, of tipping the student off about what it would be good to study, that fraud and cheating enter upon the scene.

First of all, the necessary narrowing down of the field is innocent enough and a matter of more or less public record. No one really expects that the passages to be found in the examinations will be selected from a very wide range of English writing. After all, few of the professors setting the examinations will have read, in the original English at least, more than a few chapters of one or two books by one or two authors. Everyone generally assumes that the passages will be selected from one or two novels by Maugham or Greene, and this is almost always a perfectly safe assumption. But which books by Maugham or Greene? Maugham was and Greene still is a prolific author; there are many, many titles to choose from in each case. And even within a given book, which chapter, which paragraph, which page? Without this precise narrowing down of the field, it would be folly even to begin the arduous word-for-word memorization of long passages that will, for a few fortunate students, eventually pay off with admission to a first-level Japanese university and then, four years later, with a lifetime appointment to a minor clerical position in a government or large business office— in other words, to the highest reward that the society can bestow.

There are, to be sure, many other societies in which this vital information would simply be sold behind the counter to the highest bidder. The information about which chapter, which page, which paragraph in which book is going to appear in the entrance examinations for a given university would be available in many parts of the world for cash on the line, the price for the information in question fluctuating according to market factors involved in the transaction, as for example how desirable a university the one at stake is, how many are seeking admission, and similar variables. Many other societies would work out this crude arrangement for the operation; but Japanese society is rarely if ever crude in the way it goes about its internal affairs. The way the necessary narrowing down of the field, the tipping off, the prior identification of the passages that will be selected for the university entrance examinations works in Japan is far more subtle than the simple money-down-for-goods-delivered transaction that many other cultures would favor. But because it is more subtle, it is also not only more time-consuming than such direct dealings would be; it is also far more costly, both in money and in human effort.

The necessary prior information identifying which passages will turn up in the examinations is mostly communicated slowly and subtly over a long period of time, during special courses in English given in privately operated, profit-making cram schools and other extra-official programs of after-hours instruction. In the most reliable of these schools, which means the ones at which students may be almost one-hundred-percent certain that they will eventually be told which particular passages they should memorize, the teachers who are employed (and who provide them with this information) are the same university professors who set the examinations. No student, no matter how hard-pressed, could ask for more.

During the day, these professors set the examinations, busily putting blanks into a passage laboriously extracted from Maugham or Greene. Then, during the early evening hours, these same professors give special lectures at cram schools, where students who can afford the steep tuition are drilled in English—drilled by going over the very passages that will, days or weeks later, appear in the examinations that they must pass if they are ever to be admitted to a university. The less reliable of such schools, where the tuition charges must necessarily be proportionately lower, can only employ the graduate students or teaching assistants of these same professors. This in turn makes the working out of the prior-warning system a little less automatic; but then, as in any other economic transaction in the world, you get what you pay for.

Of course, it would be crude and unsubtle simply to train the students in this sort of cram-school operation exclusively on the one short passage that will play the key role in the English-language section of their forthcoming university entrance examination. Japanese society always eschews the crude and the unsubtle in this as in all things. The teachers in these after-hours private schools will provide training in more than one such passage. The students will be forced to memorize in every detail at least four or five entire paragraphs from Maugham or Greene, commas and periods and spaces together with everything else. It is not necessary to know what these passages say, and few of the students will ever have any idea of their sense. The important thing is to memorize them, and memorize them they do.

Even at its most banal and sordid, the whole operation could not work without the really incredible willingness of the Japanese students to subject themselves to the most extraordinary feats of memorization. Just as other societies would surely have worked out some far more direct, if rather more crude, system for passing on this necessary information from the professors who set the examinations to the students who must take them, so also one suspects most other societies would also have worked out some way to free the students involved from the enormous burden of rote memory that they must undertake. But this is not the way Japanese society goes about things. Indeed, the entire arrangement might well be viewed as a microspectacle of the working of the society at large. It is always willing to become involved in tremendously complicated arrangements of detail, simply in order to accomplish what are actually rather simple ends; and it is willing also to subject its members to extraordinary expenditures of both money and effort in order to continue to work in the indirect, subtle way it generally prefers. In this particular case, the students are the ones who pay: they pay enormously in money, and they pay also in the effort that must go into memorizing several long passages of English prose.

Of course no society is totally monolithic, even one that normally seems to be as uniform as Japan's. Confronted with the highly involved, almost ritualized institution of the after-hours cram school as a subtle medium for passing from professor to student the necessary prior information about the content of the university entrance examinations, a few nonconformist individuals always surface, determined to short-circuit the system and also to make a fast yen in the process.

Each year, during the early spring months when university entrance examinations are a major concern on every level of Japanese society, the daily newspapers always manage to turn up several cases of university professors who have simply sold outright to prospective students or their parents copies of the examinations that they were involved in setting. The cases of this out-and-out vending of examination questions normally turn up in the press only when the students who have purchased the papers turn out to be too stupid to manage the feat of rote memory that still must be involved if they are going to make effective use of the information that they have spent so much money to get their hands on. Often the students who elect to do it this way are simply not bright enough to remember the correct answers very long, even though they have had copies of everything to study and commit to memory long in advance of the terrible day of examination.

Examinations in Japan are usually administered very carefully and strictly. The cruder forms of cheating, such as bringing in the correct answers concealed on the person and simply copying them out when the time comes, are virtually ruled out. The students who have simply purchased the answers often cannot remember the correct answers, or at least cannot remember enough of them long enough to get a passing score. They fail. When this happens, their parents begin to ask questions about where all that money they paid to Professor X went. These questions eventually snowball into newspaper articles headlined: "Professor X in Exam-Selling Scandal at Y University."

But these are always the exceptions, never the rule. Few professors at first-rate universities would think of becoming involved in anything as crude as the affairs one reads about in the newspapers. Besides, the long-run economic advantages of steady, year-after-year after-hours employment in the cram schools for oneself, and for one's students and teaching assistants as well, far outweigh the momentary gain possible from any single transaction.

Professors caught in the out-and-out selling of examination questions are expected to resign their posts and usually do. Each year, also, partly as fallout from these well-publicized scandals, there are shouts and murmurs in the press about the necessity for somehow restricting the employment of other professors, who have not yet been caught with their hands in the cash register, from first setting the questions on the entrance examinations and then receiving fat salaries from private cram schools whose avowed and publicly advertised aim is preparing students to pass those same examinations. Editorials are written; educators are interviewed; parents write letters to the newspapers; meanwhile, the cram schools grow larger, more important, and more expensive to attend every year.

This delicate and costly system for passing the word about the content of university entrance examinations is not restricted to those portions of the examinations that deal with English. The examinations cover a wide range of fields, including the social sciences, natural sciences, world history, and mathematics. Most non-Japanese will incidentally be surprised to learn that Japanese history is the one field that is almost completely absent from these examinations. As we have seen, after Japan's defeat in the Pacific War, it was necessary to halt all teaching of Japanese history in schools of every level, since the textbooks in use in 1945 were exclusively written from a fascist-nationalist orientation that could no longer serve the needs of the society. The plan was to halt instruction in Japanese history temporarily, until these unsatisfactory text materials could be replaced with new ones, written from a more balanced, democratic point of view. But subsequent developments within Japanese academic and educational circles have made this rewriting of the texts all but impossible. All that has resulted has been a bitter internal struggle between Marxists and political conservatives, both sides demanding exclusivity in presenting their view of history when it comes to rewriting Japanese history textbooks. Since neither side is willing to compromise in any way, hardly anything has been accomplished in revising the history textbooks in the more than three decades since Japan's defeat. The little that has emerged from this intellectual stalemate is generally Marxist in its historical approach; but the upshot of the whole sorry business in that Japanese history is hardly taught at all in the Japanese school system and also that the entire question is still far too unsettled for Japanese history to play any significant role in the university examinations.

But in each of the other fields that the examinations cover, much the same situation obtains that we have described above for English, at least as far as the employment of after-hours cram schools as a mechanism for communicating the content of examinations to students. But in most of the other fields covered by these examinations, the questions are drawn up in a more rational fashion than is true of those dealing with English, if only because the professors of mathematics, world history, and natural sciences in Japanese universities, unlike their colleagues in foreign languages, generally have excellent backgrounds in their own fields and are actually able to devise valid examinations that really do measure the student's comprehension and understanding of these subjects.

Still, the mere fact that the examinations in fields other than foreign languages are not mere abstract puzzles, but closer to genuine procedures for evaluating the student's knowledge, hardly removes these areas from the sphere of surreptitious passing down of information that will help to ensure passing the tests. The English parts of the entrance examinations are all but impossible to pass without prior information; but the other portions are also so difficult, if difficult in another way, that here too some warning of their content is necessary if the average student, no matter how diligent, is ever to be admitted to a university. In all areas and fields, then, the cram schools and their twilight business continue to flourish.

A sorry spectacle, and a sad and costly one as well—particularly in terms the wasted years of promising young lives that it consumes. This much any observer of the Japanese academic scene will be quick to admit. But the same observer might also well ask what all this elaborate subterfuge and pointless memorization has to do with the modern myth of Nihongo, the topic that remains our principal concern. Unfortunately, all this is indeed deeply intertwined with the tentacles of the Nihongo myth—unfortunately, because if it were not for this involvement, there can be little question but that Japanese society would long before now have alleviated at least the worst excesses of the university examination system, together with the largely corrupt cram schools that feed upon it.

If it were not for their involvement with the modern myth of Nihongo, the absurdities and internal contradictions of the entire university examination system in Japan would without question have been resolved in large measure long before this. But as we have seen already, any element of Japanese cultural and social behavior that becomes involved with the modern myth of Nihongo takes on, by the very fact of that involvement, many of the same unfounded assumptions, together with the stubborn determination to remain immune to all normal logic, that characterize the myth itself. English-language learning and English-language teaching in Japan both end up being tarred by the same brush with which the myth of Nihongo disfigures everything it touches.

This fatal identification of foreign-language education with the mythic approach to the Japanese language shows itself in many different ways. One striking instance of the identification concerns the same fill-in-the-blanks examination questions that we have explored above in connection with the general practices of the English-language portions of most Japanese university admission examinations. It comes as little surprise to learn that precisely the same variety of fill-in-the-blanks questions are also widely employed in the sections of those same examinations that are designed to evaluate the students' command of the Japanese language—their own native language, a language in which by definition they have native-speaker competence. The procedures are the same. A short passage is selected, ostensibly at random, from a standard Japanese author. Key words throughout the passage are replaced with blanks, and the student is expected to reconstruct the entire passage so that it will read exactly the same as it did in the original before the professor who set the examination mutilated it.

By and large, all this is precisely the same as what is done with the English-language examinations. The same opportunities abound for elaborately disguised fraud and lucrative connivance on the part of the professors who are entrusted with the job of setting these exams. An equally enormous, equally lucrative gray market of after-hours cram schools flourishes for the purpose of preparing students to succeed in these Japanese-language examinations, preparation again consisting in effect of providing prior information, for a price, about just what particular passages will be selected for use in any given entrance examination.

All this is the same, but there remains one enormous difference. This time around, the passage is in Japanese; it is in the students' native language, not in a foreign language. This is not only an enormous difference, it is also a substantial one. Testing the competence of a student in his or her own language is in both theory and practice quite a different procedure from testing in a foreign language. The same elements are not being tested in both cases; the procedures that will be effective in the one instance will not be appropriate in the other. But the overpowering impact of the modern myth of Nihongo has been to convince modern Japanese society that they are actually the same.

The myth identifies the Japanese language with Japanese race and nationality, and furthermore with anything that anyone of Japanese race and nationality does. This means that to believe in the myth is to become unable to make any distinction between testing in a foreign language—in which at best the student may be expected to have only partial competence—and testing in the student's native language—in which by definition he or she has full native-speaker competence.

Even for the student who is a native speaker of Japanese, the Japanese-language portions of the typical university entrance examination are extremely difficult. They can be selected from such an enormously wide range of literary works that without some prior clues about what passage is likely to turn up, the best-prepared student might very well find him- or herself on quite unfamiliar territory. The expensive services of the after-hours cram schools are hence quite valuable for zeroing in on this portion of the examinations. These curious institutions would hence remain both necessary for the student and extremely lucrative for their proprietors even if the university applicant were examined in no subject other than the Japanese language.

Still, while these Japanese-language sections of the entrance examinations are difficult, they are not on the face of it impossible. With the right combination of hard work, diligent rote memorization, and accurate prior information about what passages are likely to turn up on the exams, a student of normal intelligence and average mental competence may at least entertain a reasonable expectation of getting enough of the blanks filled in correctly to achieve a passing score.

When the language at issue is one's own native tongue, each of the puzzling blanks remains a difficult puzzle, but it is only a question of being more or less difficult in each case—not, as is the case when the language is not one's own, of being actually and theoretically impossible. The native speaker trying to do this sort of thing in the native speaker's own language is trying to shoot a very few small fish in a very large barrel; it is not easy, but it can be done. The student who is asked to do the same thing in a foreign language is trying to shoot an equally small number of tiny fish not in a barrel but in the open sea. And this can only be done either by a tremendously fortunate accident or by having someone tell you first where the little things are going to be swimming.

The overpowering impact of the modern myth of Nihongo upon the entire society thus manages to blur the important dividing line that separates one of these activities from the other. The myth of Nihongo takes up as its own all the functions of what is actually a quite different activity, the teaching and learning of foreign languages. And the Japanese student, together with Japanese society as a whole, is the loser. The only ones who win in any of this are the university professors who continue to moonlight lucratively in the cram schools.

It is also ultimately back to the impact of the modern myth of Nihongo that we may trace another of the limitations that continue to inhibit the learning and teaching of English throughout the Japanese educational system. Again, this is something that will most likely strike the foreign observer not already familiar with the Japanese sociolinguistic scene as being as unlikely as it is unusual.

This is the assumption that English-language training, defined as the ability to get passing scores in the English-language portions of entrance examinations, particularly those on the university level, is somehow a necessary accomplishment for everyone in the society, even though in any given instance it is unlikely that the individual concerned will ever have even the most remote opportunity or likelihood of making any practical use of English or of any other foreign language.

This deeply ingrained sociolinguistic assumption of contemporary Japanese society provides yet another demonstration of how intertwined the modern myth of Nihongo has become with foreign-language education. Everyone in Japanese society knows, and at some time or other also studies, the Japanese language. The myth extends this universality into a different and actually quite irrelevant quarter, the study of foreign languages: everyone must also, it decrees, study English as well. And study it they do, year after year, all the way through the entire system of compulsory education and on and on into the upper, elective levels of senior high school and university and graduate school—boys and girls in the rural countryside, who have never seen an English-speaking person in their lives and are unlikely ever to do so; boys and girls in great metropolitan bedroom towns who will in almost every case not be economically able to continue in school beyond the level set by Japanese law for compulsory free education; youngsters in elite private high schools, being trained like thoroughbred racing stock for eventual admission to the national university system—everyone in the society, without exception, throughout the entire enterprise that constitutes education in Japan, must and does study English. Whether or not any of them will ever use the language is a question that is never asked.

But the general silence that the society agrees to maintain on this particular score is hardly surprising, once we understand something of the way these things operate in modern Japanese life. After all, "to use English" is itself an expression capable of several different interpretations. The one that most societies would place upon this expression would imply the use of English as a foreign language for purposes of communicating with foreigners who speak English, either as a native language or as a convenient second language that they themselves have learned—in a word, as a medium for looking outside, out and away from the interior of Japanese life and society.

But while such communication remains a vital function in any society that, like modern Japan's, exists entirely on a delicate economic imbalance of unlimited foreign exports and carefully regulated imports, it is also a function that can actually be carried out by a relatively small number of persons. Such people do, of course, exist in Japanese society, in numbers that are more than adequate to the limited need that the society has for such skills. Only a tiny number of such persons are actually required, particularly in a highly efficient industrialized society like modern Japan.

One individual, after all, can write all the business letters, prepare all the bills of lading, and even handle all the customer-service complaints for the automobiles that an entire assembly line employing hundreds, even thousands, of workers can turn out. The high-school graduates who end up as workers in the factories need not know any foreign language to do their jobs, any more than do the hundreds of thousands of university graduates who end up filing receipts and counting stacks of ¥10,000 notes in Japanese offices and banks.

The relatively few people who are both necessary and actually competent enough in foreign languages to perform these highly specialized tasks for Japanese society come from widely diverse backgrounds. About all that most of them have in common is the fact that hardly any of them are products of the Japanese educational system, having acquired their language skills apart from that system, generally by some historical accident such as residence abroad or other firsthand contacts with real-life foreign-language situations.

These people do exist in modern Japan; they are the ones who conduct the necessary linguistic communication with foreigners and with foreign countries that the society demands; and none of them could probably pass the English portions of the entrance examinations for an even moderately prestigious Japanese university, any more than could the handful of native English speakers with whom they come into contact as part of their work.

But such effective, practical employment of foreign languages for communication, important though it is to the daily survival of Japanese business and trade throughout the world, is not what Japanese sociolinguistic theory has in mind by "using English." If it were, then there obviously would be no point in large numbers of the population becoming involved in the study of English. Instead, what is actually implied by "using English" in a Japanese sociolinguistic context is "using English to pass the university or other admissions examinations." Unlike interpreting for or otherwise dealing with foreigners through practical employment of linguistic skills, the necessity for passing examinations has been abstracted out of the general sociolinguistic situation to become the sole end, the ultimate goal of all English-language education in Japan.

Passing the examinations has become the only way for economic advancement within the society at large; learning to solve the perverse puzzles that constitute the English-language portions of the examinations has become the only way to get passing grades in the examinations; hence it follows—naturally, if illogically—that everyone in the society who hopes for advancement must undertake the study of English, at least that very special kind of study that will eventually ensure passing the examinations.

Thus it is hardly to be wondered at if the dividing line between this particular kind of foreign-language training and language as a whole becomes more and more blurred in the average mind. And in its turn the dividing line between Japanese and all other languages also becomes blurred, as this particular variety of examination-oriented English education becomes a desirable goal in and of itself throughout the society. Its sociolinguistic permeation through every level of Japanese life is total, and the identification of foreign-language learning with the modern myth of Nihongo becomes complete and apparently irreversible. A major opportunity has been lost here. The only ones who benefit from all this are the proprietors of the cram schools and the moonlighting university professors whom they employ. Everyone else in contemporary Japanese life is the loser. The myth has managed to extend its tentacles into yet another area of Japanese life, strangling off at their roots some of the most significant ways in which the Japanese people, even while inside their own culture and society, might otherwise better equip themselves for the task of looking out at the rest of the world.

CHAPTER TWELVE

Tomorrow the World

> *What I really want to say today is that, in actual fact,
> the time is now already past when we Japanese should
> remain passive, and simply continue to teach our
> language to the foreigners because they implore us to
> do so. Rather, I wish to advance toward the conclusion
> that it is in truth a misfortune for any member of the
> human race to go to the grave ignorant of the Japanese
> language—this is the concept that we hope to spread
> among the foreigners.* —Takao Suzuki, Lecture of
> March 18, 1978, on "Why Teach Nihongo to
> the Foreigners?"

ANY SUSTAINING myth is ideally a matter of
concern only to the society it helps sustain. This follows directly from our
definition of what such a myth consists of and also from our understanding
of what such a myth is designed to do. We have seen how the modern myth
of Nihongo, functioning as it presently does in contemporary Japanese
society, fulfills all the requirements necessary for the usual definition of a
sustaining myth; we have also seen how this same myth fully lives up to its
role by responding to the surprisingly wide range of sociolinguistic problems,
needs, and questions for which Japanese society appears otherwise to lack
useful and immediate answers.

Many, perhaps even most, of these ready answers that the myth serves up
are, as we have also seen, linguistically incorrect. But since it is a myth, this
really does not matter very much. Nor does it actually detract substantially
from the effective functioning of the myth in its ideal role as a social sustaining force.

But whether they are right or wrong, most of the instant answers that the Japanese mythmakers conjure up out of their scholarly hats are designed solely for domestic consumption. The myth's claims generally fit in with the overall role of the myth itself as a purely domestic sustaining force. Normally, most of its functions do not impinge upon linguistic contacts between Japan and the rest of the world.

Most—but unfortunately not all. In the previous chapter we have seen significant evidence for some of the ways in which the myth has managed to extend its tentacles into areas that are more and more tangential to its immediate domestic concerns. We have also seen how in the process it has managed to do great damage, especially concerning Japanese society's constant efforts to look out at the rest of the world from inside its insular confines. But the myth's enormous potential for expansionism clearly does not stop with the concerns discussed in chapter 11.

A substantial number of the myth's ready-made solutions for socio-linguistic questions prove, on closer inspection, to go far beyond the natural limits of a sustaining myth evolved solely for domestic consumption. Often we are able to observe the myth expanding itself more and more, leaving solely domestic Japanese problems and concerns further and further behind and, in the process, also managing to influence increasingly significant aspects of modern Japan's intercourse with the rest of the world.

The myth's assumptions, views, and answers, even when they are this far isolated from their original ideological home base, are still every bit as specious and erroneous as they ever were. The only difference is that now they are directed, not toward the internal concerns of Japanese society, but outward, toward the rest of the world. When the myth manages to do this, it becomes everybody's concern.

In the previous chapter we tried to consider some of the sociolinguistic questions that arise within Japanese society because of its essentially closed, isolated nature, picturing this society as a world where most individuals must remain inside, though they may keep trying to look out. The figure of speech involved, like all figures of speech, has its limitations and weaknesses as well as its instructive strengths. Much of the time, most of life for everyone in Japan certainly does focus upon the task of trying to peer out at the rest of the world from an insular inside. But we must not allow this figure of speech to carry us too far. We all know that these days great numbers of Japanese do manage to do more than simply peer out. They now go out and take a good, if generally rather quick, look at it themselves, in increasingly, and startlingly, large numbers.

Someone, only half in jest, recently suggested that the overseas Japanese tourist boom is the society's answer to its housing shortage. By keeping substantial numbers of the Japanese population constantly on the move on rapid, all-inclusive JALPAK tours through foreign countries, Japan may have worked out a way to muddle through what is a very severe crisis. If all the Japanese tourists who are absent at any given time, either in the air or busy being bussed from the Eiffel Tower to the Arc de Triomphe, were by some evil magic to be returned to the home islands at the same moment, not only would there be an insufficient number of houses and apartments to accommodate them; there most likely would not even be enough space in Japan for everyone to stand erect, much less to lie down.

The theory has its elements of exaggeration. But anyone who has observed the enormous numbers of Japanese tourists who visit Europe and North America every year may be forgiven for being tempted to take it literally. The *Asahi Shimbun* has estimated that during the summer of 1980 alone, 160,000 Japanese aged nineteen years or younger went abroad for short tours, mostly involving some opportunity for English-language training. The newspaper also estimated that such a summer tour cost the parents of each youngster between ¥300,000 and ¥500,000—roughly U.S. $1,500 to $2,500. This statistic tells us nothing of the far greater numbers of adult tourists; but it surely indicates the enormous numbers of Japanese who venture abroad every year and documents most effectively the tremendous interest that younger Japanese and their affluent parents have not only in foreign travel but also in opportunities to learn some foreign language, particularly English, in the bargain.

And what happens to them when they do manage to get abroad? How does the modern myth of Nihongo make its effect felt? How does it work to inhibit the sociolinguistic behavior of Japanese when they find themselves in a real-life foreign-language situation? An interview recently published in a widely read Japanese weekly magazine (*Shūkan Asahi*, January 18, 1980) provides an unusually candid view into the matter and deserves to be quoted at some length.

The interview in question was printed as part of a series capitalizing upon an unusual journalistic gimmick—at least, a gimmick rare in Japan: a brash, lively, unorthodox woman reporter asking frank questions of a man, rather than the other way around. In this instance the interviewer was Emi Nakao. Her subject was a fairly well-known Japanese artist and author, Masuo Ikeda, who has lived and worked in New York for a number of years, where he was also for a time married to an American.

The interview began with the usual banal formalities, but, like almost all social discourse in Japan involving anyone who has lived abroad, it soon managed to get around to sociolinguistic problems.

Ikeda is a successful artist. He also wrote a Japanese bestseller a number of years ago and, more recently, directed and produced a motion-picture version of the book. Nakao shows a necessary minimum of interest in these activities, but once that requirement is safely out of the way, she quickly manages to get the conversation turned in the direction in which she is really interested—to the problems of foreign languages in general and of English in particular. After all, it may be years before our brash girl reporter has another such chance. Here she at last has a subject to whom she can put all the questions she has always been dying to hear the answers to, but never had anyone to ask. And ask she does, in the following fashion:

Miss Nakao: . . . Anyway, Mr. Ikeda, since you've lived so long in America, there is one thing that I would like very much to ask you. . . . You see, I was born right after the end of the war, in 1946. And this means that I have this terrible complex about America.

Mr. Ikeda: That's strange. . . . Normally, I'd expect that you wouldn't have such a complex. . . .

Nakao: No, I really do have a terrible complex on the subject. I mean, after all, I grew up just when even in the matter of something to eat, it was evident that over there they had lots of things to eat that we couldn't even get hold of here in Japan, and so the whole idea that America was superior to Japan came at us in a great rush. That's why, even in the case of the English language itself, I ended up feeling a complex over the very fact that I can't understand English. Now, when I am carrying on a conversation in the way we are doing, I do really feel that Japanese are far superior to Americans—I mean, we are superior to them in our intelligence and in our attention to detail, things like that. But when I am not able to communicate all these things to the person to whom I am talking, then I end up feeling terribly frustrated.

Ikeda: In other words, by being "able to communicate to the person to whom you are talking," do you mean communication in language?

Nakao: Right! And that's why, even when I just listen to anyone speaking English, I tend to fall into a certain spirit of self-deprecation. I mean, I realize that really there is no reason why I should feel inferior in any way to those jokers who are talking English. Still, I do feel just that way, in spite of the fact that I know better. . . . Anyway, I suppose that at best, I am the kind of person who primarily makes oral contact with the other person. (*Laughter.*) So when that's not possible, then I feel frustrated.

Ikeda: Even so, it does appear strange to me that a person of your age should have such a complex.

Nakao: Maybe I shouldn't call it a complex, but if I don't call it that, I don't know what to call it. What I mean is, well, you know how American things come at us indirectly. I guess what I feel is that I would like to have them come directly instead.

Ikeda: I see, yes, I see. . . .

Nakao: What I want to do is to find out, are all those things really as wonderful as I think they are? Are they really something that should be the object of our affection or not—that's what I want to find out.

Ikeda: You'd like to find out for sure, wouldn't you. . . . Anyway, in spite of all this, and although you talk about your complex about the English language, you haven't made any effort to learn English yourself, have you?

Nakao: Ha ha ha ha ha! . . .

The interview goes on, mercifully switching to other subjects, but Nakao, the "lively, brash girl reporter who asks frank, unhesitating questions," has found out what she wanted to know—and she has also said what she wanted to say on the subject of foreign languages, which is probably even more important, at least to her.

Even Nakao's most severe critic will be forced to admit that her questions —or rather, her replies to her own questions, since she really gives Ikeda very little opportunity to say anything at all in the course of the interview— require little or nothing in the way of comment or explanation. Here we find a concentrated epitome of the way that the myth of Nihongo expands further and further away from its own concerns to inhibit and determine the course of Japanese reactions to the use of foreign languages—even when, as in the case of Nakao, the individual involved does not personally claim ever to have made any attempt to employ a foreign language as such.

This is perhaps the only feature of Nakao's self-revelations that requires particular comment, if only because it is so very unusual and unexpected. In most of her statements, she is not talking about what she experiences, or has experienced, when trying to learn or to speak English. Her idiosyncratic sociolinguistic reactions are rather directed toward quite a different object— she "tends to fall into a certain spirit of self-deprecation" simply when she "listens to anyone else speaking English." Which of course must happen a great deal when Nakao visits places like most parts of the United States, where most people are perverse enough to speak English all the time.

Ikeda's part in this interview, at least in the sections dealing with language that are translated and excerpted above, is also significant, if only in a rather negative fashion. Ikeda has actually lived abroad, in an English-speaking country, for a considerable period of time; he has been married to an English-speaking woman; and he has used English as part of his daily life during those years. It is quite clear that, among his many difficulties encountered in the course of this interview with the "brash, outspoken Miss Nakao," one of his major problems is that he simply does not know what she is talking about when she gets off on the subject of English. He genuinely does not comprehend what this foreign language, which she neither claims to know nor apparently even wishes to learn, nevertheless does to her psyche.

Ikeda shows himself to be far removed, thanks to his long residence abroad, from the major assumptions of the myth of Nihongo as they reach out to affect this sphere of Japanese social behavior. For this reason, he is frankly puzzled; he keeps trying to be polite, but he finds it difficult to think up something—anything—to say that will be along the apparent lines of the discussion without seeming rude. How happy he must have been when, finally lowering his sights a little in his last comment quoted above, he let the brash, outspoken Miss Nakao really have it. Her response, a recognized gambit in any Japanese conversation, is to signal unconditional defeat by a gale of girlish laughter. Her "Ha ha ha ha ha! . . ." has the formal sociolinguistic role of announcing her surrender and also her determination to continue the "interview," but this time with a change in subject of discussion.

What Nakao is trying to say in the segment of conversation cited above may not be expressed very clearly or very coherently, but it is nevertheless part and parcel of the modern myth of Nihongo, particularly of the portion that takes precedence when the Japanese temporarily leave their own closed society for a brief period in order to visit that great, surprising world outside. The limiting condition of a "brief period" in all this is important; we have seen how Ikeda almost fails to understand what in the world Nakao is trying to talk to him about simply because his own experience of residence in the outside world has not been brief. He has lived abroad for a substantial period of time and has had more than superficial experiences there. The mythic approach to the world outside works best when the subject concerned can observe that world for only a few moments at a time: the quick weekend in Waikiki, the bus tours of Paris, Cologne, Rome, and London, and then back to Tokyo before the precious vacation becomes only a memory.

Despite Nakao's problems in expressing herself, her opinions find expression, often in more coherent form, in much of the more serious sociolinguistic literature from Japanese academic circles. And it is particularly instructive to see how the formal, extremely serious, and highly respected scholars in the field end up putting their own words to sentiments and views all but impossible to distinguish from those of the excited if brash Nakao—or at least her sentiments before she dissolved into that fit of giggles.

One such source is a recent volume by Professor Takao Suzuki, by now an old friend to the reader. His 1975 book entitled *Tozasareta Gengo* (Language Locked-up) is an important, lengthy study of some of the ways in which he believes many Japanese react to the use of language. Here again, Suzuki appears mostly to have generalized upon the basis of his own personal views, first asking himself how he feels about this or that sociolinguistic situation and then telling us that this is the way most Japanese feel about it. Such a system may well lack something in scientific method, but his results are hardly to be neglected solely for that reason; after all, Suzuki is Japanese, and his own reactions cannot but be of interest, even though they may not be quite as universally representative as he sometimes claims.

At any rate, one particular passage in this book, in which Suzuki faces up to the main questions that arise when Japanese (like himself) appear in the outside world, repays careful study. It has much to teach us about modern Japanese life, society, and culture; it also shows us much about how the modern myth of Nihongo continues to make its cold hand felt in this area of sociolinguistic behavior:

"We [Japanese] are unable to decide our own intentions so long as the probable course of action of others involved with us is unclear. I do not think it can be denied that this psychological structuring, which makes it difficult to reach decisions concerning ourselves from our own standpoint alone, has its negative aspects. It is because of this psychological structuring that we Japanese prefer not to set up a consistent individual course of action and pursue it to its logical conclusion, but rather are skilled in sizing up a concrete situation and evolving the individual solutions that are most efficient for this time or that. Here too we see a contrast with the Western European mode of conduct, which more often than not strikes us with its authoritarian, unilateral inflexibility. It is this pattern of mutual self-recognition, depending upon the other party . . . that makes it possible to explain the psychological unrest of Japanese confronted with Europeans and Americans. For us to be able to make the necessary decisions concerning our own slot in human relations, we must first know who the other party is and whether he is of higher or lower status than ourselves. The trouble is that foreigners do not give us a single clue that would permit us to carry out this kind of ranking. The result is that since we are unable to evaluate the other party, we end up in an unstable psychological situation in which we are also unable to rank ourselves. We Japanese are famous for treating quite differently people we do not know and people with whom we are well acquainted. This happens simply because, when we encounter a second party whom we cannot rank, we find that ignoring him is the only way in which we ourselves are able to escape our own increasing sense of instability. I really do not think it is any exaggeration to say that when Japanese are faced with a second party whom they cannot completely understand or categorize, they are unable to carry on normal human intercourse with that party."

We have had occasion above, in discussing the submyths particularly relating to the much-heralded difficulty of the Japanese language, to take fairly sharp issue with a number of Suzuki's views, particularly his thesis that the Japanese writing system is superior to all other writing systems or that the Japanese "understand their own difficult language better than you foreigners do yours, with its easy writing systems." That makes it especially pleasant to be able to give Suzuki full marks this time around.

When it comes to his analysis of the sociolinguistic restraints imposed upon Japanese social behavior abroad—that closely drawn circle of restricted response to which most Japanese continue to limit themselves, thanks to the perpetuation of the mythic approach to their own language and its extension to foreign languages—Suzuki is a guide without equal. He writes easily and effectively; we never have occasion to wonder what he means; and his gift for expression is admirable. Even though we have reason to suspect that his principal source of data is nothing more than an externalization of his own soul-searching, that hardly detracts at all from the value and interest of his analysis.

Most importantly, we see at once that no particularly significant distance separates Suzuki and what he has to teach us from the brash, outspoken Miss Nakao and her effusive confession concerning the complexes and difficulties she encounters when she visits the world outside. What we have here are really only two different sides of the same coin—thin as a dime and with just as little substance in between. Heads you lose, tails I win.

Brief visits to the outside world are one thing. The best thing about them, of course, is that they are brief, and one is always back home before the new wears thin. But there is another side to the myth and its approach to the world outside of Japan that is not so easily dealt with—one that will not simply solve itself if everyone concerned waits a few minutes longer until they get home. Here the myth becomes involved with a serious, permanent problem—teaching Japanese to foreigners and encouraging foreigners to learn Japanese. Who is to do it? How is it to be done? Indeed, should it be done, and—the biggest question of all—can it be done?

In the past several years, Japanese society has seriously begun to encounter these and other related questions for the first time in its hundreds of years of continual cultural history. It has started to trouble itself concerning the feasibility, the methodology, and particularly the advisability of providing formal instruction in the Japanese language for different peoples in that enormous world outside. Today, Japanese is the language of Japan; but tomorrow . . . tomorrow it may well be the language of the world!—or so it would appear, to read some of the literature currently being generated in this particular subquarter of the mythic movement.

Of course, all this represents quite a radical departure. For most of Japanese history, there was no question of teaching the Japanese language to foreigners; indeed, there were periods in the past when to do so was against the law. The Dutch, who were permitted to trade with Japan during the so-called period of national exclusion enforced by the Tokugawa shoguns, found that a rigid prohibition against their studying the Japanese language was only one of the many annoying rules they were to obey if they wished to continue being tolerated in Japan during this difficult period. Just like trampling on the crucifix, the prohibition on studying the Japanese language was yet another of the many tiresome bureaucratic stipulations that the industrious Dutch Protestants were prepared, if not particularly pleased, to go along with in order to stay in business.

Now, of course, times have changed. The foreigner who wishes to live in Japan and help the Japanese conduct their foreign trade is no longer asked to trample on the crucifix at regular intervals. Nor is he legally forbidden to study the Japanese language. But as the Japanese now begin to realize that this question of providing instruction for foreigners who will persist in attempting to learn their language is something that, unlike Christianity, will not go away if it is simply ignored, the modern myth of Nihongo faces a potential apotheosis. Every indication is that it will soon cease to be a domestic sustaining myth, something of interest and value only to the population of a small island nation. In the process perhaps it may even transform itself into a new sociolinguistic myth of global dimension. Such a development is not intrinsically impossible. Stranger things have happened.

To say that Japanese society is now facing the problem of teaching Japanese to the rest of the world—Japanese as a foreign language, to employ the currently fashionable euphemism—for the first time in its history is, to be sure, something of an oversimplification. During World War II, the Japanese military occupation officials in some of the territories temporarily held by Japan did make limited attempts to introduce courses in Japanese —which at the time they usually insisted upon calling Nippongo—into the curricula of local schools and colleges. (The word Nippongo, with its emphatic consonant sequence -pp- replacing the weak medial -h- of the usual pronunciation as Nihongo, was much favored during the war years because of its more overtly macho acoustic effect. The same was true of the name of the country, which then tended to favor Nippon, rather than the now-usual pronunciation Nihon.) This work necessarily had to be undertaken very quickly and with little preparation on the part of all concerned; it also necessarily came to an end equally fast.

The Japanese seem to have been most successful in this wartime language teaching in Thailand, a country never officially or legally occupied by Japanese armed forces but where, throughout the war in the Pacific, a large resident Japanese garrison effectively directed and controlled a pro-Japanese puppet regime. Other significant if equally short-lived efforts toward teaching occupied peoples something of the Japanese language were made in the Philippines, where, however, in striking contrast with the situation in Thailand, the Japanese military occupation was direct, unashamed, and generally rather brutal.

The Japanese military government in the occupied Philippines asked for and received from Tokyo a considerable number of civilians sent into the area as Japanese language teachers. But the Philippines were liberated from the Japanese occupation too soon for their work to have any lasting impact;

nor were the overall circumstances under which it was conducted such as would do much to give the entire business of "teaching Japanese to foreigners" a very good name, at least in the years immediately following the debacle of 1945.

With Japan's defeat in the war and surrender to the Allied Forces, all these efforts came to a sudden halt. For the next decade, the nation had its hands full with the essential tasks of feeding, clothing, and housing its own population. The so-called Allied Occupation of Japan was, as it turned out, almost entirely an American occupation. The Supreme Commander, General Douglas MacArthur, took an extremely hard line when it came to questions of meaningful participation in the work of occupying defeated Japan by any of his wartime allies. The British and Australians were allowed to contribute only tiny, token forces to the Occupation, while the Soviets, to their great frustration, were not permitted even nominal representation. The whole business soon became a thoroughly American show; and it was also run entirely in English, not in Japanese. The American Occupation authorities routinely communicated with Japanese officialdom in English; the Japanese routinely replied in English; the work of the Occupation was conducted in English.

Several reasons lay behind this decision. The most obvious reason—namely, that English was the language of the winners, and that the winners were now in charge—is surely the principal one; but there were others. Long before the Japanese surrender in August 1945, certain elements in Washington had tried to begin planning for a long occupation of Japan. But official opinion within both American military and civilian circles sharply diverged on the question of how it should be occupied and by whom.

The American navy, already accustomed to the problems of administering islands taken in battle during the fighting in the Pacific theater, looked ahead to the problems of occupation and began training a large number of men and women in the Japanese language. The plan was to make use of these language skills during the eventual occupation of the home islands, an occupation that the navy supposed would be conducted largely through the medium of the Japanese language.

But the American army largely lacked such island-hopping experience; and for this and for other reasons they did not agree on the importance of training large numbers of persons in Japanese language or on the need for employing such trained people in the eventual occupation program.

Also important to army thinking in this connection was a view that was extremely influential in many American governmental circles near the end of the war. This held that after its surrender Japan would simply be reduced to an agricultural community of no importance to the world at large and hence would not be worth the time and trouble of a protracted military occupation. If that were to be the case, then there was no need to train large numbers of Americans for a long occupation of Japan.

What actually happened, as in much of history, followed none of these carefully evolved predictions. Japan was occupied, and the occupation lasted for a considerable period of time. But Japan was not reduced to a simple agrarian economy. Soon it was encouraged to reindustrialize, so as to serve as the weapons-maker for new American wars in the Far East. General MacArthur, who never enjoyed the company of the American navy under any conditions, passed a personal blanket-order that only United States Army personnel were to participate in his occupation of his Japan. The army had not trained its people in language skills on anything resembling the scale necessary for the Occupation to conduct its affairs in Japanese; the navy had, but now the navy was not to be allowed to take part in the Occupation. And so, out of all this involved web of historical accident further complicated by personal idiosyncrasy, the Allied Occupation of Japan soon became an all-English-speaking, all-English-writing enterprise. It was up to the Japanese to learn English if they wished to cope; and nothing could have been further from their minds at the time than the question of teaching anyone else Japanese.

Within what now seems, in retrospect, to have been an amazingly short period of time, Japanese hard work, skill, and determination, combined with material help advanced by the Occupation forces, paid off. Japanese industry recovered. Japan began to regain its foreign markets. The economy responded to ever-increasing export sales of Japanese goods throughout the world, and particularly to the United States. Slowly but surely, Japan entered a new period of growing prosperity, finally to achieve outright affluence. By 1968 the Japanese gross national product had outstripped that of West Germany. Japan now found itself in second place among the industrial powers of the West; and in the decade or more since then, it has never shown the least sign of retreating from this hard-won position of international influence, power, and wealth—and all that go with them.

With this, the stage was finally set for the revival of the modern myth of Japan. We have seen how many of the circumstances under which Japan's growing economic security and increasing affluence during the 1960s gave rise to pressing sociolinguistic questions. We have also seen a number of the ways in which the emergence of the new myth, along with some necessary refurbishing of the old, managed to respond to some of the questions that Japanese society now encountered as the nation finally arrived upon the world economic scene.

Particularly strident were the questions of national identity—the *Nihonjin-ron*—now posed by this sudden and unprecedented emergence. Japanese intellectual circles were ill prepared for the climate of power, influence, and affluence that was to be Japan's during the 1960s and 1970s. The myth now came to their assistance, providing convenient if generally specious answers to pressing questions that had never been asked before.

And, as luck would have it, some of the most pressing of all these questions turned out to involve the problem of teaching the Japanese language to foreigners. The issues presented resembled those of the general *Nihonjin-ron* in that Japanese society had never had to face up to them before; but unlike most of the *Nihonjin-ron* questions, the answers here were to prove even harder and much more difficult to answer than anyone had at first suspected.

The Japanese in the late 1960s and throughout the 1970s soon discovered that this entire area was one in which they almost entirely lacked both prior experience and prior interest. We have already noted the short-lived wartime experiences in Thailand and the Philippines; but these were hardly applicable to the present circumstances. Besides, almost none of those who had taken an active part were still around to be of any real help. During the late 1950s and into the early 1960s the Japanese government had, to be sure, started a small Japanese-language school for Southeast Asians who wished to study in Japanese colleges and universities, mostly in connection with Japanese reparation payments for wartime damages. This had been a fairly successful undertaking, but since it involved teaching Asians, not whites, it was widely felt in Japanese academic circles that the experience gained during the operation of this program would not be of any particular utility now for teaching the language to Americans and Europeans.

Meanwhile, whites who were for any reason interested in learning Japanese were forced to do it on their own, with no guidance or assistance from Japanese sources, either scholarly or official. From the end of the war on, the American academic community continued to provide a variety of programs in which Americans and other English-speakers were able to learn Japanese effectively enough to live, work, or study in Japan. By the end of the 1960s, there were a number of schools and other language-instruction programs actually operating in Japan, but they were entirely under the direction of American academic interests—and also entirely financially supported by Americans. At first this support presented no serious problem. But with the beginning of world inflation, the devaluation of American currency, and the never-ending spiral of the cost of living in Japan, the expenses involved in maintaining such language-learning facilities in Japan for foreigners soon grew to enormous proportions.

At the same time, Japanese government and educational leaders, particularly those who found themselves having frequent encounters with their opposite numbers in foreign countries, began to recognize the curious fact that Japan was the only modern industrialized nation making absolutely no effort to disseminate knowledge of its language among the people of other countries. As these people began to make more frequent and intensive trips abroad—sometimes "visits of inspection and fact finding" lasting as many as four or five days—they noticed that, for example, the British government had long sponsored English-language instruction in many different parts of the world. Indeed, the so-called British Council English-language program was a medium for learning practical English, well established in many major Japanese cities. In this particular case it was not actually necessary for the Japanese to go abroad to absorb this information.

In much the same way, the French had for decades taught the French language throughout the world through a variety of government-sponsored agencies and programs, while the prestigious Goethe Institute of the Federal Republic of Germany provided yet another example of a highly admired foreign country's taking an active interest in teaching its language to foreigners.

By the end of the 1960s, the Japanese had seen enough. A decision was reached at the highest levels of Japanese officialdom. The Japanese too would now embark on a program of teaching their language to foreigners, imitating the model that the British, French, and West German governments had set for them. The die had been cast.

The highest levels of Japanese officialdom—but in such a case, there is always the pressing question of precisely what high levels and of exactly where within the labyrinths of Japanese bureaucracy these levels are to be located.

As Japanese officials began to face up to the consequences of this decision to "do something about teaching the Japanese language to foreigners," they also found that this top-level decision had set off a bitter internecine struggle for bureaucratic territoriality. Even today, a decade or more since the original decision to become involved in teaching Japanese as a foreign language, this struggle shows few signs of being resolved, while the heavy fallout from its countless contests and confrontations continues to severely limit the overall effectiveness of much of what is now being done under Japanese government auspices in this area.

The bureaucratic struggle has centered on the question of who shall have responsibility for the official direction of Japanese-language education for foreigners. Particularly crucial has been the question of which section of the Japanese government shall be in overall charge of this sort of activity. The Foreign Office, that agency of the Japanese Government charged by law with all aspects of the conduct of Japan's foreign affairs, takes the position that teaching the Japanese language to non-Japanese is a type of international relations. As a consequence, the Foreign Office and its officials see themselves as the only ones who are legally entitled to direct and sponsor such

programs. The Ministry of Education, the agency of the Japanese government charged with the conduct of Japanese education on all levels, main-
tains that teaching Japanese to non-Japanese is a type of education. As a
consequence, its officials see themselves as the only ones legally entitled to
direct and sponsor such programs. The lines involved in the struggle are
drawn clearly enough. What is far from clear is when, if ever, the conflict
will be resolved and what form the eventual resolution of these conflicting
bureaucratic claims and interests, if indeed one is ever reached, will take.

In the meantime, and ever since this bureaucratic scramble for territorial
rights was set off by the cabinet-level decision late in the 1960s that the Japanese Government would now "do something" about the matter, these two
agencies have been engaged in a lively competition on several levels. Within
the Japanese government, they vie for appropriations of money with which
to sponsor and conduct Japanese-language instruction for non-Japanese,
both in Japan and throughout the world. Outside of Japan, they compete
for the direction of programs, for students, and along many other lines
as well.

Earlier in this chapter we noted how, by the end of the 1960s, a number
of American-sponsored academic programs concerned with providing
instruction in the Japanese language for foreigners had begun to encounter
severe financial difficulties, mostly because of changes in the Japanese economy. In their eager competition for locating ways in which to "do something" about teaching the Japanese language to non-Japanese, these two
rival agencies of the Japanese government also began to compete for the
privilege of financially bailing out the Americans and their increasingly
costly language schools—a privilege that the Americans were only too glad
to pass on to the now suddenly concerned Japanese authorities. By the early
1970s, almost all Japanese-language training conducted in Japan for non-
Japanese had in this curious crabwise fashion ended up under the direct
financial sponsorship, as well as under the direct administrative control, of
one or the other of these agencies.

But by 1978, it had also become apparent to many Japanese government
officials who were now professionally concerned with the supervision of
these inherited "Japanese as a foreign language" programs that no one in
either of the two government agencies most concerned with all this—either
the Foreign Office or the Ministry of Education—actually had any clear
idea of just how one goes about teaching the Japanese language to foreigners.

The Ministry of Education is, above everything else, concerned with the
supervision and direction of Japan's enormous, elaborate, and extremely
costly system of prestigious national universities. But the faculties of these
universities included no one who could help the ministry's bureaucrats out
with this new set of problems. After all, there were not even any foreigners

on the proper faculties of any of the national universities—Japanese law and
the ministry's regulations had taken care of that—much less anybody who
knew about how to teach anything to foreigners, especially about how to
teach them Japanese. For most of the highly trained and highly paid faculty
members of the famous national universities, a foreigner was something to
remind one of Da Ponte's well-known description of the Arabian phoenix
—a rare, strange bird that everyone talks about but that no one now alive
has ever actually seen.

Besides, if the faculty of Japan's national university system knew anything
at all, they knew that foreigners could not learn the Japanese language because of its *kotodama,* and its notorious difficulty, and all the other concepts
central to the myth of Nihongo, the same myth that many of them were
professionally involved in disseminating as their scholarly specialty. So the
Ministry of Education could expect—and got—nothing in the way of concrete help from its own people when it began to ask questions about how one
does this strange new job that they nevertheless felt must surely now be
done: teaching the Japanese language to foreigners.

The Foreign Office, for its part, was in an even less advantageous position than its archrival the Ministry of Education. The Foreign Office
types could only agree on one thing: the Ministry of Education must have
nothing to do with it, because this was an aspect of Japan's foreign relations
and clearly a Foreign Office matter.

Otherwise, they shrugged their bureaucratic shoulders firmly—a gesture
perfected over years of carefully administered snubs to applicants in visa
sections of their consular service throughout the world—and hoped that
the whole problem of teaching Japanese to foreigners, like the visa applicants,
would go away if they shrugged often and firmly enough. But it would not.

Politics is the art of the possible; the possible is identified by compromise.
Japanese bureaucratic life is very political and extremely subtle in the ways
it has for identifying areas in which compromise is feasible. By 1978, the
Foreign Office and the Ministry of Education managed to call a temporary
truce in their squabbles over this particular issue, long enough at least to
plan a joint strategy. Both parties more or less agreed that the time had arrived to arrange a halt to their internecine rivalry, to catch their bureaucratic
breaths, and to figure out where to go from there.

In order to do this, the two agencies came to the decision to employ one
of the most valuable devices Japanese society has yet developed for concealing
any unbecoming outward evidence of confrontation: the formation of a
"private, independent body" to take over the public aspects of the administrative questions involved, thus removing them, at least as far as the citi-
zenry is concerned, from the arena of open bureaucratic rivalries and visible
territorial squabbles.

This same device is well known, for example, from Japanese industry. Here private, independent bodies ostensibly organized by manufacturers or producers effectively police given sectors of the economic or business life of the country, implementing government policy on the working level, but without ever actually, formally, or directly appearing to involve government officials in the administrative and regulatory process.

In the Japanese business world, such groups are principally used in a restrictive fashion to ensure the successful operation of industry-wide monopolies and cartels. Small, independent manufacturers or producers who might try to make their way into, for example, the cultured-pearl export trade, are effectively forced out of business by a private, independent body organized by the major producers of cultured pearls. The government, for its part, will only grant the necessary export licenses to the members of such bodies; thus the bureaucrats can effectively use membership to enforce rigid controls on the quantity, price, and timing of all Japan's foreign exports, without having the bureaucrats themselves actually appear to be either responsible or liable for what happens.

The same arrangement also means, of course, that when a foreign government comes to complain that its own industry in some area or another is being destroyed by floods of Japanese imports, the Japanese Government may quite easily plead both innocence and impotence: How can we, they ask, possibly do anything about this, when such matters are all handled in Japan by nongovernmental bodies? You must take your problem to them, not to us! Whatever made you think *we* were in charge here?

Implementing this well-established pattern for exercising tight bureaucratic controls without responsibility or liability of any sort, the Foreign Office and the Ministry of Education both decided finally to cooperate in funding and setting into operation a private, independent scholarly society that would in the future be placed in charge of directing instruction in Japanese as a foreign language, whenever such instruction was sponsored by, paid for by, or otherwise conducted in the interest of the Japanese Government. As head of this new organization, which was to be known as the Nihongo Kyōiku Gakkai, The Society for Japanese Language Education, they selected a Japanese professor of French language and literature recently retired from the faculty of Tokyo University.

Japanese universities generally retire their faculty members at a ridiculous age, sometimes as early as fifty-five. This drastic action is necessary if younger members of the faculty are ever to be promoted, but it also represents a major social problem. A professor, at what would in any other country be his peak earning years, is suddenly dismissed; he still most likely has children of his own to educate, bills from cram schools to pay, and many other expenses, all of which come due just at the time when his own salary is suddenly sharply reduced.

Many government organizations and private, independent agencies take quite seriously the responsibility, as they see it, to provide employment for these early retirees. The Japanese professor of French who was selected to direct the work of the new Nihongo Kyōiku Gakkai had never taught Japanese as a foreign language; in fact, he had, by his own disarmingly frank admission, never met a foreigner who could speak Japanese until he took over his duties as head of this new group.

The title of this organization also requires a certain amount of comment; like its background, its name is a little more subtle than it might at first glance appear. The term Nihongo is simply a word meaning the Japanese language. But that is only what it means etymologically, in other words, as far as the history of the parts that go to make up this word is concerned. As we saw in chapter 9, the etymology of a word generally provides little or no clue to its meaning. "Nihon" is the name of the country; "-go" means language; and so Nihongo ostensibly means the Japanese language— but only etymologically.

What has actually been happening in connection with the meaning of this word Nihongo ever since the late 1960s is a variety of growing semantic specialization. Today, in Japanese academic and bureaucratic circles, Nihongo has become a sociolinguistic code word that—despite its etymology— actually means "the Japanese language when viewed solely as something to be taught to foreigners," or even "the special, limited kind of Japanese that foreigners are perhaps going to be able to learn."

Especially important is a strict distinction implicit in the contemporary sociolinguistic usage of this word Nihongo, a distinction that seeks to separate this special kind of foreigner's Japanese from the genuine Japanese that real Japanese people know, understand, and use in their daily lives.

That kind of Japanese—the real article, as distinct from foreigner's Japanese, is called *kokugo*, "the national language." Etymologically this word comes from *koku* (nation) plus again the same familiar element *-go* (language); but the word *kokugo* is a term that makes sense only in terms of strict sociolinguistic territoriality; *kokugo* is not just national language but *our* national language, the language of the in-group, our own thing, our own language. Hence also, by its very definition as well as by sociolinguistic convention and usage, it represents nothing that can ever be shared with foreigners. Foreigners cannot learn *kokugo*, by definition. If a foreigner says anything in Japanese, it always comes out in Nihongo, again by definition. Only a Japanese, someone who is by birth a member of the Japanese racial and sociolinguistic in-group, one of us, can learn and speak *kokugo*.

The dichotomy that divides one of these linguistic entities from the other is strict, absolute, and inviolable. Japanese students in Japanese educational institutions study *kokugo*. Foreigners, whose progress and direction in Japanese as a foreign language is now the official concern of the Nihongo Kyōiku Gakkai, must content themselves with Nihongo. And so it is no accident that this private, independent scholarly body that the Foreign Office and the Ministry of Education have set into motion in this area is called what it is. One need only know what the name of this group is, and understand a little of what that name implies, to visualize many of the problems that inevitably lie ahead of it and of its work.

With the founding of this Nihongo Kyōiku Gakkai, its leaders immediately realized that they were confronted by obvious problems in two different if closely associated areas. And despite their general lack of experience in this entire field, they set about with commendable speed to see what could be done to approach a solution for each.

The first of these areas concerned what might be called the "software" aspects of their new business. How did one go about this whole matter of providing instruction for foreigners who wished, for some reason or other, to study the Japanese language? Or, to elect the obverse side of the coin, if no foreigners turned up who wished to learn Japanese, what would be necessary to convince some of these rare birds to appear, and once they had, that they should be interested? And once given a decent supply of students, either volunteers or conscripts, what in heaven's name did one teach them? What kinds of texts, what kinds of materials, what kinds of language, what kinds of Nihongo were fit to be shared with foreigners—or, again to turn the problem inside out, what kinds of Nihongo were of so little sociolinguistic consequence to Japanese society that it was safe to allow foreigners to get at them? There was an enormous list of such questions, all on a very practical level: What are we supposed to do? And how do we do it?

The second area was more subtle, more difficult, and in the long run also more interesting to everyone concerned. No one associated with the upper-level administration of this new Nihongo Kyōiku Gakkai may have had any very clear idea of what the organization was to do, or why it was to do it, or to whom; and most of its leaders may also have lacked firsthand experience in conducting any variety of language education for non-Japanese, much less education in the Japanese language. But all of them did nevertheless share one common conviction. It was obvious that their new work, difficult and unprecedented as it would certainly be, nevertheless had something vital to do with the Japanese language. This in turn seemed to imply that their work would, from the outset, necessarily have to be involved with the modern myth of Nihongo; and this in turn meant that the myth would have to be revamped.

If the new work of the Nihongo Kyōiku Gakkai was to have the support of the myth in carrying out its official mission of teaching the Japanese language to foreigners, the necessity of its refurbishment was immediately apparent to the leadership of this group. If in nothing else, they were forced to observe this need in the semantic changes, already alluded to, that the very word Nihongo itself had begun to display.

The myth originally and essentially was itself a myth of Nihongo, but there this word simply meant the Japanese language understood in its largest sense as the language of Japan. But that largest sense had begun to show signs of being at the same time the smallest sense, now that Japanese officialdom had decreed that the language ought to be, and hence would be, taught to foreigners. With this decision, the necessity for a sharp new semantic demarcation between kokugo and Nihongo could no longer be ignored.

The first of these two terms, kokugo, was now to be made to mean the Japanese language when viewed solely as a vehicle dedicated to the needs of a sociolinguistic in-group, membership in which would as before be determined by circumstances of birth—in a word, it was now to be an even more racist category. The second term, Nihongo, was to be specialized in the sense of a related but different linguistic medium: something separate, but emphatically not equal, and something also at all costs to be kept clearly distinct from the real article, which would be kokugo. And the myth itself, originally evolved simply to serve as the sustaining force for what had now become kokugo, would have to undergo substantial refurbishment, if not radical alteration, if it were also to serve this newly isolated and conceptualized Nihongo.

To help them with their problems in designing their new software, or in other words, with the practical pedagogical considerations involved with teaching Japanese to foreigners as a foreign language, the directors of the Nihongo Kyōiku Gakkai hosted an international conference in Tokyo and Osaka in March 1978, to which they invited a small group of five foreign educators from the United States, France, and Australia, all of whom were professionally engaged in directing or supervising instruction in Japanese as a foreign language in their respective countries. In the course of a series of conferences and discussions, the leaders of the new organization exchanged views with these foreign visitors about the practical questions involved in teaching Japanese to foreigners.

During the same period, the Nihongo Kyōiku Gakkai also made substantial progress toward its goal of refurbishing the myth of Nihongo, in order to help it serve the new needs of the group and in order to fit the myth out with those additional trappings that would permit it to sustain their group's future endeavors in this area, at least as well as it had managed to sustain

Japanese society's general sociolinguistic concerns over the past many years. This vital task of polishing up the myth was entrusted to Professor Suzuki, of whose other work we have already seen a good deal in these pages.

The major address that Suzuki was invited to deliver to the Nihongo Kyōiku Gakkai in Tokyo on March 18, 1978, disappointed no one. It proved to be a sociolinguistic document of major historical importance. Fortunately, a complete stenographic transcript of the speech was later printed for internal distribution by the Japan Foundation, thus making a matter of permanent record what might otherwise have been only a well-remembered but transient afternoon of spellbinding oratory. We shall be able to learn much when we summarize its content and examine a few of its particularly salient passages later on in the present chapter.

Suzuki's speech firmly delineated the principal avenues along which the myth of Nihongo must now be reworked and redirected, in the process of refitting it to continue serving the needs of Japan in the 1980s and beyond. It outlined, to continue our computer-terminology analogy, the ideological "hardware" for this new enterprise of teaching the Japanese language to the foreigners.

But before the conference could consider Suzuki's hardware, it first had to explore the question of what was to constitute its software. In connection with the preparation of teaching materials for Japanese as a foreign language and with organizing programs for training Japanese to teach the language to non-Japanese, almost a full week of conferences and discussions were held in March 1978 both in Tokyo and in Osaka. These meetings brought together the foreign visitors who had been invited to the conference, all of whom are professionally concerned with teaching Japanese in their own countries, and their Japanese hosts. They also soon brought out into the open many interesting differences of opinion between these foreign guests and their hosts, particularly between the foreigners and the directors of the newly launched Nihongo Kyōiku Gakkai.

Most of these differences of opinion can effectively be summed up in a single question that was heard over and over again during these meetings: What kind of Japanese should the foreigners be taught?

At first hearing, the question may appear to be extremely simple and also to have a simple answer. Most non-Japanese would be inclined to answer offhand and quite directly: Why, the same kind of Japanese that the Japanese use when they talk, read, and write Japanese themselves, of course—what other kind of Japanese could there possibly be, and what utility could there be for learning any other kind of Japanese even if it existed?

Language is language, the non-Japanese observer would be tempted to reply. Japanese is the Japanese that the Japanese use; and if you are going to teach it to foreigners at all, then that is the only kind of Japanese that you must teach. To non-Japanese observers of these matters—especially to non-Japanese language-teaching specialists already engaged in teaching Japanese in several foreign countries—the answer to all this appears so simple and obvious that they are likely to wonder, at least in the beginning, if they have understood the question correctly. And even after the question has been repeated so often that it cannot possibly be misunderstood, the non-Japanese specialists in such matters may still wonder if their Japanese hosts intend this query to be taken seriously.

But then, finally, the realization dawns that all this is really in dead earnest. Now that Japanese governmental circles have finally decreed that Japanese should be taught to the foreigners, the primary concern of the administrators who have been assigned to direct and supervise this new endeavor of linguistic outreach is increasingly focused, more than anywhere else, on this single question: What *kind* of Japanese should the foreigners be taught?

Like almost everything else that relates to contemporary Japanse socio-linguistic behavior, this is a question that appears to be simple and direct, whereas in actual fact it is only the tip of an iceberg. It cannot be answered effectively—indeed, hardly at all—by responding in a simple, literal fashion to what appears to be the simple, literal meaning of the question. Before it can be answered, it must be understood; and understanding it requires that we plunge back once more into the troubled waters of the contemporary myth of Nihongo, particularly as that myth has managed to extend itself into the Japanese perception of all foreign languages, but especially into the Japanese perception of English.

In chapter 11 we have already explored some of the important ways in which the unscientific, irrational assumptions of the modern myth of Nihongo have played a major role in determining the way in which contemporary Japanese society responds to questions of foreign-language learning and teaching. We have noticed in particular the way in which the myth has managed to direct almost all English-language education in Japan toward essentially unproductive ends. This is illustrated most strikingly—and most pathetically—in the employment, at every stage of the Japanese formal educational system, of English-language tests as one of the most difficult hurdles of all to be overcome in order to advance within the society.

We have also seen how it is the myth that must be held responsible for the almost surrealistic situation that today characterizes most Japanese higher education, where passing English-language tests that no native speaker of English could possibly pass has become the only key to success—while at the same time, those fortunate few who manage to pass such tests are almost always quite incapable of saying even the simplest thing in English, much less understanding anything that might be said to them by a native speaker of the same language.

One cannot but be reminded by all this of Hermann Hesse's novel *The Glass Bead Game,* where he described how a highly advanced, extremely sophisticated society came to focus all its energies and talents upon playing a game that consisted of manipulating markers on a complex abacuslike device through infinite sets of abstract patterns. Hesse's bead-game society has neither any practical utility nor any functional goal; the only point is to play the game. The same is frighteningly true of most English-language education in modern Japan.

One of the main ways in which Japanese English-language education has been made into a bead game has been to divorce its teaching materials from anything resembling real English, meaning English as a genuine, functioning medium of daily human communication—in a word, from English as a language. After all, there are, even in Japan, native speakers of English. But none of them is or ever can be placed in charge of the society's rites of passage that hinge upon this bead-game manipulation of English-language materials under the guise of examinations. If these examinations actually made any effective use of real English-language materials or actually tested practical English-language skills, the society would by that very token be forced to turn over the direction of one of its most sacred cult rituals to the hands of foreigners. Needless to add, that is impossible even to contemplate.

We have already commented briefly on how the important differences between the real sociolinguistic article and the special artificial variety of Japanese that will have to be made up for teaching to foreigners are now symbolized by the increasingly rigid semantic differentiation between the terms *kokugo* and Nihongo. This phenomenon finds its model in the terminology under which English is customarily taught in Japan.

Quite separate terms are used in Japanese educational circles to distinguish between the kind of English one must learn to pass the university entrance examinations and the kind of English one must learn if one wishes to talk to foreigners or understand what they say. The first is *Eigo* or *Eigo kyōiku,* literally English or English education but actually understood throughout the society as meaning the abstract bead game that one must master in order to be advanced in Japanese society and survive its rites of passage. No amount of *Eigo* or *Eigo kyōiku* will make it possible for anyone to speak a single word so that a foreigner can understand what is being said, or to comprehend a single word of English as spoken by anyone not similarly adept in the same arcane game.

When, on the other hand, the Japanese wish to identify the actual, practical

study of English as a language, they call it *Eikaiwa,* literally, English conversation. The subject that you must study if you wish to talk to foreigners
or to use when you go abroad to sell transitors and automobiles is *Eikaiwa.*
This subject is not taught in Japanese universities and plays no part in university examination procedures; it must be pursued privately, in special
schools run specifically for the purpose, the same sort of school at which
one would study welding, vegetable carving, ornamental wood-burning, or
taxidermy.

By making English-language learning and English-language teaching
into this abstract bead game—by utterly separating *Eigo* and *Eigo kyōiku*
from *Eikaiwa*—Japanese educational circles have effectively ensured that
only Japanese will ever be in charge. Foreigners only know the language;
they only know *Eikaiwa.* They do not know the bead game that has been
made up to substitute for English within the sociolinguistic rites of passage
that distinguish every major stage of Japanese life.

Along these lines, then, Japanese English-language specialists long ago
evolved the special kind of English that they teach and that students have
to learn in order to play the bead game of the entrance examinations successfully. And now their colleagues are getting ready to do the same thing
for Japanese.

This, it finally became clear, was the actual thrust of the question that
was repeated time and time again in March 1978: What kind of Japanese
should the foreigners be taught? The consensus of the newly organized
Japanese academic group that government authorities have now placed in
charge of this effort to teach the language to foreigners is that they must as
quickly as possible evolve a bead-game Nihongo, some complex way for
manipulating the Japanese language along the same highly involved, quite
abstract lines that the English language is manipulated in Japan, so that teaching Japanese to the foreigners will never be in any danger of training foreigners who can really understand, or speak, or read, or write the Japanese
language. What will instead be produced are foreigners who will be alien
sociolinguistic clones of the hundreds of thousands of Japanese who each
year pass their English examinations and still are unable to speak or understand a single word of the English language as spoken by anyone but a
Japanese.

Most of the foreign guests at the March 1978 conferences naturally found
all this rather astonishing, once they had finally managed to grasp the thrust
and import of their Japanese hosts' remarks. When Japanese has been taught
as a foreign language anywhere in the world—except in Japan—the assumption has always been that what is being taught should be as close to the real
thing as possible, since the obvious purpose of learning Japanese—or of
learning any foreign language—is to understand native speakers of the lan-

guage when they speak, to be able to speak to them, and to be able to read what they have written.

This completely utilitarian approach to foreign-language education is so deeply engrained in the mentality of most persons associated with such matters in America and Europe that it took some days before most of the invited foreign guests attending the March 1978 meetings called by the Nihongo Kyōiku Gakkai even understood the full import of this question that kept coming to the fore of the discussion time and time again: What kind of Japanese should foreigners be taught? It was a classic case of not being able to see the forest for the trees. The entire concept of turning Japanese-language education for foreigners into an abstract bead game was so utterly outside the sociolinguistic experience of most of the foreign guests at the conference, and at the same time so integral a part of the thinking of their Japanese hosts, that for the first several days—and nights—of the meetings it appeared as if both sides would never be able to get together, even to the point of the one understanding what the other was talking about.

The resulting conceptual logjam was finally broken by one of the senior Japanese participants in the conference, a retired university professor who had, during his long active service on the faculty of a major Japanese national university, specialized in "English-language education." Sensing that the entire group was continuing to talk and argue at cross-purposes, largely because most of the foreign visitors did not know what their Japanese hosts were talking about when they kept asking about what "kind of Japanese" ought to be taught, this considerate gentleman mercifully cleared the air once and for all along the following unmistakably direct lines: "All of you know that when we teach English in Japan, we do not teach the Japanese to speak like Americans or Englishmen. How could learning to speak like foreigners, or to understand what foreigners are saying, possibly help anyone get admitted to a Japanese university? Well, what we are asking you foreign experts at this conference about is along those same lines. Naturally, there is no point in teaching foreigners to speak like Japanese speak, or to understand us Japanese when we speak to each other. That is the last thing in the world that we plan to do in our new Nihongo Kyōiku Gakkai. What we do want to do—and this is where we need the help of you, our foreign friends and guests—is to devise some sort of Nihongo that will stand in the same relation to the language that we Japanese use among ourselves as the English that we teach in Japanese schools and universities stands in relationship to the English that you foreigners use when you talk to each other—nothing more, nothing less."

With this admirably unambiguous statement, the matter was at last cleared up. The foreign guests at these March 1978 meetings now finally all understood what their Japanese hosts had understood all the time. The

Nihongo Kyōiku Gakkai, the official scholarly and administrative organ for implementing the new Japanese national policy of teaching the Japanese language to foreigners, has as its initial goal the creation of a special kind of Japanese language, a "Japanese for the foreigners" that will be a mirror-image of the special—and quite equally useless—"English for Japanese" that is taught throughout the Japanese educational establishment.

It would be less than fair to all concerned to neglect mentioning that in all this, there is also a characteristic element of warm, human concern for the sensibilities and feelings of the foreigners who will eventually also have to be involved with all this. It is too easy to overlook the many efforts by which our Japanese colleagues try to make things easier for us, and to do so only invites still more of the misunderstanding that we are here trying to obviate.

In this particular instance, a representative example of the constant concern for the sensibilities and special problems of foreigners was next expressed by an unidentified speaker from the floor, who responded with enthusiastic support for the clarifying declaration cited immediately above. For his part, he then added the following explanatory expression of his own purely human concern: "I am glad to learn that our guests now understand clearly why it is necessary for us to evolve a special kind of Nihongo to teach to the foreigners. It is not so much that we do not wish to teach genuine Japanese to the foreigners; it is more that we cannot. We cannot because in order to learn real Japanese—to speak it, or understand it—foreigners would have to think like we Japanese do. But this of course is impossible. So if we were to try to teach you foreigners real Japanese, we would be suggesting that you burden yourselves with an impossible task, which would be cruel and unfeeling. Making up a special kind of Japanese for the purpose of teaching it to the foreigners is, under the circumstances, not only the best thing we can do; it is also the kindest." Again, it is terribly difficult to take issue with anything that this gentleman said, and we will not try.

At any rate, and with all questions of motivation set aside, what the leaders of this new national organization are hoping to find is some way in which to generate texts, instructional manuals, and other teaching materials for "Japanese as a foreign language," which will contain only samples of this special "Japanese for the foreigners," rather than giving them specimens of the language as it is actually used by the Japanese today in Japanese society.

The task is obviously a major one. Not only must this special kind of Japanese, "suitable for teaching to the foreigners," be more or less artificially made up, and not only must textbooks and other written materials be prepared that will give the would-be foreign student of Japanese specimens of this special nonlanguage to learn, teachers must also be specially prepared in order to teach this newly invented language. No ordinary Japanese, with ordinary, normal native-speaker command of the Japanese language, will be qualified to teach this special kind of Japanese that is now to be taught to foreigners under the official auspices and direction of the Nihongo Kyōiku Gakkai, since of course this new special language by definition has no native speakers. It is never actually spoken—any more than the strange, unnatural, ungrammatical varieties of English that form the bulk of the examples in most of the English-language teaching materials employed in the Japanese educational system represent a real language spoken by anyone anywhere in the world. Having worked its perverted magic with English-language education for Japanese in Japan, the modern myth of Nihongo is now well on the way to turning the same trick with Japanese-language education for foreigners.

All that remains to be done, if this picture of perfect parallels between these two fields of language education is to be rounded out, is for the authorities to devise a system of "examinations" in this new variety of non-native-speaker "special" Japanese—examinations that in their total abstraction and isolation from practical linguistic utility will serve the same purpose for foreigners wishing to learn Japanese that the English-language portions of the usual Japanese college and university entrance examinations now do for Japanese society in general.

Such examinations, which also were widely discussed at the March 1978 meetings, seem eventually destined to play an important role in the lives of all foreigners aspiring to have some relationship with Japanese society. Like the English-language examinations of the Japanese educational system, these examinations in "Japanese as a foreign language" will serve as elaborate, extremely difficult, and highly abstract rites of passage for foreigners wishing to achieve some sort of extremely limited and rigidly prescribed entrée into Japanese life.

These examinations will not test whether or not the foreigner can understand the Japanese language, or examine whether or not he or she can use it for communicating with Japanese. What they will test instead is whether or not the foreigner in question has been willing to subject him- or herself to the pedagogical demands of the new approved courses in "Japanese for the foreigners," as taught by approved teachers using approved text materials, all carefully guaranteed not to contain any real examples of the language as it is actually used by the Japanese themselves. Like the English examinations of the Japanese universities, these testing procedures will measure social docility, not language competence.

Above everything else, the goal of Japanese-language education for foreigners that the Nihongo Kyōiku Gakkai has set for the 1980s is that of a rigidly regulated set of courses and examinations, all using officially approved texts containing officially approved language that is as far from ordinary, normal Japanese linguistic usage as it can possible be made to be—all of course to be taught by Japanese teachers specially trained for the purpose. Just as no English or American native speaker of English could possibly get a passing grade on the English-language sections of the entrance examinations for Tokyo University simply on the basis of a native speaker's command of the English language, so also—when the program of the Nihongo Kyōiku Gakkai is brought to completion—will the foreigner who has studied Japanese for many years, lived and worked in Japan for a considerable period of time, and who as a result uses the language freely every day of his life, not be considered "qualified" in this new "special kind of Japanese suitable for the foreigners." Any such individual who wishes, for any reason, to be "officially certified" by the Japanese authorities as "proficient in Japanese" will now have to start his or her study of the Japanese language all over again, learning the artificial nonlanguage of the new texts and learning to speak this new nonlanguage under the careful direction of the handful of "special" Japanese teachers who are also going to be trained in how to play this sociolinguistic bead game.

As so often in these pages, once we have described a given sociolinguistic situation or attitude as it confronts us in contemporary Japanese life, we at once risk being suspected of exaggeration, or of levity, or even of both. The reader who is unfamiliar with Japanese life, particularly the reader who is unfamiliar with the Japanese educational system, will surely ask whether or not English-language education in Japan really can be the abstract bead game that has been described. The same reader is also sure to wonder whether any modern, industrially advanced world power like Japan could now possibly be embarked upon this absurd mission of trying to make Japanese-language training for foreigners into the same totally impractical, unrealistic exercise that English-language education for Japanese has for so long been. Anyone must be forgiven for questioning, even if only silently, whether or not such things really can and do happen in modern Japan.

But anyone who has lived or worked in Japan, particularly anyone who has had any association with Japanese education, will know that the situation as described errs, if it errs at all, in the direction of understatement. No one who has not been directly involved in attempts at English-language education in Japan can really understand just how abstract, and just how divorced from sociolinguistic reality, such training is made to be. But even people who have never been in Japan will still in many cases have had a sufficient amount of firsthand contact with Japanese traveling or working abroad to make their own valid assessment of the end products of the kind of English-language education that goes on throughout the Japanese school system. For those who have encountered the results of what goes on in the

Japanese English-language classroom, no explanation is necessary; for those who have not, no explanation is possible.

Historical precedents are always important in all decisions affecting Japanese society; and it is important to note that precedents are not by any means lacking, both in early and in fairly recent Japanese history, for the wholesale creation, more or less out of the whole cloth, of nonlanguages specifically designed to serve closely defined sociolinguistic requirements. For much of their history, the Japanese have employed a nonlanguage variety of Japanese that was specially devised in order to render—but not to translate—Chinese classical and literary texts as studied in traditional Japan. The student was given a Chinese original and had to learn how to turn it into a special kind of Japanese; but the special kind of Japanese used for this purpose really made very little sense as Japanese, and it provided him with next to no information about the sense of the Chinese upon which it was based. But the point of the exercise was not to learn the Chinese language or even to understand what Chinese texts said; the point was to follow the rules and to learn to generate the prescribed, official nonlanguage version of a given Chinese original. Today the Japanese are talking about evolving a "special kind" of Nihongo for foreigners; as they go about this quest, they will surely be able to bring their centuries of rich experience, gained in evolving the special kind of Japanese that they have always used in rendering Chinese texts, into effective play.

Still another illustration of the same phenomenon is somewhat closer to the usual sociolinguistic experience of any visitor to Japan. Anyone who has spent even a single night in a Japanese hotel that "takes foreigners" will surely have noticed that the Japanese tourist and hotel industry has evolved a "special kind" of English that it uses for dealing with guests from abroad, particularly for composing written notices and instructions about how properly to use the rooms, facilities, and services of the establishments involved. Much of the grammar and many of the words of this special language are obviously borrowed from English, but the net result is quite as far from the real article as the "special kind of Nihongo for foreigners" will be from real Japanese. Documentation of this special kind of English comes too easily to hand to make it necessary to cite multiple illustrations here; the following short passage, recently noted in a leading Osaka hotel (and intending to explain why the management feels entitled to add to the bill a surcharge equivalent to several U.S. dollars, plus tax, plus service charge, for each and every outside telephone call placed from the room), will surely suffice to categorize the genre: "A NOTICE: In use of the room telephone to outside call, few additional charges to be included in accordance with the amount as for the facility."

This example shows us what the "special kind of Nihongo for foreigners" that the Nihongo Kyōiku Gakkai is currently engaged in producing will look like—it will employ some Japanese grammar and use some Japanese words, but no one who simply knows the Japanese language will ever be able to make much out of it—to do that, you will have to go to school, and train, and work very hard. And there will be those examinations to pass....

But even granted that Japanese educators have for decades been intent upon turning English-language education into a rite of passage for their society—training university graduates who after ten or fifteen years of English instruction can write the notices that tell us how "few additional charges to be included in accordance with the amount as for the facility"— does all this mean that these same educators are now really shortsighted enough to try and conjure up an equally abstract sociolinguistic bead game when faced with this new opportunity of the 1980s to teach their own language to foreigners?

Alas, and most unfortunately, it does apparently mean just that. And to understand how this could have come about, we must turn again to the modern myth of Nihongo. Once we see something of how this new bead-game approach to the teaching of Japanese to foreigners fits in with the overall structuring of that myth, we will finally be able to comprehend the major elements of motivation that lie behind the activities of such official groups as the Nihongo Kyōiku Gakkai, as well as motivating the government agencies that in turn sponsor that organization. Understanding how all this fits into the modern myth of Nihongo will go far to explain how this situation has arisen; it does not excuse that situation, or make it any better, but it does at least render it somewhat more credible. Eventually, we begin to see that there is a pattern to all this, if only we look beneath the superficially irrational and unstructured surface phenomena. And that pattern, of course, is the pattern provided by Japan's modern sustaining myth of Nihongo.

We have seen time and time again evidence that, thanks to the elaboration of the modern myth of Nihongo, the Japanese language has gradually been elevated to the position of one of the major ideological forces sustaining Japanese society, at the same time that it helps that society to close its ranks against all possible intrusions by outsiders.

This essentially defensive function of the myth is particularly striking when we consider the way in which it plays upon the fallacious identification of language with race and race with language, managing in the process to play off the one element against the other in such a way that the resulting circularity of conceptualization forms a watertight, rigidly enclosed social entity, all but impervious to penetration by any outside force. The entire mythic structure concentrates most of its energies upon erecting this impregnable sociolinguistic fortress; but even once the structure is in place, constant sociolinguistic vigilance is always the price of continued security. Japanese life and identity dwell at peace within the mythic structure of Nihongo; the door is firmly locked; the key was thrown away millennia ago.

Given the creature comforts of this impregnable fortress and the conceptual security that it provides for the society within, who now would be mad enough to throw open the main gate and welcome in the rapacious hordes of foreign invaders commonly believed to dwell out there, in the realms of night? Envious of the sociolinguistic warmth and security that it observes within this fortress of Nihongo, the rest of mankind scuttles about like great black beetles on the inhospitable plain below the myth's secure fortifications, desperately trying to devise some way to gain admission. Learning to speak, understand, read, and write the Japanese language would be a powerful tool, in the hands of these uncouth, unkempt foreigners, for breaching the fortress.

One or two stragglers from the enemy camp even appear to have pulled off the feat already—well, they can be taken care of by calling them *hen na gaijin*—crazy, crackpot foreigners. But quite obviously name-calling alone will not be the whole answer.

What the impregnable fortress of Nihongo now needs, in the 1980s, if it is to remain impregnable, is a final solution. This problem of foreigners who seek to gain admission to the inner recesses of our sociolinguistic territorial preserve must be met head-on. Apparently we cannot stop them from studying the Japanese language; if so, then we can—and will—make sure that the kind of Japanese language that they study will not help them at all in achieving their hearts' desire—mounting our walls and invading our territory.

In other words, once we evaluate these attempts to generate a "special kind of Japanese suitable for teaching to the foreigners" in the context of the overall sociolinguistic structuring of the modern myth of Nihongo, it all begins to make surprisingly good sense. The plans and programs of the Nihongo Kyōiku Gakkai, viewed in this manner, are neither irrational, illogical, nor inexplicable; considered in terms of the myth of Nihongo that sustains the conceptualization of sociolinguistic territoriality throughout contemporary Japanese society, all this actually makes quite good sense.

So much for the plans concerning the necessary new linguistic software that emerged from the discussions of the Nihongo Kyōiku Gakkai in March 1978. Once this software was out of the way, it remained only for Professor Suzuki to provide the participants in these meetings with an outline of the ideological and conceptual hardware that is also going to be necessary if the myth of Nihongo is to be refurbished effectively for the new tasks of the 1980s.

Professor Suzuki's hardware proposals proved to be very hard indeed, in every sense of the word. Many of us had until then known him only as an effective and engrossing writer. But those of us who were fortunate enough to be present at the lecture on the afternoon of Saturday, March 18, 1978, in the auditorium of Aoyama Gakuin University, Tokyo, when Professor Suzuki for the first time set forth in public his new hardware of the myth of Nihongo for the 1980s, soon discovered that he is also an enormously effective public speaker. He is able to hold a large audience in transports of rapt attention for hours at a stretch and to communicate his views with compelling force and conviction. At the conclusion of his engrossing lecture, entitled "Naze Gaikokujin ni Nihongo wo Oshieru no ka?" (Why Teach Nihongo to the Foreigners?), it is safe to say that no one in the large audience gathered for the occasion was left untouched by the thrust of his message.

But to explain in any reasonably short summary just what the thrust of Suzuki's message was, is a less than simple task. He spoke vigorously and eloquently; he carried the entire audience along with the development of his thesis and its subordinate ideas; only a few of the hundreds present on that Saturday afternoon in mid-March left the Aoyama Gakuin auditorium not in complete agreement with Suzuki. But the question of just what it was that he said is a somewhat different matter.

Fortunately, the entire lecture was recorded on one of the excellent tape devices that the Japanese produce in such abundance; and the tape was later transcribed into written text. This transcript was eventually set in type and printed for private distribution by the Japan Foundation, the principal sponsoring agency for the entire series of meetings during which the lecture in question was delivered. With this printed transcript in hand, it is somewhat easier to identify the principal themes of Suzuki's keynote address than it would be if one had only the transports of memory upon which to rely.

But only somewhat. Reading the transcript of his remarks, one is time and time again reminded that much of their initial impact necessarily was involved with Suzuki's remarkably effective method of public speaking and related to his splendid podium manner. Divorced from these qualities and reduced to the pale dimensions of the printed page, what he had to say sometimes appears to lose a good deal of the original ideological impact, not to mention the personal charm, that distinguished his original presentation.

Nor is it an easy matter to arrange Suzuki's ideas into a simple, logical outline, any more than it is to summarize their main points. What he had to say resists such arrangement just as vigorously as it thrusts off attempts at summation; to do either is to begin to destroy much of the impact of his lecture, and also to destroy much of the charisma of his remarks. One is reminded of that delicate, exotic flower of which Wilde spoke: touch it and the bloom is gone. Under these difficult circumstances, the best that can be done is probably to go through the convenient transcript of Suzuki's lecture in order, from beginning to end, selecting along the way for translation and citation here a few of his more striking passages, and introducing them with a minimum of comment and explanation, of which generally they require very little.

Essentially, Suzuki's answer to the question "Why Teach Nihongo to the Foreigners?" is a multifaceted one. He stresses that there is no single, easy answer; but there are a multitude of lesser, equally important ones, and among these, three stand out in particularly sharp relief.

First of all, Suzuki argued that Nihongo should be taught to the foreigners for the simple reason that the foreigners do not now know Nihongo. This is surely a proposition with which it is difficult to take issue, and we shall not try to do so.

His second argument was that everybody who is a human being is going to be better off for the simple fact of knowing Nihongo, an argument that is perhaps somewhat more debatable, but that we will here eagerly avoid, as eagerly as we avoided taking issue with his first point.

Suzuki's third point, however, suddenly finds us in totally unfamiliar, if equally unarguable, ground. Nihongo, he says, must be taught to the foreigners because the well-known postwar Japanese constitution outlaws war as an instrument of Japanese national policy, and so Japan does not have modern military weapons like rockets and atom bombs. What it does have is Nihongo, and we ought to use it as our weapon; it is the only one we have. Teaching Nihongo to foreigners will not only make them better people and defend weaponless Japan, it will also contribute to the peace of the world. The greatest contribution of all would be if Nihongo could be made one of the official languages of the United Nations assembly in New York.

If a reader who has available the full transcript of Suzuki's lecture objects that the above is only a list of highlights, the only excuse is that the lecture itself was really just a collection of highlights, from which the above attempt at a summary has only been able to select a few of the highest. One really had to be there, or at least to have read the completed, printed transcript, to catch the flavor of the whole thing. Anything less is as unsatisfactory as hearing Mahler played on a mouth organ or listening to someone tell about how Callas sounded when she sang *Norma*. You really had to be there.

The reader has already had the opportunity to study two short selections, translated as literally as possible from the printed transcript of Suzuki's lecture, which are used to introduce chapter 8 as well as the present chapter. Both these excerpts give an excellent idea of Suzuki's effective rhetoric at the same time that they exhibit a few of his representative themes.

But of course, two short sections can hardly do justice to a lecture that lasted well over an hour. Probably the best way to introduce the full range of his ideas is to continue here with a few more selected excerpts from that transcript, picking them up in the order in which they appear in the original, and resisting as far as possible the urge to embellish them with lengthy comments of our own.

Early in the lecture, and shortly after the excerpt quoted at the beginning of our present chapter, Suzuki addressed himself to the broader concerns of Japan's economic problems, particularly as they relate to the question of teaching Nihongo to the foreigners: "Japan's economic activities are such that, once they go beyond the boundaries of our own country, they are certain to give rise to friction. The reasons for this are simple: it is because Japan has no military forces and because Japan does not have a strong, effective religion. There would be no complaints forthcoming from abroad if Japan had a really exceptional level of military force, sufficient to subjugate other countries. Then we should simply say, 'Buy what you want to buy from us; and buy it even if you don't want it. If you won't buy, then die!' Thus, the whole world would be at peace."

But Suzuki is no economic simplist. While continuing throughout this lecture to emphasize that religious concerns can—or at least should—be fully as important as economic ones, at the same time he also stresses that economic questions of this variety can be fully as complex as are the linguistic ones: "But since the friction that Japan is currently causing cannot be settled by military force, and since at the same time it is a problem that nevertheless must be settled, how indeed shall it be resolved? The answer is that in order to solve it, we can rely upon nothing except our language. . . . Countless international meetings have been called in order to address questions of mutual benefit and disadvantage, but always, behind their words, there is the message, 'If you don't do as you are told, we will attack!' But Japan, in its constitution, has totally abandoned all the military force that would make it possible for us too to say, 'If you don't do as you are told, we will attack!' So it comes down to this: we are weaponless, unless we use our language as our weapon."

But weapons, no matter how powerful or how deadly. are always useless unless the people who possess them really know how to operate them with maximum effectiveness. Just because we have this Nihongo of ours, and just because it is potentially such a remarkable weapon for Japan's national interests, does not mean that we can use it off the cuff, without special consideration, study, and training: "What I want to say is the following: education in the Japanese language for foreigners will never be able to develop properly overseas unless we Japanese ourselves wake up to the true value of Japanese, this Japanese that is the language of our nation, and also until we wake up to the proper and correct authority of that language, and to the authority that it has in international society—until we come to have self-confidence in the Japanese language."

All this sounds like a lot of hard work, and it surely will prove to be just that; but eventually it will also be worth all the effort—not only for Japan, but also for the rest of the world: "Teaching the Japanese language to foreigners, and having foreigners learn the Japanese language, will not only be to the benefit of the Japanese. What I wish to emphasize is that this will also have an enormous significance for the peace of the world."

Japan today—tomorrow the world! And once one takes on the world, one can hardly neglect the United Nations: "Japan's reliance on foreign relations centering around the United Nations means that its foreign policy is one of language. The great difficulty here is that today, the Japanese people have not yet mastered the concept that language may serve as a military weapon. Actually, Mao Zedong, in our neighboring country (who now has passed away), and Lenin also (who passed away earlier) both clearly taught that language may be a military weapon. But this concept of language as a weapon still remains the furthest thing from the linguistic conceptualization of Japanese today. . . . This fact seems ironic when we realize that we Japanese, who have completely abandoned all such things as actual bazookas or rockets, are now only permitted the military weapon that is language. This means that until we can master the concept that language is to be employed as a military weapon, there will be nothing for the Japanese to do but to become extinct. This is why, once we Japanese have mastered this still most unfamiliar concept and have learned that language is a military weapon, then we will be able to communicate to foreign countries what Japan is thinking about, what Japan is hoping for, and what Japan wishes to accomplish. Then the Japanese language will have become an extremely powerful tool."

But to help others see ourselves as we do, we must first of all decide how we do in fact see ourselves. The metaphorical image that Suzuki suggests as maximally useful in this connection is somewhat unexpected. Not for him is the lithe, delicate Japan of the dwarf-pine bonsai or carefully arranged handful of flowers. He finds no utility in Japan as an aesthetic concept—no cherry blossoms, geisha, or Fujiyama will be allowed to confuse the issue once we really get underway with his new task of teaching Nihongo to foreigners. What is Japan? he asks rhetorically—and he replies, it is a mighty beast, a veritable mammoth: "There is this great beast, indeed, this mammoth, called Japan, which the people of the other nations of the world cannot ignore. If this mammoth continues to walk ponderously and silently along its way, the rest of the world might very well be crushed under it, as they seek to escape from its path, first thinking it is going to come this way, or sometimes that it is about to turn to the left, or that it is suddenly going into reverse. But once we have taught the Japanese language to many foreigners, we will simply be able to announce, in plain and simple Japanese, that the beast is about to go into reverse, so that those who are in our path may be sufficiently warned to get out of our way."

Like many observers of world affairs today, Suzuki admits to some disappointment about the apparent lack of effective action on the part of the UN in confronting a number of serious crisis situations. But unlike many, Suzuki has a concrete suggestion to make in order to help the UN get its act in order: "What I mean to stress is my thesis that the reason why the UN does not now function effectively is because Japanese is not one of its official languages."

To teach Nihongo effectively to the foreigners, it is of course not only necessary to understand all about Nihongo; we will also have to understand all about foreigners. But this, Suzuki reassured his audience, is a comparatively easy thing to do. Only one thing really must be kept firmly in mind at all times: "Foreigners are keen on calculating profit and loss. If something does not harm them, they will pay no attention to it."

Few potential students of any given subject, whether Nihongo or nuclear physics, would be likely to remain obdurate, or less than maximally diligent, under the tutelage of such effectively directed educational psychology.

But if Suzuki here begins to sound a little harsh, this does not mean that his approach to teaching Nihongo to the foreigners will be totally unleavened. Earlier we saw how he considers economics and religion to be twin strings both ideally fitted to his sociolinguistic bow; and later on in his lecture, he returned more than once to the second of these themes, that of religion.

Teaching Nihongo to the foreigners, he told us, will not be a dull linguistic or pedagogical endeavor. Rather, it will incorporate much of the comfort of a new religion. The foreigner who learns this new foreigner's Nihongo will find him- or herself caught up by that variety of lofty aspiration toward higher and better things that has always provided mankind with one of its principal consolations in times of troubles.

The special kind of Nihongo that Suzuki and the Nihongo Kyōiku Gakkai are now getting prepared to teach to the foreigner will not, of course, equip foreigners to talk to Japanese people or to understand Japanese people when they talk to one another. Nothing could be further removed from its goals. But it will provide foreigners with the solace of one of the world's higher religions—not to mention the consolation of philosophy, if anyone is still interested in that old thing these days. All this for the price of memorizing a few easy words of special, made-for-foreigners-only Nihongo—surely a bargain, no matter how one looks at it.

But as usual, Suzuki is the best exponent of his own doctrines. We can hardly do better than to end this selection of extracts from his lecture with his following stirring call to worship at the altar of Nihongo: "The nation of Japan . . . is one in which religious ideology has always been quite shallow. We Japanese have been a docile race. We have not developed ideologies or principles that explicitly define things in definite terms. We have lacked a messianic urge, the ideological strength to spread our ideas aggressively to other countries. For us Japanese now to found a new religion, something that we could spread throughout the entire world, would be a task requiring enormous time; nor are the other usual possibilities for extending our influence abroad any more feasible. What we must do, therefore, is to make a religion of Nihongo. We must think of the Japanese language as the Nihongo Creed, and spread this new religion of Nihongo throughout the nations of the earth."

A standing ovation followed, as well it might, when Suzuki finally concluded his lecture at the Aoyama Gakuin auditorium in Tokyo on the afternoon of March 18, 1978. Unfortunately, no one there that day had the presence of mind to take up a collection or even to make provision for a free-will offering. If they had, it seems certain that a considerable sum could have been realized, for there were few in the large and appreciative audience who were not moved by the force and persuaded by the eloquence of Suzuki's remarks.

And even those who still had certain reservations about his views could nevertheless hardly resist joining in the general acclamation that greeted the conclusion of his remarks: O wonder, O brave new world, that has such a language in it.

Bibliographical Notes

The following is not a comprehensive bibliography; it aims only to document the principal published sources upon which the present book draws. In the case of sources originally published and here cited, in Japanese, all translations of excerpts in this book are the author's, unless otherwise specified.

Bird, Isabella Lucy. *Unbeaten Tracks in Japan: An Account of Travels in the Interior Including Visits to the Aborigines of Yezo and the Shrine of Nikko*. New York: G. P. Putnam's Sons, 1880; reprinted Rutland, Vermont & Tokyo: Charles E. Tuttle Co., 1973.

Bloomfield, Leonard. *Language*. New York: Henry Holt, 1933.

Gauntlett, John Owen, trans. and Robert King Hall, ed. *Kokutai no Hongi, Cardinal Principles of the National Entity of Japan*. Cambridge: Harvard University Press, 1949.

Kindaichi, Haruhiko. *Nihongo*. Iwanami Shinsho, 265. Tokyo: Iwanami Shoten, 1957.

———. *Nihongo e no Kibō*. Tokyo: Taishūkan Shoten, 1976.

———. *The Japanese Language*. Umeyo Hirano, trans. Rutland, Vermont & Tokyo: Charles E. Tuttle Co., 1978.

Kokusai Kōryū Kikin. *Nihongo Kyōiku Kokusai Kaigi*. Tokyo: Kokusai Kōryū Kikin, 1978.

Kokutai no Hongi [author not given]. [Tokyo:] Mombu-shō, 1937.

Lewin, Bruno. "Zur japanischen Sprache in der frühen Shôwa-Zeit." *Oriens Extremus* 26: 1/2 (1979): 38–47.

Miller, Roy Andrew. *The Japanese Language*. Chicago: University of Chicago Press, 1967.

———. *The Japanese Language in Contemporary Japan: Some Sociolinguistic Observations*. AEI-Hoover Policy Studies, 22. American Enterprise Institute for Public Policy Research, Washington, D.C., & Hoover Institution on War, Revolution and Peace, Stanford University, Stanford, California, 1977.

———. "The 'Spirit' of the Japanese Language." *Journal of Japanese Studies* 3: 2 (Summer, 1977): 251–98.

———. *Origins of the Japanese Language, Lectures in Japan during the Academic Year 1977–78*. Seattle: University of Washington Press, 1980.

Miyoshi, Masao. *Accomplices of Silence: The Modern Japanese Novel*. Berkeley: University of California Press, 1974.

Mochida, Takeshi. "*Japan Echo*, A Journal of Opinion to Bridge the Communication Gap." *Japan Foundation*

Newsletter 6: 3 (August-September, 1978): 28–29.

Moore, Charles A., ed. *The Japanese Mind, Essentials of Japanese Philosophy and Culture.* Honolulu: East-West Center Press & University of Hawaii Press, 1967.

Okonogi, Keigo. "The Ajase Complex of the Japanese (2)." *Japan Echo* 6: 1 (1979): 104–18.

Said, Edward W. *Orientalism.* New York: Random House, 1978 and New York: Vintage Books, 1979.

Seward, Jack. *The Japanese.* New York: William Morrow & Co., 1972.

Steiner, George. *After Babel: Aspects of Language and Translation.* New York & London: Oxford University Press, 1975.

Suzuki, Takao. *Kotoba to Shakai.* Tokyo: Chūō Kōron-sha, 1975.

———. *Tozasareta Gengo—Nihongo no Sekai.* Tokyo: Shinchō-sha, 1975.

———. "Writing is not Language, or is it?" *Journal of Pragmatics* 1: 4 (December, 1977): 407–19.

———. "Naze Gaikokujin ni Nihongo wo Oshieru no ka?" in Kokusai Kōryū Kikin, *Nihongo Kyōiku Kokusai Kaigi,* 1978, pp. 104–20.

Tanizaki, Jun'ichirō. *Bunshō Tokuhon.* Tokyo: Chūō Kōron-sha, 1934; reprinted 1960.

Toyoda, Kunio. *Nihonjin no Kotodama Shisō.* Kōdansha Gakujutsu Bunko, 483. Tokyo: Kōdansha, 1980.

Tsunoda, Tadanobu. *Nihonjin no Nō.* Tokyo: Taishūkan Shoten, 1978.

———. "Hidari no Nō to Nihongo." *Kokusai Kōryū* 16 (Winter, 1978): 13–21.

———. "The Left Cerebral Hemisphere of the Brain and the Japanese Language." *Japan Foundation Newsletter* 6: 1 (April-May, 1978): 3–7.

Watanabe, Shōichi. "On the Japanese Language." *Japan Echo* 1: 2 (1974): 9–20.

Documentation of a number of minor published sources follows, together with the identification of specific passages from the more important of the sources cited above.

Chapter 1, p. 3: Kindaichi, 1957, p. 10; Kindaichi, 1978, p. 30. P. 18: a convenient checklist of the contents of the first five years of the *Japan Echo* was published *Japan Echo* 5: 1 (1978): 122–24.

Chapter 2, p. 21: Arnoldus Montanus (1625?–83), first English edition, J. Ogilby, trans., London, 1670, p. 366.

Chapter 3, p. 41: Bloomfield, p. 508. P. 57: Kindaichi, 1976, p. 36. Pp. 59–60: Miller, *Japanese Language: Sociolinguistic Observations,* p. 50, and Wm. F. Sibley, *The Shiga Hero* (Chicago: University of Chicago Press, 1979), p. 101. P. 61: Donald Richie, "The Asian

Bookshelf," *Japan Times,* February 16, 1979. P. 62: full bibliographic data on the Lati "purity of language" charade are published in the journal *Language Problems and Language Planning* 6: 1 (Spring, 1982), in the author's review of the Hirano translation of Kindaichi's *Nihongo.*

Chapter 4, p. 69: Bloomfield, p. 36. P. 78: an article by Atuhiro Sibatani in *Science 80* 1:8 (December, 1980): 24–26, published by the American Association for the Advancement of Science, represents yet another recycling of the *Japan Foundation Newsletter* article earlier cited. Pp. 79–80: see the review of Tsunoda's book by Dr. Kiyoshi Makita in *Journal of Japanese Studies* 5 (1979): 439–49. Pp. 81–82: see the author, on Tsunoda's linguistics, in *Journal of Japanese Studies* 5 (1979): 449–50.

Chapter 5, p. 86: Miyoshi, p. xv. P. 91: Bird, pp. xxiii, 185. P. 94: the official post-1945 position, to the effect that no one in Japan had ever taken the *Kokutai no Hongi* seriously, found its way into print as early as a review by E. O. Reischauer, *Harvard Journal of Asiatic Studies* 13 (1950): 250; for a recent documentation of the lasting impact of this document on Japanese intellectuals, see the author's "Plus ça Change . . . ," *Journal of Asian Studies* 39: 4 (1980): 771–82. P. 101: *New York Times Magazine,* November 21, 1976, pp. 106–7.

Chapter 6, p. 102: Kindaichi, 1976, p. 48. P. 103: the slur on Arabic is cited from Jonathan Raban, *Arabia: A Journey Through the Labyrinth* (New York: Simon & Shuster, 1980), by John Updike in "Journeyers," *The New Yorker,* March 10, 1980, p. 150. Pp. 108–9: details on Mori and Whitney in Miller, *Japanese Language: Sociolinguistic Observations,* p. 42. Pp. 109–13: Shiga cited in, and translated from, Suzuki, *Tozasareta Gengo,* p. 21 ff. P. 110: "*Kokugo Undō*" originally appeared in the journal *Kaizō,* April, 1946. P. 114: Tanizaki, *Bunshō Tokuhon,* pp. 44–47. Pp. 114–15: Hagiwara and Yanagita cited in, and translated from, Kindaichi, 1957, pp. 22, 100. Pp. 115–16: the haiku problem, *Mainichi Shimbun,* July 3, 1971. P. 116: Nakamura cited in English in Moore, p. 195. P. 117: Yukawa cited in English in Moore, pp. 56–57. P. 120: Chinese and Korean as "sick languages," Kindaichi, 1976, pp. 130–31 (*kono yō na kokugo wa yahari, byōki to iu hoka wa nai*). Pp. 121–23: Suzuki, *Tozasareta Gengo,* pp.

31–35 and *passim.* Pp. 125–26: Claude Ciari, "My 'Adopted' Country—The Immigration Blues," *PHP* 10:10 (109) (October, 1979): 31–34, 59–62.

Chapter 7: *Kokutai no Hongi* translations from Gauntlett & Hall, except for p. 133, where their version, pp. 101–2, has been retranslated in part after the original, pp. 61–62. P. 136: Genesis 32: 23–31. P. 138: Watanabe, pp. 10, 12. P. 139: Watanabe, p. 16. P. 140: Steiner, pp. 266, 381.

Chapter 8, p. 144: Suzuki, "Naze . . . Oshieru no ka?" p. 113b. Pp. 151–52: Takayasu Higuchi, *Nihonjin wa doko kara kita ka?* Kōdansha Gendai Shinsho, 265 (Tokyo: Kōdansha, 1971), pp. 12–13. P. 155: Basil Hall Chamberlain, *Things Japanese . . . ,* 1904, reprinted as *Japanese Things* (Rutland, Vermont & Tokyo: Charles E. Tuttle Co., 1974), p. 382. P. 155 ff.: Suzuki, *Tozasareta Gengo,* pp. 174–75 and *passim.* P. 157: Suzuki, *Tozasareta Gengo,* pp. 176–77. Pp. 163–64: Andrew Horvat, personal communication of February 25, 1979.

Chapter 9, pp. 183–84: Samuel Greenberg, "I Can Teach You All the Japanese You'll Ever Need to Know," *New York Times Magazine,* January 10, 1971. Pp. 185–86: Deng on the subjects of Chinese script and Confucianism, speaking in June 1974, and quoted in the *Asahi Shimbun,* July 20, 1977, morning editions (in connection with his latest rehabilitation). Pp. 187–89: Suzuki, *Tozasareta Gengo,* p. 86 ff. Pp. 194–95: Seward, pp. 180, 178. P. 198: Strauss, cited by Elizabeth Drew, "Profiles," *The New Yorker,* May 7, 1979.

Chapter 10, p. 200: *Mombu hōrei,* cited after Gauntlett & Hall, p. 194. Pp. 206–7: Kaname Saruya, "Sambyakumannin no Daigaku, 5, Kokusai Kirisutokyō Daigaku," *Asahi Journal,* April 20, 1979, pp. 44–50; on the university as atonement for the atomic bombing, p. 46. Pp. 207–8: Ray A. Moore, *Journal of Japanese Studies* 6: 2 (1980): 400n2 cites Etō's November 7, 1979, Foreign Service Institute Lecture on Taoka's memorandum. P. 209: Said, p. 1. P. 212 ff.: Edward Seidensticker, Review of *The Japanese Language in Contemporary Japan, Journal of the Association of Teachers of Japanese* 13 (November, 1978): 200–204. P. 213: Paul Theroux, *The Great Railway Bazaar* (New York: Ballantine Books, 1975), p. 290 has a true-to-life account of a chance encounter with a sensei whose entire life revolves around reading—and teaching—a single book. P. 217: Seidensticker on the perils of the *shakaika*, p. 200.

Chapter 11: p. 219, *The Economist*, April 21, 1979, p. 96, cited by Chalmers Johnson, *Journal of Japanese Studies* 6 (1980): 115.

Chapter 12, p. 255: Suzuki, "Naze... Oshieru no ka?" p. 105a. P. 257: "Tensei Jingo," *Asahi Shimbun*, August 11, 1980. Pp. 257–59: "Onna ga semaru, 37," *Shūkan Asahi*, January 18, 1980, pp. 126–30. P. 261: Suzuki, *Tozasareta Gengo*, pp. 186–87. P. 269: Lorenzo da Ponte, *Così fan tutte*, 1.2: "... come l'araba fenice, / che vi sia ciascun lo dice, / dove sia nessun lo sa." P. 273 ff.: the primary published source for the March 1978 conference is the volume Kokusai Kōryū Kikin, *Nihongo Kyōiku Kokusai Kaigi*, 1978, already cited; a *zadankai* with the foreign guests is reported in "Nihongo kyōshi ōi ni kataru," *Kokusai Kōryū* 18 (Summer, 1978): 39–59; in English,

there appears at present to be only the short account by Eleanor H. Jorden, "The 1st International Conference on Japanese Language Teaching, A Retrospect," *Japan Foundation Newsletter* 6: 2 (June–July, 1978): 3–5. P. 276: Hermann Hesse, *Das Glasperlenspiel. Gesammelte Werke*, 9. (Frankfurt/M.: Suhrkamp Verlag, 1970, reprint of Zürich: Fretz & Wasmuth Verlag AG, 1943). Subsequently translated variously as *The Glass Bead Game* or *Magister Ludi*. P. 285: the transcript of the Suzuki lecture appears on pp. 104–20 in Kokusai Kōryū Kikin, *Nihongo Kyōiku Kokusai Kaigi*, 1978, to which the following citations of specific passages refer (*a* and *b* identify top and bottom columns on the page cited): p. 286, "everybody who is a human being ...," p. 119*b*; p. 287, "Japan's economic activities...," p. 108*b*; "But since the friction...," p. 108*b*; "Countless international meetings...," p. 109*a*; pp. 287–88, "What I want to say...," p. 115*b*; p. 288, "Japan's reliance on foreign relations...," p. 117*a*; pp. 288–89, "There is this great beast...," p. 117*a*–*b*; p. 289, "What I mean to stress...," p. 118*b*; "Foreigners are keen...," p. 118*b*; p. 290, "The nation of Japan...," p. 119*a*–*b*.

The epigraph on page 1 was attributed to Fr. Rolfe by the Rev. R. Hugh Benson in a letter of February 1905 cited in A. J. A. Symons, *The Quest for Corvo* (Middlesex: Penguin Books Ltd., 1966), p. 199.

Index

The "weathermark" identifies this book as a production of John Weatherhill, Inc., publishers of fine books on Asia and the Pacific. Book design and typography: Meredith Weatherby and Margaret Taylor. Composition, printing, and binding: Korea Textbook Company, Inc., Seoul. The typeface used is Monotype Bembo.